TAKING SIDES

**Clashing Views on
Controversial Issues in American History
Volume I, Second Edition**
The Colonial Period to Reconstruction

*We are not afraid to follow truth wherever it may lead, nor to
tolerate any error so long as reason is left free to combat it.*
—Thomas Jefferson

STAFF

Jeremy Brenner   Program Manager
Brenda Filley   Production Manager
Lynn Shannon   Designer
Libra Ann Cusack   Typesetting Coordinator
Diane Barker   Copy Editor

TAKING SIDES

Clashing Views on Controversial Issues in American History
Volume I, Second Edition
The Colonial Period to Reconstruction

Edited, Selected and with Introductions by

EUGENE KUZIRIAN, University of Texas, El Paso
and
LARRY MADARAS, Howard Community College, Columbia, Maryland

The Dushkin Publishing Group, Inc.
Guilford, Connecticut 06437

Library of Congress Catalogue Card Number: 86-48001

Manufactured in the United States of America

Second Edition, First Printing

ISBN: 0-87967-658-2

To Odile and Maggie

CONTENTS

Professor Schlesinger argues that the environment of the American
frontier created a unique society based on agrarian values. Professor Hayes presents the American experience in the context of the
Atlantic community.

Professors Boyer and Nissenbaum present their argument that economic and social tensions motivated the Salem witchhunts. Professor Hansen cites evidence to support his belief in the reality of
pathological bewitchment.

Professor Vaughan presents the Native American as a victim of color symbolism, racial differences and non-conformity to European cultural traditions. Professor Johnson chronicles cooperative relations between settlers and natives in the New World.

Professor Rossiter presents demographic statistics as evidence of widespread ethnic pluralism in the colonies. Historian Gipson argues that a "broad conformity" existed in England's North American colonies.

Professor Phillips considers slavery a necessary component of the plantation system. Professor Stampp considers slave labor as a deliberate choice made to maximize profits.

Professor Simpson, while noting both the negative and positive effects of Puritanism, believes it had a continuing influence on American society. Professor Wertenbaker acknowledges the importance of Puritanism in the history of seventeenth-century New England but denies its impact on subsequent American development.

PART II: THE NEW NATION

Professor Jameson enumerates several ways in which the American Revolution greatly changed society. Professor Tolles counters with a view of change in eighteenth-century America which takes exception to many of Jameson's conclusions.

Professor Beard argues that economic interests determined the political structure of the federal government. Professor McDonald contradicts Beard with evidence that many delegates voted against policies which would benefit them economically.

Historian Leonard Levy contends that Jefferson was a messianic nationalist who often violated in practice the lofty theoretical standards of civil liberties that he espoused. Historian Morton Borden believes that Jefferson was a moderate and pragmatic politician who placed the nation's best interests above those of individual states.

Professor Woloch describes the exercise of autonomy and authority in the domestic role of middle-class wives. Historian Lerner considers a spectrum of women's roles, emphasizing the subservient position of female industrial workers.

PART III: ANTEBELLUM AMERICA

Professor Robert V. Remini argues that the 1828 presidential election symbolized the people's arrival at political responsibility and began a genuine two-party system that came of age in the 1830s. Historian Richard C. McCormick maintains that statistics demonstrate that a genuine revolution in the nature of US politics did not take place until the presidential elections of 1840.

Journalist T.D. Allman argues that President Monroe's original policy of nonintervention in Latin America was subverted by later presidents to justify US military intervention there. Diplomatic historian Robert Ferrell believes that although the American government waged an aggressive war in Mexico, our actions were not imperialistic in nature.

Professor C. Vann Woodward argues that the South's different historical experiences of frustration and failure make a unique section in America. Professor Thomas P. Govan believes that historians have exaggerated sectional differences between the so-called industrial North and the agrarian South.

Professor Craven emphasizes that how the war came about, through a breakdown of the democratic process, is more important than the causes of the war. Professor Schlesinger criticizes Craven and other revisionists, because they ignore the moral issues which justified civil war as a means of ending slavery.

Professor Donald argues that Lincoln concentrated all his energies and presidential powers on winning the war. Professor Stampp explains why the South subconsciously desired to lose.

Author Randall argues that Reconstruction failed because carpetbaggers and their Negro allies misgoverned the South and looted its treasuries. Professor Eric Foner believes that, although Reconstruction was nonrevolutionary and conservative, it was a splendid failure because it offered blacks a temporary vision of a free society.

PREFACE TO THE SECOND EDITION

In the first edition of this book we pointed out that too often the history of America is taught as if it were a lesson in civics. The heroic exploits of our outstanding political and military leaders have been emphasized *ad nauseum*. On the other hand, the darker side of our treatment of minorities and weaker nations has been ignored or glossed over with phrases like "the peculiar institution," "melting pot," "Manifest Destiny," and "national security."

The editors grew up at a time when students were expected to learn the names of all the presidents of the United States in chronological order and to know the capitals of all the states. Times have changed. Recently, one free-lance journalist (in an admittedly casual survey) revealed the appalling level of ignorance about American history held by college students in southern California. No more than one could place the date of the Declaration of Independence. Only two could approximately identify Thomas Jefferson. None could name any of the first ten amendments to the Constitution or connect them with the Bill of Rights. One individual displayed his awareness of the Great Depression: "Was that right after World War II when Elvis Presley came along?"

The same writer discovered that these teenagers' knowledge of world history was just as bad. No one had ever heard of Vladmir Ilyich Lenin ("Was he the drummer with the Beatles before Ringo Starr?"). One correctly identified Stalin though another thought "he was president just before Roosevelt." Should such answers be tolerated from journalism majors at a prestigious university in southern California?

We are not upset if students fail to recite the names of all the presidents in chronological order. We *are* concerned that students complete a college survey course with an awareness of the complexities of the major issues which have confronted our society in the past and which raise questions about our future.

This volume treats nineteen issues in the period from the settlement of the American colonies to Reconstruction following the Civil War. In volume two, there are seventeen important issues from Reconstruction to modern times that concern us now and into the future. These issues are: Was Reconstruction a Total Failure?; Was the American Farmer Responsible for the Agricultural Problems of the Late Nineteenth Century?; Was John D. Rockefeller a "Robber Baron"?; Was the American Labor Movement Conservative?; Was the Immigrants' Old World Culture Destroyed as they Adjusted to American Life?; Was Urban America A Healthy Place to Live By 1900?; Should Historians Abandon the Concept of a Progressive Movement?; Have the Antitrust Laws Preserved Competition in the American Economic System?; Did Prohibition Work?; Was the New Deal an Effective Answer to the Great Depression?; Was 1898 the Decisive Year for the US as a World Power?; Was Woodrow Wilson a Great President?; Was It Necessary to Drop the Atomic Bomb on Japan to End World War II?; Has America's Distrust of Soviet Policy Been Justified?; Could the United States Have Prevented the Fall of South Vietnam to the Communists?; Has the Women's Movement Failed Because It Lacks a Radical Ideology?; Have the Presidential Elections of the 1980s Created a New Conservative Majority Republic Party?

We have aimed at a balanced collection of issues covering both the traditional political and diplomatic topics as well as social and cultural concerns. We welcome suggestions for topics and articles to be excluded or included in future editions. Those of you who wish to discover how other social scientists have made use of *Taking Sides* books in their respective disciplines should write or call the publisher for a complementary copy of *Using Taking Sides in the Classroom: Methods, Systems, and Techniques for the Teaching of Controversial Issues*. The manuscript for this manual was based on the classroom experiences of many instructors from across the country.

ACKNOWLEDGEMENTS

Those who were kind enough to share their ideas with us for this second edition include Maggie Cullen, Barry Crouch, Jean Soto, Sandra Harding, and Odile Kuzirian. We also wish to thank the users of the first edition who shared with us their experiences and comments. They were: Sister Carol Berg, Dr. Joseph A. Stout, Dr. Ray Broussard, Professor John Buchanan, Professor Brendan Burns, Professor Robert Campbell, Professor John Crevelli, Professor Roger Davis, Professor Joseph Dawson, Dr. Lawrence H. Douglas, Professor Larry Easley, Dr. Jeremy P. Felt, Professor Dean Frazer, Professor James Hillesheim, Dr. James P. Keenen III, Professor Gerald Keete, Professor Ronald A. Petrin, Professor Jim Reithmiller, Professor Barbara Lacey, Professor Constance Maas, Professor George Monies, Professor James Moriarty, Professor Patrick Reed, Dr. Ronald H. Ridgely, Sister M. Eucharia Ryan, Dr. Neil Sapper, Professor Jerry Thompson, Professor Roberta Weil and Professor Irv Zisselman.

A big thanks goes to senior editor Jeremy Brenner who initiated the idea for a *Taking Sides* reader in American history and kept the authors moving when the going got rough. The last round of applause goes to typists Bonnie Mikkelsen and Susan Block who had to read our awful handwriting. Librarians Ann Schultis, Diana Twelves, and Helen Bell facilitated research. Flo Dick not only processed words but also contributed her knowledge of history and English usage.

Eugene E. Kuzirian, El Paso, Texas
Larry Madaras, Columbia, Maryland
January 1987

INTRODUCTION:
"EVERYMAN HIS OWN HISTORIAN"

Eugene Kuzirian
Larry Madaras

The phrase, everyman his own historian, was coined by Professor Carl Becker over fifty years ago at a meeting of the American Historical Association. Becker, in his presidential address to his colleagues, summarized the characteristics of modern historiography. These qualities have not changed significantly during the half century which had passed. If anything, they have greater currency today than they did in 1931, the year of Becker's speech.

Becker insisted, for example, that "it is impossible to divorce history from life." Then he proceeded to show how mundane activities such as paying a coal bill involved activities quite similar to those associated with historical research. These were, according to Becker, recalling things said and done, examining records to uncover necessary details, comparing various sources of information, drawing conclusions based on a "selected series of historical events." One of Becker's main purposes was, of course, to demonstrate that history was a part of Everyman's daily life. He was as concerned about the process of reaching conclusions as he was about the conclusions themselves. Indirectly he seemed to be implying that an understanding of history requires thinking and making decisions.

Becker remained aware of the macrocosm as well as the minutiae of Everyman's daily life. As the democratic, even egalitarian, title of his essay suggests, there is considerable political importance to Everyman's "historical research" when paying his bills. The transference which Becker insists takes place between paying bills and historical research must be carried to the conclusions at which Becker only hinted. If Everyman understood the steps necessary to pay his coal bill to the firm which actually delivered it rather than to the firm from which it had been ordered, then the skills exercised might be used to understand the difficult topics which citizens in a democratic society need to think about if a government of the people, by the people and for the people is to function.

Becker relied on a belief that the average person could understand the events of the day and make decisions affecting his political and economic life. By 1931, however, there was considerable evidence that the kinds of democratic institutions which had been developing for several centuries were on the defensive. Historians had an important role to play if the democratic process were to resist the tide of dictatorship. Everyman required knowledge of the past and would obtain it wherever possible, Becker insisted, if professional historians failed to meet the needs of society. Historians needed to interpret the past for Everyman, in terms which he could understand. Otherwise, Becker continued, historians would be conversing only with each other and their books would remain unopened on library shelves.

In a pluralistic society such as ours students are bombarded with many different interpretations of the past as well as the present. Consequently, understanding history presupposes the evaluation of information, a task sometimes comparable to searching in a haystack for a needle. The various interpretations of a historical person or event need to be compared and contrasted as well as subjected to internal analysis to establish both absolute and relative value. This process is all the more difficult because historical interpretations rarely arrange themselves as indisputably right or wrong, black or white, left or right. Internal analysis, comparison, contrast and evaluation imply careful thinking. The difficulty of thinking in a pluralistic society is, first of all, the variety of opinions available and, secondly, the subtleties which distinguish one of those opinions from the others.

RELATIVISM AND REVISIONISM

Change dominates our twentieth-century lives. News updates on television, headlines in the newspapers, specialized newsletters inform us, perhaps more often than we are prepared to accept, of the latest developments on the other side of the globe or of advances in medicine, tax reform and the opening prices of gold, silver and the dollar in the European markets. Historiography, as the writing of history is known, reflects this symptom of our times as much as the stock market or the prices of new automobiles. We have had to reconcile, for example, myths with reality. Three of the most popular presidents of the twentieth century, Roosevelt, Eisenhower and Kennedy, have had the most intimate secrets of their private lives revealed in books and newspaper articles. We have been informed that the Allies in World War II knew about the Nazi extermination camps like Auschwitz but took no steps to eliminate them through precision bombing. Perhaps the most notorious example of the changes affecting historiography in the United States is the topic of slavery both for its effects on black Americans and as a cause of the Civil War. We have been told, alternatively, that the moral struggle over slavery caused and did not cause the war between the states. We have been informed that the oppression of plantation life, on one hand destroyed black culture, while another view insists black society developed its own values in the face of the servile conditions of life in the South. Even in the Soviet Union where the party line simplifies historical interpretation, change has caused, for example, Stalin's reputation to experience extreme ups and downs, from the victorious warlord of World War II to the paranoiac dictator who ordered the executions of millions of Soviet citizens.

An understanding of history in the pluralistic society implies the acceptance of historical relativism. History is no more absolute than medical knowledge or the law. All three have undergone modifications associated with relativism. Vitamin therapy and herbal remedies challenge prescription pharmaceuticals as a means to wellness and conservative management, usually in the form of physical therapy, competes with surgery. Good behavior, parole and social factors frequently mitigate the penalties to which the guilty have been sentenced in court.

The choice of historical interpretations requires the active involvement of the audience for whom it is intended. The choices are far from simple if only because it is not enough to accept one view, rather than another, wholesale. Very often part of one interpretation must be welded to a section of another, while the conclusions but not the premises of a third are combined with the evidence but not the conclusions of a fourth. The task remains to create an intelligible whole despite the eclectic accumulation of the parts. The goal becomes accuracy, not the truth, and certainly not logic.

Relativism encourages revisionism. The maxim that the past must remain useful to the present and the truism that the present is always undergoing change further argue for historical reinterpretation. Every generation should write its own history, thereby issuing a mandate for the continuous examination and reexamination of history.

Of course, there are other, more clear-cut reasons for rewriting history. The discovery of new information (documents, letters, photographs, diaries) necessitates reevaluation. New methodologies such as quantification and the use of computers, oral history built upon interviews and local history which emphasized families, neighborhoods and cities modify traditional generalizations. Historians have expanded their discipline in other ways as well. They have borrowed the knowledge and methodologies of political science, economics, sociology, anthropology, and psychology for historical investigations. They have engaged in comparative studies of southern slavery and the American Revolution with similar events in other countries.

The proliferation of historical approaches, which are reflected in the debate issues, has had mixed results. On the one hand, historians have become so specialized in their respective time periods and methodological styles that it has become difficult to synthesize the recent scholarship into a comprehensive text for the general reader. On the other hand, historians know more about the American past than at any other time in our history. They have dared to ask questions never thought of before or which were considered to be of importance only to other disciplines. There is little agreement about the answers to these new questions. But the search for answers to these questions makes history an exciting field to study.

History, consequently, does not remain static. Almost all historians commit themselves to revising "older" interpretations, synthesizing particular revisionist writing into new macro-interpretations or revising the revisionists. Historical revisionism and reform politics have traveled hand in hand throughout the twentieth century. The most recent phase began in the late 1960s and continues today. Known respectively as the "new history" and the "new left," these attempts at redoing history have profoundly affected Everyman as well as professional historians. The past and the present have been fused together and Everyman has become absorbed in his genealogy, nostalgic about period clothes and curious about daily living in times past. The ultimate task, of course, is to convince Everyman that the great issues affecting his life, just like the practical history he seems most concerned with, do not exist in a vacuum. They must be placed in a historical context.

HISTORICAL SKILLS AND HISTORICAL KNOWLEDGE

The study of history is a process which combines skills and knowledge. An understanding of the past requires learning the techniques of inquiry as well as memorizing a body of knowledge. Two of the earliest influences in the study of history were Thucydides and Socrates, both ancient Greeks who lived during the Athenian Golden Age. Thucydides, a participant in the events he recorded, set a standard of objectivity for future historians. His contemporary, Socrates, offered a technique, rather than a goal, by asking questions as a method of obtaining information.

The initial steps of historical inquiry rely on basic questions people usually ask: when, where, who, what. Such questions provide a framework for historical investigation. Interrogation limited to these fundamentals, however, leads to a dead end. When and where, who and what do not provide explanations. More sophisticated inquiry uses probes such as how and why, analyze, evaluate, compare and contrast. These imperatives help to create historical interpretations and, as a part of the intellectual milieu of a pluralistic society such as ours, indicate that history is not cut and dry. Our understanding of the past is open to a variety of explanations.

The topics in these volumes represent both mainstream and radical historical perspectives. Many reflect the most recent methodological approaches in the writing of American history: quantitative analysis of political elections; psycho-historical portraits of individuals and institutions; relations between the United States and other nations; social approaches to the history of native Americans, Afro-Americans, white ethnics, and women from the point of view of their respective cultures; and historical explorations of the relevant issues studied by social scientists—family, religion, sports, drugs, and crime.

Each of these controversial issues stands alone on its individual merit. At the same time, however, they also interact with each other to illustrate larger historical themes. The issues, when grouped thematically, reveal continuing motifs in the development of American history.

1. *The National Scene.* Some of the issues below explore questions which survey large segments of United States history. A general view of our past, seen through the dimension of the national character, finds expression in Issue 1. This issue provides an introduction to Volume Two as well as Volume One of *Taking Sides: Clashing Views in American History* because it juxtaposes two different hypotheses about the overall development of American history. Arthur M. Schlesinger, Sr., enumerates a series of values and characteristics which he labels uniquely American. His grand interpretation of American history provoked Carleton J.H. Hayes, three years later, to a rebuttal. Hayes insisted American history

belongs within the pattern of western civilization stretching back to the ancient Greeks. Both these historians attempted synthesized interpretations which affect, directly or indirectly, all the other issues in both volumes. "Have Puritan Values Had Lasting Effects on American Society?" Issue 6 inquires. Alan Simpson offers an affirmative interpretation which needs the wide expanse of our history from its beginnings to the present as a backdrop. Thomas J. Wertenbaker's negative reply to Simpson also takes into account the general development of the United States but Wertenbaker confines Puritan influence to a particular time (the seventeenth century) and specific place (New England). Frederick Jackson Turner's frontier hypothesis, discussed in Issue 14, presents another opportunity to consider American historical development as a whole. Turner attempted to explain American institutions and values, such as individualism, democracy and nationalism, by expounding the importance of the frontier. George W. Pierson takes exception to this monolithic interpretation by pointing out important historical topics which Turner ignored because they had little or no connection with the frontier. Turner, in Pierson's view, exaggerated the significance of the frontier and omitted subjects such as industrialization, commercial development and cultural history. The topic of reform presented in Issue 15 as "Antebellum Reform: Did It Have a Great Impact on the Nation?" offers a fourth topic which investigates the national scene over a period of several decades. The selection written by Arthur Schlesinger, Sr., comes from his survey of reform as a major aspect of United States history. Antebellum reform in his opinion produced some of the most intense change in American history. Ronald G. Walters pays lip service to reform in the twentieth century in his conclusion but his point of view, that antebellum reformers were failures, is based on an examination of the first few decades of the nineteenth century. Nevertheless, his discussion covers forty-five years of history, a significant timeframe of the American past.

2. *Assimilation and Ethnic Conflict.* These broad concepts, relying heavily on anthropology, form the basis for three issues: the give-and-take relationship between the colonists and Indians, ethnic diversity among the colonists themselves, and the development of the black American family within the environment of servitude. Alden T. Vaughn in Issue 3 relies on the concept of historical change to explain how Europeans initially thought Native Americans were Caucasians like themselves but later condemned them to racial inferiority as "redskins." This attempt at cultural interchange (acculturation) degenerated into ethnic conflict. Richard C. Johnson, on the other hand, rejects a generalized picture in favor of specific examples of cooperation between various tribes and colonists in New England. His conclusion presents the Indians as active participants, not impassive victims of colonial policy. Issue 4 compares and contrasts English and Continental ethnic influences among the colonists. In the eighteenth century more and more immigrants to the "English" colonies in North America came from the Continent or non-English parts of the British Isles. Clinton Rossiter argues that the ethnic diversity in the colonies weakened England's control over its North American possessions. Lawrence H. Gipson sees unity rather than diver-

sity in the British colonies. British institutions and values, in his view, dominated colonial life. Issue 4 raises this question: How did ethnic diversity affect English institutions with which some of these newcomers were unfamiliar and in some cases even hostile?

Did ethnic diversity help establish the pluralistic society in North America? For many years it was assumed that slavery destroyed the black family. Twenty years ago Senator Daniel Moynihan wrote his famous report for President Lyndon Johnson in which he asserted that the legacy of slavery was responsible for the large number of single-parent families in the black community today. Issue 13 discusses the effects of slavery upon the black family. Stanley Elkins employs two approaches to probe for the personality of the slave: theoretical knowledge drawn from modern psychology and an analogy developed from the literature on concentration camps. He concludes that slavery became a closed system of total control run by a perverted patriarchy who turned the culturally-uprooted African slave into a passive and childlike "Sambo." Employing a more traditional search through the plantation records, with a careful reading of slave autobiographies, the controversial records of ex-slaves, and interviews conducted by federal governmental workers in the 1930s led Eugene Genovese to different conclusions from Elkins. As a Marxist, Genovese argues that southern slavery existed in a pre-capitalistic society dominated by a paternalistic ruling clan of white slaveholders who ruled over their white and slave families. Genovese reflects the views of most historians who wrote about slavery in the 1970s that blacks developed their own system of family and cultural values in the slave quarters.

3. *Political Compromise and Discord.* Political pluralism in America developed with the appearance of each new English colony. Variations in society, geography, economy and ethnicity reinforced the initial religious differences among the founding groups. The two extremes of political pluralism, discord and compromise, figure prominently in four issues in this volume. Issue 8, "Did Economic Self-Interest Motivate the Writing and Ratification of the Federal Constitution?" raises questions of political controversy and compromise at the inception of the federal period. Charles A. Beard argues that the political structure of the federal government owes its characteristics to the selfish interests of the Constitution makers in Philadelphia. The national political structure they created reflected their own economic interests, Beard insists. Forrest McDonald's research, on the other hand, presents evidence which shows that many of those who voted for the Constitution put the national interest above any personal benefits. The eleventh election held under the auspices of that Constitution, in 1828, has raised questions about its importance as a turning point in the nation's political life. Did it represent a "democratic revolt of the people?" Robert Rimini thinks that it did through the medium of a two-party system organized on a national scale. Richard P. McCormick dissents from this view. In his opinion significant political change occurred not in the election of 1828 but three elections later, in 1840. This major change in American political life occurred peacefully but Issue 17 considers politics within the context of the causes of the

Civil War. Avery Craven explains that a breakdown in the political system led to war—one definition of which is "the conduct of politics by other means." Americans failed to compromise, Craven insists, as they had so many times in the past. It was the breakdown in this process rather than any issue which explains the coming of the war. Arthur Schlesinger, Jr., takes an extremely different position on this issue. There was a moral imperative for the North to end slavery and by 1860 war was the only method which could accomplish that aim. The enormity of the immorality of slavery, he argues, required an equally powerful response, a war between the states. The aftermath of Civil War, the Reconstruction period, raises a multitude of questions about American political life. Issue 18 focuses on the South in the post-Civil War years. Was reconstruction a complete fiasco? J.G. Randall presents the traditional viewpoint that reconstruction was a total failure because carpetbaggers and their ignorant Negro allies misgoverned the South and looted its treasuries. Professor Eric Foner rejects the ideas that blacks were intellectually inferior to whites and also that the South was unfairly punished after the Civil War. Although reconstruction was nonrevolutionary and conservative, it was, in Foner's words, a "splendid failure" because it offered blacks a temporary vision of a free society as well as an opportunity to participate in politics.

4. *The Importance of Individuals.* The people who make history range from the members of the power elite like presidents on one hand, to Carl Becker's Everyman on the other. The former cannot be ignored because of their overwhelming significance. The latter often write diaries and letters or make penetrating observations which reveal important details about daily life. Two of our most important presidents, Thomas Jefferson and Abraham Lincoln, are discussed in this volume. Was Jefferson, often called a renaissance man and certainly our most intellectual president, also a shady politician who violated his philosophical principles during his presidency? In Issue 9 Leonard Levy presents an unusually caustic view of President Jefferson and contends he was a messianic nationalist who often violated in practice the lofty theoretical standards of civil liberties which he philosophically supported. Morton Borden, however, views the "sage of Monticello" as a moderate and pragmatic politician who placed the nation's best interests above those of the individual states during his eight years in the oval office. Discussions of individual presidents lead to broader historical questions. How much are individuals products of the times in which they live? Why are some presidents led by the events of their times while others alter the course of history? Issue 18 compares and contrasts reasons why the Union won the Civil War. Was it Lincoln's attributes as an outstanding war leader as David Donald suggests? Kenneth Stampp takes a radically different approach. He looks at the impersonal forces which appear to minimize the human factor. Stampp argues that the Confederacy wanted to fight but lost the war to save face over the abolition of slavery.

5. *Economic and Geographical Determinism.* Did Southern plantations, Issue 5 asks, demand slave labor? There are many historical approaches to the issue of slavery and its impact on the development of

the United States. Issue 5 seeks out the heart of the matter, the economic question. Why was slave labor used in the first place? Ulrich B. Phillips presents the classic argument for the necessity of slave labor for the plantation system. As a native of Georgia, Phillips grew up in the midst of the vestiges of the plantation system and slavery. He accepted them and spent his life amassing statistics and other evidence to explain life in the Old South. Kenneth M. Stampp disputes this traditional view, as the title of his book, *The Peculiar Institution,* indicates. Stampp became the first of a series of scholars to criticize slavery, euphemistically known as "the peculiar institution." Stampp's attack on Phillips is one of several examples of one historian deliberately refuting the views of another. Similarly pointed dialogues appear in Issues 1, 7, 8, 14 and 17.

The surveying of the Mason-Dixon line to settle boundary disputes also raises questions beyond the matter at hand. The surveyor's line, it seems, did more than settle territorial disputes which originated in overlapping colonial land grants. It also became a line of demarcation between free and slave states, between the North and the South in terms of culture, society, and politics as well as the economy. There are almost as many books about the American South as there are about the lives of Christ and Shakespeare. Was the South different from the rest of America? In Issue 16, C. Vann Woodward argues that the South's different historical experiences of frustration and failure make it a unique section in American history. But Thomas Govans dissents from this view. With the exception of the slavery issue which becomes the paramount issue after 1850, Govans believes that historians have projected a false and oversimplified dichotomy of industrialism versus agrarianism and have exaggerated the differences between the North and the South. A discussion of early nineteenth-century foreign policy in Issue 12 examines economic and geographical determinism in light of both our diplomatic relations with the rest of the world and our self-perception within the world of nations. Did we conceive of our power as continental, hemispheric, or world wide? T.D. Allman believes that President Polk as well as future twentieth-century presidents distorted President Monroe's original policy of nonintervention in Latin America in order to justify expansionist military excursions by the United States in that continent. But Robert Ferrell justifies American expansionist policies against Mexico in terms of the nineteenth-century ideology of manifest destiny. Although he admits the American government waged an aggressive war against Mexico, Ferrell argues it was inevitable for the United States to possess Texas, New Mexico, and California.

6. *Social Changes.* Social distinctions in the New World might not be as clear cut as they once were in Europe or the Orient. Nevertheless, they exist and need to be placed in a historical context. Controversy over the accusations of witchcraft (Issue 2) arose among contemporary observers and subsequently ensconced itself in American historiography. Paul Boyer and Stephen Nissenbaum have uncovered evidence which suggests that social differences motivated the charges of black magic. Hansen Chadwick takes the appearance of witchery in Salem at face value. He believes in the pathology of witchcraft and that its symptoms

in Salem were genuine. Issue 7 directly tackles the question of change as it relates to the American Revolution. Did fundamental change occur only after the War for Independence had commenced, as Franklin Jameson advocates? Frederick Tolles argues the reverse. Changes occurred throughout the eighteenth century, he insists. In Issue 10 Nancy Woloch and Gerda Lerner present sharply contrasting descriptions of early nineteenth century women. Woloch insists domesticity provided women with a strong power base. Lerner, however, finds that the position of large numbers of women had deteriorated after the colonial period.

The study of history in a pluralistic society allows each citizen the opportunity to reach independent conclusions about the past. Since most, if not all historical issues affect the present and future, understanding the past becomes necessary if the pluralistic society is to continue. All citizens are involved in contemporary public issues part of the time and some citizens are absorbed in them all the time. Many of today's problems have a direct connection with the past. They have a history just as there is a history of science or family histories of the Mayflower passengers. Other contemporary issues may lack obvious direct antecedents from the past but, at least, a study of history will provide analogies to illuminate them.

The diversity of pluralism, however, does create some obstacles to comprehending the past. The spectrum of differing opinions on any particular subject eliminates the possibility of quick and easy answers. The variety of thought demands thorough comparison and contrast. In the last analysis, conclusions are often built through a synthesis of several different interpretations. Even then, they may be partial and tentative. Historical relativism is alive and well in the pluralistic society.

The process of history relies more on thinking than on memorizing data. Once the basics (when, where, who, what) are revealed, historical thinking shifts to a higher gear. Analysis, comparison and contrast, evaluation and explanation take command. These skills not only increase our knowledge of the past but also they are general tools for the comprehension of all the topics human beings think about. As Carl Becker pointed out in "Everyman His Own Historian," the essentials of historical research are not far removed from the steps necessary to pay a coal bill.

Those who may remain unconvinced of the usefulness of historical study will argue that history is irrelevant. History's supposed inconsequence, however, serves an extremely important purpose. Thinking about subjects which possess no apparent utility for the here and now, ironically does offer an opportunity to exercise the thinking process without the handicap of emotional involvement. As a result, when extremely "relevant" issues present themselves for consideration, previous experience facilitates comprehension.

The difficulty of thinking in a pluralistic society is, first of all, caused by the variety of opinions available and, secondly, the subtleties which distinguish one of those opinions from another. At first, it may appear confusing to read and to think about opposing historical views. In the end, however, the survival of the pluralistic society will depend on such critical thinking by acute and discerning minds.

The brave old Hendrick the great SACHEM or Chief ... one of the Six Nations now in Alliance with & Subject to ...

Jebuick Indians
Great Britain

PART 1
FROM SETTLEMENT
TO REVOLUTION

The settlement of the colonies took place in the context of conditions that were unique to that time and place. The ethnic identity of the colonists affected relations with the Native Americans and each other, influenced the nature of the institutions that developed, and perhaps led inevitably to revolutionary change. Many of the institutions and ideals that grew out of the colonial experience served the early settlers well and are still emulated today. Others, such as slavery, have left a less positive legacy.

Is the American National Character Unique?

Did Social Tensions in Salem Motivate the Witchhunt of 1692?

Was a Conflict Unavoidable Between Native Americans and Colonists?

Were the Colonists Losing Their English Identity in the Eighteenth Century?

Was Slavery an Economic Necessity in the Old South?

Have Puritan Values Had Lasting Effects on American Society?

ISSUE I

IS THE AMERICAN NATIONAL CHARACTER UNIQUE?

YES: Arthur M. Schlesinger, Sr., from "What Then Is the American, This New Man?" *The American Historical Review,* January 1943

NO: Carlton J.H. Hayes, from "The American Frontier—Frontier of What?" *The American Historical Review,* January 1946

ISSUE SUMMARY

YES: Professor Schlesinger, argues that the environment of the American frontier created a unique society based on agrarian values.
NO: Professor Hayes presents the American experience in the context of the Atlantic Community.

Is it valid to argue as Arthur Schlesinger, Sr. does in this issue, that Americans possess a unique national character? Did ocean boundaries separate Americans from their ancestors, creating a people distinct from the various ethnic groups which immigrants left behind in Europe, Africa, Asia, and the Middle East? Carlton J.H. Hayes challenges Schlesinger's interpretation, insisting that American development must be placed in the context of Western civilization.

The notion of a unique American character emerged in the eighteenth century. In 1782, St. John de Crèvecoeur, an immigrant from France, observed that Americans were "new men," molded by the wilderness environment and the mixture of different European nationalities. Americans, Crèvecoeur pointed out, modified the traditions they brought with them to the New World, created new ones when necessary, and jettisoned those which were inappropriate. The success of the Revolution underscored the eighteenth-century perception of unique American qualities. At the same time, presidential authority extended the concept of unique Americans to a unique America. Washington cautioned in his

Farewell Address (1796), "Europe has a set of primary interests which to us have none or a very remote relation." Washington's foreign policy reflected the concept of the uniqueness of Americans and America. This connection reappeared in Jefferson's first inaugural address in 1801 with the phrase, "peace, commerce, and honest friendship with all nations, entangling alliances with none."

America's separateness from European politics reinforced the concept that Americans were a breed apart. Greater elaboration came in the Monroe Doctrine (1823). Monroe insisted that the United States policy toward Europe remain, as before, "not to interfere in the internal concerns of any of its powers." This meant, of course, that the Europeans should reciprocate. The Atlantic, according to these presidents, was no longer the center of a civilization connecting the Old and New worlds. The Atlantic now kept the continents and their peoples distinct and separated by more than geographical distance.

Developments in the United States during the nineteenth century encouraged the theme of American uniqueness. Tremendous internal improvements gave the impression that Americans could exist and, for that matter, prosper within a self-contained hemisphere. The opportunities in American society (universal education, male suffrage, unparalleled availability of property) helped create the impression of uniqueness.

In the twentieth century, although the trauma of war partially destroyed the *myth* of American separateness it also strengthened it. Freedom of the seas, particularly the Atlantic, involved the United States in what appeared, at first, to be strictly a European conflict. Americans fought in the last stages of World War I "to make the world safe for democracy," and Wilson's Fourteen Points helped bring about an armistice in 1918. But our refusal to join the League of Nations, along with the Neutrality Acts (1935-1939), reconfirmed ethnocentric attitudes that stretched back to the eighteenth century. However, the devastation of World War II brought a transformation in policies which reflected a change in the self-image of both Americans and the nation itself. Americans were still proud of the capabilities that enabled the United States to be "the arsenal of democracy." But it was no longer possible for us to disassociate ourselves from the rest of the world. Between 1947 and 1949 massive economic assistance to Europe (the Marshall Plan), military aid (particularly to Greece and Turkey [the Truman Doctrine]), and the actual deployment of permanent troops and war materiel (the NATO Alliance) revolutionized American foreign policy in thought and deed.

In their addresses to the American Historical Association, written in the midst of this shift in opinion, Professor Schlesinger in 1943 and Professor Hayes in 1946 infused the weight of historical scholarship into this issue. Schlesinger insisted that America was fundamentally different from Europe. Professor Hayes preferred to demonstrate the acculturation of European values in the United States.

YES — Arthur M. Schlesinger, Sr.

"WHAT THEN IS THE AMERICAN, THIS NEW MAN?"

This question, posed in the last years of the Revolution by a Frenchman long resident in America, has never ceased to be of challenging interest. It lies at the heart of every inquiry into the national past and of every attempt to understand the present or peer into the future. It concerns specialists in economics, political science, and sociology no less than historians; students of religion, literature, and the arts no less than social scientists; statesmen no less than scholars. If we can once learn why the American has come to be as he is, what his instinctive reactions are to life, how he differs from the people of other lands, we shall have gained a deep insight into the springs of national thought and action.

Crèvecoeur's own answer to his question can still be read with profit. He was, of course, one of a long procession of Europeans who have tried to describe and appraise the American character. Their writings, though of varying merit, possess the common advantage of presenting an outsider's point of view, free from the predilections and prepossessions which blur the American's vision of himself. Viewing the scene from a different background, they are also sensitive to national divergences of which most Americans are unaware. Though bias may influence the individual observer's judgment, the total number of visitors has been so great as to render far more significant their points of agreement.

The composite portrait that emerges deserves our thoughtful consideration. The attributes most frequently noted are a belief in the universal obligation to work; the urge to move about; a high standard of comfort for the average man; faith in progress; the eternal pursuit of material gain; an absence of permanent class barriers; the neglect of abstract thinking and of the aesthetic side of life; boastfulness; a deference for women; the blight of spoiled children; the general restlessness and hurry of life, always illustrated by the practice of fast eating; and certain miscellaneous traits such as overheated houses, the habit of spitting, and the passion for rocking chairs and ice water.

Excerpted by special permission from, "What Then Is the American, This New Man?" by Arthur Schlesinger, Sr., *American Historical Review*, Volume XLVIII, Number 2, January 1943. Copyright © The American Historical Association.

This inventory, so far as it goes, reveals qualities and attitudes recognizably American. Moreover, the travelers express no doubt as to the existence of a distinctive national character. Americans looking at their fellow countrymen readily identify them as New Englanders or Middle Westerners or Southerners, as products of old native stock or newcomers of immigrant origin, and they remember that at one period of their history the differences between Northerner and Southerner sharpened into a sword, causing a tragic civil war. But the detached observer from Europe has always been less impressed by these variations than by the evidences of fundamental kinship, even in slavery times. James Bryce, most perspicacious of the commentators, goes so far as to say: "Scotchmen and Irishmen are more unlike Englishmen, the native of Normandy more unlike the native of Provence, the Pomeranian more unlike the Wurtemberger, the Piedmontese more unlike the Neapolitan, the Basque more unlike the Andalusian, than the American from any part of the country is to the American from any other part." His conclusion is that "it is rather more difficult to take any assemblage of attributes in any of these European countries and call it the national type than it is to do the like in the United States." The preoccupation of American historians with local and sectional diversities has tended to obscure this underlying reality. . . .

The Old World heritage consisted merely of that part of European culture which the people who settled America had shared. The great bulk of the colonists, like the immigrants of later times, belonged to the poorer classes. Whether in England or on the Continent, they and their ancestors had been artisans, small tradesmen, farmers, day laborers—the firm foundation upon which rested the superstructure of European cultivation. Shut out from a life of wealth, leisure, and aesthetic enjoyment, they had tended to regard the ways of their social superiors with misgiving, if not resentment, and, by the same token, they magnified the virtues of sobriety, diligence, and thrift that characterized their own order. Even when many of them, notably in England, improved their economic position as a result of the great growth of commerce and industry in the sixteenth and seventeenth centuries, they continued to exalt the ancient proprieties. This attitude found its classic spiritual expression in Calvinism. As Professor Tawney has said, Calvinism was "perhaps the first systematic body of religious teaching which can be said to recognize and applaud the economic virtues." It neatly fitted the glove of divine sanction to the hand of prudential conduct, thus giving a sense of personal rectitude to the business of getting ahead in the world. But whether in Britain or elsewhere, whether in the religious groups directly affected or those more remotely influenced, Calvinism merely intensified a pre-existing bent. It is similarly true that the stringent code of morals often attributed to Calvinism, and more particularly to Puritanism, represented a lower-middle-class mentality long antedating the Geneva teachings.

This, then, was the type of human breed upon which the untamed New World exerted its will. It has often been observed that the plants and animals of foreign lands undergo change when removed to America. These mutations arise from differences in climate and geography. But other influences also affected the transplanted European man. One was the temperament of the settler, the fact that he was more adventurous, or more ambitious, or more rebellious against conditions at home than his fellows who stayed put. It is not

15

necessary to believe with William Stoughton that "God sifted a whole Nation that he might send Choice Grain over into this Wilderness," but undoubtedly the act of quitting a familiar life for a strange and perilous one demanded uncommon qualities of hardihood, self-reliance, and imagination. Once the ocean was crossed, sheer distance and the impact of novel experiences further weakened the bonds of custom, evoked unsuspected capacities, and awakened the settler to possibilities of improvement which his forebears had never known.

The conditions offered by an undeveloped continent fixed the frame within which the new life must be lived, the mold within which the American character took form. Farming was the primary occupation. At first resorted to by the settlers to keep from starvation, it quickly became the mainstay of their existence. The Revolution was fought by a people of whom nineteen out of twenty were farmers. With good soil easily obtainable for over a century more, agriculture continued, though with gradually diminishing effect, to provide the pervasive atmosphere of American life and thought. "The vast majority of the people of this country live by the land, and carry its quality in their manners and opinions," wrote Emerson in 1844. Even when the hosts from Continental Europe began to swell the population in the nineteenth century, the rural temper of the nation continued unaltered, for most of the immigrants also turned to farming. This long apprenticeship to the soil made an indelible impress on the developing American character, with results which the modern age of the city has not wholly effaced.

The agriculture of the New World, however, differed from the agriculture of the Old. This was the initial lesson which the colonial newcomers were compelled to learn. Those who had been bred to husbandry in their homelands found many of the traditional methods unsuitable. Those who had worked at urban occupations suffered from an even greater handicap. Densely forested land must be cleared, the wildness taken out of the soil, a knowledge gained of indigenous plants and of the best means of growing them. The settlers of Jamestown were barely able to struggle through the early years. "There were never Englishmen left in a forreigne Country in such miserie as wee were in this new discovered Virginia," wrote one of them. "Unsufferable hunger" caused them to eat horses, dogs, rats, and snakes, and instances even of cannibalism are recorded. As is well known, the Plymouth colonists experienced similar trials. Yet in both cases the woods abounded with native fruits, berries, roots, and nuts; wild game was plentiful; and the near-by waters teemed with fish.

Had these Englishmen been more readily adaptable, they could have enjoyed a gastronomic abundance beyond the reach of even the nobility at home. But reversion to a stage of civilization which the white man had long since outgrown was not easy. At the very first, all the early settlements actually imported food supplies. The Swedish colony on the Delaware did so for twenty years. A knowledge of self-sufficient farming came slowly and painfully, with untold numbers of men, women, and children perishing in the process. In the long run, however, the settlers learned to master their environment. Utilizing native crops and Indian methods of tillage, they abandoned the intensive cultivation required by the limited land resources of the Old World. It was simpler to move on to new fields when the fertility of the old was exhausted. The typical farm was a small one, worked by the owner and his family. Even when the system of staple production emerged in the South, the small independent farmers considerably outnumbered the great slaveholding planters.

Though the colonial agriculturist owed much to the Indians, his European heritage restrained him from imitating them more than he must. Unlike the aborigines, he thirsted for the simple mechanical aids and other amenities which he and his kind had enjoyed in the Old World, and, lacking other means, he proceeded as best he could to reproduce them for himself. Besides wrestling with the soil, every husbandman was a manufacturer and every home a factory, engaged in grinding grain, making soap and candles, preparing the family meat supply, tanning skins, fabricating nails, harness, hats, shoes, and rugs, contriving tools, churns, casks, beds, chairs, and tables. Occasionally he did some of these things for his neighbors for hire. Such activities were supplemented by hunting, trapping, and fishing. As cold weather closed in, the men used their spare time in getting out rough timber products, such as shingles and planks, or spent the long winter evenings before the open fireplace carving gunstocks or making brooms while the womenfolk knitted, spun, or wove.

Under the pressure of circumstances the farmer became a Jack-of-all-trades. As Chancellor Livingston later wrote, "being habituated from early life to rely upon himself he acquires a skill in every branch of his profession, which is unknown in countries where labour is more divided." Take the case of an undistinguished New Englander, John Marshall of Braintree, early in the eighteenth century. Besides tending his farm, he was painter, brickmaker, and carpenter, turned out as many as three hundred laths in a day, bought and sold hogs, and served as a precinct constable. The primitive state of society fostered a similar omnicompetence in other walks of life, as the career of Benjamin Franklin so well exemplifies. Lord Cornbury, the governor of New York, characterized Francis Makemie as "a Preacher, a Doctor of Physick, a Merchant, an Attorney, or Counsellor at Law, and," he added for good measure, "which is worse of all, a Disturber of Governments."

The pioneer farmer of later times was the colonial farmer reborn. Up and down the Mississippi Valley he faced the same difficulties and the same opportunities as his forefathers, and he dealt with them in much the same way. As time went on, he managed to secure from independent craftsmen and factories certain of his tools and household conveniences; he took advantage of newly invented laborsaving appliances, such as the iron plow and the reaper; and more and more he raised crops for sale in a general market. Along the Atlantic seaboard similar alterations occurred. But whether in the older or the new communities, these innovations affected the surface rather than the substance of the traditional way of life. Nor did the advent of towns and cities at first do much to change the situation. Mere islands in a sea of population, they long retained marked rural characteristics and depended for a large part of their growth on continued accessions from the country side.

What qualities of the national character are attributable to this long-persistent agrarian setting? First and foremost is the habit of work. For the colonial farmer ceaseless exertion was the price of survival. Every member of the community must be up and doing. If a contrary spirit showed itself, the authorities, whether Anglican,

1. IS THE AMERICAN NATIONAL CHARACTER UNIQUE?

Puritan, or of a different faith, laid a heavy hand upon the culprit. . . .

Probably no legacy from our farmer forebears has entered more deeply into the national psychology. If an American has no purposeful work on hand, the fever in his blood impels him nevertheless to some form of visible activity. When seated he keeps moving in a rocking chair. A European visitor in the 1890's found more fact than fiction in a magazine caricature which pictured a foreigner as saying to his American hostess, "It's a defect in your country, that you have no leisured classes." "But we have them," she replied, "only we call them tramps." The traveler's own comment was: "America is the only country in the world, where one is ashamed of having nothing to do."

This worship of work has rendered it difficult for Americans to learn how to play. As Poor Richard saw it, "Leisure is the Time for doing something useful"; and James Russell Lowell confessed,

Pleasure doos make us Yankees kind o' winch,
Ez though 't wuz sunthin' paid for by the inch;
But yit we du contrive to worry thru,
Ef Dooty tells us thet the thing's to du. . . .

The first deviations from the daily grind took the form of hunting, fishing, barn-raisings, and logrollings—activities that contributed directly to the basic needs of living. As the years went on, the great Southern planters developed rural diversions into a sort of ritual, but their example, like that of the fashionable circles in the cities, made the common man all the more self-conscious when he sought recreation. Nor did the spontaneous gaiety that marked the idle hours of the Germans and Irish who came in the mid-nineteenth century have any other effect than to rein-

force suspicions of them formed on other scores. "The American," wrote a New Yorker of his compatriots in 1857, "enters into festivity as if it were a serious business. . . ." And a serious business it has continued to be ever since. Into it goes all the fierce energy that once felled the forests and broke the prairies. We play games not for their own sake but in order to win them. We attend social gatherings grimly determined to have "a good time." Maxim Gorky said of Coney Island, "What an unhappy people it must be that turns for happiness here." The "rich gift of extemporizing pleasures," of enjoying leisure leisurely, has, for the most part, been denied us. It is significant that the English *Who's Who* lists hobbies while the American still excludes them.

The importance attached to useful work had the further effect of helping to render "this new man" indifferent to aesthetic considerations. To the farmer a tree was not a symbol of Nature's unity but an obstacle to be reduced to a stump and then quickly replaced with a patch of corn or vegetables. . . . The cult of beauty, in other words, had nothing to contribute to the stern business of living; it wasn't "practical." The bias thus given to the national mentality lasted well into America's urban age. One result has been the architectural monotony and ugliness which have invariably offended travelers accustomed to the picturesque charm of Old World cities.

On the other hand, the complicated nature of the farmer's job, especially during the first two and a half centuries, provided an unexcelled training in mechanical ingenuity. These ex-Europeans and their descendants became a race of whittlers and tinkers, daily engaged in devising, improving, and repairing tools and other things until, as Emerson said, they had "the power and habit of invention in their brain." "Would any one but an American, asked one of Emerson's contemporaries, "have ever invented a milking machine? or a machine to beat eggs? or machines to black boots, scour knives, pare apples, and do a hundred things that all other peoples have done with their ten fingers from time immemorial?" As population increased and manufacturing developed on a commercial scale, men merely turned to new purposes the skills and aptitudes that had become second nature to them. Thus Eli Whitney, who as a Massachusetts farm youth had made nails and hatpins for sale to his neighbors, later contrived the cotton gin and successfully applied the principle of interchangeable parts to the making of muskets; and Theodore T. Woodruff, a New York farm boy, won subsequent fame as the inventor of a sleeping car, a coffee-hulling machine, and a steam plow. In this manner another trait became imbedded in the American character.

The farmer's success in coping with his multitudinous tasks aroused a pride of accomplishment that made him scorn the specialist or expert. As a Jack-of-all-trades he was content to be master of none, choosing to do many things well enough rather than anything supremely well. Thus versatility became an outstanding American attribute. In public affairs the common man agreed with President Jackson that any intelligent person could discharge the duties of any governmental office. He had an abiding suspicion of the theorist or the "scholar in politics," preferring to trust his own quick perceptions and to deal from day to day with matters as they arose. In his breadwinning pursuits the American flitted freely from job to job in marked contrast to the European custom of following permanent occupations which often de-

scended from father to son. The most casual scrutiny of the *Dictionary of American Biography* discloses countless instances reminiscent of John Marshall and Francis Makemie in colonial times. Thomas Buchanan Read, born on a Pennsylvania farm, was in turn a tailor's apprentice, grocer's assistant, cigar maker, tombstone carver, sign painter, and actor before he became a portrait painter, novelist, poet, and Civil War officer. Another personage is listed as "ornithologist and wholesale druggist"; another as "preacher, railway president, author"; and still another as "physician, merchant, political leader, magazine editor, poet, and critic." The wonder is that, despite such a squandering of energies, they could yet gain sufficient distinction in any phase of their activities to be recalled by posterity.

Even in his principal occupation of growing food, the farmer encountered harsh criticism from foreign visitors because of his practice of wearing out the land, his neglect of livestock, and his destruction of forest resources. But Old World agriculture was based on a ratio of man to land which in the New World was reversed. It was as natural for the American farmer to "mine the soil" and pass on to a virgin tract as it was for the European peasant to husband his few acres in the interest of generations unborn. Not till the opening years of the twentieth century, when the pressure of population dramatized the evils of past misuse, did the conservation of physical resources become a deliberate national policy.

Meanwhile the tradition of wasteful living, fostered by an environment of abundance, had fastened itself on the American character, disposing men to condone extravagance in public as well as in private life. Even official corruption could be winked at on the ground that a wealthy country such as the United States could afford it. In their personal lives Americans were improvident of riches that another people would have saved or frugally used. One recent arrival from England in the early nineteenth century wrote that the apples and peaches rotting in Ohio orchards were more "than would sink the British fleet." Another immigrant said of her adopted countrymen that she wished "the poor people in England had the leavings of their tables, that goes to their dogs and hogs." A national crisis like the present reveals the ravages of this proclivity. By a sudden inversion of time-honored values the salvaging of kitchen fats, waste paper, abandoned tools, and other discarded materials has become a mark of patriotism.

Toward women the American male early acquired an attitude which sharply distinguished him from his brother in the Old World. As in every new country, women had a high scarcity value, both in the colonies and later in the settling West. They were in demand not only for reasons of affection but also because of their economic importance, for they performed the endless work about the house and helped with the heavy farm labor. "The cry is everywhere for girls; girls, and more girls!" wrote a traveler in 1866. He noted that men outnumbered women in thirty-eight of the forty-five states and territories. In California the ratio was three to one; in Colorado, twenty to one. "Guess my husband's got to look after me, and make himself agreeable to me, if he can," a pretty Western girl remarked—"if he don't, there's plenty will." In the circumstances men paid women a deference and accorded them a status unknown in older societies. European observers attributed the high standard of sex morals largely to this fact, and it is significant that the most rapid strides toward equal suffrage took place in those commonwealths where the conditions of rural life had lingered longest.

Since the agriculturist regarded his farm only as a temporary abode, an investment rather than a home, he soon contracted the habit of being "permanently transitory." Distances that would have daunted the stoutest-hearted European deterred "this new man" not at all. Many an Atlantic Coast family migrated from place to place across the continent until the second or third generation reached the rim of the Pacific and the next one began the journey back. "In no State of the Union," wrote James Bryce in 1888, "is the bulk of the population so fixed in its residence as everywhere in Europe; in many it is almost nomadic." But for this constant mingling of people and ideas the spirit of sectionalism would have opened far deeper fissures in American society than it did, for the breadth of the land, the regional diversification of economic interests, and the concentration of European immigrants in certain areas were all factors conducive to separatism and disunity. Instead of one great civil war there might have been many. Apart from the crisis of 1860, however, it has always been possible to adjust sectional differences peaceably. The war between North and South might itself have been avoided if the slave-centered plantation system of agriculture had not increasingly stopped the inflow of persons from other parts of the country as well as from Europe. Denied such infusions of new blood, the Southerners lived more and more to themselves, came to value their peculiarities above the traits they shared with their fellow countrymen, and, in the end, resolved to strike for an independent existence.

As the country grew older and its institutions assumed a more settled aspect, the locomotive tendencies of the Americans showed no signs of abatement. The wanderlust had entered their blood stream. According to a study of population redistribution in 1936, "over the last few decades mobility has been increasing rather than decreasing." The Department of Agriculture reports that the average farm family remains on the same farm for only five or six years and that nearly half the children ultimately go to the towns and cities. Urban dwellers take flight with equal facility. On the principle of the man biting the dog, the New York *Times*, June 14, 1942, reported that a resident of the California town of Sebastapol had lived in the same house for fifty years, although it admitted he was the only one of eleven children who had not gone to other parts. With the advent of the cheap automobile and the passion for long-distance touring, the rippling movement of humanity came to resemble the waves of the ocean. In 1940 the American people owned more motorcars than bathtubs. The pursuit of happiness was transformed into the happiness of pursuit. Foreigners had earlier expressed amazement at the spectacle of dwellings being hauled by horses along the streets from one site to another, but by means of the automobile trailer more than half a million Americans have now discovered a way of living constantly on wheels. The nation appears to be on the point of solving the riddle of perpetual motion.

Geographic or horizontal mobility was the concomitant of a still more fundamental aspect of American life: social or vertical mobility. The European notion of a graded society in which each class everlastingly performed its allotted function vanished quickly amidst primitive surroundings that invited the humblest persons to move upward as well as outward.

Instead of everybody being nobody, they found that everybody might become somebody. In the language of James Russell Lowell, "Here, on the edge of the forest, where civilized man was brought face to face again with nature and taught mainly to rely on himself, mere manhood became a fact of prime importance." This emancipation from hoary custom was "no bantling of theory, no fruit of forethought," but "a gift of the sky and of the forest." In this manner there arose the ingrained belief in equality of opportunity, the right of every man to a free and fair start—a view which in one of its most significant ramifications led to the establishment of free tax-supported schools. This belief was far from being a dogma of enforced equality. The feeling of the American was "I'm as good as you are" rather than "I'm no better than anyone else." To benefit from equality of opportunity a man must be equal to his opportunities. The government existed principally as an umpire to supervise the game with a minimum of rules. The upshot was a conception of democracy rigorously qualified by individualism. . . .

If this analysis of American characteristics is well founded, then certain modifications might be expected as the primacy of rural life yielded to the rise of urbanism. In the latter decades of the nineteenth century a rapidly increasing proportion of the people found themselves dwelling under conditions different from those of earlier times. In 1860 only a sixth of the nation lived in towns of 8,000 or more, but by 1900 a third resided in urban communities, and today well over half do. Moreover, throughout these years, places of 25,000 or more attracted a majority of the city dwellers. Paralleling this urban growth occurred a remarkable development of new means of communication and transport that carried city ideas and

1. IS THE AMERICAN NATIONAL CHARACTER UNIQUE?

ways to "the very fingertips of the whole land": the telephone, rural free delivery, good roads, interurban electric transit, the automobile, the movie, the radio. In this changed environment of American society many of the historic national traits flourished; others were tempered or transformed. . . .

The national character, as we at present know it, is thus a mixture of long-persistent traits and newly acquired characteristics. Based upon the solid qualities of those Europeans who dared to start life anew across the Atlantic, it assumed distinctive form under the pressure of adaptation to a radically different environment. "Our ancestors sought a new country," said James Russell Lowell. "What they found was a new condition of mind." The long tutelage to the soil acted as the chief formative influence, removing ancient inhibitions, freeing latent energies, revamping mental attitudes. The rise of the city confirmed or strengthened many of the earlier attributes while altering others. Probably none of the traits is peculiar to the American people; some of them we may regard with more humility than pride; but the sum total represents a way of life unlike that of any other nation.

Just as the American character has undergone modification in the past, so it will doubtless undergo modification in the future. Nevertheless, certain of its elements seem so deeply rooted as to defy the erosion of time and circumstance. Of this order are the qualities that made possible the occupying and development of the continent, the building of a democratic society, and the continuing concern for the welfare of the underprivileged. These are attributes better suited to peace than to war, yet every great crisis has found the people ready to die for their conception of life so that their children might live it. . . . The American character, whatever its shortcomings, abounds in courage, creative energy, and resourcefulness and is bottomed upon the profound conviction that nothing in the world is beyond its power to accomplish.

NO

Carlton J. H. Hayes

THE AMERICAN FRONTIER— FRONTIER OF WHAT?

... We used to know that we were Europeans as well as Americans, that we were not Indians or a people miraculously sprung from virgin forests like the primitive Germans described by Tacitus, but modern Europeans living in America on a frontier of Europe. All our original white ancestors on this continent knew they came from Europe. They and their sons and grandsons knew they had ties with Englishmen, Spaniards, Portuguese, Hollanders, or Frenchmen, as the case might be, not only on this side of the ocean but on the other. And generation after generation of their descendants on this side, no matter on what segment of the frontier they chanced to be, and no matter how intent on clearing new lands, were concerned and found themselves participants in all the successive major wars of Europe from the sixteenth century to the twentieth: the English-Spanish wars, the English-Dutch wars, the War of the League of Augsburg, the War of the Spanish Succession, the War of the Austrian Succession, the Seven Years' War, the Revolutionary and Napoleonic Wars, the war of 1914, the war of 1939. From the first, moreover, it has been known or knowable, if latterly obscured, that our language, our religion, our culture are rooted in Europe, that our ideals of liberty and constitutional government are a heritage of Europe.

In paying tribute to the members of the Constitutional Convention of 1787, Charles A. Beard has remarked:

> It is not merely patriotic pride that compels one to assert that never in the history of assemblies has there been a convention of men richer in political experience and in practical knowledge, or endowed with a profounder insight into the springs of human action and the intimate essence of government. It is indeed an astounding fact that at one time so many men skilled in statecraft could be found on the very frontiers of civilization among a population numbering about four million whites.

It is not quite so astounding, I would add, if one bears in mind that those men "on the very frontiers of civilization" possessed lively contacts with, and solid knowledge of, the European civilization on whose frontiers they were.

Excerpted by special permission from, "The American Frontier—Frontier of What?" by Carlton J.H. Hayes, *The American Historical Review*, Volume LI, Number 2, January 1946. Copyright © The American Historical Association.

1. IS THE AMERICAN NATIONAL CHARACTER UNIQUE?

One has only to run through the numbers of the *Federalist* to recognize the sure and firm grasp of such men as Hamilton, Madison, and Jay on the history and political experience of ancient Greece and Rome and of the countries of medieval and modern Europe—Britain, Germany, France, Poland, the Netherlands, Switzerland. The founding fathers may have been frontiersmen and greatly influenced by economic conditions in the New World, but they could readily have passed a searching examination for the doctorate in European history and European comparative government, which, I dare say, is more than the majority of our senators or even of our Ph.D.'s in American history could now do.

That the United States could become an independent nation and enjoy the freedom and opportunity to extend its frontiers and greatly to increase its population and prosperity and strength during the perilous fifty years of Revolutionary and Napoleonic Wars and Metternichean reaction, from 1775 to 1825, is attributable less to American aloofness from Europe than to the informed statecraft of Americans who were then in familiar touch with Europe and equipped to treat with it intelligently and realistically. Almost without exception, our presidents and secretaries of state and key diplomatists of that time had practical experience in European, as well as American, affairs—Franklin, Jefferson, Jay, Marshall, Madison, Monroe, John Adams, John Quincy Adams. Monroe, for example, served in diplomatic posts in France, England, and Spain for six years before he became Madison's Secretary of State, and his own Secretary of State, John Quincy Adams, had been a student at Paris and Leiden and had had twenty years' diplomatic experience in France, the Netherlands, Prussia, Russia, and Great Britain. The words which this qualified statesman put into Monroe's celebrated message of 1823 to the Congress expressed an enlightened realism in notable contrast with utterances and actions of certain American statesmen of a later date less in touch with the realities of Europe and more with ideological propaganda in America.

Said the message of 1823, without trace of a holier-than-thou attitude:

> Our policy in regard to Europe . . . remains the same, which is, not to interfere in the internal affairs of any of its powers; to consider the Government *de facto* as the legitimate Government for us; to cultivate friendly relations with it, and to preserve those relations by a frank, firm, and manly policy; meeting, in all instances, the just claims of every power; submitting to injuries from none.

It was not only our statesmen of that time who knew and appreciated the relationship between Europe and America. Our colleges and academies, with their classical curriculum, and our literary men and publicists, with their extensive reading of British and French philosophers of the seventeenth and eighteenth centuries, possessed like knowledge and appreciation. Our commercial classes, including our cotton planters, had it, too. To protect our commerce with Europe, Jefferson dispatched to the Mediterranean an American armed expeditionary force which made landings in North Africa nearly a century and a half before the recent repetition of American campaigning in the Mediterranean. And what a reading public there was in the United States for those literary historians in our "middle period"—Irving, Prescott, Motley, and Parkman—who dwelt on exploits of Spanish, Dutch, and French. It might well be envied by any historian of the American frontier or even by the Book-of-the-Month Club. The Mediterranean Sea was not then so far off, or the Atlantic Ocean so wide, as our developing isolationist nationalism later made them.

Our successive American generations of frontiersmen on the eastern seaboard, in the piedmont, across the Alleghenies, along the Ohio, the Great Lakes, and the Mississippi, over the prairies, and into and beyond the Rockies, may have thought of themselves as Americans first. They may have adopted Indian dress and Indian usages in hunting and fishing and scalping. They may have exerted, and doubtless did exert, a profound and lasting influence on the nationalist evolution of the United States. But all this did not make them Indians or immunize them against the superior and eventually mastering civilization which emanated from Europe and relentlessly followed them. They remained Europeans and retained at least the rudiments of European civilization. After all, the American frontier, as Professor Turner so ably and perhaps regretfully showed, was an evanescent phenomenon, ever passing from primitiveness toward the social and intellectual pattern of the area in back of it. In other words, the abiding heritage of traditional civilization outweighed, in a relatively brief period, the novelties acquired from Indians and wilderness. Continuity proved stronger than change. The transit of culture was not so much *from* as *to* the frontier.

Differences admittedly obtain between Americans in the United States and the peoples in Europe from whom they are descended, but the differences are not greater in kind, and hardly greater in degree, than those obtaining between Englishmen and Spaniards or between Germans and Italians, or between the people of the United States and the peoples of Central and South America. True, the nationalism which has progressively infected all peoples of Europe and America during the last hundred and fifty years has grossly exaggerated the differences and given wide currency to the notion of distinctive and self-contained national cultures—a French culture, a Norwegian culture, a Spanish culture, an American culture. The result has been an obscuring and neglect of what these several national cultures have in common, a European or "Western" culture, the community of heritage and outlook and interests in Europe and its whole American frontier.

Actual differences are differences of emphasis and detail, associated with political sovereignty and independence, and arising from variant geographical and historical circumstances. Back of them all, however, is a unifying fact and force, which is describable as "European" or "Western," and which, now more than ever before, needs to be appreciated and applied. Actually and fundamentally, just as the European remains a European while thinking of himself first as an Englishman, a Frenchman, a German, or a Spaniard, so the descendants of Europeans in America remain European even while insisting that they are Americans first.

The frontier has undoubtedly been a very important source of what is distinctive and peculiar in the national evolution of the United States. But few European nations have been without a frontier in the American sense at some time in their history and without significant lasting effects of that frontier. Contemporary peculiarities in the life and customs of Spain, for instance, cannot be dissociated from the slow advance, during several centuries, of a frontier of conquest of Moorish lands; nor Germany's, from an analogous frontier in barbarous regions ofnorth central Europe. In a larger way, all America is a frontier: Latin America, of Spain and Por-

1. IS THE AMERICAN NATIONAL CHARACTER UNIQUE?

tugal; Quebec, of France; the United States, of Great Britain and Holland, Spain and France, Germany and Ireland, Scandinavia and Italy and Poland. Our Negroes and Indians, as these have been civilized, have been Europeanized as well as Americanized. The "melting pot" is no novelty in the history of Western civilization; it has latterly been doing in America, on a large scale, the same sort of fusing which at earlier dates produced the chief nations of modern Europe. Comparative study of frontiers in Europe and America, together with comparative study of melting pots and nationalisms in both, might serve to demonstrate that obvious differences between nations of European tradition are fewer and relatively less significant than their similarities.

"European," as I here use the term, does not refer merely to a detached piece of geography or to a continent by itself, and not to another "hemisphere" or a hoary and pitiable "Old World." Rather, it refers to a great historic culture, the "Western" civilization, which, taking its rise around the Mediterranean, has long since embraced the Atlantic, creating what Mr. Walter Lippmann has appropriately designated the "Atlantic Community." As Professor Ross Hoffman says:

> Every state of the North and South American continents originated from Western European Christendom which Voltaire, in the age before the independence movements, characterized so well as a "great republic." Englishmen, Frenchmen, Spaniards, Portuguese, Dutchmen and Danes in the early modern centuries made the Atlantic Ocean the inland sea of Western civilization; they made it an historical and geographical extension of the Mediterranean. . . . Many of these early-forged bonds still span the Atlantic, and the spread of British, French, and American ideals of liberty and constitutional government has

made this oceanic region the citadel of what today is rather loosely called Democracy.

Of such an Atlantic community and the European civilization basic to it, we Americans are co-heirs and co-developers, and probably in the future the leaders. If we are successfully to discharge our heavy and difficult postwar responsibilities, we shall not further weaken, but rather strengthen, the consciousness and bonds of this cultural community.

Against it, militate two current trends of quite contradictory character. One, which I have already indicated, is the nationalistic tendency to view each nation as *sui generis,* and to attribute to it an independent and distinctive culture all its own. The second is the hypothesizing of a "world civilization." This has already passed from the fictional titles of high-school textbooks to the solemn pronouncements of statesmen. It represents a leap from myopic nationalism to starry-eyed universalism. I, for one, have not the faintest idea what world civilization is. I know there are enduring and respectable civilizations in Moslem areas, in India, in China, and presumably in Japan. I also know there are considerable influences of such civilizations upon ours, and, especially in the material domain, heavy impacts by ours upon them. But the many existing civilizations still do not constitute a single "world civilization," and for a long time to come, I hazard, the common denominator among them is likely to be low—as low, I should suppose, as unadorned "human nature."

Neither devotion to one's nation nor idealization of the world at large should obscure the important cultural entities which lie between. These are the powerhouses of civilization for their constituent nationalities, and the units which must be brought into co-operation for any world order of the future. The one to which Americans belong is the "European" or "Western." It has conditioned our past. And whether we are aware of it, or not, it conditions our present and future.

In what does it consist? First, in the Greco-Roman tradition, with its rich heritage of literature and language, of philosophy, of architecture and art, of law and political concepts. Second, in the Judeo-Christian tradition, with its fructifying ethos and ethics, its abiding and permeating influence on personal and social behavior, its constant distinctions between the individual and the race, between liberty and authority, between mercy and justice, between what is Caesar's and what is God's. Third, proceeding from joint effects of the first two, it comprises traditions of individualism, of limitations on the state, of social responsibility, of revolt and revolution. Fourth, likewise proceeding from the others, particularly from the Christian tradition, it includes a tradition of expansiveness, of missionary and crusading zeal, which has inspired not merely a spasmodic but a steady pushing outward of European frontiers—from the Mediterranean to the Arctic and across the Atlantic, in turn over lands of Celts, Germans, Slavs, Magyars, and Scandinavians, over the full width of both American continents, and beyond to the Philippines and Australasia and into Africa.

In all these characteristics of European or Western civilization, every nationality of central and western Europe and of America shares. In measure as the frontier advances and is civilized, it is these characteristics which actuate and are embodied in the civilization. The United States is no exception.

One does not have to go to Athens and Rome to behold Greek and Roman architecture, or to Palestine and Europe to see Jewish synagogues and Christian churches. There are more churches and synagogues in the United States than in any other country in the world. There is more classical architecture in Leningrad or London than in Athens, and still more in Washington. It is indeed the practically official architecture of our American democracy from Jefferson to Hoover, and the favorite style for bank buildings, railway stations, and public schools, whether in Virginia or Illinois or the Far West. Our prevailing language continues to be transatlantic English, and distinctively American only in pronunciation and raciness of idiom. Shakespeare and Milton are as much ours as England's. Our juristic conceptions and legal usages are likewise transatlantic, and I know of no philosophical speculation on this continent, in the whole gamut from the pragmatic to the Thomistic, or on any subject from theological to scientific, including political and economic, which has not had its equivalent and usually its antecedent in Europe.

If we belonged to a Moslem or Confucian culture, or to a purely indigenous one, we would not have the mores which we have. We would not, for instance, be free on Sundays for church or golf or for surreptitious privacy in library or laboratory. Probably we would not use knives and forks, and we would wear different clothes. We might be more ceremonial and more externally polite. We might think, as well as behave, differently. Our sense of values and our frames of references could not be quite the same. We are what we are only in part because of biological heredity and physical environment. In larger part it is because we are stamped from infancy with a historic culture of singularly educative and perduring potency. . . .

There will doubtless be dissent from the thesis I have here advanced, and from its implications. May I suggest, however, that, among us, dissent be attended by informed thought rather than by nationalist emotion. In the past, American historians, by concentrating their thought and labor more and more on the United States and its western frontier, have contributed immeasurably to the conscious solidifying, in time and space, of the great independent Republic of the New World. Now, when the Republic's old frontier, completing its western march, has disappeared from the American continent and been superseded by new and quite different frontiers on distant isles of the Pacific, in the Azores, and on the Rhine and Danube, our historians, whether they agree or not with my particular views, might appropriately devote more attention to fields which have hitherto been relatively neglected and whose cultivation will be conducive to clearer appreciation in this country of its historic setting and current responsibilities.

It is no longer a question of creating a great American nation. It is now a question of preserving and securing this nation in a world of nations. Nor is it now a question of isolationism versus internationalism. This has finally been determined by the Senate's almost unanimous ratification of the Charter of the United Nations. The question now is whether as a nation we are going to be sufficiently informed and intelligent about foreign conditions, sufficiently freed from provincialism, to ensure the effective operation of the United Nations' organization in the best interest of ourselves and of world peace. Toward satisfactory solution of this question, American historians, if they will, can make major contributions.

One contribution would be to put much greater emphasis than in the past on cultural history—on the history of language and literature, of religion and church, of art and science, of intellectual currents, and of the transit of culture. Our national past and present, like the world's at large, are only partially explicable in terms of industrial and material development; and I would hope that the "economic interpretation," which has had such stimulating and valuable influence on historical research and writing during the past half century, might now be qualified and supplemented by a broader "cultural interpretation." There is doubtless already a trend in this direction. It is evidenced in a considerable number of recent monographs, and especially in the important co-operative *History of American Life* edited by Professor Schlesinger and the late President Fox. It requires, however, for its confirmation and proper fruitage much deepening and broadening and a much larger number of scholarly investigators and writers. It is cultural considerations, let me stress, which most profoundly affect American relationships with the world, not only of the past, but of the present and future.

I hope, too, that we shall not lose sight of the continuity of history. There is a pronounced tendency in the United States to dwell on the "newness" and "uniqueness" of the "New World" and our "new nation"—new freedom, new frontier, new deal, new knowledge, new thought—and to accept a cataclysmic view of history. Serious historical scholars know—or should know—that such striking events as the invention of gunpowder or of printing, the discovery of America, the Protestant Reformation, the French Revolution, the American Revolution, were not really cataclysmic, that they merely speeded some continuous process long previously under way and left untouched vastly more habits of human thought and action than they altered. With this knowledge well in mind, we should be very skeptical of contemporary popular notions concerning the cataclysmic character of the Russian Revolution, the second World War, or even the atomic bomb. We may confidently expect that the world of the future will continue to be mainly the world of the past. The principal threads of our historic Western culture, like those of the Chinese or Moslem cultures, have not suddenly been cut in A.D. 1945. Unconsciously if not consciously, whether we like it or not, we shall go right on in the Greco-Roman and Judeo-Christian traditions. It would be realistic to recognize the fact.

Of course, there is change, and what may properly be called progress, in America and in the world. But how are we to gauge it or to try intelligently to direct it without relating it to the constants and continuities in human experience? American history should, of course, be taught in our schools—more, rather than less, American history—but it should not be taught as beginning with the political independence of a new nation in 1776 or even with the discovery of a New World in 1492. To understand what America really is, of what actually it is a frontier, its history should be studied continuously from at least the ancient Greeks and the first Christians.

Finally, I would earnestly urge that greater attention be paid to comparative history. The comparative method is the surest means of diminishing racial, political, religious, and national prejudices. As the distinguished Belgian historian Henri Pirenne has written:

> These prejudices ensnare him who, confined within the narrow limits of national history, is condemned to understand it badly becaue he is incapable of comprehending the bonds attaching it to the histories of other nations. It is not due to *parti pris*

but because of insufficient information that so many historians lack impartiality. One who is lost in admiration of his own people will inevitably exaggerate their originality and give them the honor for discoveries which are in reality only borrowed. He is unjust to others because he fails to understand them, and the exclusiveness of his knowledge lays him open to the deceptions of the idols set up by sentiment. The comparative method permits history to appear in its true perspective. What was believed to be a mountain is razed to the size of a molehill, and the thing for which national genius was honored is often revealed as a simple manifestation of the imitative spirit.

The student of the history of the United States, whether dealing with its political, economic, or cultural development, would be the better historian and the more enlightening if he was a specialist also in the history of a foreign country from which comparisons and contrasts could be drawn. Similarly, the student of the history of a foreign country could profitably extend his study beyond that country. Most of all, the historian of a particular phenomenon, such as nationalism, slavery, democracy, the frontier, etc., however specific in time or space may be his immediate work, must needs possess, if his work is to be informed and judicious, a wide background of acquaintance with other and comparable examples of the phenomenon.

In summary, the American frontier is a frontier of European or "Western" culture. This culture, however modified by or adapted to peculiar geographical and social conditions in America or elsewhere, is still, in essential respects, the culture and hence a continuous bond of the regional community of nations on both sides of the Atlantic. Like its predecessor and inspirer, the Mediterranean community of ancient times, the Atlantic community has been an outstanding fact and a prime factor of modern history. Despite the growth in latter years of an anarchical nationalism and isolationism on one hand, and of a utopian universalism on the other, the Atlantic community has lost none of its potential importance for us and for the world. We must look anew to it and strengthen our ties with it, if we are to escape the tragedy of another world war and ensure the blessings of liberty and democracy to future generations. To this end the historical guild in America can immeasurably contribute by extending the use of the comparative method, by emphasizing the continuity of history, and by stressing cultural and social, equally with political and economic, history.

POSTSCRIPT

IS THE AMERICAN NATIONAL
CHARACTER UNIQUE?

Both Schlesinger and Hayes built their interpretations around concepts of expansion as analyzed in Frederick Jackson Turner's "The Significance of the Frontier in American History," read in 1893 at Chicago's Columbian Exposition.

Their disagreements reflect different approaches to historical study. Schlesinger wrote social history, while Hayes concentrated on cultural values. Schlesinger believed strongly in the concept of national character. He discussed characteristics such as the work ethic and practicality as uniquely American, as if these qualities were absent in other peoples. Hayes was considerably less ethnocentric than Schlesinger and more familiar with American historiography than Schlesinger was with European historical writing. Hayes incorporated Turner's frontier thesis into the larger picture, the macrocosm of the Atlantic community. Schlesinger's nationalistic approach, on the other hand, revealed a microcosmic viewpoint. Hayes was inclusive, Schlesinger exclusive. But isn't there some validity in each interpretation? If there are distinctions that separate Europe and the United States, are they differences of kind or of degree? Are the values of the United States those of farmers conditioned primarily by an expanding frontier? Is there no place for the Hellenistic traditions in literature, art, architecture, thought, or the Judaic-Christian religious tradition in the Mediterranean world?

The Comparative Approach to American History (Basic Books, 1968), edited by C. Vann Woodward, presents essays from the colonial period to the cold war in an international context. Frederick Jackson Turner augmented his original essay with others in *The Frontier in American History* (Holt, 1920). Ray Allen Billington, Turner's heir as advocate of the frontier thesis, has numerous works on the West. R.R. Palmer's two-volume *The Age of the Democratic Revolution* (Princeton University Press, 1959, 1964) develops the idea of the Atlantic community in the late eighteenth century through the study of comparative revolutions.

Neither Schlesinger nor Hayes discussed the important contributions made by Africans, Native Americans, and Asians to American society. Nevertheless, their thoughts provide a framework for the subsequent issues in this volume.

ISSUE 2

DID SOCIAL TENSIONS IN SALEM MOTIVATE THE WITCHHUNTS OF 1692?

YES: Paul Boyer and Stephen Nissenbaum, from *Salem Possessed: The Social Origins of Witchcraft* (Harvard University Press, 1974)

NO: Chadwick Hansen, from *Witchcraft at Salem* (George Braziller, 1969)

ISSUE SUMMARY

YES: Professors Boyer and Nissenbaum think economic and social tensions motivated the Salem witchhunts.
NO: Professor Hansen believes in the reality of pathological bewitchment.

Proof that witchcraft has existed since prehistoric times is evident from paintings on the walls of caves throughout Europe, from Russia to Spain. However, the most intense eruptions in its long history appeared during the religious turmoil of the sixteenth and seventeenth centuries. There were over one hundred witchcraft trials in seventeenth-century New England alone, and forty percent of those accused were executed. The Salem trials in 1692 accounted for half of these hangings. While religion played an important part in the accusations at Salem there were other determining factors.

Accusations of witchcraft have followed certain patterns, occurring usually in times of social stress, economic dislocation, or political turmoil. Salem's bout with black magic reflected these characteristics. The indictments ripped Salem apart and revealed deep social divisions between Salem Town and Salem Village (the latter a kind of suburb which sought independence from the former) as well as within the village itself. Economic tensions between commercial and agricultural interests, microcosmic disagreements between town and village, and a macrocosmic political impasse between English authorities and the

Massachusetts Bay Colony formed the backdrop to the legal drama. In addition, foreign affairs played an important role; the accusations commenced shortly after an expensive and abortive invasion of New France.

By 1692 these various problems coalesced in Salem Village in Reverend Samuel Parris's kitchen. His West-Indian slave girl, Tituba, and several of her friends were trying to guess the future by reading messages in the white of a raw egg dropped into a glass of water. The tragic results of this seemingly innocent diversion scandalized the Salem community and reverberated all the way to Boston. One of the girls insisted she saw the spectre of a coffin when she examined the egg white/water solution. Soon after, the girls began to display the hysterical symptoms of the possessed. One of the first to recognize the omens of black magic was Tituba, who prepared an antidote, a witch's cake. Tituba's remedy failed and not long after she and two old, eccentric women were charged with practicing magic. This development fit the traditional pattern of alleged witches frequently being old women of eccentric behavior. In Salem, however, there was an additional generational factor—those initially possessed were children or teenagers; the tormentors they accused were adults.

Subsequent events uncovered the dark side of life in Salem and lent American witchhunting an enduring and unsavory reputation. Allegations spread, followed by indictments. Their frequency and intensity underscored economic, social and political anxieties. Tituba confessed to sorcery. Although two explicit references in the Old Testament (Leviticus 20:27 and Exodus 22:18) condemn witches to death, Salem Christians were willing to spare *confessed* witches. Ironically, confession, as dangerous as that might be, assured acquittal. Those who risked trials gambled with their lives. (One man refused to enter a plea of guilt or innocence and was pressed to death by weights in an attempt to bring him before a jury.)

After Tituba admitted her offenses, and thereby established her credibility as a sorceress, she corroborated the possessed girls' claims. Tituba acknowledged the existence of other witches but refused to name them. The possession spread as did the accusations. Paranoia in the community reflected the hysterics of the bewitched. Between May and September 1692 hundreds of people were arrested. Nineteen were convicted and hanged. Accusations had been hurled at very prominent persons including the wife of Sir William Phipps, the Royal Governor, and in September 1692 court proceedings were halted. In May 1693 Phipps ordered those in jail to be released.

"Those who defended the witches were generally their neighbors," Boyer and Nissenbaum concluded, "often their immediate neighbors. Those who accused them were not." Hansen, basing his views on modern studies of emotional disturbances, insisted "With minor exceptions the girls' behavior belongs to the history of pathology rather than the history of fraud."

YES

Paul Boyer and Stephen Nissenbaum

SALEM POSSESSED: THE SOCIAL ORIGINS OF WITCHCRAFT

1692: SOME NEW PERSPECTIVES

Salem witchcraft. For most Americans the episode ranks in familiarity somewhere between Plymouth Rock and Custer's Last Stand. This very familiarity, though, has made it something of a problem for historians. As a dramatic package, the events of 1692 are just too neat, highlighted but also insulated from serious research by the very floodlights which illuminate them. "Rebecca Nurse," "Ann Putnam," "Samuel Parris"—they all endlessly glide onto the stage, play their appointed scenes, and disappear again into the void. It is no coincidence that the Salem witch trials are best known today through the work of a playwright, not a historian. It was, after all, a series of historians from George Bancroft to Marion Starkey who first treated the event as a dramatic set piece, unconnected with the major issues of American colonial history. When Arthur Miller published *The Crucible* in the early 1950's, he simply outdid the historians at their own game.

After nearly three centuries of retelling in history books, poems, stories, and plays, the whole affair has taken on a foreordained quality. It is hard to conceive that the events of 1692 could have gone in any other direction or led to any other outcome. It is like imagining the *Mayflower* sinking in midpassage, or General Custer at the Little Big Horn surrendering to Sitting Bull without a fight.

And yet speculation as to where events might have led in 1692 is one way of recapturing the import of where they did lead. And if one reconstructs those events bit by bit, as they happened, without too quickly categorizing them, it is striking how long they resist settling into the neat and familiar pattern one expects. A full month, maybe more, elapsed between the time the girls began to exhibit strange behavior and the point at which the first accusations of witchcraft were made; and in the haze of those first uncertain weeks, it is possible to discern the shadows of what might have been.

Bewitchment and Conversion

Imagine, for instance, how easily the finger of witchcraft could have been pointed back at the afflicted girls themselves. It was they, after all, who first began to toy with the supernatural. At least one neighboring minister, the Reverend John Hale of Beverly, eventually became convinced that a large measure of blame rested with these girls who, in their "vain curiosity to know their future condition," had "tampered with the devil's tools." And Hale's judgment in the matter was shared by his far more influential colleague Cotton Mather, who pinpointed as the cause of the outbreak the "conjurations" of thoughtless youths, including, of course, the suffering girls themselves.

Why then, during 1692, were the girls so consistently treated as innocent victims? Why were they not, at the very least, chastised for behavior which itself verged on witchcraft? Clearly, the decisive factor was the interpretation which adults—adults who had the power to make their interpretation stick—chose to place on events whose intrinsic meaning was, to begin with, dangerously ambiguous.

The adults, indeed, determined not only the direction the witchcraft accusations would take; it was they, it seems, who first concluded that witchcraft was even in the picture at all. "[W]hen these calamities first began," reported Samuel Parris in March 1692, "... the affliction was several weeks before such hellish operations as witchcraft was suspected." Only in response to urgent questioning—"Who is it that afflicts you?"—did the girls at last begin to point their fingers at others in the Village.

It is not at all clear that the girls' affliction was initially unpleasant or, indeed, that they experienced it as an "affliction" at all. Unquestionably it could be harrowing enough once witchcraft became the ac-cepted diagnosis, but the little evidence available from late February, before the agreed-upon explanation had been arrived at, makes the girls' behavior seem more exhilarated than tormented, more liberating than oppressive. One of the early published accounts of the outbreak, that of Robert Calef in 1700, described the girls' initial manifestations as "getting into holes, and creeping under chairs and stools..., [with] sundry odd postures and antic gestures, [and] uttering foolish, ridiculous speeches which neither they themselves nor any others could make sense of." ...

Some Patterns of Accusation

Pace. By the time the storm subsided in October, several hundred persons had been accused of witchcraft, about 150 of them formally charged and imprisoned, and nineteen executed. But when it first broke out in February, there had been no indication that it would reach such proportions, or that it would be any more serious than the numerous isolated witchcraft outbreaks that had periodically plagued New England since at least 1647—outbreaks that had resulted in a total of only fifteen or so executions. The initial accusations at the end of February had named three witches, and most people outside Salem Village, if they heard of the matter at all, probably assumed that it would end there. But the symptoms of the afflicted girls did not subside, and toward the end of March the girls accused three more persons of tormenting them. Still, by early April (a month and a half after the accusations began) only six people had come under public suspicion of witchcraft.

It was at this time, however, that the pace of accusations picked up sharply, and the whole situation began to assume unusual and menacing proportions. Twenty-two witches were accused in April, thirty-nine more in May. After a dip in June, probably reflecting the impact of the first actual execution on June 10, the arrests picked up again and increased steadily from July through September. Indeed, toward the end of the summer, accusations were being made so freely and widely that accurate records of the official proceedings were no longer kept.

Status. But it was not only in the matter of numbers that the episode changed dramatically as it ran its course; there was a qualitative change as well. The first three women to be accused could be seen as "deviants" or "outcasts" in their community—the kinds of people who anthropologists have suggested are particularly susceptible to such accusations. Tituba, as we have seen, was a West Indian slave; Sarah Good was a pauper who went around the Village begging aggressively for food and lodging; "Gammer" Osborne, while somewhat better off, was a bedridden old woman.

In March, however, a new pattern began to emerge. Two of the three witches accused in that month—the third was little Dorcas Good—were church members (a sign of real respectability in the seventeenth century) and the wives of prosperous freeholders. This pattern continued and even intensified for the duration of the outbreak: the twenty-two persons accused in April included the wealthiest shipowner in Salem (Phillip English) and a minister of the gospel who was a Harvard graduate with a considerable estate in England (George Burroughs). By mid-May warrants had been issued against two of the seven selectmen of Salem Town; and by the end of the summer some of the most prominent people in Massachusetts and their close kin had been accused if not officially charged. . . .

True, none of these persons of quality was ever brought to trial, much less executed. Some escaped from jail or house arrest, others were simply never arraigned. Nevertheless, the overall direction of the accusations remains clear: up the social ladder, fitfully but perceptibly, to its very top. Whatever else they may have been, the Salem witch trials cannot be written off as a communal effort to purge the poor, the deviant, or the outcast.

Geography. Just as the accusations thrust steadily upward through the social strata of provincial society, so, too, they pressed outward across geographic boundaries. Beginning within Salem Village itself, the accusations moved steadily into an increasingly wide orbit. The first twelve witches were either residents of the Village or persons who lived just beyond its borders. But of all the indictments which followed this initial dozen, only fifteen were directed against people in the immediate vicinity of Salem Village. The other victims came from virtually every town in Essex County, including the five which surrounded the Village. (In the town of Andover alone, there were more arrests than in Salem Village itself.)

While almost all these arrests were made on the basis of testimony given by the ten or so afflicted girls of Salem Village (although in some cases they merely confirmed the validity of others' accusations), it is clear that the girls themselves did not actually know most of the people they named. . . .

Accusers and accused, then, were in many if not most cases personally unacquainted. Whatever was troubling the girls and those who encouraged them, it was something deeper than the kind of chronic, petty squabbles between near neighbors which seem to have been at the root of earlier and far less severe witchcraft episodes in New England.

But if the outbreak's geographic pattern tends to belie certain traditional explanations, it raises other, more intriguing, interpretive possibilities. More than a hundred years ago, Charles W. Upham, a public figure in Salem whose lifelong avocation was the study of the witch trials, published a map which located with some precision the home of nearly every Salem Village resident at the beginning of 1692. Using Upham's careful map as a basis, it is possible to pinpoint the place of residence of every Villager who testified for or against any of the accused witches and also of those accused who themselves lived within the Village bounds. A pattern emerges from this exercise—a pattern which further reinforces the conclusion that neighborhood quarrels, in the narrow sense of the phrase, played a minor role indeed in generating witchcraft accusations:

There were fourteen accused witches who lived within the bounds of Salem Village. Twelve of these fourteen lived in the eastern section of the Village.

There were thirty-two adult Villagers who testified against these accused witches. Only two of these lived in that eastern section. The other thirty lived on the western side. In other words, the alleged witches and those who accused them resided on opposite sides of the Village.

There were twenty-nine Villagers who publicly showed their skepticism about the trials or came to the defense of one or more of the accused witches. Twenty-four of these lived in the eastern part of the Village—the same side on which the witches lived—and only five of them in the west. Those who defended the witches were generally their neighbors, often their immediate neighbors. Those who accused them were not. . . .

What we have been attempting . . . is to convey something of the deeper historical resonances of our story while still respecting its uniqueness. We see no real conflict between these two purposes. To be sure, no other community was precisely like Salem Village, and no other men were exactly like embittered Samuel Parris, cool and ambitious Israel Porter, or Thomas Putnam, Jr., grimly watching the steady diminution of his worldly estate.

This irreducible particularity, these intensely personal aspirations and private fears, fairly leap from the documents these Salem Villagers, and others, left behind them. And had we been able to learn to know them better—heard the timbre of their voices, watched the play of emotion across their faces, observed even a few of those countless moments in their lives which went unrecorded—we might have been able to apprehend with even greater force the pungent flavor of their individuality.

But the more we have come to know these men for something like what they really were, the more we have also come to realize how profoundly they were shaped by the times in which they lived. For if they were unlike any other men, so was their world unlike any other world before or since; and they shared that world with other people living in other places. Parris and Putnam and the rest were, after all, not only Salem Villagers: they were also men of the seventeenth century; they were New Englanders; and, finally, they were Puritans.

If the large concepts with which historians conventionally deal are to have any meaning, it is only as they can be made manifest in individual cases like these. The problems which confronted Salem Village in fact encompassed some of the central issues of New England society in the late seventeenth century: the resistance of back-country farmers to the pressures of commercial capitalism and the social style that accompanied it; the breaking away of outlying areas from parent towns; difficulties between ministers and their congregations; the crowding of third-generation sons from family lands; the shifting locus of authority within individual communities and society as a whole; the very quality of life in an unsettled age. But for men like Samuel Parris and Thomas Putnam, Jr., these issues were not abstractions. They emerged as upsetting personal encounters with people like Israel Porter and Daniel Andrew, and as unfavorable decisions handed down in places like Boston and Salem Town.

It was in 1692 that these men for the first time attempted to piece together the shards of their experience, to shape their malaise into some broader theoretical pattern, and to comprehend the full dimensions of those forces which they vaguely sensed were shaping their private destinies. Oddly enough, it has been through our sense of "collaborating" with Parris and the Putnams in their effort to delineate the larger contours of their world, and our sympathy, at least on the level of metaphor, with certain of their perceptions, that we have come to feel a curious bond with the "witch hunters" of 1692.

But one advantage we as outsiders have had over the people of Salem Village is that we can afford to recognize the degree to which the menace they were fighting off had taken root within each of them almost as deeply as it had in Salem Town or along the Ipswich Road. It is at this level, indeed, that we have most clearly come to recognize the implications of their travail for our understanding of what might be called the Puritan temper during that final, often intense, and occasionally lurid

efflorescence which signaled the end of its century-long history. For Samuel Parris and Thomas Putnam, Jr., were part of a vast company, on both sides of the Atlantic, who were trying to expunge the lure of a new order from their own souls by doing battle with it in the real world. While this company of Puritans were not the purveyors of the spirit of capitalism that historians once made them out to be, neither were they simple peasants clinging blindly to the imagined security of a receding medieval culture. What seems above all to characterize them, and even to help define their identity as "Puritans," is the precarious way in which they managed to inhabit both these worlds at once.

The inner tensions that shaped the Puritan temper were inherent in it from the very start, but rarely did they emerge with such raw force as in 1692, in little Salem Village. For here was a community in which these tensions were exacerbated by a tangle of external circumstances: a community so situated geographically that its inhabitants experienced two different economic systems, two different ways of life, at unavoidably close range; and so structured politically that it was next to impossible to locate, either within the Village or outside it, a dependable and unambiguous center of authority which might hold in check the effects of these accidents of geography.

The spark which finally set off this volatile mix came with the unlikely convergence of a set of chance factors in the early 1690's: the arrival of a new minister who brought with him a slave acquainted with West Indian voodoo lore; the heightened interest throughout New England in fortune telling and the occult, taken up in Salem Village by an intense group of adolescent girls related by blood and faction to the master of that slave; the coming-of-age of Joseph Putnam, who bore the name of one of Salem Village's two controlling families while owing his allegiance to the other; the political and legal developments in Boston and London which hamstrung provincial authorities for several crucial months early in 1692.

But beyond these proximate causes lie the deeper and more inexorable ones we have already discussed. For in the witchcraft outburst in Salem Village, perhaps the most exceptional event in American colonial history, certainly the most bizarre, one finds laid bare the central concerns of the era. And so once again, for a final time, we must return to the Village in the sorest year of its affliction.

Witchcraft and Factionalism

Predictably enough, the witchcraft accusations of 1692 moved in channels which were determined by years of factional strife in Salem Village. The charges against Daniel Andrew and Phillip English, for example, followed closely upon their election as Salem Town selectmen—in a vote which underscored the collapse of the Putnam effort to stage a comeback in Town politics. And Francis Nurse, the husband of accused witch Rebecca Nurse, was a member of the anti-Parris Village Committee which took office in October 1691.

Other accusations, less openly political, suggest a tentative probing around the fringes of the anti-Parris leadership. For example, George Jacobs, Jr.—accused with several members of his family—was a brother-in-law of Daniel Andrew, whose lands he helped farm. Jacobs was close to the Porter group in other ways as well. In 1695, for example, he was on hand as the will of the dying Mary Veren Putnam was drawn up, and his name appears with Israel Porter's as a witness to that controversial document. In May 1692 Daniel Andrew and George Jacobs, Jr., were named in the same arrest warrant, and they evidently went into hiding together.

Another of Daniel Andrew's tenants was Peter Cloyce whose wife, Sarah (a sister of Rebecca Nurse) was among the accused in 1692. And Michael DeRich, whose wife Mary was also charged that year, seems at one time to have been a retainer or servant in the household of the elder John Porter, and his ties to the family may well have continued into the next generation. (Mary DeRich, in turn, was a close relative—perhaps even a sister—of Elizabeth Proctor, convicted of witchcraft along with her husband John.)

Indeed, as the accused are examined from the perspective of Village factionalism, they begin to arrange themselves into a series of interconnected networks. These networks were not formally organized or rigidly structured, but they were nonetheless real enough. The kinds of associations which underlay them were varied: kinship and marriage ties were crucial, but marriage, in all likelihood, was simply the final step, the institutionalization of less tangible bonds built up gradually over a period of time. The traces of such bonds lie buried in a wide variety of sources, including real-estate transactions, court testimony, genealogies, and lists of witnesses and executors in wills and estate settlements. Ultimately, the evidence for these relationships fades off into shadowy associations which are frustratingly difficult to document with precision—although they were certainly well known at the time. . . .

Given all this, it is not surprising to discover a high correlation between Salem Village factionalism and the way the Village divided in 1692 over the witchcraft outbreak. There are forty-seven Villagers whose position can be determined both in 1692 (by their testimonies or other involvement in the witchcraft trials) and in 1695 (by their signatures on one or the other of the two key petitions). Of the twenty-seven of those who supported the trials by testifying against one or more of the accused witches, twenty-one later signed the pro-Parris petition, and only six the anti-Parris document. Of the twenty who registered their opposition to the trials, either by defending an accused person or by casting doubt on the testimony of the afflicted girls, only one supported Parris in 1695, while nineteen opposed him. In short, supporters of the trials generally belonged to the pro-Parris faction, and opponents of the trials were overwhelmingly anti-Parris.

Almost every indicator by which the two Village factions may be distinguished, in fact, also neatly separates the supporters and opponents of the witchcraft trials. . . . The connection is clear: that part of Salem Village which was an anti-Parris stronghold in 1695 (the part nearest Salem Town) had also been a center of resistance to the witchcraft trials, while the more distant western part of the Village, where pro-Parris sentiment was dominant, contained an extremely high concentration of accusers in 1692.

Similarly with wealth: just as the average member of the anti-Parris faction paid about 40 percent more in Village taxes than his counterpart in the pro-Parris faction, so the average 1695-96 tax of the Villagers who publicly opposed the trials was 67 percent higher than that of people who pushed the trials forward—18.3 shillings as opposed to 11 shillings.

NO

Chadwick Hansen

WITCHCRAFT AT SALEM

... The traditional interpretation of what happened at Salem is as much the product of casual journalism and imaginative literature as it is of historical scholarship. It might be summarized as follows: (1) no witchcraft was practiced in Massachusetts; (2) the behavior of the "afflicted" persons, including their convulsive fits, was fraudulent and designed chiefly to call attention to themselves; (3) the afflicted persons were inspired, stimulated, and encouraged by the clergy (especially Cotton Mather), who used the fear of witchcraft as a means of bolstering their flagging power in the community; (4) the clergy whipped the general populace into a state of "mass hysteria" with their sermons and writings on witchcraft; (5) the only significant opposition to the proceedings at Salem came from the merchant class, specifically from Thomas Brattle and Robert Calef; and (6) the executions were unique in Western civilization, and therefore monstrous, and attributable to some narrowness or fanaticism or repressiveness peculiar to Puritans.

Yet the facts are quite contrary to these common assumptions. To begin with, witchcraft actually did exist and was widely practiced in seventeenth-century New England, as it was in Europe at that time (and still is, for that matter, among the unlearned majority of mankind). It worked then as it works now in witchcraft societies like those of the West Indies, through psychogenic rather than occult means, commonly producing hysterical symptoms as a result of the victim's fear, and sometimes, when fear was succeeded by a profound sense of hopelessness, even producing death.

The behavior of the afflicted persons was not fraudulent but pathological. They were hysterics, and in the clinical rather than the popular sense of that term. These people were not merely overexcited; they were mentally ill. Furthermore, they were ill long before any clergyman got to them.

The general populace did reach that state of public excitement inaccurately called "mass hysteria," but this was due to the popular fear of witchcraft rather than to the preachings of the clergy. The public excitement continued well after the leadership, both clerical and secular, had called a halt to the witchcraft proceedings. In fact the clergy were, from beginning to end, the chief opponents to the events at Salem. In particular, Cotton Mather was anything but the wild-eyed fanatic of tradition. Throughout most of the proceedings he was a model of restraint and caution, and at one point he went further than any of his colleagues dared go in proposing a method to protect the innocent.

The writings of Brattle and Calef came too late to have any significant influence on the course of events in Massachusetts.

Finally, the executions at Salem were by no means unique. Belief in witchcraft was quite as common among seventeenth-century Anglicans, Quakers, Lutherans, and Catholics as it was among Puritans. Executions for witchcraft reached their height in Western civilization during the seventeenth century and continued in Europe until the end of the following century, more than a hundred years after the outbreak at Salem. . . .

WITCHCRAFT

Early in the year 1692 several girls at Salem Village (now Danvers), Massachusetts, began to sicken and display alarming symptoms. The most disturbing and most frequent of these symptoms was convulsive fits: fits so grotesque and so violent that eyewitnesses agreed the girls could not possibly be acting. "Their motions in their fits," wrote the Reverend Deodat Lawson, "are preternatural, both as to the manner, which is so strange as a well person could not screw their body into; and as to the violence also it is preternatural, being much beyond the ordinary force of the same person when they are in their right mind."

The Reverend John Hale of Beverly confirmed Lawson's description. "Their arms, necks, and backs," he wrote, "were turned this way and that way, and returned back again, so as it was impossible for them to do of themselves, and beyond the power of any epileptic fits, or natural disease to effect."

There were other symptoms almost equally alarming: temporary loss of hearing, speech, and sight; loss of memory, so that some of the girls could not recall what had happened to them in their fits; a choking sensation in the throat; loss of appetite. Later there were terrifying hallucinations; they saw specters who tormented them in a variety of ingenious and cruel ways. They felt themselves pinched and bitten, and often there were actual marks upon the skin.

These symptoms are readily recognizable. The most cursory examination of the classic studies of hysteria—of Charcot, of Janet, of Breuer and Freud—will demonstrate that the afflicted girls in Salem were hysterical in the scientific sense of that term. It has, of course, been customary to call these girls hysterical, but only in the loosest and most popular sense of the word. Thus the same historians who have called them hysterical have also called them liars, although the terms are mutually exclusive so far as conscious motivation is concerned. With minor exceptions the girls' behavior belongs to the history of pathology rather than the history of fraud.

In any case, their behavior was both conspicuous and distressing. Two of them, Elizabeth Parris and Abigail Williams, were the daughter and niece of the Reverend Samuel Parris of Salem Village, and the Reverend Mr. Parris treated their affliction with those universal remedies of seventeenth-century Massachusetts, prayer and fasting. But he also did what you or I would do if our children began behaving in that fashion: he took them to the doctor—to a series of doctors, in fact—and he persuaded other parents and guardians to do the same. For some time the physicians were puzzled, but eventually one of them—tradition says it was Dr. William Griggs of Salem Village—produced a diagnosis. "The evil hand," he announced, "is upon them"; the girls were victims of malefic witchcraft.

The diagnosis was in no way unusual. The overwhelming majority of seventeenth-century physicians, like other learned men, believed in witchcraft and considered it the cause of some diseases. An instructive parallel to Doctor Griggs's opinion is that of Sir Thomas Browne, the celebrated author of *Religio Medici*, who was called as expert witness by an English witchcraft court convened at Bury St. Edmunds in 1664. He gave as his opinion:

> that these swooning fits were natural, and nothing else but what they call the mother, but only heightened to a great excess by the subtlety of the Devil, co-operating with the malice of these which we term witches, at whose instance he doth these villainies.

"The mother" was the common abbreviation for "the suffocation of the mother," one of the seventeenth-century English terms for hysteria; it referred to the choking sensation in the throat that was one of the commoner symptoms. Thus, Sir Thomas Browne was entirely correct in his identification of the illness, and it is quite possible that Dr. Griggs, too, was right in whatever identification he made of the Salem symptoms.

What is more surprising is that Dr. Griggs was probably also correct in his identification of the cause. It does seem to have been witchcraft that was reponsible for the girls' afflictions. . . .

It should be emphasized that all of the learned, whether believers or skeptics in principle, were skeptical of the majority of witchcraft cases that came to their attention, because they were all too well aware of the abysmal depth and infinite extent of popular credulity. Every accident, every sudden or unusual illness of man or of beast, every inexplicable or menacing circumstance of any sort was apt to raise the cry of witchcraft among the common people. The learned knew this, and were disposed to approach the individual case with skepticism. We should beware, however, of making a general principle of this statistical skepticism. In 1711 Bishop Berkeley, the philosopher, wrote to a friend that "I do not believe one in a thousand of these stories to be true." But, he added, "neither on the other hand do I see sufficient grounds to conclude peremptorily against plain matter of fact well attested." He enclosed with his letter one such instance of "plain matter of fact"; an account of an Irish case which Berkeley firmly believed to be an instance of malefic witchcraft. The "plain matter of fact" is no more convincing—indeed is less convincing—than the facts produced in Massachusetts.

We must bear in mind that in a society which believes in witchcraft, it works. If you believe in witchcraft and you discover that someone has been melting your wax image over a slow fire or muttering charms over your nail-parings, the probability is that you will get extremely sick. To be sure, your symptoms will be psychosomatic rather than organic. But the fact that they are obviously not organic will make them only more terrible, since they will seem the result of malefic and demonic power. So it was in seventeenth-century Europe, and so it was in seventeenth-century Massachusetts.

The hideous convulsive fits were thought to be the result of witches and demons wrenching the bodies of their victims into tortuous postures. The loss of hearing, speech, sight, appetite, and memory were deprivations caused by Satan himself. The contraction of the throat—the *globus hystericus*—was seen as an attempt by demons to make the victim swallow occult poisons. And when she swallowed rapidly and her belly swelled (what is actually involved here is a kind of accelerated ulcer formation), it was thought the demons had succeeded. When blisters appeared upon the skin (many skin diseases are functional rather than organic), they were thought to have been raised by brimstone out of Hell. Many of these symptoms, including the skin lesions, would pass fairly rapidly. Cotton Mather, who was a Fellow of the Royal Society, a former medical student, and a thorough and careful observer, remarked more than once on the surprising rapidity with which "witchwounds" healed. But other symptoms would persist. And a new fit would bring a repetition of the old afflictions, or new ones equally alarming.

The cause of these hysterical symptoms, of course, was not witchcraft itself but the victim's fear of it, and that is why so many innocent persons were executed. It is impossible now, and was in many instances impossible then, to tell how many of the persons executed for witchcraft were actually guilty of practicing it. It is surely no exaggeration to say that the majority, even the vast majority, were innocent victims of hysterical fears. But we should again be wary of converting a statistical truth into a general principle. While it is clearly true that the majority of persons executed for witchcraft were innocent, it is equally true

that some of them, in Massachusetts and elsewhere, were guilty. . . .

The examinations of Sarah Good and Sarah Osburn afforded grounds for suspicion and for further examination. But the major event of that first day of March was the examination of Tituba. It began like the others, but it changed very quickly:

> "Tituba, what evil spirit have you familiarity with?"
> "None."
> "Why do you hurt these children?"
> "I do not hurt them."
> "Who is it then?"
> "The Devil, for aught I know."
> "Did you never see the Devil?"
> "The Devil," said Tituba, "came to me and bid me serve him."

She went on, with a minimum of judicial prodding, to provide a detailed confession of witchcraft, the first of approximately fifty that were made during the Salem trials. The number and the character of these confessions we shall deal with later, but for the present let us limit ourselves to what Tituba had to say in her examinations of March first and second.

The Devil had come to her in the shape of a man—a tall man in black, with white hair. Other times he had come in the shape of an animal. He had told her he was God, that she must believe in him and serve him six years, and he would give her many fine things. He had shown her a book and she had made a mark in it, a mark that was "red like blood." There were nine marks in the book, and two of them had been made by Good and Osburn. Goody Good had told Tituba she had made her mark there, "but Goody Osburn would not tell; she was cross to me." Sometimes the black man had brought four witches with him—Good and Osburn and two women from Boston whose names she did not know—and they had forced her to go with them and afflict the children. She had gone "upon a stick or pole and Good and Osburn behind me. We ride taking hold of one another; don't know how we go, for I saw no trees nor path but was presently there." Both Good and Osburn had familiars. Sarah Good had a cat and a yellow bird sucked her "between the fore-finger and long-finger upon the right hand." Sarah Osburn had a thing with "wings and two legs and a head like a woman." The children had seen it on February 29, after which it turned into a woman. She also had "a thing all over hairy, all the face hairy, and a long nose, and I don't know how to tell how the face looks." The thing had two legs "and is about two or three foot high, and goeth upright like a man, and last night it stood before the fire in Mr. Parris' hall."

At the end of Tituba's first examination the children were in fits, and Hathorne asked who afflicted them. Tituba said she saw the shape of Sarah Good tormenting them, and the girls confirmed it. The convulsions of Elizabeth Hubbard grew suddenly more violent, and Hathorne asked who afflicted her. "I am blind now," said Tituba. "I cannot see." Shortly afterward she had spells of losing her speech as well, and fell eventually into fits.

Tituba's confession is in general similar to witchcraft confessions from other times and places. Part of it may have been suggested to her. But not all. It is far too detailed and far too original in some of its details to have been merely the product of the magistrates' leading questions. Her concluding line, of course, suggests the experienced medium, and her loss of sight and loss of speech as well as her fits suggest the hysteric. The most likely conclusion is that her confession was the product both of experience with the occult and of hysteri-cal hallucinations as vivid and as terrifying as those of the afflicted girls.

We do not know in detail how the community reacted to it. One would give much to have seen the expression on the Reverend Mr. Parris' face when he heard what had been warming itself only the night before at his domestic fire. One immediate reaction was the committing of the three accused women to jail. Sarah Osburn was to die there on the tenth of May. Tituba, like later confessors, was never brought to trial. She lay in jail until she was sold to pay the jailer's fees, her master refusing to pay them. Sarah Good was brought to trial, and we shall meet with her again.

Another reaction to Tituba's confession was to confirm the community in its fear of witchcraft, and particularly its fear of the three accused women. The night of March first William Allen and John Hughes heard a strange noise; it continued, frightening them, but they approached and "saw a strange and unusual beast lying on the ground. . . . Going up to it, the said beast vanished away and in the said place started up two or three women and fled, . . . not after the manner of other women but swiftly vanished out of our sight, which women we took to be Sarah Good, Sarah Osburn and Tituba." The next night William Allen again had hallucinations: "Sarah Good visibly appeared to him in his chamber, said Allen being in bed, and brought an unusual light in with her. The said Sarah came and sat upon his foot. The said Allen went to kick at her, upon which she vanished and the light with her." Notice that in this hallucination as in many others the hallucination stops as soon as the subject is able to move or speak. . . .

2. DID SOCIAL TENSIONS MOTIVATE THE WITCHHUNTS OF 1692?

A COUNTRY FULL OF LIES

Our seventeenth-century ancestors differed from us in most ways, but in nothing did they differ more than in their attitude toward the truth. In this they were closer to the Middle Ages than to us. For them a lie—a breaking of one's faith—was the worst of sins. Today we do not regard lying as a serious moral wrong. If the word "morality" is mentioned we think immediately of our bodily appetites, especially of sex, and drugs, and alcohol. We take our appetites very seriously—perhaps too seriously—but we do not regard lying as a mortal sin. We are one of the few civilizations in which entire professions (advertising, for example, and public relations) are seriously devoted to bending the truth.

Dante, in his *Divine Comedy,* divided sins into three kinds: those of lust, those of violence, and those of fraud. The sins of lust—those we tend to take most seriously—were those that Dante thought most trivial; the sins of fraud—which we take lightly—were for Dante the worst of all. To create a "credibility gap" as our revealing phrase has it (as though the only relevant issue is whether a statement will compel belief), to lie, was for the medieval man to break one's faith, and it was faith which constituted the bonds between man and his fellow-man, between man and the state, between man and God. To lie was to reduce all the most valuable relationships of life to chaos. And the seventeenth-century Puritan, like Dante, was still living by his faith.

Just how important the truth was to the seventeenth-century Puritan may be gathered from the fact that all of the innocent persons who were executed—and the majority of those executed were innocent—could have saved themselves by lying. After the first execution—that of Bridget Bishop—took place in June it became obvious to everyone that persons who confessed, like Tituba and Dorcas Good, were not being brought to trial. Thus any suspected person might have his life by confessing. Twenty people died, nineteen of them hanged and one pressed for refusing to plead. Bridget Bishop, Mammy Redd, and George Burroughs were three of these. One cannot be at all certain of the guilt or innocence of several more. But at least a dozen now seem to be clearly innocent. Twelve people, and probably more, chose to die rather than belie themselves. It is impressive evidence of the Puritan's attachment to the truth.

Yet it was not really so simple as that, because the truth was not easy to find in Salem in 1692. . . .

46

POSTSCRIPT

DID SOCIAL TENSIONS IN SALEM
MOTIVATE THE WITCHHUNTS OF 1692?

Although witchcraft and devil worship apparently enjoy a minor vogue today, the last two hundred and fifty years have witnessed a decline in mystical beliefs. A few witches were tried after Salem: in 1706 in Virginia, in 1712 in North Carolina, and in 1728 in Rhode Island. The last execution for witchcraft in England occurred in 1712 and fifteen years later in Scotland. On the Continent, royal edicts put an end to the persecution before the end of the seventeenth century.

Is it possible for a society that does not readily accept the existence of witches to understand the events in Salem? On the other hand, perhaps we have our own kinds of witchhunts. Many writers compared the search for Communists, particularly in the federal government in the 1950s, to the hysteria at Salem. Arthur Miller's play, *The Crucible* (Viking, 1953), accomplishes this parallel through historical innuendo. The search for historical accuracy involves many variables and the issue of possession at Salem raises some of the most important of these. How should eyewitness' accounts of hysteria be evaluated? Did the prevalent belief in magic in seventeenth century Salem cause the afflicted to simulate their hysteria? Did the belief that witches could bedevil their victims cause the girls' imaginations to run wild? How about coincidence? Could bona fide instances of hysteria, as Hansen suggests, have occurred side by side with the social and economic tensions portrayed by Boyer and Nissenbaum? Is it possible to reach any consensus on a historical topic as elusive as witchcraft at Salem?

Documentary evidence of seventeenth century witchcraft may be examined in G.L. Burr (ed.), *Narratives of the Witchcraft Cases, 1648-1706 (Barnes and Noble, 1975)*, and Boyer and Nissenbaum's primary source companion to Salem Possessed, *Witchcraft in Salem Village* (Wadsworth, 1972). For comparative history, consult G.L. Kittridge, *Witchcraft in Old and New England* (Harvard University Press, 1929), and A.D.J. Macfarlane, *Witchcraft in Tudor and Stuart England* (Harper and Row, 1970). John Demos helps to clarify the larger picture in his article, "Underlying Themes in the Witchcraft of Seventeenth-Century New England," *The American Historical Review*, 75 (June 1970), 1311-1326.

ISSUE 3

WAS A CONFLICT BETWEEN NATIVE AMERICANS AND COLONISTS UNAVOIDABLE?

YES: Alden T. Vaughan, from "White Man to Redskin," *The American Historical Review,* October 1982

NO: Richard R. Johnson, from "The Search for a Usable Indian," *The Journal of American History,* December 1977

ISSUE SUMMARY

YES: Professor Vaughan presents the Native American as a victim of color symbolism, racial differences and non-conformity to European culture.
NO: Professor Johnson chronicles co-operative relations between settlers and natives in the New World.

Relations between Native Americans and Europeans were marred by the difficulties arising from people of very different cultures encountering each other for the first time. These encounters led to inaccurate perceptions, misunderstandings, and failed expectations. While at first the American Indians deified the explorers, experience soon taught them to do otherwise. European opinion ran the gamut from poets and painters who admired the Noble Savage to the avaricious and acquisitive who held "the only good savage is a dead one" as a rationalization for genocide.

Spanish, French, and English treatment of Native Americans differed and was based to a considerable extent on each nation's hopes about how the New World could be subordinated to the Old. The Spanish exploited the Indians most directly, taking their gold and silver, transforming their government, religion and society, even occasionally enslaving them. The French were less of a menace than the others because there were fewer of them and because many French immigrants were itinerant trappers and priests rather than settlers. In the long run, the emigration from England was the most threatening of all. Entire families came from Albion and they were determined to establish a permanent home in the wilderness.

The juxtaposition of Native American and English from the Atlantic to the Appalachians resulted sometimes in coexistence, other times in enmity. The English depended on the Indians' generosity in sharing the techniques of wilderness survival. Puritan clergymen tried to save their neighbors' souls, going so far as to translate the Bible into dialects, but they were not as successful at conversion as the French Jesuits and Spanish Franciscans. Attempts at coexistence did not smooth over the tension between the English and the Indians. They did not see eye to eye about the uses of the environment. Indian agriculture, in the eyes of English settlers, was neither intense nor efficient. Native Americans noticed white settlers consumed larger amounts of food per person and cultivated not only for themselves but also for towns and villages which bought the surplus. Subsistence farming collided with the market economy.

Large-scale violence erupted in the 1670s. Throughout New England the Wampanoags, Narragansets, Mohegans, Podunks and Nipmucks united to stop the encroachments into their woodlands and hunting grounds, while in the Virginia piedmont, frontiersmen led by Nathaniel Bacon attacked tribes living in the Appalachian foothills. Hostilities, known as King Philip's War, lasted from June 1675 to September 1676 with isolated raids stretching on until 1678. Casualties rose into the high hundreds and Anglo-Indian relations deteriorated.

In the next century Spain, France, and England disputed each other's North American claims and Native Americans joined sides, usually as the allies of France against England. These great wars of the eighteenth century ended in 1763 with England's victory but disputes over territorial expansion continued. Colonial officials disagreed with the imperial government when King George III forbade his subjects to settle west of the Appalachian watershed. The area from those mountains to the Mississippi River, acquired from France at the recently negotiated Peace of Paris, was designated as an Indian reservation. From 1763 to 1783, as Anglo-colonial relations changed from argument to combat to independence, the London government consistently sided with the Native Americans. Desire to acquire Indian territory lurked behind the American drive for freedom.

Both Professor Vaughan and Professor Johnson focus their interpretations on the importance of military developments between Native Americans and colonists. Vaughan concludes, "It was only a short step from regarding the Indians as bloodthirsty foes to perceiving them as naturally inferior in morality and humanity, and eventually in color." On the other hand, "There was a complex Indian dependence on white society," Johnson writes. "This dependence," he continues, "in turn, resulted from the fundamental shift in the balance of Indian-white relations that occurred over the course of the seventeenth century."

YES
Alden T. Vaughan

FROM WHITE MAN TO REDSKIN: CHANGING ANGLO-AMERICAN PERCEPTIONS OF THE AMERICAN INDIAN

. . . Documenting the shifts in the Anglo-American perceptions of Indian color is easier than explaining them. Contemporary authors were oblivious to the changes; they were too close to the phenomena and too involved in them. To a large extent, of course, the reasons for changing attitudes can only be surmised, for they reflect a vast and complicated alteration in millions of disparate individuals whose perceptions of the Indian cannot be precisely reconstructed. Nonetheless, Anglo-American writings of the eighteenth century offer important clues to the psychological imperatives that encouraged "white" Americans to believe that Indians were significantly and irrevocably darker than themselves. At least three major interrelated and mutually reinforcing influences are apparent: the Anglo-Americans' anger at Indian hostility, their frustration over Indian rejection of Christianity and "civility," and their adoption of eighteenth-century racial theories.

First, chronologically, was the transformation of the Indian in English eyes from potential friend to inveterate enemy. That change took place gradually and unevenly, occurring at different times in different places, as military conflict increasingly characterized Indian-English contact. From the standpoint of Anglo-American attitudes, the causes of conflict were irrelevant: Englishmen at home or in America almost invariably blamed the Indians for hostilities and, hence, came to think of them as incorrigibly aggressive and ruthless. It was only a short step from regarding the indians as bloodthirsty foes to perceiving them as naturally inferior in morality and humanity, and eventually in color.

The initial Anglo-American view of the Indians was largely amiable and optimistic. Most of the "savages," imperial spokesmen contended, would be friendly. They would also be eager for commerce and the gospel, partly because it would be in their own self-interest but mainly because the English prefessed to come peacefully, offering voluntary acceptance of English culture and religion. (By contrast, English imperialists viewed Spanish settlement as a model of how to alienate and exterminate the natives.) The Indians would therefore welcome English outposts, willingly sell surplus land, engage in mutually profitable trade, and enthusiatically embrace Protestantism. Yet, from the earliest days of English colonialism, its champions predicted—judging from a century of European experience in America—that some natives would oppose settlement no matter how fairly they were treated. And Indians who persisted in hostility or obstinately rejected free trade and proselytizing, the imperialists argued, deserved no quarter; the English never seriously questioned their own right to occupy part of America, by force if necessary. England's deeply ingrained ethnocentrism (a characteristic other European nations possessed, but apparently to a lesser degree), and England's determination to make profits and converts, which it hoped would emulate Spanish success but not Spanish methods, would brook no native opposition. Even the usually benign younger Hakluyt minced no words on this point: "To handle them gently, while gentle courses may be found to serve . . . be without comparison the best: but if gentle polishing will not serve, then we shall not want hammerours and rough masons enow, I meane our old soldiours trained up in the Netherlands, to square and prepare them to our Preachers hands." With the few recalcitrants chastised, colonization would proceed peacefully, to the benefit of settlers and Indians alike.

Such expectations died early. At Roanoke Island in the 1580s, most of the Indians turned against the colonists, for justifiable reasons, and the neighboring Powhatans probably exterminated the "Lost Colony" of 1587. In Virginia, settlers and natives clashed almost incessantly from 1607 to 1613, often in open warfare, sometimes in sporadic skirmishes, occasionally in bloodless but hostile negotiations. Nearly a decade of relative calm followed the captivity and conversion of Pocahontas in 1613; the brief and imperfect respite from hostilities ended suddenly with the massacre of 1622, which almost exterminated the colony. Even though responsibility for the massacre ultimately belonged with the English, as their own accounts unwittingly reveal, the Anglo-American attitude toward the Indians quickly shifted from contempt to hatred—a sentiment intensified by the ensuing decade of blatant carnage and by a similar massacre in 1644.

New England's experience offers some parallels and some marked contrasts to Virginia's. Unlike Virginia, the New England colonies had generally peaceful relations with the local tribes until 1675. To a considerable extent that reflected New England's unusual population ratio: epidemics in 1616-17 and 1633-34 greatly reduced the natives while barely touching the colonists, which lessened Indian resistance and further encouraged Puritan immigrants to believe that God intended them to create a New English Zion. So did the Pequot War of 1637, which briefly threatened New England's view of the Indians as potential friends and converts. The decisive victory over the Pequots further reduced Indian numbers, and, when most of the tribes remained neutral or actively supported the colonists, the Puritans' confidence in their own invincibility and in the Indians' vulnerability was reinforced rather than undermined. By contrast, early Virginians faced an Indian population that vastly outnumbered them and that had enough political cohesion to use its numerical strength effectively.

But numbers do not tell the whole story. Important too was the strong missionary impulse among New England's founders, an impulse that eventually enjoyed a quarter-century of modest achievement. New England's missionary activity began belatedly in the 1640s, but its success from then until King Philip's War seemed to justify earlier expectations. The uprisings of 1675—once again an Indian response to colonial encroachment and abuses—dashed Puritan assumptions about the eventual transformation of the Indians into proper Englishmen. Henceforth, the British colonists in New England joined those in the Chesapeake and elsewhere in a growing conviction that Indians in general were their enemies. That conviction hardened in the late seventeenth century and throughout the eighteenth as the British colonial frontier became a vast English-Indian battleground, often exacerbated by troops or agents from other colonial powers. Even Pennsylvania, after the effective withdrawal of the Quakers from political control and after the influx of a predominantly non-Quaker population, had its share of racial conflict.

Frequent and ferocious hostilities, regardless of who was at fault, inevitably corroded the earlier Anglo-American view of the Indians and reshaped its vocabulary. References to the Indians, never especially flattering, now became almost universally disparaging. In the aftermath of 1622, Anglo-American spokesmen portrayed the Virginia native as "having little of Humanitie but shape," "more brutish than the beasts they hunt," and "naturally born slaves." New Englanders reacted similarly to King Philip's War. The Indians were "Monsters shapt and fac'd like men," wrote one New England poet, and most of his compatriots undoubtedly agreed. Even book titles reflect the shift in attitude. In 1655 John Eliot could write hopefully of the Indians' progress toward conversion in *A Late and Further Manifestation of the Progress of the Gospell amongst the In-dians in New England: Declaring Their Constant Love and Zeal to the Truth, with a Readiness to Give Account of Their Faith and Hope, as of Their Desire to Be Partakers of the Ordinances of Christ.* Twenty years later, in the midst of New England's struggle for survival, an anonymous pamphleteer suggested a far different view of the Indians in a *Brief and True Narration of the Late Wars Risen in New-England, Occasioned by the Quarrelsome Disposition, and Perfidious Carriage of the Barbarous, Savage, and Heathenish Natives there.* As warfare increasingly became the dominant mode of English-Indian contact, the image of the Indian as vicious savage made deep inroads on the Anglo-American psyche. Cotton Mather, whose rhetorical flights often exaggerated but seldom misrepresented colonial sentiments, gave revealing advice to New England's soldiers in King William's War: "Once you have but got the Track of those Ravenous howling Wolves, then pursue them vigourously; *Turn not back till they are consumed. . . . Beat them small as the Dust before the Wind . . . Sacrifice them to the Ghosts of Christians whom they have Murdered. . . . Vengance, Dear Countrymen! Vengance upon our Murderers.*" The culmination of a century and a half of military escalation came in 1776 in the Declaration of Independence's only reference to the Indians: The king "has endeavored to bring on the inhabitants of our frontiers, the merciless Indian savages, whose known rule of warfare is an undistinguished destruction of all ages, sexes and conditions." Nearly a decade of border warfare exacerbated the revoluntionaries' fear and hatred of the Indians. "The white Americans," observed a British traveler in 1784, "have the most rancorous antipathy to the whole race of Indians; and nothing is more common than to hear them talk of extirpating them totally from the face of the earth, men, women, and children."

War-bred animosities did not require a difference in color perception, but the unconscious temptation to tar the Indian with the brush of physical inferiority—to differentiate and denigrate the enemy—appears to have been irresistible. Wartime epithets have often invoked outward appearance, however irrelevant (witness the "yellow Japs" of World War II), and British Americans frequently resorted to pejorative color labels. In the late seventeenth and early eighteenth centuries, as war raged along the northern New England frontier, Cotton Mather castigated "those Tawny Pagans, than which there are not worse Divels Incarnate upon Earth," and "a *swarthy* Generation of *Philistines* here; the *Indian* Natives, I mean, whom alone we are like to have any *Warrs withal*." Nearly a century later, when the bulk of the Indians sided with Great Britain during the American Revolution, Henry Dwight complained of "copper Colour'd Vermine" and hoped that an American army would "Massacre those Infernal Savages to such a degree that [there] may'nt be a pair of them left, to continue the Breed upon the Earth." Logically enough, "redskins" eventually emerged as the epithet for enemies who usually used red paint on the warpath. Not coincidentally, perhaps, the first reported use of that term appears in a passage about Indian assaults on frontier settlements. In a sentence that suggests the impact of war on changing English attitudes, Samuel Smith of Hadley, Massachusetts, recalled in 1699 that several decades earlier his father had endured Indian raids in the Connecticut Valley. "My Father ever declardt," Smith remembered, "there would not be so much to feare iff ye Red Skins was treated with suche mixture of Justice & Authority as they cld understand, but iff he was living now he must see that wee can do nought but *fight* em & that right heavily."

The Indians' refusal to adopt English concepts of civility and religion poisoned Anglo-American attitudes as thoroughly as did warfare. Sixteenth- and seventeenth-century expectations of rapid and wholesale anglicization met constant rebuff; by the end of the seventeenth century it must have been clear to all but the more optimistic missionaries that most Indians would never be Christian in faith or English in allegiance and customs. Converts in the southern and middle colonies numbered only a handful; most of John Eliot's "praying towns" had been scuttled by King Philip's War and its aftermath; and even the Quakers in Pennsylvania, despite a commendable effort to treat the Indians fairly, had won few to English ways or beliefs. Occasional successes notwithstanding, the missionary movement had failed. Even less successful was the broader mission of eliminating customs that Englishmen subsumed under the heading of "savagery," such as nakedness, scarification, tribal law and government, hunting instead of herding, and, perhaps most important of all, an exclusively oral language. Some technological assimilation had occurred, as had some imaginative blending of religious ideas, but the overwhelming majority of Indians steadfastly held to their traditional ways and rejected most of the alien culture's offerings.

Who was to blame? The most obvious scapegoat was the Indian himself. He stubbornly resisted spiritual and material improvement, his critics charged, and they eventually concluded that his resistance stemmed either from a deeply ingrained antipathy to "civilization" or from a natural incapacity for improvement. Benjamin Franklin explained to a correspondent in 1753 that "Little Success . . . has hitherto attended every attempt to Civilize our American Indians in their present way of living. . . . When an Indian Child has been brought up among us, taught our language and habituated to Our Customs, yet if he goes to see his relations and make one Indian Ramble with them, there is no perswading him ever to return." Franklin did not consider the Indians inherently incapable of adopting English ways; they simply and obstinately preferred their own. Many of Franklin's contemporaries were less charitable. The editor of the 1764 edition of William Wood's *New England's Prospect,* for example, thought the Indians incurably barbarian and pagan. "The christianizing the Indians," he peevishly noted,

> scarcely affords a probability of success; for their immense sloth, their incapacity to consider abstract truth . . . and their perpetual wanderings, which prevent a steady worship, greatly impede the progress of Christianity, a mode of religion adapted to the most refined temper of the human mind. . . . The feroce manners of a native Indian can never be effaced, nor can the most finished politeness totally eradicate the wild lines of his education.

Almost predictably, the editor believed that Indians were not born white: with few exceptions, contempt for Indians correlated highly with a belief in their innate darkness.

A third major influence toward perceiving the Indians as inherently tawny or red came from eighteenth-century naturalists. Few of them had first-hand information about the American Indians—most were European scholars who never visited the New World—but in their frantic attempt to classify systematically all plant and animal life, including the principal divisions of mankind, they contributed directly to the notion of Indians as inherently red and indirectly at least to the belief in their inferiority.

Initially, the naturalists' categories had no hierarchical intent. Their taxonomies were horizontal, not vertical, and each branch of humanity enjoyed equality with all others. Before long, however, the subdivisions of *homo sapiens* acquired descriptive judgments that suggest a relative superiority in Europeans and corresponding inferiority in other races. Such a view meshed perfectly with the eighteenth century's emphatic belief in natural order, mataphorically expressed as a "Great Chain of Being," in which all creatures from microorganisms to angels had permanent places on a hierarchical continuum. The idea of an orderly chain of life had existed for centuries; it flourished in the fifteenth century, for example, when Sir John Fortescue recorded a classic description: "In this order angel is set over angel, rank upon rank in the Kingdom of Heaven; man is set over man, beast over beast, bird over bird, and fish over fish . . . so that there is no worm that crawls upon the ground, no bird that flies on high, no fish that swims in the depths, which the chain of this order binds not in most harmonious concord." Not until the eighteenth century, however, did ranks *within* humankind receive much attention. Then, because natural scientists almost invariably chose skin color as the principal criterion of racial identity, darkness of hue became "scientifically" linked to other undesirable qualities. As Winthrop Jordan has pointed out, for Africans the "Great Chain of Being" soon became a "Great Chain of Color" on which whites regarded blacks as divinely relegated to a lesser rank of humanity. In the eighteenth century, American Indians also became victims, though not quite so pejoratively, of the color chain's invidious implications. . . .

American racial thought in the post-Revolutionary era underwent subtle but significant changes. Ever since the sixteenth century, Europeans had viewed Africans and Indians as fundamentally different from each other in postdiluvian biological development and in their prospects for absorption into British-American society. In the eighteenth century, the gap gradually closed as the Indian became, in the eyes of most white observers, inherently tawny. As earlier, most Anglo-Americans considered Africans immutably black; in the late eighteenth and early nineteenth centuries some writers further debased the Afro-American by contriving polygenic theories to explain what they believed to be the black race's irredeemable physical and behavioral inferiority. Indians, by contrast, were sometimes lauded for superior appearance, virtue, or ability, yet increasingly they too suffered the stigma that white America attached to peoples of darker skin.

That the Indian was, in fact, inherently darker than the European, and that his pigmentation was the sign of a separate branch of mankind, had become axiomatic by the outbreak of the American Revolution. What remained for the Jeffersonian generation and its early nineteenth-century successors was to determine the Indians' proper color label and to reach a rough consensus on the implications of a racial status that was clearly inferior to the white man's but also superior to the black's. . . .

Once red became a viable designation, it seems to have satisfied everyone. To the Indians' bitterest critics, red could signify ferocity, blood, and anger; to their most avid supporters and to the Indians themselves, red could suggest bravery, health, and passion; to those who fell between the judgmental extremes, red could mean almost anything or nothing. In short, red was sufficiently flexible and ambiguous to meet the metaphysical imperatives of a society that did not wholly agree about the Indian's basic character or social and political fate. . . .

Even among their supposed supporters, however, the Indians fared badly, as a host of examples from Jefferson through Thomas McKenney and Lewis Cass amply illustrate. Such "friends" of the Indians contended that in the long run the Indian must be incorporated into the American mainstream, but increasingly in the nineteenth century the number of such advocates declined and the duration of the Indians' expected tutelage expanded. The Indians, assimilationists argued, must become farmers, landowners, and citizens; they must adopt "white" America's language, laws, and customs. They must cease to be Indians—even if it took centuries to reach that end. Along the way, Indian desires were rarely considered. Although the overwhelming majority wanted to retain their land and their culture, the Eastern tribes had little choice. In the first half of the nineteenth century, the basic options were assimilation or extermination, with removal to the West as a temporary stage in either case.

Some assimilationists advocated miscegenation as the surest path to de-Indianization. Ironically, the biological solution emerged almost simultaneously with laws in many states against Indian-white intermarriage. Such laws hint at hypocrisy and racial intransigence among the majority of Americans and reveal the implausibility of intermarriage as a solution to race relations in nineteenth-century America. But whatever the solution—miscegenation, allotment of farmlands in the East, removal to the West, or education in white-controlled

3. WAS A CONFLICT UNAVOIDABLE?

boarding schools—the Indian was marked for gradual extinction by the uneasy coalition of his friends and foes. For both groups, as well as for the bulk of Americans who were neither friend nor foe but merely indifferent, the conviction that the Indians were innately and ineradicably "redmen" underlay their concern, or lack of it, for the Indians' fate. And to most white observers—certainly to the Indians' foes and almost certainly to the millions who scarcely cared—the stereotypical color carried a host of unfavorable associations that prevented the Indians' full assimilation into the Anglo-American community and simultaneously precluded their acceptance as a separate and equal peo-

ple. Although a few dissenters resisted the prevailing color taxonomy and its correlative racial policies, the surviving literature, both factual and fictional, shows that the Indian was no longer considered a member of the same race; he remained forever distinct in color and character. Even relatively sympathetic spokesmen now believed the Indians to be permanently different. "No Christianizing," declares Natty Bumppo in Cooper's *Pathfinder* (1840), "will ever make even a Delaware [Indian] a white man, nor any whopping and yelling convert a paleface into a redskin." Bumppo earlier—in *The Prairie* (1827)—puts the same idea more succinctly: "Red natur' is red natur'. ". . .

NO

Richard R. Johnson

THE SEARCH FOR A USABLE INDIAN: AN ASPECT OF THE DEFENSE OF COLONIAL NEW ENGLAND

. . . Two questions remain. [Why] did the Indians, for their part, cooperate with the whites? [What] does this episode contribute to an understanding of relations between the races in this period? Answers to both these questions are, unfortunately, limited by the same deficiencies of evidence that have largely restricted the study of the Indian's relations with the white to that of white attitudes toward the Indian. There are very few materials on which to base an interpretation of the Indian's side of the relationship and fewer still that have not passed through the refracting glass of white transcription. Nevertheless, by attempting to understand the wider context of white and Indian cooperation, it is possible to suggest motives and effects to an extent that casts some additional light upon the character of racial relations in early America.

The Iroquois' motives for encouraging New England's courtship are the least difficult to reconstruct. They risked little and gained much by its prolongation. Indeed, only if their warriors had tried and failed to subdue the eastern Indians might the bubble of illusion have been pricked. Clearly, the very lack of evidence concerning Indian motives may mislead scholars into reading diplomatic skills into what may have been no more than a profiting from fortunate circumstances. In the case of the Iroquois, however, both the relative abundance of the records of their diplomacy and its conspicuous success in preserving the confederacy as a major independent power in North America until the Revolution attest to their consistent and clear-sighted realism. Their negotiations with New England were characteristic. In return for a purely rhetorical commitment, they reaped a harvest of political prestige, several hundred pounds' worth of presents, and even, as in 1689, military assistance.

The motives of the New England Indians who served with the colonial forces are necessarily more conjectural. The frequent wranglings over money and the care taken by such leaders as Church to ensure that the Indians and their families received their due compensation indicate that pay and bounties were as powerful an inducement for Indian volunteers as for white. At a time when

Excerpted from "The Search for a Usable Indian: An Aspect of the Defense of Colonial New England," by Richard R. Johnson, *Journal of American History*, LXIV, No. 3, December 1977. Footnotes omitted.

3. WAS A CONFLICT UNAVOIDABLE?

the New England Indians were being stripped of their lands, military service was an important source of income. In addition, and in contrast to such alternatives as apprenticeship, whaling, and domestic service, it allowed young men to earn their manhood in the traditional ways frowned upon by a surrounding white society. The ease with which Church often persuaded former Indian adversaries to enlist under his command demonstrates that Europeans were not the only race whose members sometimes found the attractions of waging war as a way of life greater than other, more social, loyalties.

A study of those groups that furnished New England with the bulk of its Indian auxiliaries—the Mohegans of Connecticut and the Praying Indians of Massachusetts and Plymouth—suggests, however, that these economic and cultural motives were but a part of a more complex Indian dependence on white society. This dependence, in turn, resulted from the fundamental shift in the balance of Indian-white relations that occurred over the course of the seventeenth century. The first military alliances between white and Indian in New England had been those of independent peoples seeking mutual advantage, as when Pilgrim and Wampanoag formed common front against the Narragansetts, or when the latter in turn joined forces with the Connecticut settlers in 1637 to exterminate their troublesome Pequot neighbors. The colonists' arrival initially added only a new ingredient to conflict still centered around domestic Indian factionalism and inter-tribal rivalries. But the growing predominance of the whites tilted the balance of these relationships, compelling their Indian allies in turn to reassess their commitments. Some, like the Narragansetts and the Wampanoags, ultimately forsook old enmities in a last attempt to stem the English tide, only to meet with defeat and dispersal in King Philip's War. And those others, such as the Mohegans and the Praying Indians, who chose to remain committed to the whites, emerged from the struggle more dependent clients than allies as the very aid they furnished to the colonists enabled the latter to achieve a decisive local supremacy. None succeeded in preserving or profiting from a balance of forces of the kind which enabled the Iroquois to remain at once indispensable and autonomous.

Those Indians remaining within "white" New England by the last years of the seventeenth century, therefore, were necessarily those who had best accommodated themselves to the colonists' ways and needs. In addition, the Mohegans and the Praying Indians were peculiarly bound into a close relationship with the whites by the circumstances under which they had first established their separate identities. For the Praying Indians, this identity was defined by their acceptance of the colonists' religious beliefs and by the processes of socialization and acculturation that accompanied conversion. As recent studies have shown, the missionary program promoted by the Massachusetts and Plymouth governments was not limited to the provision of churches and schools for the Indians; it also resettled them in "praying towns" safely removed from tribal influences, set them under the supervision of English guardians, and commenced the reshaping of their behavior to "civilized" white Christian standards with codes of conduct suppressing many of the remaining manifestations of Indian cultural life. The thoroughness of this training in conformity to white practices and beliefs and its considerable measure of success in comparison to the efforts of colonial governments elsewhere does much to explain the willingness of a majority of Praying Indians to side with the English in time of war. Similarly, the early expression of this conformity in the practice of Indians from the praying towns hiring themselves out as laborers to neighboring farmers doubtless prepared the way, on both sides, for their subsequent employment as soldiers.

The Mohegans were also a product of the period of white colonization, but under circumstances that were primarily political rather than religious or social. They were born of intra-tribal factionalism, in a struggle over leadership within the Pequots that resulted in the secession in 1636 of a dissident group of "Mohegans" headed by the unsuccessful claimant, Uncas. They elected from the first to consolidate their separate identity through alliance with the whites, as when they promptly joined in the coalition already forming against their own Pequot kinsmen and shared the spoils of victory. This balanced and mutually profitable interdependence remained the theme of subsequent Mohegan-white relations, as Uncas deftly maneuvered the colonists into eliminating all rivals to his local hegemony, and they in turn profited from the Mohegans' military skills and willingness to admit new settlers to their lands. Moreover, by rebuffing the half-hearted proselytizings of the Connecticut authorities, Uncas and his successors succeeded in staving off the cultural and political pressures that had overwhelmed the Praying Indians. A measure of their success in preserving their traditional authority and their people's cohesion can be seen in the manner of their military service: the Mohegans continued to fight in separate companies alongside the whites at a time when the Massachusetts Indians were generally conscripted on an individual basis.

Ultimately, of course, the enveloping pressures of white settlement overwhelmed Mohegans and Praying Indians alike. By the mid-eighteenth century, the allies of King Philip's War had dissolved into scattered bands confined to shrinking reservations and fast disappearing amidst the surrounding English. This deepening dependence was clearly instrumental in inducing the New England Indians to remain in the service of the whites. Enlistment was even then, as it had continued to be, the refuge of those newly rootless or in transition between two worlds. Those Indian peoples whose way of life or political status had been most deeply affected by association with white society served in greatest numbers with the colonial forces. Yet the evident complexity of this association does not show that this service was a form of tribute paid by subservient peoples, and this does not support the modern moral that New England Indians were never more than either the white man's victims or his dupes. The example of the Mohegans demonstrates how even Indian peoples directly in the path of white expansion could turn the newcomers' presence to their own advantage, to the extent that some were able to found their own brief power and prosperity upon the trading of one form of assistance for another. Others were less fortunately situated or less skillful in their diplomacy. But even those who, like the Praying Indians, acquiesced in the pressures exerted upon them by white society, chose a path of accommodation over the alternatives of resistance or withdrawal. From this perspective, the Indians of New England were not merely being used by the whites; their military service was also a personal strategy for survival, a revealing and neglected phase in their response to the dislocations inflicted by European colonization.

3. WAS A CONFLICT UNAVOIDABLE?

This examination of the motives behind the military cooperation of Indian and white has already led far into the field of relations between the two races in the early colonial period. The search for the usable Indian can properly be seen as a significant phase in the evolution of these relations; to what extent did it also influence their subsequent development, shaping the ways in which Indian and white regarded and treated one another in New England? Did it heighten or alleviate the tensions between the races?

Prejudice is commonly tempered by the hope of advantage, and the policies and attitudes of the New England governments often reflected their recognition of the value of Indian aid. They learned to cater to the Indians' own shrewd assessment of their bargaining power. "If now our Indians are kindly used," wrote James Fitch to Massachusetts in 1696, "you may hereafter have more, if other wise non will stir." Grumblings at such presumption gave way to acquiescence; by 1712, Dudley was pressing a New Hampshire subordinate to treat the enlisted Indians with justice, for "I shall never get an Indian to serve for your province again if they want a shilling of their due." Public recognition was less apparent, but it evidently extended to the point of tolerating an integrated indulgence in the white man's vices. John Neesnummin, an Indian minister visiting Boston, was denied lodging in the town, but Indian recruits were freely entertained at local taverns, hospitality to which sympathetic observers attributed their notorious weakness for liquor.

Appropriately, the greatest solicitude was lavished on those most conscious of their strength and from whom most was expected: the Five Nations of the Iroquois. The Massachusetts magistrates suppressed the province's first newspaper partly on account of a disparaging reference to the Mohawks, and in 1709, a year after Neesnummin had been refused accommodation, two successive delegations of Iroquois chiefs were royally entertained in Boston at the province's expense. The extent to which a desire for cordial relations with the confederacy could govern official policy was graphically demonstrated after the killing of several settlers at Deerfield and Hadley in 1693 and 1696. In both cases the evidence pointed to the Iroquois or their allies as the culprits—at Deerfield a wounded settler identified several Mohawks as his assailants. But urgent representations from Boston, Hartford, and New York pointed out the dangers of any verdict which might alienate the confederacy. After much correspondence two of the four suspects at Hadley were executed. But at Deerfield political considerations—"the English Interest"—outweighed "the Inquisition after Blood" as the Boston government took advantage of some flimsy circumstantial evidence throwing the blame on French Indians to order the prisoners' release.

Yet expediency rather than trust and affection inspired this solicitude and, in the long term, it would seem that the colonists' perception of the Indian's military potential did more to deepen than to heal divisions between the races. It prompted the employment of the Mohegans and missions to the Iroquois, but it also reinforced the image of the Indian as a dangerous and incorrigible warrior. The early settlers had anticipated that the Indian could be civilized out of his savagery. Conversion would distinguish Christian from pagan, not white from red. But by the late seventeenth century this optimism had subsided into the grimmer realization that Indians—all Indians—were somehow irredeemably different from the whites.

Hopes of assimilation gave way to policies of segregation and discriminatory legislation. The use of Indian aid did not cause this change: both were consequences of the conflict that set the seal upon the breakdown of racial and cultural coexistence. Within the context of such prejudice, however, the colonists' perception of the Indians' military skills heightened their suspicions of those who remained in New England, Indians who had now, in the words of one Rhode Islander, "seen ye Englishes Slowness & therein weaknes & thyr owne nimblenes & strength." Hence the frequent questioning of the surviving Indians' loyalty, the proposals that those accounted but "pretended Freinds" should be driven from New England, and the widespread rumors that new uprisings backed by "Popish Treachery" were in preparation amongst the tribes. Fairness to the Indians, therefore, remained a pragmatic rather than a moral obligation, designed, in the revealing phrase of one frontier leader, "Least we or till we declare all indians to be Enemyes."

The search for Indian aid was not wholly devoid of warmer feelings. Among whites who served with the Indians, wartime comradeship often spun lasting bonds of loyalty and friendship. Aspinwall rescued from jail two Indians he believed to have been unjustly convicted of complicity in the murder of a settler; Fitch, Mason, and Avery spoke out boldly in defense of the Mohegans and Pequots they befriended; and Church successfully lobbied for a grant of land at Tiverton for the families of his Indian veterans. But such ties were uncommon, and, like the efforts of Gookin and his fellow "Indian-lovers" to protect the Praying Indians during King Philip's War, their character demonstrates more the reality of prejudice than its absence. Moreover, the very nature of the search for a usable

Indian fostered a darker view of the Indian. It not only led the colonists to discover the Indian's military potential but also to desire that potential's most effective expression. In seeking Indian aid, the whites were requiring the Indian to be precisely what they most detested in him—savage, bloodthirsty, relentless, skulking, terrorizing and tearing the scalp from his opponents. Ironically, these qualities were in many ways more akin to white methods of total warfare than to the traditional Indian preference for a more symbolic and less destructive form of combat. But the whites ascribed to others what they feared to perceive in themselves, thereby moving a further step toward the belief that all Indians, because they embodied qualities deemed to be characteristically Indian, were too dangerous and different to be allowed to remain in contact with white society.

The Indian played the martial role allotted to him too well to allay these feelings. They burst out most strongly upon the frontier where, as one observer noted in 1696, the settlers were "exceedingly possessed with a vehement spirit against all Indians not indureing the sight of them as to the present." Certainly the frontier regions bore the brunt of suffering and attack. The perennial political division between angry frontiersmen demanding protection and coastal settlers and governments more concerned with matters of trade and taxes was already taking shape. Yet, a part of that anger and that "vehement spirit against all Indians" also grew out of the frontiersmen's impotent frustration at the Indian's superiority in border warfare—a superiority made all the more galling by the attempts of their own governments to enlist the Indian to protect them. If so, then the roots of racial prejudice lay in envy as well as ignorance and fear. One outlet for this frustration was the mistreatment of those Indians remaining within reach, as during King Philip's War. As one perceptive contemporary noted, "the vollgar cry is kill all indians when they cannot kill one."

New England's search for Indian aid serves in microcosm to illuminate the development and interrelation of larger themes of the roots of prejudice, the pattern of Indian-white relations, the changing face of war in America, and the colonists' adjustment to a world of international conflict. As policy, it proved to be a temporary expedient rather than a lasting solution. Yet, Indian auxiliaries shouldered much of the burden of defending New England for almost half a century; and the colonists' determined pursuit of aid from the Iroquois left a lasting imprint on their diplomatic and strategic perspectives. Moreover, its very transitoriness sets it more firmly in the stream of early American history. It mirrors New England's passage through a period when its colonists found themselves forced to look beyond their own resources, to the Indians and ultimately to England, for assistance. And it exemplifies an often neglected stage in early Indian-white relations, one where illusions and optimism had subsided but where the elements of a mutual dependence remained. From this longer perspective, New England's search for a usable Indian forms a strand in the fragile thread of collaboration between Indian and white that runs beyond the colonial period to reappear in such unexpected forms as the Indian auxiliaries of Andrew Jackson and George Custer and the Navaho radio operators of World War II. Sadly, such collaboration between the two races had bred no enduring coexistence; as in the case of New England, its character has served rather to define the terms of their segregation.

POSTSCRIPT

WAS A CONFLICT BETWEEN NATIVE AMERICANS AND COLONISTS UNAVOIDABLE?

Are relations between peoples of different races and cultural traditions necessarily tense? Do they deteriorate into hostility because of factors which are ancillary to color, race, or culture? Should relations between Indians and white settlers be evaluated by distinguishing between the primary and the secondary causes of conflict? How did the United States government treat Native Americans after the Revolution?

The policy of containing Native Americans on reservations began in 1786, on the eve of the Constitutional Convention in Philadelphia. The purchase of Louisiana in 1803 raised the possibility of the forced removal of Indians to areas west of the Mississippi. The most notorious removal, the Long Trek of the Five Civilized Tribes from their homelands in the Gulf Plains to Oklahoma, resulted in the deaths of thousands from hunger, cold and disease. During the Civil War many tribes, particularly those that owned slaves, allied with the Confederacy. They continued to battle the federal government until 1868. After a brief hiatus, the carnage recommenced between 1875 and 1890.

Oklahoma, which had originally been designated as "Indian Territory," offers a microscopic example of the Indian policy of the United States government. In 1866 the Five Civilized Tribes were ordered to relinquish the western half of Oklahoma for the relocation of other tribes. In 1899 white homesteaders were allowed to settle in "Indian Territory," and after 1900 the area was regrouped and statehood was obtained in 1907.

The demands for minority rights in American society have been accompanied by a strong interest in Native Americans by scholars. A panoramic consideration appears in Robert Berkhofer's *The White Man's Indian: Images of the American Indian from Columbus to the Present* (Random House, 1978). Reginald Horsman discusses the question of racial attitudes and territoriality in *Race and Manifest Destiny: The Origins of American Racial Anglo-Saxonism* (Harvard University Press, 1981). Grant Foreman narrates the migration of the Five Civilized Tribes with a sympathetic understanding in *Indian Removal: The Emigration of the Five Civilized Tribes of Indians* (University of Oklahoma Press, 1932).

ISSUE 4

WERE THE COLONIES LOSING THEIR ENGLISH IDENTITY IN THE EIGHTEENTH CENTURY?

YES: Clinton Rossiter, from *The First American Revolution: The American Colonies on the Eve of the Revolution* (Harcourt, Brace and World, 1953)

NO: Lawrence Henry Gipson, from *The Coming of the Revolution, 1763-1775* (Harper and Row, 1954)

ISSUE SUMMARY

YES: The late Professor Rossiter presented demographic statistics as evidence of widespread ethnic pluralism in the colonies.
NO: Historian Gipson argues that a "broad uniformity" existed in England's North American colonies.

Colonial North America reflected great ethnic diversity during the seventeenth century. The Spanish moved north from Mexico City to Santa Fe in the Rocky Mountains. The French established Quebec and Montreal along the St. Lawrence River. From the Connecticut River to the Delaware, New Netherland and New Sweden bisected the area under English control until 1655 when New Sweden was conquered by the Dutch (who themselves came under English control a decade later). By the mid 1660s England's possessions stretched from southern Chesapeake Bay to the north shore of Massachusetts Bay. To refer to these settlements as "English," however, would be erroneous. Certainly this area belonged to England and its political institutions were English. Legal disputes were settled according to English Common Law. Financial ties led directly to London and foreign policy, which often led to wars on both sides of the Atlantic, was also decided there. But the pluralistic society had taken root. Pluralism, which established the privilege of voluntary choice, had a strong ethnic character in England's colonies. There were diverse languages with distinct names for places and their inhabitants, heterogeneous foods, and apparel. Many occupations were exclusive to certain ethnic groups. The best example of pluralism, however, was the variety of religious sects.

From 1621 to 1678 hundreds of Irish families settled in Virginia and the Carolinas. A decade after the first Irish arrived in Virginia, Norwegian families began to settle in New England. New England also became home to Jews after 1662 and Latvians arrived there in 1687. French Huguenots, encouraged by Charles II, started to arrive in South Carolina in the 1680s when religious persecution at home intensified. Mennonites also sought religious freedom in England's possessions; they came from Germany and Lithuania in the second half of the seventeenth century and built new lives in Pennsylvania.

The remarkable effect of this European mixture was the lack of discord. How might that be explained? Did the search for religious freedom overcome linguistic incompatibilities? Was space a factor? Did the wilderness cushion the shocks of ethnic disagreement? Perhaps the racial disparity of white, black, and red curtailed the kind of squabbling Europeans would have engaged in at home. Some emigrants from the Continent sojourned in England on their way to America. Did they, perhaps, begin an Anglicization process there?

Most non-English emigrants readily accustomed themselves to the English institution of trials by juries of their peers and a defendant's presumed innocence until proven guilty. The establishment of colonial assemblies assured that legislative consent to taxation (an issue over which the English had fought a civil war in the 1640s), and the right to initiate legislation would continue in the New World. In 1619 Virginia's House of Burgesses became the first of these assemblies. Others followed, in most cases, immediately after colonies were founded.

The unconditional religious toleration of the New World attracted both English and Continentals who had been denied absolute freedom of worship, while the prospect of economic security caught the attention of those suffering from economic hardship.

In the eighteenth century, improvements in travel and communications served to bind people closer together. Coaches regularly traveled on roads reinforced with wooden surfaces in places which might otherwise have been impassable. There was increased coastal traffic as well. After 1692 one single postal system delivered mail to all the colonies. Newspapers and pamphlets were distributed beyond their local boundaries. At least two organizations, the Society of Friends (Quakers) and the Masons, had members throughout the colonies.

Non-material values wove invisible threads among colonists. They shared one literary heritage regardless of language or religious sect: the Bible. Those who read extensively were influenced by the philosophies which reinforced colonial beliefs in life, liberty, property and the equality of opportunity. The elite knew Latin as well and the literature of ancient Rome provided timely political messages: resistance to tyrannical monarchs and the superiority of republican government with political power balanced among government institutions and offices.

Professor Rossiter has written, "The arrival of non-English immigrants did much to weaken the hold of the mother country." He reinforced this generalization by specifying that "the Scotch-Irishman was America's typical frontiersman, the German was its typical farmer." Professor Gipson counters by pointing out "in 1763 all colonials were Britons—at least those who were white and either born within the Empire or naturalized."

YES   Clinton Rossiter

THE FIRST AMERICAN REVOLUTION:
The American Colonies on the
Eve of Independence

. . . The clash of imperial policy and colonial self-reliance is almost always productive of the spirit of liberty. This is especially true if the policy of the parent state is conceived purely in its own interests, and if the colonists are men of high political aptitude and proud descent. Such was the pattern of Anglo-American relations in the colonial period. From the time of the earliest settlement, which like all the important settlements was the result of private initiative, English and American opinions on the political and economic status of the colonies were in sharp conflict.

The conduct of colonial affairs by the English government rested on these assumptions: The colonies were dependents of the parent state. Since their interests were subordinate to those of England, the welfare of the latter was to be the one concern of all agencies charged with governing them. They were therefore to serve, apparently forever, as a source of wealth and support for the land out of which their inhabitants had departed. If the English government had acted on these assumptions consistently throughout the colonial period, the contrasting ideas of the colonists would have had less chance to strike deep root. But confusion at the beginning, domestic troubles in the middle, and "salutary neglect" throughout most of this period permitted the colonists to build not only a theory but a condition of self-government. And it was this condition, of course, as some perceptive Englishmen were aware, that helped the colonies develop into prizes worth retaining by force of arms. The interests of England were, in this important sense, fatally self-contradictory.

The views of the colonists on their place in the imperial structure were somewhat mixed, ranging from the arrogant independence asserted by Massachusetts in the seventeenth century to the abject dependence argued by a handful of Tory apologists in the eighteenth. In general, the colonial attitude was one looking to near-equality in the present and some sort of full partnership in the future, all within the confines of a benevolent and protecting empire. The colonist acknowledged that for certain diplomatic and commercial purposes his destiny would rest for some time to come in the hands of men in London. But in all other matters, especially in that of political self-determination, he considered himself a "freeborn subject of the Crown of England." Theories of the origin and nature of the colonial assemblies are a good example of these divergent views. In English eyes the assemblies were founded by royal grant and existed at royal pleasure; in American eyes they existed as a matter of right. The Board of Trade looked upon them as inferior bodies enjoying rule-making powers under the terms of their charters; the men of Virginia and Massachusetts looked upon them as miniature Houses of Commons with power to make all laws they could get away with in practice. The struggle between these assemblies and the royal governors sent to control them was the focus of conflict of colonial and imperial interests. . . .

. . . The early colonists, thrown willy-nilly on their own devices, developed habits of self-government and passed them on to their descendants. The descendants, still just as far if not farther from London, fell naturally into an attitude of provincialism well suited to their condition but corrosive of empire. The lack of contact between one colony and another, the result of distance and unbelievably bad roads, allowed each to develop on its own. The diversity in character of the key colonies of Virginia, Massachusetts, New York, and Pennsylvania made a mockery of any notion of uniform imperial policy.

Worst of all from the imperial point of view, the ill effects of the inconsistency, inefficiency, corruption, stupidity, arrogance, and ignorance displayed to some degree at all times and to a perilous degree at some times by the English authorities were doubled and redoubled by the rolling seas and passing months. English laxity in enforcing the Navigation Acts and colonial habits of disobeying them were one instance of the extent to which three thousand miles of ocean could water down a policy of strict control. The technique of royal disallowance, which seemed so perfectly designed to keep the colonial assemblies in check, was likewise weakened by the mere fact of distance. For example, the disallowance in 1706 of two New Hampshire judiciary acts passed in 1699 and 1701 was never reported properly to the province, and the judiciary in that colony continued to function under these laws for a half century. And the royal governor, the linchpin of empire, was a far more accommodating fellow in Boston or Charleston that he appeared in his commissions and instructions issued from London. A governor like Sir Matthew Johnson of North Carolina, whose reports to the Board of Trade went astray four years in a row, could not have been much of a buffer against colonial urges to independence. When we realize that no regular mail-service of any kind existed until 1755, and that war disrupted communications more than one-third of the time between 1689 and 1763, we can understand how the ocean was at once a highway to freedom and a barrier to imperialism. Rarely in history have the laws of geopolitics worked so powerfully for liberty.

Had Burke ever lived in the colonies, he might have listed still another "capital source" to explain the rise of liberty in America, and thus have anticipated Frederick Jackson Turner and his celebrated thesis. We need not go all the way with Turner—"American democracy is fundamentally the outcome of the experiences of the American people in dealing with the West"—to acknowledge the significance of the frontier in early American history. Whatever the extent of that influence in the nineteenth century, in the seventeenth and eighteenth centuries—when America was one vast frontier and perhaps one in three Americans a frontiersman at some time in his life—it was clearly of the first importance. If we may take the word "frontiers" to mean not only the line of farthest settlement to the west, but also the primitive conditions of life and thought which extended throughout the colonies in the seventeenth century and continued to prevail in many areas east of the Appalachians during most of the eighteenth, we may point to at least a half-dozen indications of the influence of the American environment.

First, the frontier impeded the transfer to America of outworn attitudes and institutions. The wilderness frustrated completely such attempts to plant feudalism in America as the schemes of Sir Ferdinando Gorges and the stillborn Fundamental Constitutions of Carolina, and everywhere archaic laws and customs were simplified, liberalized, or rudely abandoned. In the matter of church-state relations the frontier was especially influential as a decentralizing and democratizing force. The positive result of this process of sloughing off the old ways was an increase in mobility, experimentation, and self-reliance among the settlers.

The wilderness demanded of those who would conquer it that they spend their lives in unremitting toil. Unable to devote any sizable part of their energies to government, the settlers insisted that government let them alone and perform its severely limited tasks at the amateur level. The early American definition of liberty as freedom *from* government was given added popularity and meaning by frontier conditions. It was a new and invigorating experience for tens of thousands of Englishmen, Germans, and Scotch-Irish to be able to build a home where they would at last be "let alone."

The frontier produced, in ways that Turner and his followers have made clear, a new kind of individual and new doctrines of individualism. The wilderness did not of itself create democracy; indeed, it often encouraged the growth of ideas and institutions hostile to it. But it did help produce some of the raw materials of American democracy—self-reliance, social fluidity, simplicity, equality, dislike of privilege, optimism, and devotion to liberty. At the same time, it emphasized the importance of voluntary co-operation. The group, too, had its uses on the frontier, whether for defense or barn-raising or cornhusking. The phrases "free association," "mutual subjection," and "the consent of the governed" were given new content in the wilderness.

Next, the fact that wages were generally higher and working conditions better in the colonies than in England did much to advance the cause of liberty. The reason for this happy condition was a distinct shortage of labor, and a prime reason for the shortage was land for the asking. The frontier population was made up of thousands of men who had left the seaboard to toil for themselves in the great forest. The results of this constant migration were as important for the seaboard as they were for the wilderness.

From the beginning the frontier was an area of protest and thus a nursery of republican notions. Under-represented in assemblies that made a habit of overtaxing them, scornful of the privileges and leadership assumed by the tidewater aristocracy, resentful of attempts to saddle them with unwanted ministers and officials, the men of the back country were in fact if not in print the most determined radicals of the colonial period. If their quaint and strangely deferential protests contributed very little to the literature of a rising democracy, they nevertheless made more popular the arguments for liberty and self-government.

Finally, all these factors combined to give new force to the English heritage of law, liberty, and self-government. The over-refined and often archaic institutions that the settlers brought along as part of their intellectual baggage were thrust once again into the crucible of primitive conditions. If these institutions emerged in shapes that horrified royal governors, they were nevertheless more simple, workable, and popular than they had been for several centuries in England. The laws and institutions of early Rhode Island or North Carolina would not have worked in more civilized societies, but they had abandoned most of their outworn features and were ready to develop along American lines. The hardworking, long-suffering men and women of the frontier—"People a litle wilful Inclined to doe when and how they please or not at al"—were themselves a primary force in the rise of colonial self-government.

The English descent and heritage of the colonists, the conflict of imperial and colonial interests, the rolling ocean, the all-pervading frontier—these were the "forces-behind-the-forces" that shaped the history of the colonies and spurred the peaceful revolution that preceded the bloody one of 1776. . . .

Well before 1765 the colonies had begun to take on a pattern of national origins that was "characteristically American": They looked to one country for their language, institutions, and paramount culture, but to many for their population. Americans were predominantly English in origin, but they were also Scotch, Irish, German, French, Swiss, Dutch, Swedish, and African. . . .

I turn now to a brief reckoning of the national elements in this population and begin, of course, with the English majority. The fact that America's career as asylum of the oppressed of many nations was well under way in 1765 should not obscure the predominantly English character of the colonial population. Seven in ten were of English blood, almost nine in ten were British. Although immigration from England tapered off sharply after 1689, the high rate of natural increase among the early families of New England and the tidewater had by 1750 produced a basic stock of perhaps one million English-Americans. It was these people, of course, who controlled America—politically, linguistically, culturally, and institutionally. The Dutch, French, Germans, and Scotch-Irish were energizing transfusions, but the English were, from beginning to end, the body and blood of colonial society. Even Pennsylvania, the most thoroughly cosmopolitan colony, had almost as many people of English descent as of all other nationalities put together. This is a plain truth that historians of this or that national group would do well to keep in mind.

From the North of Britain came two elements in the population: the Scots, who drifted in directly from their home country throughout the latter part of the colonial period, and the so-called Scotch-Irish, or the "Scots settled in Ireland," who had been living in the North of Ireland since early in the seventeenth century. The Scots, an unpopular people in colonial days, came from both lowlands and highlands. The Scotch clergyman, factor, and schoolmaster from the lowlands—all familiar figures in the colonies—were often quite English in character and outlook even before emigration. Highlanders, who left Scotland in largest numbers in the hard times after the rebellions of 1715 and 1746, were a more alien element, generally preferring to settle in their own isolated communities. Wherever he came from and wherever he settled, the industrious Scot was a man who fitted naturally into the American scene.

The Scotch-Irish of Ulster, who numbered thousands of Englishmen and Irishmen along with the predominant Scots, began to come to America around 1715. These people, for the most part lowlanders, had first been settled in northern Ireland in the reign of James I, had added to their numbers after 1685, and had prospered entirely too much for their own good. Harassed repeatedly by acts of Parliament that excluded their products, the Scotch-Irish were driven to seek a refuge in America. They came by tens of thousands, first to New England, where they were not very enthusiastically welcomed, then to Pennsylvania and the frontier countries to the south. The old colonists called them Irish, but they called themselves British. . . . Many Scotch-Irish came as indentured servants, but as servants who had every intention of ending up free, self-supporting farmers. By 1765 there were several hundred settlements in the western counties in which Scotch-Irish held sway. Natural-born frontiersmen, these hardy people were the most powerful national influence for western expansion, religious dissent, and democratic politics in the eighteenth century.

Catholic or southern Irish, as distinguished from Calvinist or northern Scotch-Irish, were also to be found in every colony, but especially in Maryland and Pennsylvania. Most of them came as individuals or in families, often abandoning their religion in order to win a friendlier reception. The average southern Irish immigrant failed

to preserve his national identity. The fact that the Scotch, Irish, and English strands of the total Irish migration of the eighteenth century are hopelessly snarled has persuaded some patriots to make ridiculous claims for the "pure" Irish. Yet the claims of the Scotch-Irish must not be pushed too far in the other direction. At least 20 per cent of the "Irish" of the eighteenth-century migration must have actually been Irish in national origin.

The largest national element with a character distinctly alien to the dominant English strain was the German population in the middle and Southern colonies. Poverty, war, and religious persecution drove so many thousands of Rhinelanders to Pennsylvania in the eighteenth century that Franklin and others predicted a Germanic future for the colony. In upstate New York, the western counties of the South, and above all in Pennsylvania, Germans settled in great swarms, more often than not retaining their language, customs, and culture. Although they took a small part in the political and social life of the colonies, their superior farming skill, thrift, and industry made them important in the economy, while their multiform Protestantism was a spur to religious liberty. Pennsylvania was the breadbasket of the American Revolution not least because it was one-third German. . . .

Perhaps fifteen to twenty thousand Swiss migrated to America from the German-speaking cantons between 1700 and 1765, fully half of them arriving in the decade 1734–1744. Pennsylvania and the Carolinas were the main destinations of these valuable immigrants, most of whom were regarded as another of the numerous breeds of German immigrant. A few French-speaking Swiss were also in the colonies.

It has been variously estimated that

between twenty and forty thousand French Protestants settled in the colonies after the revocation of the Edict of Nantes in 1685, most of them coming by way of England and Holland. Several features made this migration one of the most influential in colonial times: the way in which the French scattered themselves throughout the colonies; the high proportion of gentle blood, intelligence, and professional skill they brought with them; and the almost effortless manner in which they were assimilated into the colonial population. In religion, speech, and culture the French Huguenot became an authentic English-American. . . .

The story of New Netherland and New Amsterdam is such common American property that it is easy to overestimate the influence of Dutch blood and culture in the development of the colonies. It is generally agreed that there were only ten thousand Dutch in the colonies in 1700, that perhaps fifty to sixty thousand persons had predominantly Dutch blood in 1765, and that in eighteenth-century New York and New Jersey, where this stock was concentrated, roughly 15 to 20 per cent of the total white population could be classified as Dutch. Dutch immigration and influence were largely confined to the seventeenth century and the middle colonies. Dutch institutions were quickly scrapped after the English conquest of 1664, while the language, although some Hudson River farmers and Dutch Reformed pastors clung to it tenaciously, was in decline long before the end of the colonial period. The main contributions of the Dutch to the colonies were a good national stock, some expressive words, and a policy of colonization that made New York a cosmopolitan city from the beginning. The first permanent settlers of New Netherland were thirty families of Protestant, French-speaking Walloons from the southern Netherlands. Comparatively

few Dutch were prepared to leave home and settle permanently in the new world, yet those who did fathered a breed of typical colonists. . . .

Some ten to fifteen thousand colonists in 1765 had predominantly Swedish blood. Most of these were descendants of the few hundred settlers of New Sweden on the Delaware, which was founded as a fur-trading center in 1638 and was taken over by the Dutch in 1655. Although many of these sturdy farmers and traders migrated to other parts of the middle colonies, the original area of settlement maintained cultural and ecclesiastical ties with the homeland well into the eighteenth century. Over the years the Swedes proved to be a reasonably assimilable national element, as did also the small number of Finns and even smaller sprinkling of Danes who helped plant the tiny colony at Fort Christina.

The total number of Jews in the colonies in 1765 could not have been more than 1,500, most of them Spanish or Portuguese in immediate origin. Newport, New York, Charleston, and Savannah were the principal havens of this trading people, but they could also be found in individual families or tiny groups through all the colonies. Jews suffered the expected social and political discrimination, but in the field of business they were first-class citizens. Many of them lived, as one traveler observed of the New York Jews, in highly respectable style. . . .

What was the total effect on society, culture, and government of this influx of nationalities into the American settlement? I will attempt to evaluate English influence at several points in the course of this book. But what of the other nationalities, especially the Scotch-Irish and Germans? What did they do to reshape or improve the dominant English strain?

First, the melting pot had only just

71

begun to heat up in the latter part of the eighteenth century. Crèvecoeur's example of the English-French-Dutch family "whose present four sons have now four wives of four different nations" was a phenomenon more prophetic of the Republic than typical of the colonies. The great process of national fusion had made little progress by 1765. Assimilation into the English stock rather than the creation of a new people was the result of such intermarriage as took place in colonial times. Nor were all the ingredients yet in the pot; the essential racial (Teutonic-Celtic) and religious (Protestant) unity of the population must not be overlooked.

The arrival of non-English immigrants did much to weaken the hold of the mother country. The newcomer wanted to be as loyal as anyone else, but his allegiance to the Crown could have little real emotional content. The Germans were inclined to be conservatively neutral about English dominion; the Scots and Irish were, for all the loyal humility that oozed from their petitions, innately hostile to the Georges and their agents. They lacked, as one traveler put it, the "same filial attachment" to England "which her own immediate offspring have."

Next, the influx of aliens did much to strengthen the Protestant, dissenting, individualistic character of colonial religion. The Presbyterian, Lutheran, Baptist, and German Pietist churches were the chief beneficiaries of this immigration. The numbers and enthusiasm of these dissenting groups gave a tremendous lift to the cause of religious liberty in the colonies south of Pennsylvania.

The eighteenth-century immigrants helped democratize the political institutions that had been brought over from England and put to work in the wilderness. This was especially true of the Scotch-Irish, whose only quarrel with the representative governments of their adopted colonies was that they were not representative enough. The Germans were inclined to be politically passive; their major contribution to the coming democracy was the support they brought to the middle-class creed of industry, frugality, and self-reliance. The Scotch-Irish, on the other hand, were more politically conscious. If the controlling groups of the coastal counties refused to honor their legitimate claims to participation in public life, this rebuff served only to make their radicalism more insistent. They had little intention of altering the English-American scheme of government, but they did mean to show the world how democratic it could be. The sentiments of "leveling republicanism" were especially active on the Scotch-Irish frontier; here the "real American Revolution" went on apace.

Finally, the mere volume of immigration from Germany and Ireland had a pronounced effect on colonial life. The swarming of these industrious peoples made possible the remarkable expansion in territory and population that marked the eighteenth century in America. If the Scotch-Irishman was America's typical frontiersman, the German was its typical farmer; and between them they made it possible for cities like Philadelphia and towns like Lancaster to grow and flourish. Though they were men of different natures, both sought the same blessing. "And what but LIBERTY, charming LIBERTY, is the resistless Magnet that attracts so many different Nations into that flourishing Colony?"

NO

Lawrence Henry Gipson

THE COMING OF THE REVOLUTION

THE BRITISH EMPIRE IN 1763

... In 1763 all colonials were Britons—at least those who were white and either born within the Empire or naturalized. The Empire was their own and they were proud of membership in it. There were good reasons for this pride. Its government rested fundamentally on law and not on men. Both in Great Britain and the colonies in the eighteenth century the law of the land that bound all men, even the King, was a mixture of common and statutory law; that is, law based upon judicial interpretation of common custom, on the one hand, and on formal legislative enactment, on the other. Despite the striking contrasts in the seventeenth century between the codes enforced within some of the colonies and the legal system of the mother country, in the course of the eighteenth century colonial law and British law were in substantial harmony by 1763. This degree of uniformity was reached not only as a result of the adoption of English law by colonial assemblies, particularly Pennsylvania, but by reason of the exercise by the King's Privy Council of the power both to disallow colonial legislation and to review colonial judicial decisions. In substance, the colonies acquiesced in the exercise of these supervisory powers. Further, although all the older and more mature colonies legislated for themselves, by 1763 many statutes of Parliament extended throughout the Empire by express enactment and covered a multiplicity of subjects, from such external matters as the regulation of imports and exports and the naturalization of foreigners to such internal matters as the regulation of currency, the operations of stock companies, and the cutting of timber.

The instrumentalities of lawmaking and enforcement within the colonies were about as similar to those of Great Britain as could be expected under differing conditions. Indeed, the colonial assemblies not only consciously adopted as far as was possible the forms and procedures of the House of

4. WERE THE COLONISTS LOSING THEIR ENGLISH IDENTITY?

Commons but constantly sought to acquire its powers. With respect to the electorate that selected the lawmakers, everywhere, as was true in England, there existed what might be called a political aristocracy made up of qualified males who enjoyed the right of franchise and a monopoly of public offices—as against others who were of the disenfranchised, whose persons and property were subject to regulation and taxation without true representation.

In short, the popular branches of the colonial assemblies were consciously evolving from the earlier purely dependent ordinance-making bodies, and in structure and powers approaching the likeness of the House of Commons. Moreover, other features of the colonial governments were just as consciously patterned after the institutions of the mother country. The colonial governor was regarded as one who, to a greater or less extent, represented the King, either directly under royal commission and royal instruction, as in the royal colonies, or less directly, as in the proprietary and the corporate colonies. At least, in every instance this official as the chief executive was under heavy bond to see that imperial regulations were enforced; he also had an advisory council not unlike the King's Cabinet Council. Likewise, the English offices of sheriff and of justice of the peace, county or parish courts, courts of oyer and terminer, and courts of appeal had made their appearance in the colonies. In fact, these and other institutions transplanted from the mother country were so well adapted to meet the divergent needs of Americans that, even with the establishment of their independence from Great Britain, they were, with some modifications, preserved and are still regarded as among the most cherished possessions of most North Americans.

Not only were the inhabitants of the Empire bound together by similar, if not identical, systems of law and institutions of government but the religious, ethical, intellectual, and social conceptions of the mother country were still largely those of the English-speaking colonials and increasingly those of the non-English transplanted elements. An important factor in producing this broad uniformity, with infinite variations, was the fact that the British people of both the Old and New World were by and large not only literate but were eager readers of weekly newspapers and pamphlets concerned with contemporary world developments; most of them also read the King James version of the Holy Scriptures, thus drawing their religious inspiration from the same source. Then, too, large numbers of colonials perused the works of British theologians, philosophers, scientists, essayists, poets, novelists, and dramatists. Further, English etiquette, dress, architecture, and home furnishings, as well as other English practices, exerted a profound influence, especially on the more settled communities of the eastern Atlantic seaboard. Moreover, one must take into account the connections existing between Anglicans, Quakers, Baptists, Presbyterians, and other religious groups in the colonies and the parent organizations in Great Britain.

While these common conceptions, common legal and social codes, and common institutions produced a very great degree of cultural homogeneity within the British Empire, there were, nevertheless, divergencies that are equally important to recognize.

The American frontier was creating a new type of Briton—the American—one who was less and less, as time elapsed, under the influence of tradition and inherited cultural patterns and more and more shaped by his contest with nature and the necessity to improvise if he were to survive. The King, the Privy Council, the ministers of state, and the Parliament, established as they were beyond the intervening forest and the rushing rivers and across the wide Atlantic, were quite lost to his view. Indeed, only in time of great emergency, when things were beyond his and his fellow pioneers' control—as in the face of the threat of annihilation in the early years of the late war—did the wilderness dweller heed the existence of or value of the imperial connections that still bound him to Great Britain. His recognized leader was not, as a rule, even the colonial governor of the colony in which he had his isolated western home, or even the sheriff or lieutenant of his country, but rather the most enterprising and daring of his wilderness companions. In other words, the form of social structure that the backwoodsman knew and the only one that to him had significance was a rude but true type of democratic society, with authority, such as it was, exercised by those who by common consent had shown superior capacity to face the hard conditions of life on the frontier.

Even along the settled Atlantic seaboard, where conditions of living were far less fluid and primitive than those of the wilderness, there were likewise deviations from the institutions of England. While here an aristocracy of wealth enjoying political and social domination was firmly planted, there was no aristocracy of title, nor was there a hereditary body clothed with legislative and judicial power as was the case in the British Isles. In contrast, while the status of slavery was not recognized in English law, a substantial percentage of the population in the southern provinces and at least a small percentage in every colony were slaves whose status was recognized and defined by local law. These cultural variations sprang largely from differences in environment....

In America, a pioneer outlook combined with a Puritan tradition ran counter to the setting up of a hereditary titled class—and this in spite of the existence in some of the colonies of such feudal institutions as primogeniture and entail, which in England had helped create and preserve a hereditary landed aristocracy. However, the institution of slavery had fastened itself on American life, not only by reason of the activities of British slavers—at first directed toward the carrying of Africans to the Spanish possessions—but primarily because it offered to colonials an easy and profitable means of rolling back the North American wilderness and thereby laying out and exploiting plantations, and staffing the households of the wealthy with permanent servants. So between the years 1763 and 1775 fiery advocates of liberty—planters, merchants, lawyers, and even ministers of the Gospel—saw apparently no moral inconsistency in openly offering rewards in newspapers for the return into captivity of some runaway black, while at the time denouncing as "slavery" restrictions that the mother country had seen fit to place upon their freedom of action.

Indeed, the sharp accent upon colonial rights after 1763, the rapid development of sectionalism within the Empire, the armed revolt of the thirteen colonies, the declaration of American independence, and, finally, the creation of a new nation followed one after the other with almost breath-taking speed. All were accomplished facts twenty-five years after Great Britain and the colonies had in closest association won the most spectacular and also by far the most important military successes in the history of the old Empire.

This overwhelming victory doubtless seemed to most people to portend that the Empire, for more than a century to follow, would by the utilization of its varied talents and vast material resources be not only dominant on the seas but also a most potent force in two hemispheres, both in peace and in war. It was an empire without an emperor, setting an example to the rest of mankind as to how liberty could be reconciled with law, even within physical boundaries as widespread as those of the autocratic Spanish Empire and much more extended than those of imperial Rome at the height of its glory—a living testimony that there could exist in the midst of a world of despotisms the unity of a great, free, and enlightened society, where men could worship, speak and write, and mold their own lives with remarkably few restraints and with a sense of personal security and dignity. Where else in the contemporary world of the eighteenth century, people could ask, had a whole literature flowered, based upon conceptions of the rights and privileges of the individual? Where else could men point with pride to a series of great constitutional documents, stemming from past centuries, as the symbols of their liberties?

As tokens of their common sense of security and freedom from fear, the inhabitants of the Empire in 1763 could point to the fact that they were protected not only by a victorious army but, what was of greater assurance, by the most powerful fleet that had ever sailed the seas. Their merchant marine was also vastly larger than that of any other nation, and in its bottoms they exported to foreign ports a greater surplus of cereals and meat products than was exported by all the rest of the world combined, obtaining in return a bewildering variety of commodities to add to the satisfactions of life. They ranked first in the iron industry and in shipbuilding, as well as in other fields. In fact, despite squalor and poverty to be found here and there and especially in the British Isles, in the eyes of contemporaries most of King George III's subjects enjoyed an enviable standard of living: they were, by and large, better fed, better clothed, better sheltered, better rewarded for their efforts, than any other people with the possible exception of the Dutch. This was particularly true of those freemen dwelling in the American colonies.

Men, however, do not live by bread alone. What of the higher satisfactions of life and the evidences of civilized living within the Empire? By any standard that might be applied, the epoch now under consideration was indubitably one of the greatest in the history of the English-speaking people; indeed, the pages of its annals were crowded with the achievements of men of commanding capacity. Consider the statesman William Pitt, the Great Commoner, who by his superb organizing ability and dynamic qualities of leadership in the late war had brought victory to the Empire; Edmund Burke, who as an orator surpassed him in profundity; and Charles James Fox, Burke's brilliant and radical political rival. There were David Hume, the philosopher, and Samuel Johnson, the writer and lexicographer, each an intellectual colossus in his own field—men would later refer to "the age of Johnson" and could with equal reason refer to "the age of Hume." There were the historians, such as William Robertson and Edward Gibbon, the latter to leave to the world his *Decline and Fall of the Roman Empire*, a historical work still to be eclipsed by any other yet produced in the English-speaking world. There were the distinguished jurist William Blackstone and equally distinguished political economist

Adam Smith, both to publish in this era the results of massive learning: the one in his classic *Commentaries on the Laws* and the other in his equally classic *The Wealth of Nations.* John Wesley, the most outstanding English religious reformer since the days of John Wycliffe, was still active in his Christian ministry, with a message destined to transform the lives of countless people and to inject into the harsh criminal law of both the Old and the New World a new humanitarian spirit; and George Whitefield, a former colleague in the Methodist movement, and the most powerful field evangelist that England has ever produced or America has ever heard, was still going from city cross to village cemetery speaking with a voice of deep conviction to even tens of thousands of forgotten men, drawn together and held spellbound by his burning exhortations. There were Thomas Gray, the poet; Oliver Goldsmith, the dramatist; James Boswell, greatest of all British biographers; David Garrick, perhaps the first among a galaxy of Shakespearean actors; and Sir Joshua Reynolds, George Romney, and Thomas Gainsborough, three of the most gifted of portrait painters, together with William Hogarth, whose inimitable caricatures of his own age have amused and sobered generations of people. Samuel Richardson, the father of the English novel, died only in 1761 and his successor, Tobias Smollett, not until 1771. Nor must one forget the brothers Robert and James Adam, great architects and designers of furniture, who together with Thomas Chippendale and young Thomas Sheraton were to leave a lasting influence on the beauty of living and good taste of the English-speaking world. Finally, there were James Watt, who gave to his generation the improved steam engine in 1764— shortly followed by James Hargreaves's spinning jenny and a little later by Richard

Arkwright's spinning water frame—and the young scientist, Henry Cavendish, already embarked upon his remarkable series of investigation into the properties of gases and electricity. All four were heralds of a new age of science and technology.

Although the overseas English-speaking peoples up to 1763 had been largely preoccupied with conquering the wilderness, they, too, could point to some notable personalities. Jonathan Edwards, theologian and metaphysician, whose treatise on the *Freedom of the Will* has been called "the one large contribution that America has made to the deeper philosophic thought of the world," died only in 1758; the fame of Benjamin Franklin, whose impressive achievements in many fields were to gain for him world-wide recognition, had already spread to Great Britain, where he had received not only the gift of the freedom of the city from the corporation of Edinburgh but honorary degrees from the ancient universities of St. Andrews and Oxford; and his friend John Bartram, distinguished as one of the leading eighteenth-century naturalists and a tireless collector of New World flora, was in the midst of his life work. Further, the eve of the Revolution ushered in a new generation of American political philosophers and statesmen—such men as John Dickinson, John Adams, Thomas Jefferson, and young James Madison—who would leave a lasting imprint on the institutions and political ideals of the Western Hemisphere. Finally, living in quiet retirement in Virginia, was the planter George Washington, destined to display such wisdom, such patience, such strength of character and purpose, such utter self-dedication to the fulfillment of the tasks that he was to undertake both in war and in peace, that by the universal verdict of mankind he would be accorded a place among the world's greatest men.

Only in Ireland—cursed for two centuries with strife engendered by the interfusion of religious, ecclesiastical, and political issues—was there within the Empire in 1763 any noticeable discontent among the people with their lot, and rightly so. Yet before the outbreak of the American Revolution even this unhappy land was to find in Henry Flood and Henry Grattan not unworthy champions of Irish rights, and was thus to see the beginnings of the long travail that would ultimately bring about the birth of a free nation.

In short, the British Empire in 1763 was perhaps more economically self-contained and more prosperous than any other that had ever before existed. Nor is this all. No better testimony to its enlightened character can be offered than the fact that between 1763 and 1775 there existed not simply one religion, as was the case within the French, Spanish, and Portuguese empires, but four different Christian faiths which were established by law in various areas: the Anglican, the Presbyterian, the Congregational, and the Roman Catholic; while many other faiths were quietly tolerated. In addition there were even colonies with no religious establishment. These varied achievements together with the spirit of enlightenment stamped the old Empire as truly the wonder of the world. Yet within a decade it was to be torn asunder by internecine strife. . . .

AMERICA WAXES RICH AND STRONG

. . . To repeat, the great wilderness of North America was slowly helping to create a new kind of Briton—the American. But the American was not shaped from any one mold. Certainly the ranchers of the western Carolinas, who tended the great herds of cattle that roamed and fattened upon the marshy uplands about the sources of the Santee and other rivers, were by 1763 as distinct in pattern of living as were the cowboys of the western plains in the nineteenth century. Quite distinct were the western traders and trappers, who lived a life not unlike that of the Indians and one very different from other frontiersmen primarily interested in husbandry and homebuilding. In the more settled parts of the colonies, not only the wealthy tobacco and rice planters of the South but the merchant princes of the North had become as dissimilar from their prototypes in England as were American farmers, sailors, fishermen, small tradesmen, and mechanics. Moreover, the woodsmen, both of Maine and New Hampshire and of the pine barrens of the Carolinas, represented types that had no counterpart in the mother country. There were also extensive communities of German-speaking people in Pennsylvania, western Maryland, and western Virginia who preserved much of the culture of their ancestral homeland, as did the Ulster Scots—more familiarly known as Scotch-Irish—who remained a border people much like their ancestors in northern Ireland and earlier in the Lowlands of Scotland. Finally, there were the Negroes, probably numbering by 1763 almost 175,000. The impact of their mores, as well as their mere presence as slaves, upon the English civilization of the New World was clearly evident and as much as any other social institution distinguished it sharply from that of the mother country.

In short, many distinct groups were jostling one another in the British North America of 1763. Some were pacifistic like the Quakers, the Mennonites, and Dunkards in Pennsylvania, and others decidedly militant, like the Presbyterian Ulster Scots and the New England Congregationalists; many were devout communicants and others were apparently disassociated from any church or religion; most of them used the tongue of England, and yet thousands spoke some other language. Thus, there was a vital need of the spirit of tolerance in the colonies, were conditions of living not to be rendered unbearable. That this spirit of toleration was growing cannot be doubted; that it still fell far short of the present American ideal is not to be denied. In 1763, Roman Catholics as well as non-Christians, including Jews, were denied the franchise and other rights of citizenship even in Rhode Island, that colony of "soul freedom." Nor was religious freedom of Catholics protected in Massachusetts Bay under its charter, while in the province of Maryland a harsh code directed toward the complete suppression of their religion still remained on the statute books. In Connecticut men were being haled into court and fined or imprisoned for the crime of separatism; neither "unitarians" nor "deists" were capable of holding any office. In Virginia, Baptist and other dissenting preachers were liable to persecution for carrying on their activities, and so late as 1768 many of them were actually imprisoned as disturbers of the peace. Nevertheless, the spirit of the times was hostile to this intolerance, under whatever name it presented itself, and such popular leaders as Patrick Henry came powerfully to the defense of those who suffered for their nonconformity.

It is quite evident, in surveying their progress in the eighteenth century, that the American continental colonies had attained a large measure of maturity by 1763. Since this maturity had a very direct bearing upon their ultimate relationship to the rest of the British Empire and particu-larly to the mother country, it is important to indicate its characteristics with some clearness. . . .

It should be understood that fundamentally the elaborate system of economic controls that were supposed to bind the British Empire in 1763 was in essence not only a protectionist system but one designed to make the Empire as nearly as possible economically self-contained. In other words, as least from about the middle of the seventeenth century the government of England sought to realize in the planting of colonies the ideal of having each new establishment supplement rather that supplant the gainful activities of the people of the mother country and those of the other possessions. Nor, on the other hand, were the inhabitants of England permitted to depress the condition of Englishmen overseas who had discovered profitable means of gaining a livelihood in harmony with this objective. Therefore, those in southwestern England who in the seventeenth century had established tobacco plantations were compelled by law and the use of force to cease activities. Consistent with this conception, when, in 1663, Carolina was established, it was hoped by those close to King Charles II that the new colony would devote itself to providing many commodities not as yet produced in England and the other English colonies rather than compete in established fields, and this also was true when Georgia was founded in 1732.

The steady growth of the Empire brought about not only an increasing realization of the goal of economic self-containment, but a vast increase in the cost of military and naval security. Even in times of peace the charges upon the government steadily rose. By 1700 these charges averaged over £3,750,000 a year, including debt retirement; between 1715 and 1739 they averaged about £5,750,000; and between 1750 and 1755 they reached over £6,500,000. Moreover, the wars in which England had been engaged since the days of William III, and upon the successful outcome of which the welfare, if not the fate, of the colonies depended, had been very costly. Between 1693 and the end of 1749, over £144,649,000 had been spent on them alone. Yet the national debt in 1755, as the result of steady, heavy taxation of the people of England, stood at a sum but slightly over £75,000,000. This result could only have been achieved by an England permitted to prosper. Therefore, the restrictive system that sought not only to make the mother country the center of the commercial life of the Empire, but also to protect it from competition in such special fields as the manufacturing of woolen and iron commodities, upon which English economic stability so largely depended, was designed to serve this end. Furthermore, by means of this system the colonies were able to make an indirect contribution to the end of sustaining both the public credit of England and the means of their own security. While it is true that much has been written against the system, it is difficult to visualize one that would under given conditions have been better adapted to serve the ends of preserving and nurturing the colonies embraced within the old British Empire before 1763. That they themselves were among its chief beneficiaries can hardly be questioned in view of the impressive evidence of their unprecedented development in the course of the eighteenth century. . . .

POSTSCRIPT

WERE THE COLONIES LOSING THEIR ENGLISH IDENTITY IN THE EIGHTEENTH CENTURY?

In many ways the war for independence provides a clue to answering this question. Washington's troops starved and froze at Valley Forge while Pennsylvanians sold food and fuel to the Redcoats. British General Howe was accompanied by one thousand Bostonians when he evacuated the city. As many as fifty thousand Loyalists fought *against* independence and in 1783, at the war's conclusion, one hundred thousand Loyalists went into exile.

The events which led up to the war provide other insights. Changes during the eighteenth century transformed the many variables of colonial society. Events blended the diverse subcultures of Europe, the English traditions and institutions, and the values which had developed in the new world into a new definition of America. No longer did that word have only a geographical meaning; it now also reflected a state of mind—intangible, yet effective. Between 1765 and 1776 the Stamp Act Congress, the Committees of Correspondence, the Continental Congresses, and the Declaration of Independence all contributed to this new definition.

Wallace Notestein's, *The English People on the Eve of Colonization* (Harper and Row, 1954), describes English society, its emigrants and their movitations. George L. Smith's, *Religion and Trade in New Netherland: Dutch Origins and American Development* (Cornell University Press, 1973), documents the important contributions of one particular ethnic group to religious pluralism. Wesley F. Craven's *The Colonies in Transition* (Harper and Row, 1966), is a good introduction to the multivolume works of Charles M. Andrews's, *The Colonial Period in American History*, 4 volumes (Yale University Press, 1934-1937), and Lawrence H. Gipson's, *The British Empire Before the American Revolution*, 15 volumes (Alfred A. Knopf, 1936-1970). The *Ethnic Chronology Series* (Oceana Publications, 1972-1978 with updates to 1982), provides the dates and places of arrival for virtually all ethnic groups. Individuals and families are identified when possible.

ISSUE 5

WAS SLAVERY AN ECONOMIC NECESSITY IN THE AMERICAN SOUTH?

YES: Ulrich B. Phillips, from *American Negro Slavery* (D. Appleton and Co., 1918)

NO: Kenneth M. Stampp, from *The Peculiar Institution* (Alfred A. Knopf, 1956)

ISSUE SUMMARY

YES: Professor Phillips considered slavery a necessary component of the plantation system.
NO: Professor Stampp considers slave labor as a deliberate choice made to maximize profits.

By the time the Thirteenth Amendment abolished slavery in 1865, the history of that peculiar institution had stretched back two hundred years. It was as old as Harvard in New England and the House of Burgesses in Virginia. Those institutions were not at all unique to the New World however, having their roots in Parliament and the Universities of Oxford and Cambridge. Slavery, on the other hand, did not exist in England at this time. The paradox which needs explanation, then, is why did slavery develop in settlements which were inhabited by English people searching for freedom of religion and the freedom of economic opportunity?

The London companies whose investments underwrote the colonization of Massachusetts and Virginia intended to earn a profit on their capital. Slavery had always held an attraction for entrepreneurs who believed that the costs of labor determine prices. When the Europeans found Native Americans unsuited to enslavement, they did not abandon their interest in servitude. Instead they imported Black Africans as bondsmen.

Why were they available? The forced migration of Black Africans who became slaves in the New World resulted from several factors. Initially, and with supreme irony, many were sold to European slave traders by other Blacks. Defeat and capture in tribal warfare forced them down a path of exploitation and alienation which led from the interior of Africa to the western edges of the Atlantic. Starting in 1502 when the Spanish slave trade commenced, ten to fifteen million Blacks were brought to the Americas over the next three hundred years. Often the journey across the Atlantic, known as the Middle Passage, meant changing masters who bought and sold human beings for a profit. The labor shortage in the New World settlements explain the large profits that were available.

The South lacked workers in the same way other colonies did but particularly because of the kind of agriculture developed there. Labor-intensive staples such as tobacco, rice, indigo, cotton and sugar dominated the Southern economy. The toil required to transplant tobacco seedlings on wet days or to pick hornworms off the maturing leaves partially explains why a subservient and cowed work force appeared attractive. Workers with any semblance of choice avoided not only the tobacco fields but also the cultivation of rice and indigo, often grown on the same plantation. Both kinds of work were tedious and unhealthy. Rice was planted in reclaimed swampland, and slaves worked submissively from dawn to dusk. The processing of indigo blooms, cotton, and sugar cane demanded around the clock work. Finally, there were fewer out of pocket expenses with slaves than there were when using indentured servants (who had to be searched for continuously and paid for in cash). Slaves, on the other hand, proved to be a wise investment because their offspring eliminated the need for continuing importation. The slaveholders in the older colonies actually found themselves supplying the Gulf and Trans-Appalachian region with slaves as this institution spread.

Phillips, who was born in Georgia in 1877, thought slave labor necessary for southern agriculture. "If the plantation system were to be perpetuated an entirely different labor supply must be had," he wrote of Jamestown, Virginia, before 1619. Stampp, who critically revised Phillips' interpretation, countered, "Actually the southern plantation system was older than slavery and survived its abolition."

YES

Ulrich B. Phillips

AMERICAN NEGRO SLAVERY

PLANTATION TENDENCIES

Every typical settlement in English America was in its first phase a bit of the frontier. Commerce was rudimentary, capital scant, and industry primitive. Each family had to suffice itself in the main with its own direct produce. No one could afford to specialize his calling, for the versatility of the individual was wellnigh a necessity of life. This phase lasted only until some staple of export was found which permitted the rise of external trade. Then the fruit of such energy as could be spared from the works of bodily sustenance was exchanged for the goods of the outer world; and finally in districts of special favor for staples, the bulk of the community became absorbed in the special industry and procured most of its consumption goods from without.

In the hidden coves of the Southern Alleghanies the primitive régime has proved permanent. In New England where it was but gradually replaced through the influence first of the fisheries and then of manufacturing, it survived long enough to leave an enduring spirit of versatile enterprise, evidenced in the plenitude of "Yankee notions." In the Southern lowlands and Piedmont, however, the pristine advantages of self-sufficing industry were so soon eclipsed by the profits to be had from tobacco, rice, indigo, sugar or cotton, that in large degree the whole community adopted a stereotyped economy with staple production as its cardinal feature. The earnings obtained by the more efficient producers brought an early accumulation of capital, and at the same time the peculiar adaptability of all the Southern staples to production on a large scale by unfree labor prompted the devotion of most of the capital to the purchase of servants and slaves. Thus in every district suited to any of these staples, the growth of an industrial and social system like that of Europe and the Northern States was cut short and the distinctive Southern scheme of things developed instead.

Excerpted from *American Negro Slavery* by Ulrich B. Phillips. Copyright ©1918, Appleton Century Crofts, Inc. Footnotes have been omitted.

This régime was conditioned by its habitat, its products and the racial quality of its labor supply, as well as by the institution of slavery and the traditional predilections of the masters. The climate of the South was generally favorable to one or another of the staples except in the elevated tracts in and about the mountain ranges. The soil also was favorable except in the pine barrens which skirted the seaboard. Everywhere but in the alluvial districts, however, the land had only a surface fertility, and all the staples, as well as their great auxiliary Indian corn, required the fields to be kept clean and exposed to the weather; and the heavy rainfall of the region was prone to wash off the soil from the hillsides and to leach the fertile ingredients through the sands of the plains. But so spacious was the Southern area that the people never lacked fresh fields when their old ones were outworn. Hence, while public economy for the long run might well have suggested a conservation of soil at the expense of immediate crops, private economy for the time being dictated the opposite policy; and its dictation prevailed, as it has done in virtually all countries and all ages. Slaves working in squads might spread manure and sow soiling crops if so directed, as well as freemen working individually; and their failure to do so was fully paralleled by similar neglect at the North in the same period. New England, indeed, was only less noted than the South for exhausted fields and abandoned farms. The newness of the country, the sparseness of population and the cheapness of land conspired with crops, climate and geological conditions to promote exploitive methods. The planters were by no means alone in shaping their program to fit these circumstances. The heightened speed of the consequences was in a sense merely an unwelcome proof of their system's efficiency. Their laborers, by reason of being slaves, must at word of command set forth on a trek of a hundred or a thousand miles. No racial inertia could hinder nor local attachments hold them. In the knowledge of this the masters were even more alert than other men of the time for advantageous new locations; and they were accordingly fain to be content with rude houses and flimsy fences in any place of sojourn, and to let their hills remain studded with stumps as well as to take the exhaustion of the soil as a matter of course. . . .

In the oldest districts of all, however, the lowlands about the Chesapeake, the process went on to a final stage in which the bulk of the planters, after exhausting the soil for staple purposes, departed westward and were succeeded in their turn by farmers, partly native whites and free negroes and partly Northerners trickling in, who raised melons, peanuts, potatoes, and garden truck for the Northern city markets.

Throughout the Southern staple areas the plantations waxed and waned in a territorial progression. The régime was a broad billow moving irresistibly westward and leaving a trough behind. At the middle of the nineteenth century it was entering Texas, its last available province, whose cotton area it would have duly filled had its career escaped its catastrophic interruption. What would have occurred after that completion, without the war, it is interesting to surmise. Probably the crest of the billow would have subsided through the effect of an undertow setting eastward again. Belated immigrants, finding the good lands all engrossed, would have returned to their earlier homes, to hold their partially exhausted soils in higher esteem than before and to remedy the depletion by reformed cultivation. That the

5. WAS SLAVERY AN ECONOMIC NECESSITY?

billow did not earlier give place to a level flood was partly due to the shortage of slaves; for the African trade was closed too soon for the stock to fill the country in these decades. To the same shortage was owing such opportunity as the white yeomanry had in staple production. The world offered a market, though not at high prices, for a greater volume of the crops than the plantation slaves could furnish; the farmers supplied the deficit.

Free workingmen in general, whether farmers, artisans or unskilled wage earners, merely filled the interstices in and about the slave plantations. One year in the eighteen-forties a planter near New Orleans, attempting to dispense with slave labor, assembled a force of about a hundred Irish and German immigrants for his crop routine. Things went smoothly until the midst of the grinding season, when with one accord the gang struck for double pay. Rejecting the demand the planter was unable to proceed with his harvest and lost some ten thousand dollars worth of his crop. The generality of the planters realized, without such a demonstration, that each year must bring its crop crisis during which an overindulgence by the laborers in the privileges of liberty might bring ruin to the employers. To secure immunity from this they were the more fully reconciled to the limitations of their peculiar labor supply. Freemen white or black might be convenient as auxiliaries, and were indeed employed in many instances whether on annual contract as blacksmiths and the like or temporarily as emergency helpers in the fields; but negro slaves were the standard composition of the gangs. This brought it about that whithersoever the planters went they carried with them crowds of negro slaves and all the problems and influences to which the presence of negroes and the prevalence of slavery gave rise.

One of the consequences was to keep foreign immigration small. In the colonial period the trade in indentured servants recruited the white population, and most of those who came in that status remained as permanent citizens of the South; but such Europeans as came during the nineteenth century were free to follow their own reactions without submitting to a compulsory adjustment. Many of them found the wage-earning opportunity scant, for the slaves were given preference by their masters when steady occupations were to be filled, and odd jobs were often the only recourse for outsiders. This was an effect of the slavery system. Still more important, however, was the repugnance which the newcomers felt at working and living alongside the blacks; and this was a consequence not of the negroes being slaves so much as of the slaves being negroes. It was a racial antipathy which when added to the experience of industrial disadvantage pressed the bulk of the newcomers northwestward beyond the confines of the Southern staple belts, and pressed even many of the native whites in the same direction.

This intrenched the slave plantations yet more strongly in their local domination, and by that very fact it hampered industrial development. Great landed proprietors, it is true, have oftentimes been essential for making beneficial innovations. Thus the remodeling of English agriculture which Jethro Tull and Lord Townsend instituted in the eighteenth century could not have been set in progress by any who did not possess their combination of talent and capital. In the ante-bellum South, likewise, it was the planters, and necessarily so, who introduced the new staples of sea-island cotton and sugar, the new devices of horizontal plowing and hillside terracing, the new practice of seed selection, and the new resource of commercial fertilizers. Yet their constant bondage to the staples debarred the whole community in large degree from agricultural diversification, and their dependence upon gangs of negro slaves kept the average of skill and assiduity at a low level.

The negroes furnished inertly obeying minds and muscles; slavery provided a police; and the plantation system contributed the machinery of direction. The assignment of special functions to slaves of special aptitudes would enhance the general efficiency; the coordination of tasks would prevent waste of effort; and the conduct of a steady routine would lessen the mischiefs of irresponsibility. But in the work of a plantation squad no delicate implements could be employed, for they would be broken; and no discriminating care in the handling of crops could be had except at a cost of supervision which was generally prohibitive. The whole establishment would work with success only when the management fully recognized and allowed for the crudity of the labor.

The planters faced this fact with mingled resolution and resignation. The sluggishness of the bulk of their slaves they took as a racial trait to be conquered by discipline, even though their ineptitude was not to be eradicated; the talents and vigor of their exceptional negroes and mulattoes, on the other hand, they sought to foster by special training and rewards. But the prevalence of slavery which aided them in the one policy hampered them in the other, for it made the rewards arbitrary instead of automatic and it restricted the scope of the laborers' employments and of their ambitions as well. The device of hiring slaves to themselves, which had an invigorating effect here and there in the towns, could find little application in the country; and the paternalism of the planters would provide no fully effective substitute. Hence the achievements of the exceptional workmen were limited by the status of slavery as surely as the progress of the generality was restricted by the fact of their being negroes. . . .

Every plantation of the standard Southern type was, in fact, a school constantly training and controlling pupils who were in a backward state of civilization. Slave youths of special promise, or when special purposes were in view, might be bound as apprentices to craftsmen at a distance. Thus James H. Hammond in 1859 apprenticed a fourteen-year-old mulatto boy, named Henderson, for four years to Charles Axt, of Crawfordville, Georgia, that he might be taught vine culture. Axt agreed in the indenture to feed and clothe the boy, pay for any necessary medical attention, teach him his trade, and treat him with proper kindness. Before six months were ended Alexander H. Stephens, who was a neighbor of Axt and a friend of Hammond, wrote the latter that Henderson had run away and that Axt was unfit to have the care of slaves, especially when on hire, and advised Hammond to take the boy home. Soon afterward Stephens reported that Henderson had returned and had been whipped, though not cruelly, by Axt. The further history of this episode is not ascertainable. Enough of it is on record, however, to suggest reasons why for the generality of slaves home training was thought best.

This, rudimentary as it necessarily was, was in fact just what the bulk of the negroes most needed. They were in an alien land, in an essentially slow process of transition from barbarism to civilization. New industrial methods of a simple sort they might learn from precepts and occasional demonstrations; the habits and standards of civilized life they could only

87

acquire in the main through examples reinforced with discipline. These the plantation régime supplied. Each white family served very much the function of a modern social settlement, setting patterns of orderly, well bred conduct which the negroes were encouraged to emulate; and the planters furthermore were vested with a coercive power, salutary in the premises, of which settlement workers are deprived. The very aristocratic nature of the system permitted a vigor of discipline which democracy cannot possess. On the whole the plantations were the best schools yet invented for the mass training of that sort of inert and backward people which the bulk of the American negroes represented. The lack of any regular provision for the discharge of pupils upon the completion of their training was, of course, a cardinal shortcoming which the laws of slavery imposed; but even in view of this, the slave plantation régime, after having wrought the initial and irreparable misfortune of causing the negroes to be imported, did at least as much as any system possible in the period could have done toward adapting the bulk of them to life in a civilized community. . . .

ECONOMIC VIEWS OF SLAVERY: A SURVEY OF THE LITERATURE

In barbaric society slavery is a normal means of conquering the isolation of workers and assembling them in more productive coordination. Where population is scant and money little used it is almost a necessity in the conduct of large undertakings, and therefore more or less essential for the advancement of civilization. It is a means of domesticating savage or barbarous men, analogous in kind and in consequence to the domestication of the beasts of the field. It was even of advantage to some of the people enslaved, in that it saved them from extermination when defeated in war, and in that it gave them touch with more advanced communities than their own. But this was counterbalanced by the stimulus which the profits of slave catching gave to wars and raids with all their attendant injuries. Any benefit to the slave, indeed, was purely incidental. The reason for the institution's existence was the advantage which accrued to the masters. So positive and pronounced was this reckoned to be, that such highly enlightened people as the Greeks and Romans maintained it in the palmiest days of their supremacies.

Western Europe in primitive times was no exception. Slavery in a more or less fully typical form was widespread. When the migrations ended in the Middle Ages, however, the rise of feudalism gave the people a thorough territorial regimentation. The dearth of commerce whether in goods or in men led gradually to the conversion of the unfree laborers from slaves into serfs or villeins attached for generations to the lands on which they wrought. Finally, the people multiplied so greatly and the landless were so pressed for livelihood that at the beginning of modern times European society found the removal of bonds conducive to the common advantage. Serfs freed from their inherited obligations could now seek employment wherever they would, and landowners, now no longer lords, might employ whom they pleased. Bondmen gave place to hirelings and peasant proprietors, status gave place to contract, industrial society was enabled to make redistributions and readjustments at will, as it had never been before. In view of the prevailing traits and the density of the population a general return whether to slavery or serfdom was economically unthinkable. An intelligent Scotch philanthropist, Fletcher of Saltoun, it is true, proposed at the end of the seventeenth century that the indigent and their children be bound as slaves to selected masters as a means of relieving the terrible distresses of unemployment in his times; but his project appears to have received no public sanction whatever. The fact that he published such a plan is more a curious antiquarian item than one of significance in the history of slavery. Not even the thin edge of a wedge could possibly be inserted which might open a way to restore what everyone was on virtually all counts glad to be free of.

When the American mining and plantation colonies were established, however, some phases of the most ancient labor problems recurred. Natural resources invited industry in large units but wage labor was not to be had. The Spaniards found a temporary solution in impressing the tropical American aborigines, and the English in a recourse to indented white immigrants. But both resorted predominantly for plantation purposes to the importation of Africans, for whom the ancient institution of slavery was revived. Thus from purely economic considerations the sophisticated European colonists of the sixteenth and seventeenth centuries involved themselves and their descendants, with the connivance of their home governments, in the toils of a system which on the one hand had served their remote forbears with good effect, but which on the other hand civilized peoples had long and almost universally discarded as an incubus. In these colonial beginnings the negroes were to be had so cheaply and slavery seemed such a simple and advantageous device when applied to them, that no qualms as to the future were felt. At least no expressions of them appear in the records of thought extant for the first century and more of English colonial experience. And when apprehensions did arise they were concerned with the dangers of servile revolt, not with any deleterious effects to arise from the economic nature of slavery in time of peace . . . .

NO

Kenneth M. Stampp

THE PECULIAR INSTITUTION
Slavery in the Ante-Bellum South

THE SETTING

To understand the South is to feel the pathos in its history. This aura of pathos is more than a delusion of historians, more than the vague sensation one gets when looking down an avenue of somber, moss-draped live oaks leading to stately ruins or to nothing at all. For Southerners live in the shadow of a real tragedy; they know, better than most other Americans, that little ironies fill the history of mankind and that large disasters from time to time unexpectedly help to shape its course.

Their tragedy did not begin with the ordeal of Reconstruction, or with the agony of civil war, but with the growth of a "peculiar institution" (as they called it) in ante-bellum days. It began, in short, with chattel slavery whose spiritual stresses and unremitting social tensions became an inescapable part of life in the Old South.

What caused the growth of this institutional affliction which had so severe an impact upon the lives of so many Southerners? Some historians have traced the origin of southern slavery to a morbific quality in the southern climate. Though admitting great climatic variations within the South and the normal mildness of the winter season, they have emphasized the weather's fiercer moods—the torrential rains, the searing droughts, above all, the humid heat of subtropical summers. Since Southerners were unable to control the weather, they had to come to terms with it. So it was the climate that determined the nature of their institutions and the structure of their society. "Let us begin by discussing the weather," wrote one historian who saw here "the chief agency in making the South distinctive." To such climatic determinists the social significance of "ninety degrees in the shade" was too real to be ignored.

If climate alone could not explain everything, then perhaps certain additional factors, such as soil, topography, and watercourses, contributed to a broader geographical determinism. Combine the hot summers and long growing seasons with the rich southern soils—the alluvial river bottoms, the sandy loams of the coastal plains, the silt loams of the Black Belt, and the red clays of the piedmont—and an agricultural economy was the logical result. Add the many navigable rivers which facilitated the movement of bulky staples from considerable distances inland to coastal ports, and all the requirements for a commercial form of agriculture were at hand. Commercial agriculture induced a trend toward large landholdings which in turn created a demand for labor. Thus some have argued the Southerners, in permitting slavery to grow, had merely submitted to compelling natural forces.

Human institutions, however, have not been formed by forces as rigidly deterministic as this. To be sure, men must inevitably make certain adjustments to fixed environmental conditions. But, within limits, these adjustments may take a variety of forms. At different times and in different places roughly similar environmental conditions have produced vastly different human responses. Some human adaptations have been far more successful than others. For this reason one must examine the forms of southern institutions as closely as the facts of the southern environment.

It may be that unfree labor alone made possible the early rise of the plantation system, but this proves neither the necessity nor the inevitability of slavery. Actually, the southern plantation was older than slavery and survived its abolition. More important, there was nothing inevitable about the plantation. Without a continuing supply of bondsmen southern agriculture, in its early development at least, would probably have depended more upon small-farm units and given less emphasis to the production of staple crops. Under these circumstances the South might have developed more

slowly, but it would not have remained a wilderness. There was no crop cultivated by slaves that could not have been cultivated by other forms of labor, no area fit for human habitation that would have been passed by for want of a slave force. The slave-plantation system answered no "specific need" that could not have been answered in some other way.

Slavery, then, cannot be attributed to some deadly atmospheric miasma or some irresistible force in the South's economic evolution. The use of slaves in southern agriculture was a deliberate choice (among several alternatives) made by men who sought greater returns than they could obtain from their own labor alone, and who found other types of labor more expensive. "For what purpose does the master hold the servant?" asked an ante-bellum Southerner. "Is it not that by his labor he, the master, may accumulate wealth?" The rise of slavery in the South was inevitable only in the sense that every event in history seems inevitable after it has occurred.

Southerners who chose to develop and to preserve slavery could not more escape responsibility for their action than they could escape its consequences. But to judge them without compassion is to lack both the insight and the sensitivity needed to understand the nature of their tragedy. For the South began with good human material; its tragedy did not spring from the inherent depravity of its people. Southerners did not create the slave system all at once in 1619; rather, they built it little by little, step by step, choice by choice, over a period of many years; and all the while most of them were more or less blind to the ultimate consequences of the choices they were making. Somehow, at crucial times, their vision failed them; somehow it was their misfortune to have built a social structure wanting in flexibility. Ultimately Southerners became the victims of their own peculiar institution; they were unwilling to adjust it, or themselves, to the ideological and cultural realities of the nineteenth century.

Not that slavery failed as a practical labor system. In that narrow sense it was a success, and it was still flourishing as late as 1860. In terms of its broad social consequences for the South as a whole, however, slavery must be adjudged a failure. Few slaves ever really adapted successfully to their servitude, and few whites could defend the system without betraying the emotional stresses to which slavery subjected them. Eventually the omnipresent slave became the symbol of the South and the cornerstone of its culture. When that happened, disaster was close at hand—in fact, that in itself was a disaster.

An essential point about the South's peculiar institution was this: its slaves were Negroes (that is, they possessed one or more Negro ancestors). The presence of Negroes in the South was indeed significant, but the significance of their presence must be neither exaggerated nor misunderstood. The folklore regarding the Negro and his role in southern history must not be mistaken for fact.

According to tradition, Negroes had to be brought to the South for labor that Europeans themselves could not perform. "The white man will never raise—can never raise a cotton or a sugar crop in the United States. In our swamps and under our suns the negro thrives, but the white man dies." Without the productive power of the African whom an "all-wise Creator" had perfectly adapted to the labor needs of the South, its lands would have remained "a howling wilderness."

Such is the myth. The fact is that, ever since the founding of Jamestown, white men have performed much of the South's heavy agricultural labor. For a century and a half white farmers have tended their own cotton fields in every part of the Deep South. In the 1850's Frederick Law Olmsted saw many white women in Mississippi and Alabama "at work in the hottest sunshine . . . in the regular cultivation of cotton." In 1855, even a South Carolinian vigorously disputed "the opinion frequently put forth, that white labor is unsuited to the agriculture of this State." All that such laborers required was to be properly acclimatized. "The white man—born, raised and habituated to exposure and labor in the field in our climate—will be found equal to the task in any part of this State free from the influence of the excessive malaria of stagnant waters." Then this Carolinian observed an important fact: in the swamplands Negroes did not thrive any better than white men. But Negro slaves, unlike free whites, could be forced to toil in the rice swamps regardless of the effect upon their health. That was the difference. . . .

PROFIT AND LOSS

In searching for evidence to justify their cause, southern proslavery writers showed remarkable resourcefulness. In persuasive prose their polemical essays spun out religious, historical, scientific, and sociological arguments to demonstrate that slavery was a positive good for both Negroes and white—that it was the very cornerstone of southern civilization. But they rarely resorted to the most obvious and most practical argument of all: the argument that the peculiar institution was economically profitable to those who invested in it. Rather, most of the polemicists insisted that slaves were a financial burden and that the institution continued to exist for noneconomic reasons. They apparently thought that to admit that men could make money from slave labor would seriously damage their cause. "In an economical point of view," wrote James H. Hammond, "slavery presents some difficulties. As a general rule, I agree that . . . free labor is cheaper than slave labor. . . . We must, therefore, content ourselves with . . . the consoling reflection, that what is lost to us is gained to humanity."

Outside the South, doctrinaire liberals, with whom the major tenets of Adam Smith were articles of faith, supported the defenders of slavery on this point at least. The liberals, to be sure, criticized slavery because they believed in the moral goodness of a competitive society of free men, a society in which labor is rewarded with the fruits of its toil. But they also criticized slavery because they were convinced that free labor was, for a number of reasons, cheaper to employ. John E. Cairnes, the English economist, could reason from his liberal assumptions that slavery was unprofitable. Olmsted, though his position was somewhat ambiguous and his evidence conflicting, also reached the general conclusion that slave labor was more costly than free. Solon Robinson, a northern agricultural expert, reported after a tour of the South that planters were earning meager returns on their investments.

Numerous historical treatises on slavery accept the verdict of these contemporaries; they agree that, except on the fresh lands of the Southwest, slavery had nearly ceased to be profitable by the close of the ante-bellum period—that some masters made money "in spite of slavery rather than because of it." Indeed, a doubt has been raised about whether slaves were a

sound investment "year in and year out" even in Mississippi.

If the employment of slaves was unprofitable (or nearly so), it must somehow be explained why slaves brought high prices in the market and why masters continued to use them. To say that no other form of labor was available hardly answers the question, for slave labor could have been converted into free labor by emancipation. And would not an employer use no labor at all in preference to a kind that gave him no return on his investment? Perhaps it was the mere expectation of profit, though seldom or never realized, that kept him going from year to year. Perhaps the slaveholder did not keep careful and accurate business records and therefore did not realize that he was on an economic treadmill. Or perhaps slavery, having been profitable in the past, survived now only because of custom and habit— because of a kind of economic lethargy. These are possible explanations, or partial explanations, why an unprofitable labor system might survive for a considerable length of time.

Moreover, slavery in the ante-bellum South was not purely or exclusively an economic institution: it was also part of a social pattern made venerable by long tradition and much philosophizing. One cannot assume that a Southerner would have promptly liquidated his investment in land and slaves whenever he found some other form of investment that promised him larger returns. For many slaveholders were emotionally and ideologically committed to the agrarian way of life—to the Jeffersonian idea that those who lived on the land were more virtuous than those who engaged in commerce or industry. "To day Mr T L Pleasants came over to consult about breaking up and going into a mercantile business," wrote a small Virginia planter. "To me it seems to be a wild idea, hope he will give it up and be satisfied to Farm." An Alabamian refused to abandon farming to engage in mining operations, for "I believe Farming is the safest and most honorable *calling* after all."

No other profession gave a Southerner such dignity and importance as the cultivation of the soil with slave labor. The ownership of slaves, affirmed Cairnes, had become "a fashionable taste, a social passion"; it had become a symbol of success like "the possession of a horse among the Arabs: it brings the owner into connexion with the privileged class; it forms the presumption that he has attained a certain social position." Slaves, therefore, were "coveted with an eagerness far beyond what the intrinsic utility of their services would explain." Cairnes concluded that it would be futile to propose compensated emancipation, for this would be asking slaveholders to renounce their power and prestige "for a sum of money which, if well invested, might perhaps enable them and their descendants to vegetate in peaceful obscurity!"

Southern merchants often put at least part of their savings in slaves and plantations, as did lawyers, doctors, and clergymen, without always considering whether this was the most profitable investment. In 1834, Henry Watson, Jr., of East Windsor, Connecticut, moved to Greensboro, Alabama, and after the Panic of 1837 made a modest fortune as a lawyer. Then, like numerous other Yankees in the South, Watson sought admission to the gentry through the purchase of land and Negroes. Since he bought wisely at depression prices, his investment proved to be rewarding economically as well as socially; but it would be hard to say which reward he found more gratifying.

The desire for profits was no more the exclusive factor in the use and management of slaves than it was in their accumulation. Because masters enjoyed status from the ownership of a large force, they sometimes supported more field-hands and domestics than they could employ with maximum efficiency. Nor did planters think only in economic terms when they debated leaving their exhausted lands in the East for fresh lands in the West. One North Carolinian refused to move because of his "local attachments"; another decided not to settle in Louisiana because the country was "sickly" and lacked "good society." "This is a miserably poor place," wrote James H. Hammond of his South Carolina plantation. Yet, "I have hung on here . . . partly because I did not wish to remove from my native state and carry a family into the savage semi-barbarous west." Far from being strictly economic men, southern masters permitted numerous other considerations to help shape their decisions about the acquisition and utilization of slave labor.

The proslavery writer's favorite explanation for the survival of an allegedly unprofitable labor system was that Negroes were unfit for freedom. Slavery existed because of the "race problem"—because the presence of a horde of free Negroes would pose an immense social danger and threaten southern civilization. Slavery was, above all, a method of regulating race relations, an instrument of social control. The master kept possession of his slaves from a sense of duty to society and to his "people." To destroy the system, according to the proslavery argument, would be a tragedy for both races.

But surely there are limits beyond which it is unreasonable to credit noneconomic factors for the survival of slavery. One can concede that the desire for status stimulated the acquisition of slave property, that fear of the free Negro created a demand for a system of social control, and that some masters had a paternalistic quality in their make-up. Forces even as strong as these, however, could not long prevent an archaic labor system from collapsing of its own weight. There is no evidence that a substantial number of masters held their human property *chiefly* to gain status, or to help the South solve its "race problem," or from a patriarchal sense of duty to the Negroes. Had the possession of slaves been a severe economic burden, it is certain that the great mass of slaveholders would have thrown them on the market— or, if necessary, abandoned them. Even Cairnes conceded that the survival of bondage warranted the inference that the institution was at least self-supporting.

As long as slavery showed no sign of decline or decay, the system was probably accomplishing a good deal more than merely supporting itself. If slavery appeared to be flourishing, it must have been justifying itself economically and not simply surviving on the strength of a sentimental tradition. And during the 1850's slavery did in fact give much evidence of continued vigorous growth. Slave prices were higher than ever before, and everywhere in the South the demand for Negro labor exceeded the supply. The railroads were just beginning to open new cotton lands which had not previously been exploited for lack of transportation. Even Virginians were complaining about a labor shortage, and slavery was, if anything, more securely entrenched in the Old Dominion than it had been a generation earlier. Hence, the claim that slavery had "about reached its zenith by 1860" and was on the verge of collapse is far from convincing. It appears that the noneconomic factors involved in the survival of slavery

have been overemphasized; for the realities of 1860 create a presumption that the institution was still functioning profitably.

If one is to investigate the profitability or unprofitability of slavery, it is essential to define the problem precisely. Profitable for whom? Bondage was obviously not very profitable for the bondsmen whose standard of living was kept at the subsistence level; but bondage was not designed to enrich its victims. Nor was it introduced or preserved to promote the general welfare of the majority of white Southerners, who were nonslaveholders. The question is not whether the great mass of southern people of both races profited materially from slavery.

Moreover, the question is not whether a Southerner would have gained by selling his slaves, leaving his section, settling somewhere in the North, and investing in commerce or industry. He might have, but this involves the question of whether agriculture, in the long run, ever yields profits equal to those gained from manufacturing and trade. With or without slavery, planters and farmers were the victims of uncontrolled and wildly fluctuating prices, of insect pests, and of the weather. The year 1846, mourned one Mississippi planter, "will ever be memorable in the history of cotton planting from the ravages of the army worm which has no doubt curtailed the crop . . . at least Six Hundred Thousand Bales, worth Twenty Millions of Dollars." A rice planter surveyed the ruin following a "violent gale accompanied by immense rain. . . . The little that remained of the Crop after the two last gales, may now be abandoned. Not even the fragments of the wreck are left. Such is planting." Time after time the growers of southern staples saw their crops wither in severe droughts during the growing season—or rot in heavy rains at harvest time. Everything, concluded a discouraged planter, "seems to be against Cotton, not only the Abolitionists: but frost, snow, worms, and water." These were the hazards of husbandry in an age without crop insurance, price supports, or acreage restrictions. But they have no bearing upon the question of whether those who chose to risk them found it profitable to employ slave labor.

Here, then, is the problem: allowing for the risks of a laissez-faire economy, did the average ante-bellum slaveholder, over the years, earn a reasonably satisfactory return from his investment? One must necessarily be a little vague about what constitutes a satisfactory return—whether it is five percent, or eight, or more—because any figure is the arbitrary choice of the person who picks it. The slaveholders themselves drew no clear and consistent line between satisfactory and unsatisfactory returns. In an absolute sense, of course, anything earned above operating expenses and depreciation is a profit. The question is whether it was substantial enough to be satisfactory.

It may be conceded at the outset that possession of a supply of cheap slave labor carried with it no automatic guarantee of economic solvency, much less affluence. An incompetent manager moved with steady pace toward insolvency and the inevitable execution sale. Even an efficient manager found that his margin of profit depended upon the fertility of his land, proximity to cheap transportation, and the ability to benefit from the economics of large-scale production. Moreover, nearly every slaveholder saw his profits shrink painfully during periods of agricultural depression such as the one following the Panic of 1837; and many who had borrowed capital to speculate in lands and slaves were ruined. In short, there were enormous variations in the returns upon investments in slave labor from master to master and from year to year. For the "average slaveholder" is, of course, an economic abstraction, albeit a useful one. . . .

POSTSCRIPT

WAS SLAVERY AN ECONOMIC NECESSITY IN THE AMERICAN SOUTH?

In 1776 and 1787 there were opportunities for changing the status of Black Americans but in both instances the Declaration of Independence and United States Constitution, which provide fundamental freedoms to most Americans, ignored them. The prohibition of the foreign slave trade, Article One, Section Nine of the Constitution, did not eliminate slave markets within the United States. The freedom enjoyed by some Black Americans after independence was granted by states which abolished slavery. Even the Thirteenth Amendment, which legalized the effects of the Civil War and the Emancipation Proclamation, left the nation with schizophrenic policies. The eradication of the long-term effects of the peculiar institution required Supreme Court decisions in the 1950s and civil rights legislation in the 1960s.

A broad perspective on slavery appears in David Brion Davis's, *The Problem of Slavery in Western Culture* (Cornell University Press, 1966). John Hope Franklin surveys the history of Black Americans in *From Slavery to Freedom* (Third Edition, Knopf, 1967). The history of the slave trade appears in Basil Davidson's, *Black Mother: The Years of the African Slave Trade* (Little, Brown, 1961). Winthrop Jordan discusses racial attitudes in *White Over Black: American Attitudes Toward the Negro, 1550-1812* (University of North Carolina Press, 1968).

As with most of the issues in this volume, the question of slavery is not only historical in its importance but it also raises issues of continuing interest.

ISSUE 6

HAVE PURITAN VALUES HAD LASTING EFFECTS ON AMERICAN SOCIETY?

YES: Alan Simpson, from *Puritanism in Old and New England* (University of Chicago Press, 1955)

NO: Thomas J. Wertenbaker, from *The Puritan Oligarchy: The Founding of American Civilization* (Charles Scribner's Sons, 1947)

ISSUE SUMMARY

YES: Professor Alan Simpson, while noting both the negative and positive effects of Puritanism, believes it had a continuing influence on American society.

NO: Professor Thomas Wertenbaker acknowledges the importance of Puritanism in the history of seventeenth-century New England but denies its impact on subsequent American development.

Myths about Puritanism abound and they inhibit our understanding of this significant aspect of modern history. Historians find it easier to describe the origins of the Puritan movement in Tudor England, than to analyze its characteristics or to evaluate its effects on American society. Also, there is a semantic problem. Does Puritan refer only to the Pilgrims who settled in Massachusetts Bay Colony? Or, can it include all the early English Protestants? The pejorative connotations of Puritan and Puritanism create other difficulties. As Professor Simpson has noted about the historical development of Puritan as a word: "It began as a sneer, was taken up in self-defense, and has established itself as a convenient label." Thomas B. Macauley's jibe, that "the Puritan hated bear-baiting, not because it gave pain to the bear, but because it gave pleasure to the spectators," reflects not only nineteenth-century attitudes but also our own. Ridiculing Puritans is a major subject in American humor if the cartoons in popular magazines may be taken as evidence.

In addition to making Puritans the butt of jokes, social myths about them limit our understanding. Puritans and New England are synonymous in American folklore. Thanksgiving, turkeys and Pilgrims comprise the first history American schoolchildren learn. These superficialities of Puritan culture precondition us, making it difficult to probe beyond them to the essentials of Puritan values. Negativism lies in wait, along with ridicule and superficialities, as another roadblock to understanding. The witches of Salem along with the sinner incarcerated in the stocks complete with a sign admonishing "Ye shall not . . ." falsely symbolize New England Puritanism as much as turkeys and pumpkins.

The Puritan story, even if kept to the essentials, is beset with serious contradictions. First of all, the impact of Puritanism went far beyond religion. As James Russell Lowell observed, "Puritanism, believing itself quick with the seed of religious liberty laid, without knowing it, the egg of democracy." In other words, the study of Puritan values demands an evaluation of the implicit as well as the explicit. It requires separating the causes, effects and the historical development in between. To do so often results in paradox and irony. For example, the Puritans demanded religious liberty in England but would not allow it to others in Massachusetts. This policy led to the development of other New England settlements such as Rhode Island and parts of New Hampshire. The demand for a well-educated clergy necessitated the founding of the colonial colleges not only in New England but also in the Middle Atlantic colonies and Virginia. A final example which illustrates the complexity inherent in Puritanism is the splintering of English Protestantism. Well within the first century of its development, from about 1550 until 1650, Protestantism grew in numbers but remained limited in its ability to change the basics of religion beyond the moderate concessions of the Elizabethan settlement. The divisiveness within the movement resulted in the appearance of the Congregationalists, Presbyterians, Baptists and Quakers, to mention only the most important groups. This fragmentation diluted any political effectiveness Puritanism may have had. These groups shared enough basic characteristics to be labeled Puritans but they also disagreed on enough specific points to deny Puritanism any real political clout in England even during the seventeenth century.

Neither Professor Simpson nor Professor Wertenbaker takes an extreme point of view in their conclusions about Puritanism. Simpson clearly sees the effects of Puritanism in American society, especially in the nineteenth century, as generally beneficial. He also notes shortcomings and failures. Simpson concludes, "The Puritan Code had its repellent features, but it is no bad thing to have habits of honesty, sobriety, responsibility, and hard work impressed on a community." Both Simpson and Wertenbaker agree on the intellectual contributions made by Puritan thinkers in New England, but that is about as far as Wertenbaker will go. Otherwise, he concludes, "No truthful historian will withhold from New England the credit due her for her part in the creation and moulding of the nation." He quickly adds, after listing these contributions, "But most of the contributions were made after the fall of the Puritan oligarchy, and the men to whom the chief credit is due were not its supporters, but, on the contrary, those who rebelled against it."

YES

Alan Simpson

PURITANISM IN
OLD AND NEW ENGLAND

THE PURITAN TRADITION

How does one assess the influence of some profound experience on the subsequent history of a people? The effort of [Puritan] saints to seize and dominate the life of English-speaking people in the seventeenth century was obviously such an experience, and everyone who inspects the national consciousness of Englishmen and Americans today finds Puritanism a part of its makeup, whether the inspection is made by ourselves or by strangers who look at us with the incredulity— sometimes kindly, sometimes irritated—of visitors from another world. But what is this Puritanism which has a continuing history? Obviously, it is not the Puritanism which I have been discussing [elsewhere]. That is a historical movement with a beginning and an end. It does not repeat itself. Nor is the Puritanism with a continuing history the sum total of the connections which can be traced to Puritanism. Unitarianism can be traced to Puritanism and Transcendentalism to Unitarianism, but is Emerson to be regarded as part of the Puritan tradition? I should say "Yes" only if it could be shown that Emerson was attempting to solve his problems as he believed that Puritans tried to solve theirs or if his solutions bore some direct resemblance to Puritan solutions. Let me foreshorten this type of question and make it more extreme. There were Puritans in the seventeenth century who telescoped into their own lives a history which might take fifty years to work itself out in a dissenting congregation; that is to say, they began as dogmatic Puritans with an intense conviction of their election and ended as lukewarm deists with a few Puritan inhibitions. Is such a man to be considered a Puritan after he has worked his passage from the ages of faith into the ages of reason? I should say not, if the term is to have any meaning at all. Similarly, I should say that the continuing history of Puritanism, if it is to have any useful meaning, must be the continuing history of attempts to solve problems in a Puritan spirit. . . .

If one is looking for the broadest definition of the original Puritanism, it obviously falls into the category of religious revivals. This has been a recurring rhythm in the history of Christian culture, and a more general view than I am taking in these essays would relate Puritanism to earlier revivals. However, if one is to ignore this previous history, and to start with Puritanism, one finds that it has certain drive and that it goes through the typical history of self-discovery, enthusiasm, organization, and decay. It derives its drive from its view of the human predicament. When the Puritan surveys the world within the terms laid down by Christian tradition, he is struck by the profundity of human sin, by the necessity for a work of grace in his own soul to redeem him from the lot of fallen humanity, and by the demand for a disciplined warfare against sin which God makes on those he has saved. His pilgrimage is therefore a search for regeneration, which is usually achieved through an experience of conversion, and for the development of the type of character which is appropriate to the regenerate—a character marked by an intense sense of personal responsibility to God and his moral law, which expresses itself in a strenuous life of self-examination and self-denial. So much for the drive. As for the typical history, it takes rather more than a century to work itself out. The origins of English Puritanism are to be found among the Protestant Reformers of the mid-sixteenth century; it takes shape in the reign of Elizabeth; produces thrust after thrust of energy in the seventeenth century, until the final thrust throws up the Quakers; and then ebbs away. . . .

One contrast lies in the relationship between the Puritan and the intellect of his age. Though I have said in a previous chapter that I think the picture of the Puritan as an intellectual has been overdrawn, to the extent that Puritanism was always more an affair of the heart than of the head, the fact remains that the earlier Puritan did not have to maintain his faith in spite of or against the evidences of philosophy or science. Many Puritans, in my definition, which includes the anti-intellectuals as well as the intellectuals, were neither interested in these evidences nor capable of judging them, but those who were could feel that the truths of Scripture were in harmony with all learning and experience. There was much in the philosophic tradition to support the Puritan. There is little in historical science to shake his faith in Scripture or his conception of human history as the field in which God gathers his elect. There was nothing in the older physical science to cause him great concern: no mechanistic theory of the universe, no displacement of this planet from its central place, no doctrine of evolution. His use of the prophetic books of the Bible to interpret human history, his doctrine of special providences in which God was constantly setting aside the ordinary operations of nature to achieve his purposes, seemed eminently reasonable to him. The result was that among the Puritan scholastics—the last representatives of the medieval ambition to synthesize all experience—it was possible to achieve a fusion of intellect and emotion that was less and less possible for their descendants. Increasingly, it becomes necessary to bury difficult questions in a wise silence or to compromise with them in a way which robs the Puritan impulse of some of its otherworldliness or to shunt them aside. On the whole, evangelism has chosen either to bury or to shunt. Although it has been able to impart its ethical impulse to almost all classes of society, so that even the high aristocrat in Victorian England cultivates a sense of duty and the agnostic himself is a very earnest moralist, it has been less and less able to sound intellectually respectable. And in its extremer forms it becomes a religion of feeling without any intellectual structure at all.

The second contrast lies in the relationship between the Puritan and the religious organization of his society. When the first revival began, his society had a dogmatic religious commitment, and no such thing as toleration existed, apart from the concessions which politicians have always made to expediency. Working within this tradition, the first impulse of the Puritan was to turn his community into a rigorous theocracy. Government of the people, by and for the saints, might be described as his idea of good government. However, partly as a result of divisions among the saints, and of the genuine theory of religious liberty which some saints developed, and partly as the result of developments for which the saints can claim no credit, what emerged from that enterprise was not a theocracy but a regime of toleration. The second revival begins under that regime. In America it is turned into a regime of religious liberty, with the state separated from the church. The diversity of religions left no alternative so far as the federal government was concerned, and the rationalists combined with the evangelicals to get the state churches disestablished. In Britain, religious toleration is turned into a system where no religion is discriminated against, but an established church remains. All this means that the second revival is working within either a liberal or a democratic community. But its theocratic impulse dies hard. The converted soul is likely to cling to its conviction that it has a superior insight into God's design for the social order—a conviction which irritates the un-

converted and which is not based on any experience. The belief of Roger Williams that the state should be left to the natural reason which God has bestowed on all his creatures, with the Christian only playing his part as one witness, would seem to be more appropriate. However, if political leaders, like Lincoln, are sometimes afflicted by preachers who insist that God demands the immediate abolition of slavery, these reformers are no longer in a position to use any force but argument.

So much for the obvious contrasts. As for the comparisons, there is the conversion experience, which I have chosen as the central feature of the original Puritanism. There is the fission process, the endless splintering, the Babel of heresies, or the flowering of the sects, whichever you prefer to call it—a process which demonstrates once again how fundamental the individualism of the Protestant Reformation has proved to be compared with its superficial collectivism. There is, furthermore, the same bewildering variety of consequences which the search for regeneration can have; the same variety as it had during the Puritan Revolution. Some activities no doubt tend to be shared: an educational mission, a philanthropic mission, a mission to preserve Sabbatarianism or to promote the adoption of Puritan morals, an evangelical impulse which prompts the converted to adopt causes of one description or another. But in this last category it is noticeable that the southern churches feel little disposition to adopt the antislavery cause and that the conversion experience is compatible with every kind of social outlook. John Wesley is a Tory, but the movement he starts will produce liberals, chartists, and socialists. English nonconformity, smarting under the legal privileges and social snobberies of parsons and squires, is either middle or lower class; but English evangelicalism will make as many converts within the privileged classes as outside. Jacksonian democrats like Orestes Brownson are in the tradition of seventeenth-century Levellers, and they are resisted by Puritans in the tradition of the seventeenth-century Brahmins. Evangelicalism can mean an individualistic capitalism or produce experiments in communism. It can sustain the privileged or rally the underprivileged. The insights of the converted, as they survey the social scene, are simply not to be marshaled under any single formula.

The final similarity is, of course, in the character. I have said enough in this book about the heroic virtues. The defects have often been made the subject of jibes, and I shall try to restrain myself.

The Puritan has a very limited sense of humor, as one can see from a glance at his portrait. I am thinking not of Grant Wood's "American Gothic" but of seventeenth-century portraits. The corners of the mouths in the divines, at least, are almost invariably pulled down. Emerson has a good phrase for his ancestors. He calls them "the great grim earnest men who solemnized the heyday of their strength by planting New England." I will only add that life seldom struck them as funny. I know that the historian of New England can produce one humorist in Nathaniel Ward; but I have not been so fortunate with the English Puritans. The nearest I came to it was in a Puritan diary, where the author admits he cannot repress his desire to tell a good story, but he tries to keep the account straight by capping every joke with what he calls "a savoury morsel" of divinity. Cromwell's characteristic humor is a sort of horseplay; this is the Cromwell who throws cushions at his officers, who is said to have spattered an officer's face with ink

while they were signing the king's death warrant, or who gets a good laugh watching a soldier tip a pail of milk over another soldier's head. Perhaps it is a relief from tension with a touch of hysteria about it; or perhaps it is just the bucolic antics of a plain russet-coated captain. Later in the history of Puritanism a certain humor develops, but it is naturally rather wry—or it has to be indulged when the great Taskmaster is not looking. Of course I do not want to imply that the Puritan, while he is being a Puritan, cannot make a good remark. I have always liked the reply of the revivalist preacher who had not much grammar and was one day ridiculed for it. "That's all right, brother; what little I have I use for the Lord. What do you do with yours?" But you see he is keeping his eye on the main business. . . .

CONCLUSION

In conclusion, let us return to the Puritan's impact on politics. Among his virtues I would list:

1. *His contribution to our system of limited government.*—The original Puritans had a genuine basis for their distrust of arbitrary power in addition to their experience of arbitrary government. They thought that man was too sinful to be trusted with too much power. They were likely to make an exception of the saint, but, once saints were prevented from ruling, they have kept their conviction that nobody else should be trusted. The Puritan tradition, with its everlasting insistence that only God is worthy of worship, is one insurance among Anglo-Saxon people that the state has no claim to worship. Fortunately, there are many other securities, but no one will undervalue the stubbornness of this one. They have defended, in season and out of season, the right to preach, to criticize,

and to judge. A shrewd observer of the English scene after the Puritan Revolution was struck by the difference it had made to the power of authority to procure respect for its pronouncements: "He [the author] thinketh that the Liberty of the late times gave men so much Light, and diffused it so universally amongst the people, that they are not now to be dealt with, as they might have been in Ages of less enquiry; and therefore tho in some well chosen and dearly beloved Auditories, good resolute Nonsense back'd with Authority may prevail, yet generally Men are become so good Judges of what they hear, that the Clergy ought to be very wary how they go about to impose upon their Understandings, which are grown less humble than they were in former times, when the Men in black had made Learning such a sin in the Laity, that for fear of offending, they made a Conscience of being able to read; but now the World is grown sawcy, and expecteth Reasons, and good ones too, before they give up their own Opinions to other Mens Dictates, tho never so Magisterially deliver'd to them."

2. *His contribution to self-government— to the development of initiative and self-reliance in the body of the community.*—The Puritan pilgrimage has been a perpetual pilgrimage in self-help. The significance of the dissenting chapel as a training ground for working-class leadership in English history has often been emphasized, and much the same services have been performed by the free church tradition in America. Nor should we forget, in the nineteenth century as in the seventeenth, the direct transfer from church affairs to political affairs of certain techniques of action. The political meeting of the nineteenth century owes an obvious, if not wholly healthy, debt to the camp meeting of the revivalist preacher.

3. *His contribution to education.*—The most anti-intellectual Puritan has been obliged to master at least one book—and that a great one. The most intellectual Puritans, in their desire to promote saving knowledge, have thrown up academy after academy, college after college, until their influence has been writ large over the history of education in England and America.

4. *His contribution to morality.*—The Puritan code has its repellent features, but it is no bad thing to have habits of honesty, sobriety, responsibility, and hard work impressed on a community. It seems probable that the acquisitive energy of the nineteenth century would have created far more havoc than it did without the restraining influence of this evangelical spirit.

Finally, there is the contribution which Puritanism, within the religious tradition of Anglo-Saxon peoples, has made to "the class peace." Almost the worst thing that can happen to the politics of a modern society is to have them polarized around social classes. Any force which works across these divisions, and either conceals or cements them, has a permanent claim on our gratitude.

As the limitations of Puritanism have been sufficiently stressed in these essays, I shall quote only one passage which seems to sum them up. I might have chosen for censure the *cri de coeur* of the nonconformist conscience in nineteenth-century English politics as it appears in the protest of the famous preacher Hugh Price Hughes: "What is morally wrong can never be politically right." Instead, I shall take a passage from an American sermon called "Puritan Principles and the Modern World," which was delivered in 1897:

"Puritanism stands for reality; for character; for clean living as a condition of public service; for recognition of responsibility to God; for the supremacy of the spirit. When

Oliver Cromwell entered Parliament in 1653, and said, pointing to one member, 'There sits a taker of bribes'; to another, 'There sits a man whose religion is a farce'; to another, using the hardest name possible, which I soften, 'These sits a man whose personal conduct is impure and foul'; and then in the name of Almighty God broke up the Parliament, he was the impersonation of Puritanism; and for one, I wish he would rise from his grave and in the same spirit enter some of our halls of legislation, both state and national."

That passage, with its conviction that righteousness ought to prevail, with its tendency to make the Puritan's own moral character a test of political fitness, and with its pressure to turn politics, which ought to be the art of reconciliation, into a moral crusade, reminds us of the darkest blot on his political record.

NO

Thomas Jefferson Wertenbaker

THE PURITAN OLIGARCHY
THE FOUNDING OF AMERICAN CIVILIZATION

. . . Puritanism found its truest expression, not in England, but in New England. The Bible Commonwealth envisaged by Ames, Baynes, Bradshaw and others was never established in the mother country. It was not so much the opposition of the King and the bishops which thwarted the Puritan leaders as the fact that a large part of the people, perhaps a decided majority, were not in sympathy with the reform movement. Even in their hour of triumph, when the monarchy had been overthrown by Cromwell's Ironsides, the Puritan leaders found themselves powerless to set up the government by the elect of which they had so long dreamed. The very suggestion, when made in the famous Barebones Parliament, led to the dissolution of that body and the proclaiming of the Protectorate. As for Oliver Cromwell, stern Independent though he was, his ideals were far from squaring with those of a Cotton or a Norton.

So it is to New England we must turn if we are to study the true Puritan State with all its distinctive features—congregations whose autonomy was derived from a covenant with God, a civil government in which only Church members participated, an educational system designed to buttress the orthodox religion, a rigid code of morals, the suppression of heresy. In fact, New England may be considered a laboratory of Puritan civilization.

The founders of the Massachusetts Bible State confidently expected it to endure forever. To them it was no social and religious experiment, but the carrying out of God's commands. Yet they had been in America but five or six years and were still struggling to clear the forests, lay out their meager crops and build their houses, when alarming weaknesses appeared. A few decades later the ministers were bewailing the general decline of godliness, were searching their souls for the cause of the general "decay," were warning the people that God had a controversy with them. Before the end of the seventeenth century it was apparent to all who had eyes to see that the Puritan experiment had failed.

The reforming synod of 1679, despite their earnest debates, their fasting and their prayers, threw little light upon the causes of decline. There had been heresy in the colony, they pointed out, swearing and drinking to excess had become common, the Sabbath day had been broken, love of wealth was supplanting the love of God, parents had been lax with their children, Christian education was being neglected. But they failed to see that these things were symptoms rather than causes. Had they looked deeper they would have found behind them all human nature itself—man's natural desire to acquire the good things of this world, and his instinctive dislike of restraint, whether of his personal conduct or his freedom of thought or his conscience, or his right to have a voice in the conduct of the state.

There is no reason to doubt the sincere belief of Winthrop and Cotton and Shepard that their Bible State was shaped according to God's directions and that in consequence it was as near perfect as man could make it, a civil and religious Utopia. To those who complained that this structure was undemocratic they replied that it was intended to be so. But they would have been indignant had one stigmatized it as a tyranny. Yet in some respects a tyranny it was, a tyranny over men's minds, a restriction upon one's right to think, imposed by sermons, laws against heresy and the control of education and the press. In early Massachusetts one disagreed with the minister at one's peril.

The ministers and magistrates would have been even more indignant at the accusation that the structure of Church and State was designed with the end of bestowing upon them special privilege and power. Certainly such a charge would have been unjust. Nonetheless special privilege and power it did give them. And though the ministers spoke of themselves as "God's poor servants," they valued their influence to the full and battled fiercely to retain it. In reading the election sermons one cannot escape the impression that a Norton or an Oakes or a Torrey took deep satisfaction in the privilege of scolding Magistrates and Deputies, of instructing them as to their duties and telling them what to do and what not to do. And in his own community the minister, even though perhaps a loving shepherd to his flock, demanded obedience as well as affection.

But the power of the few over the many, whether exercised by an aristocracy or a plutocracy or a theocracy, always is vulnerable to attack. If it is based on wealth, wealth may be confiscated; if it is based on military strength, arms may overcome arms; if it is based on ascendency over men's minds, reason may overthrow it. When the Puritans left England they fled from the things which seemed to them to threaten their souls, from a hostile King, from the bishops, from Church ceremonials, from lax morals, from disobedience to God's "ordinances"; but they could not flee from human nature, they could not flee from themselves. Upon landing on the shores of Massachusetts Bay they might fall on their knees to ask God to bless their great venture, but it was they themselves who brought the germs of failure.

As we have seen, economic conditions in New England—the expansion of foreign trade, the growth of fisheries, the shift from the agricultural village to the farm—tended to undermine the Puritan State. Yet it is doubtful whether any other place on the American continent would have been more favorable. Had the Puritans planted themselves on the banks of the Potomac they would almost certainly have established the plantation economy so unfavorable to religion, and have sacrificed the autonomy they valued so highly for a binding trade with England. Had they landed on the Delaware they would have found conditions there, too, far from ideal. It was on the Delaware that Penn tried his Holy Experiment, and, it will be remembered, the Holy Experiment failed. As for New Jersey, a Puritan community based upon the ideals of Ames, Cotton and Davenport was actually established there in 1666, but before five decades had passed it lay in ruins.

Even had Winthrop and the other leaders of the Great Exodus led their followers into the very heart of the American continent to establish their Zion on the banks of the Ohio or the Mississippi, the results would not have been greatly different. Though there they might have found the complete isolation they so highly valued, though no heresies from without might have filtered in, though they might have enjoyed complete political and economic independence, though the supernatural might not have grown dim before the glaring light of rationalism, the experiment would certainly have failed. It probably would have endured longer than in New England, but its ultimate fate would have been just as certain.

The temple of American Puritanism fell because it was built, had to be built, on the sands of human nature. When the pillars of the structure—political autonomy, the close alliance of Church and State, the control of education, orthodoxy, the stern code of morals, isolation—one after another began to sag, it was not so much the pillars themselves as the sand which caused the trouble. It was from beneath that came the succession of shocks which threatened the whole structure—the Roger Williams heresy, the Anne Hutchinson heresy, the Child petition, the Halfway Covenant, the demand for a wider franchise, the liberalizing of Harvard, the defeat of the clergy and magistrates in the witchcraft prosecution, the growing laxness in morals.

In bringing to the New World a society which was largely the product of sixteenth-century thought and defending it there against change in a changing world, the Puritans attempted the impossible. As the decades of the seventeenth century passed, men's minds expanded to keep pace with new scientific discoveries, with new ideals of human rights, with new conceptions of man's relation to God. The leaders of the old order in Massachusetts might as well have attempted to interfere with the movement of the moon around the earth as to block these changes. While they were vainly trying to crystallize the Puritan spirit of the time of Winthrop and Cotton, the tide of a new civilization swept over and past them.

But failure did not bring immediate destruction. Certain features of the Puritan State survived not only the loss of the charter, the Glorious Revolution, the advance of rationalism, the weakening of the moral code, but even the American Revolution and the creation of a Federal Union. When the nineteenth century dawned New England society was still undemocratic; the clergy and the moneyed classes were still entrenched behind a barrier of statutes, patronage, election devices and traditions. In Massachusetts no atheist, no Jew, no man of meager income could be Governor; in Connecticut no Roman Catholic could be Governor. To be eligible for the Upper House in Massachusetts one must have a freehold of £300 or personal property valued at £600; in New Hampshire, a freehold of £200. "We have lived in a State which exhibits to the world a democratic exterior," one New Englander remarked, "but which actually practices all the arts of an organized aristocracy under the management of the old firm of Moses and Aaron."

It was this remnant of the Puritan Oligarchy which Thomas Jefferson and his New England henchmen of the Democratic-Republican Party attacked so fiercely in the early decades of the nineteenth century. In Connecticut Abraham Bishop denounced the old charter of Charles II, upon which the government based its authority. "Let us sweep it away for a Constitution based on the will of the people," he said. The reformers denounced the clergy as a pack of privileged reactionaries who strutted around with queues and cocked hats and prated about government by the wisest and best. The conservatives fought back with every available weapon. From one pulpit after another Jefferson was denounced as an atheist, a liar, an enemy of the Churches, a Jacobin. "Let us not destroy the fabric erected by our fathers," the clergy pleaded. "The issue is clearly between religion and infidelity, morality and sin, sound government and anarchy." But they pleaded in vain. Election after election went against them, and new and more liberal Constitutions replaced the old governments. The day after the final defeat of the Connecticut conservatives, Lyman Beecher found his father seated with his head drooping on his breast. "Father, what are you thinking of?" he asked. "I am thinking of the Church of God," was the answer.

Despite the failure of the Puritan experiment it is a widely accepted belief that it was largely instrumental in moulding the character not only of modern New England, but of the entire United States. Plymouth is spoken of as the birthplace of the nation; the Puritans, it is claimed, came to America as the champions of re-ligious freedom, they founded American democracy, they gave us the public school system, they lit the torch of learning to shine in every corner of the country, they contributed an element of stern morality.

Obviously this rests more upon fiction than reality. Plymouth was not the birthplace of the nation, for the nation was founded neither upon the ideals and institutions of the Pilgrims nor of the Puritans who followed them to New England. In fact, the use of the word "birthplace" as a metaphor to explain the origin of the country is quite misleading. When the English colonized America they established not just one beachhead on the coast, but a half dozen or more. And it was from each of these beachheads that European civilization swept westward or northwestward or southwestward too create what later became the United States. The founders of St. Mary's, Charleston, and Philadelphia were as truly founders of this nation as those of Jamestown and Plymouth.

The belief that the Puritans came to the New World in the cause of religious freedom is, of course, completely erroneous. The battle for toleration in this country was won in the face of their bitter opposition. It would have seemed to Mary Dyer, William Robinson, Marmaduke Stevenson and William Leddra, as they went to their fate on the gallows, ironical indeed that three centuries later their executioners should win applause as champions of religious freedom.

Nor did American democracy have its origin in New England. American democracy was born in England, it was defended and enlarged in Westminster Hall and upon many an English battlefield, it was brought to America by the settlers and there given a new expression, a new growth under the influence of frontier conditions. There were noble men in New England, as in other colonies, who fought the good fight for democracy, but they were rebels against the old Puritan order, not its defenders. An oligarchy of Church members has no more place in the American system than Locke's feudal system, or a slave-holding aristocracy, or a plutocracy based on big business, or a proletarian dictatorship.

As for the Puritan code of morals and the Puritan Sabbath observance, despite the many lapses in colonial New England itself they have left an imprint on life in many parts of the United States which has not yet been entirely erased. Blue-laws are often ignored, but they remain on the statute books. Yet it is in the South that blue-laws have the greatest vitality, and the Southern inheritance is Presbyterian, Baptist and Methodist, not Congregationalist.

A better case can be made for the influence of the Massachusetts school system, which was the most efficient in the colonies, the first to receive support from public funds, the first to be capped by a college. Yet the chief indebtedness of the United States is not to the founders of the Puritan educational system but to the men who so reconstructed it as to make it fit the needs of a democratic society. It was only under the pressure of Jeffersonian ideals that New England, two centuries after its founding, accepted the vital principle that public education should not be affiliated with any religious sect and should make civic duty rather than religion its chief objective.

But it is to the everlasting credit of the founders of New England that they lit and kept alive in infant America the fires of scholarship. The great importance they attached to learning, the readiness with which they accepted the findings of noted scientists, their own scientific strivings bore rich fruit for New England and the United States. The fact that eleven New Englanders were invited to join the Royal Society of London during the colonial period testifies to the intellectual activity of the region.

No truthful historian will withhold from New England the credit due her for her part in the creation and moulding of the nation. Her sons were among the most active in winning independence, they did their full share in shaping the Constitution, they were pioneers in opening western New York, northern Pennsylvania and the Great Lakes region, they gave the country its first American literature, they made noble contributions in the fields of invention, science, art, architecture. But most of the contributions were made after the fall of the Puritan oligarchy, and the men to whom the chief credit is due were not its supporters, but, on the contrary, those who rebelled against it.

POSTSCRIPT

HAVE PURITAN VALUES HAD LASTING EFFECTS ON AMERICAN SOCIETY?

The question of time dominates this issue. Professor Simpsonn takes a larger view than Professor Wertenbaker in considering when Puritan influence affected society. While Simpson admits Puritanism had a beginning and an end as a historical phenomenon, there is also a continuing tradition in his opinion. Wertenbaker, in his pithy analysis, attempts to restrict Puritanism as much as possible. As he notes near the end of his conclusion, "Despite the failure of the Puritan experiment, it is a widely accepted belief that it was largely instrumental in moulding the character not only of modern New England, but of the entire United States." Wertenbaker argues against such sweeping conclusions.

Both historians seem to be saying that Puritanism had direct and indirect effects. Both appear to agree that many of the direct effects, those associated with seventeenth-century Puritanism, contain negative elements. Then the two part company. Simpson develops a moderately positive interpretation by looking at the eighteenth- and nineteenth-century absorption of certain values he attributes to Puritans. Is he suggesting that hard work, responsibility, sobriety and honesty are exclusively Puritan values? Perhaps Wertenbaker argues more subtly. Is there not a connection between his two main points, that the Puritan experiment failed and that the New Englanders who made important contributions were those who rebelled against that experiment? Again, the irony of cause and effect intrudes in this controversial issue. Also, the question of time must be considered. The Puritan experiment may have failed to dominate New England, even Massachusetts, society but it did succeed in establishing communities in the wilderness. And the first Puritan generations might be credited indirectly with contributing to New England's achievements because their actions created the rebels who Wertenbaker insists, "were among the most active in winning independence, they did their full share in shaping the Constitution, they were pioneers in opening western New York, northern Pennsylvania and the Great Lakes region, they gave the country its first American literature, they made contributions in the fields of science, art, and architecture."

In addition to the paradoxes inherent in the study of Puritanism, the two historians whose views are presented here present another. Have they, in balancing their views and admitting both positive and negative characteristics, made an assessment of their interpretations more, not less, difficult?

Perry Miller's opera on Puritan ideas make him the dean of this subject. See his *Orthodoxy in Massachusetts, 1630–1650* (Cambridge: Harvard University Press, 1933), *The New England Mind: The Seventeenth Century* (New York: Macmillan, 1939) and *The New England Mind: From Colony to Province* (Cambridge: Harvard University Press, 1953). Recent studies emphasize social history. Among these are Darrett B. Rutman, *Winthrop's Boston: Portrait of a Puritan Town, 1630–1649* (Chapel Hill: University of North Carolina Press, 1965); Kenneth A. Lockridge, *A New England Town: The First One Hundred Years* (New York: Norton, 1970); and Philip Greven, *Four Generations: Population, Land and Family in Colonial Andover, Massachusetts* (Ithaca: Cornell University Press, 1970).

The BOSTONIAN'S Paying the EXCISE-MAN, or TAR[...]

Plate I

London Printed for Rob.t Sayer & J.Bennett, Map & Printseller, N°53 Fleet Street as the Act [...]

PART 2
THE NEW NATION

As America grew and became more established, its people and leaders struggled with the implementation of the ideals that had sparked a revolution. What had been abstractions before the formation of the government had to be applied and refined in day-to-day practice. The nature of post-revolutionary America, the place of religion in America, as well as the role of women and the reality of civil rights, had to be determined in a process that continues today.

Did the Revolution Significantly Change American Society?

Did Economic Self-interest Motivate the Writing and Ratification of the Federal Constitution?

Was President Jefferson an Opponent of Civil Rights?

Did Women Achieve Greater Autonomy in the New World?

ISSUE 7

DID THE REVOLUTION SIGNIFICANTLY CHANGE AMERICAN SOCIETY?

YES: J. Franklin Jameson, from *The American Revolution Considered as a Social Movement* (Princeton University Press, 1926)

NO: Frederick B. Tolles, from "The American Revolution Considered as a Social Movement: A Re-Evaluation," in *The American Historical Review,* October 1954

ISSUE SUMMARY

YES: Professor J. Franklin Jameson enumerates several ways in which the American Revolution greatly changed society.
NO: Professor Frederick Tolles counters with a view of change in eighteenth-century America which takes exception to many of Jameson's conclusions.

"What do we mean by the Revolution?" John Adams asked Thomas Jefferson in 1815. The second president of the United States might have been addressing a historical meeting rather than his successor in the White House. His question focused on one of the central issues of this great event in American history. In doing so, Adams raised a question which has perplexed historians as well as the men who made the Revolution. Before attempting an analysis of the *American* Revolution, the word revolution itself needs definition. Most historians would agree that, in modern times, revolution implies fundamental change. To confine the word in this manner is what Carl Becker referred to as reducing history to its common denominator as if it were a mathematical exercise. "In order to understand the essential nature of anything it is well to strip it of all superficial and irrelevant accretions," Becker wrote in *Everyman His Own Historian.*

The debate over the American Revolution involves at least three distinctive topics: the event itself, its causes and its effects. Perhaps the first step in evaluating the American Revolution is to ask, did it cause fundamental changes? Next, the process by which the changes occurred needs analysis. Motivation must not be ignored: why was fundamental change necessary? The kinds of changes produced should be considered. Were they political, social, economic, cultural? When historians have asked these questions, they have often restricted their answers by studying one kind of cause or effect at the expense of others. Since these topics ultimately overlap, it is not possible to isolate them completely from each other.

In addition, the historiography of the American Revolution has raised another question. Those who argue that fundamental changes occurred before 1775, as does Professor Tolles, introduce the question of dating the effects. John Adams, again in his letter to Jefferson, referred to this issue as well. "What do we mean by the Revolution? The war? That was no part of the Revolution; it was only an effect and consequence of it," Adams wrote. Those who interpret the Revolution as a gradual development which took place largely, if not entirely, before 1775 must by necessity minimize the importance of the Revolutionary War battles. While this approach emphasizes the importance of less dramatic events at the expense of the obvious, it is not possible to ignore the effects of the war entirely. The War for Independence had to be fought if independence were to become reality.

It seems that dating the occurrence of the Revolution and the use of descriptors such as political, social, economic and cultural, are intertwined. A historian's conclusions depend heavily on the adjectives used to describe the causes and effects under consideration. Major economic and cultural changes did occur independently of military conflict and they did occur before 1775. Is it possible to draw the same conclusions about political and social changes?

Both the selections below raise other questions. Which changes took place in all thirteen territories? Which were restricted to one government or another? For example, the effects of political change were both regional (within a particular jurisdiction such as North Carolina) and national with the adoption of the Articles of Confederation and the Federal Constitution. On the other hand, social change, if the abolition of slavery might be used as an example, affected each area differently. In 1790, Massachusetts was the only state which had no slaves. In short, if changes did take place as a consequence of the War for Independence, it must not be assumed that the changes, even if recognized as fundamental, were sweeping and affected all the thirteen states in the same way.

Jameson quotes an eighteenth-century South Carolinian who observed, "The American war is over, but this is far from being the case with the American Revolution. On the contrary, nothing but the first act of the great drama is closed." Building on this point of view he concludes, "Thus in many ways the successful struggle for the independence of the United States affected the character of American society by altering the status of persons." Tolles, in his rebuttal nearly thirty years later, states "Indeed the points at which the supports to Jameson's thesis seem weakest—where for example he argues for sharper changes in the political and social status of individuals than can be justified on the evidence—are precisely those points at which he overlooked or underestimated dynamic forces already present in the society of late colonial America."

YES
J. Franklin Jameson

THE AMERICAN REVOLUTION CONSIDERED AS A SOCIAL MOVEMENT

THE REVOLUTION AND THE STATUS OF PERSONS

... If [it] is rational to suppose that the American Revolution has some social consequences, what would they be likely to be? It would be natural to reply that it depends on the question, who caused the Revolution, and that therefore it becomes important to inquire what manner of men they were, and what they would be likely, consciously or unconsciously, to desire. In reality, the matter is not quite so simple as that. Allowance has to be made for one important fact in the natural history of revolutions, and that is that, as they progress, they tend to fall into the hands of men holding more and more advanced or extreme views, less and less restrained by traditional attachment to the old order of things. Therefore the social consequences of a revolution are not necessarily shaped by the conscious or unconscious desires of those who started it, but more likely by the desires of those who came into control of it at later stages of its development.

You know how it was with the English Revolution of the seventeenth century. At first it was the affair of moderate statesmen, like Pym and Hampden, or moderate generals like Essex or Manchester, earls, who would not push the king too hard, but before long it fell into the hands of men like Cromwell, whose spirit is shown by his bold declaration, "If I should meet the king in battle, I would as soon fire my pistol at him as at any man." Now when we examine the interesting mass of constitutional and social legislation enacted by the parliaments of the Commonwealth, we see in it the work of men of far more advanced views than those of Pym and Hampden, to wit, of radicals who had come into control of the movement in its latest stages.

Or again, take the French Revolution. Everyone knows how its history is marked by distinct successive periods, in each of which the control is exercised by a group more radical and extreme than its predecessors; and the same has been true of the great Russian revolution. Now, widely as our American

Revolution differed from these, do not let us suppose that it escaped every trait of conformity to the natural history of such movements. Certain it is that, in some of our states at least, it fell ultimately into quite other hands than those that set it in motion.

Well, then, we may ask, who were in favor of the Revolution, and who were against it? The answer of course varies with the different stages of its development. In 1774 the partisans of American independence were very few, though there had long been those who thought, in an academic way, that it would soon take place. In most years after 1776 the partisans of American independence were the great majority. But what sort of man became a Tory as it gradually became necessary to take sides? What sort of man became a Whig? As a matter of course, almost all persons who enjoyed office under the Crown became Tories, and these were a large number. In an age when the king's turnspit was a member of Parliament, and under a king whose chief means of political action was the distribution of offices, officeholders were certain to be numerous, and their pay was, in proportion to the wealth of the country and the work they had to do, much greater than it is now. If the natural desire of all mankind to hold on to a lucrative office (a desire which is said sometimes to influence political action even in this age) did not make an officeholder a Tory, there was another motive arising from the fact that he had been appointed and had sworn to execute the laws, and might therefore feel in duty bound to obey the instructions, of the ministers in England. As for the merchants, many, who had extensive interests that were imperilled by rebellion, adhered to the royal cause. But on the whole the great body of the merchants of the thirteen colonies were Whigs, for of the deep underlying causes, which for a generation had been moving the American mind in the direction of independence, none was so potent, according to all the best testimony, as the parliamentary restrictions on the trade of the colonies. Among farmers many of the richest took the royalist side. Probably most Episcopalians did so, except in the South. Everywhere the debtor class was, as was natural, and as has been true the whole world over, mainly on the side of revolution.

If we speak of professions, we should note that probably most of the clergy were Whigs, with the exception of nearly all the clergymen of the Church of England in the northern colonies. Most lawyers were Whigs, but most of the most eminent and of those enjoying the largest practice were Tories. John Adams says that, of the eight lawyers who had an important practice before the Superior Court of Massachusetts at the time of the Stamp Act, only Otis and he were Whigs ten years later. One of the others had died, and remaining five were Tories. Among physicians the proportion of Tories was quite as large as among lawyers.

A word as to race and nationality. Colonists who had very recently arrived from England were likely to take the Tory side. Immigrants from Scotland, also, were usually Tories. A hundred and fifty years ago the Scots at home were among the warmest of Tories; Hume's *History of England* is typical of their feelings. Perhaps, too, their well-known clannishness gave them, in America, the position of aliens who held together, and would not assimilate with the rest of the population. Of the Irish, on the other hand, and those of the Scotch-Irish stock, Protestants from the north of Ireland, it is customary to hold that they were warmly and by vast majority on the side of revolution. It is not so certain. Industrious efforts have been made to show that they formed the backbone of the Revolutionary army—efforts partly based on a misinterpretation of a single passage in Joseph Galloway's testimony before a committee of the House of Commons. On the other hand, I have observed that, in the two large lists of Loyalist claimants that give the country of birth, 146 out of 1,358 claimants, or eleven percent, say that they were born in Ireland—a larger number than were born in England. Yet in Pennsylvania, where the proportion of Irish or Scotch-Irish population was greatest, it was unquestionably their influence that carried the state for independence, at the same time breaking the power in state affairs of the Philadelphia conservatives, and bestowing upon the state a radically democratic constitution. In all the colonies the Germans generally adhered to the party of independence, but not with great ardency.

As is usually the case, the revolutionary side was more frequently espoused by young men, the conservative cause by their elders. There were not a few conspicuous cases, such as that of Sir John Randolph, the king's attorney-general in Virginia, and his son Edmund Randolph, in which the son adopted the former, the father the latter cause, and other cases, like that of Samuel and Josiah Quincy, in which an elder and a younger brother were thus divided. Among all the leaders of the Revolution, very few were forty-five years old in 1775; most were under forty. But think for a moment of the leaders of the French Revolution—Robespierre thirty-one years old when the Revolution began, Danton thirty, Camille Desmoulins twenty-seven, Collot-d'Herbois thirty-nine, Couthon thirty-three, Lebas twenty-four, Saint-Just twenty-one—and we shall see

cause to be glad that our Revolution was carried through by men who, though still young, had at any rate reached their full maturity of thought and of character.

If we should investigate the Tory party in the several colonies in detail, we should be forced to the conviction that, in New England, it comprised in 1775 a very great share, probably more than half, of the most educated, wealthy, and hitherto respected classes. In March 1776, when Howe evacuated Boston, eleven hundred refugees sailed away with him. These eleven hundred, and the thousand or more who subsequently followed them, bore away perhaps a majority of the old aristocracy of Massachusetts. The act of banishment which the state legislature passed in 1778, to punish the Tories, includes among its three hundred-odd names some representatives of most of the families which had been distinguished in the earlier days of the colony. The loss of this important element, cultivated, experienced, and public-spirited, was a very serious one. It is true that many Tories returned after the war, but their fortunes were usually much broken, and they could never regain their influence. In New England, in short, it appears that the Revolution brought new strata everywhere to the surface.

In New York it seem probable that, in the height of the war at least, the bulk of the property-owners belonged to the Tory party, and it was strong also among the middle classes of the towns and among the country population. On the large manorial estates the tenant farmers sided with their landlords if they took sides at all. The city of New York and the county of Westchester were strongly Tory during at least the period of the British occupation, and Westchester very likely before. So were Staten Island and the three counties of Long Island.

In Pennsylvania it is probable that during the critical years of the war, at least, the majority of the population was on the side of the Crown, and that majority seems to have included many persons of eminence, and many Quakers. On the other hand, as is well known, the Virginian aristocracy in general, living somewhat remote from the influence of the royal officials, upon their secluded estates, were full of the spirit of local independence. Quite unlike their New England compeers, they took the Whig side, and that almost unanimously. It was the Virginian planters who formed the local committees, seized from the outset the control of the movement, and made it impossible for loyalty to show itself in concerted or effective action. And it is well known how numerous and active were the Tories in the Carolinas. But, says Dr. Ramsay, speaking of South Carolina, "Beside their superiority in numbers, there was an ardour and enthusiasm in the friends of Congress which was generally wanting in the advocates for royal government." Is not this a most significant touch? After all the evidence as to classes and numbers—for perhaps there were a hundred thousand Loyalist exiles, to say nothing of the many more who did not emigrate—the ultimate success of the American cause might well seem to us a miracle. But the fact remains that the Revolutionary party knew what they wanted. They had a definite programme, they had boldness and resolution, while those averse to independence were divided in their counsels, and paralyzed by the timidity which naturally cleaves to conservative minds. The first scientific observer of political revolutions, Thucydides, pointed out, and every subsequent revolution has accentuated his words, that in such times boldness and energy are more important requisites to success than intelligence or all other qualities put together. This is the secret of the whole matter. "There was an ardour and enthusiasm in the friends of Congress which was generally wanting in the advocates for royal government."

All things considered, it seems clear that in most states the strength of the revolutionary party lay most largely in the plain people, as distinguished from the aristocracy. It lay not in the mob or rabble, for American society was overwhelmingly rural and not urban, and had no sufficient amount of mob or rabble to control the movement, but in the peasantry, substantial and energetic though poor, in the small farmers and frontiersmen. And so, although there were men of great possessions like George Washington and Charles Carroll of Carrollton who contributed a conservative element, in the main we must expect to see our social changes tending in the direction of levelling democracy. . . .

The workings of the popular sentiment in favor of equality may of course be plainly seen in the legislation abolishing rights of primogeniture and distributing more or less equally the estates of persons dying intestate, but this movement may perhaps be more conveniently considered in a lecture devoted to the Revolution and the Land. We might also expect the equalitarian or humane spirit to show itself in alterations of the laws respecting redemptioners or indented servants. Those laws, however, seem not to have been changed in the Revolutionary period. We may infer that the laws protecting the interests of such persons, a very numerous class in years just preceding the Revolution, either were, or were deemed to be, adequate already for their humane purpose, and that the status of the indented, who after all had but a few years to serve and then would have all the rights of other poor people,

7. DID THE REVOLUTION CHANGE AMERICAN SOCIETY?

was not regarded as seriously unsatisfactory.

A far more serious question, in any consideration of the effect of the American Revolution on the status of persons, is that of its influence on the institution of slavery, for at this time the contrast between American freedom and American slavery comes out, for the first time, with startling distinctness. It has often been asked: How could men who were engaged in a great and inspiring struggle for liberty fail to perceive the inconsistency between their professions and endeavors in that contest and their actions with respect to their bondmen? How could they fail to see the application of their doctrines respecting the rights of man to the black men who were held among them in bondage far more reprehensible than that to which they indignantly proclaimed themselves to have been subjected by the King of Great Britain?

At the time when the Revolution broke out there were about a half-million of slaves in the Thirteen Colonies, the figures probably running about as follows: 200,000 in Virginia, 100,000 in South Carolina, 70,000 or 80,000 each in Maryland and in North Carolina, 25,000 perhaps in New York, 10,000 in New Jersey, 6,000 in Pennsylvania, 6,000 in Connecticut, 5,000 in Massachusetts, 4,000 in Rhode Island. Slavery in the continental colonies at that time was no doubt less harsh than in the West Indies, and milder than it has been in many other countries and times. An English parson, preaching to a Virginian congregation in 1763, says: "I do you no more than justice in bearing witness, that in no part of the world were slaves ever better treated than, in general, they are in the colonies." But slavery is slavery, and already before the Revolution many hearts had been stirred against

it. It is of course true that other influences than those of the American Revolution were abroad in the world at the same time which would surely work in some degree against the institution of human slavery. On the one hand Voltaire has raised a powerful, if at times a grating, voice in favor of a rational humanitarianism, and Rousseau had poured upon time-worn institutions the active solvent of abounding sentimentality. Quite at another extreme of human thought from them, Wesley and Whitefield had stirred the English nation into a warmth of religious feeling of which Methodism was only one result, and with it came a revived interest in all varieties of philanthropic endeavor. . . .

In actual results of the growing sentiment, we may note, first of all, the checking of the importation of slaves, and thus of the horrors of the trans-Atlantic slave trade. The Continental Congress of 1774 had been in session but a few days when they decreed an "American Association," or non-importation agreement, in which one section read: "That we will neither import nor purchase any slave imported after the first day of December next, after which we will wholly discontinue the slave trade, and will neither be concerned in it ourselves, not will we hire our vessels nor sell our commodities or manufactures to those who are concerned in it"; and the evidence seems to be that the terms of this agreement were enforced throughout the war with little evasion.

States also acted. Four months before this, in July 1774, Rhode Island had passed a law to the effect that all slaves thereafter brought into the colony should be free. The influence under which it was passed may be seen from the preamble. "Whereas," it begins, "the inhabitants of America are generally engaged in the preservation of their own rights and liberties, among which that of personal freedom must be considered as the greatest, and as those who are desirous of enjoying all the advantages of liberty themselves should be willing to extend personal liberty to others," etc. A similar law was passed that same year in Connecticut. Delaware prohibited importation in 1776, Virginia in 1778, Maryland in 1783, South Carolina in 1787, for a term of years, and North Carolina, in 1786, imposed a larger duty on each negro imported.

Still further, the states in which slaves were few proceeded, directly as a consequence of the Revolutionary movement, to effect the immediate or gradual abolition of slavery itself. Vermont had never recognized its existence, but Vermont was not recognized as a state. Pennsylvania in 1780 provided for gradual abolition, by an act which declared that no negro born after that date should be held in any sort of bondage after he became twenty-eight years old, and that up to that time his service should be simply like that of an indented servant or apprentice. Now what says the preamble of this act? That when we consider our deliverance from the abhorrent condition to which Great Britain has tried to reduce us, we are called on to manifest the sincerity of our professions of freedom, and to give substantial proof of gratitude, by extending a portion of our freedom to others, who, though of a different color, are the work of the same Almighty hand. Evidently here also the leaven of the Revolution was working as a prime cause in this philanthropic endeavor.

The Superior Court of Massachusetts declared that slavery had been abolished in that state by the mere declaration of its constitution that "all men are born free and equal." In 1784 Connecticut and Rhode Island passed acts which gradually extinguished slavery. In other states, ameliorations of the law respecting slaves were effected even though the abolition of slavery could not be brought about. Thus in 1782 Virginia passed an act which provided that any owner might, by an instrument properly attested, freely manumit all his slaves, if he gave security that their maintenance should not become a public charge. It may seem but a slight thing, this law making private manumission easy where before it had been difficult. But it appears to have led in eight years to the freeing of more than ten thousand slaves, twice as great a number as were freed by reason of the Massachusetts constitution, and as many as there were in Rhode Island and Connecticut together when the war broke out.

That all was not done that might have been done for the removal or amelioration of slavery we cannot deny, nor that there was in many places a glaring contrast between the principles avowed by the men of the Revolution and their acts respecting slavery; yet very substantial progress was made, and that more was made in this period than in any other until a much later time may be taken as clear evidence of a pronounced influence of the Revolution upon the status of persons in the realm where that status stood most in need of amelioration.

Thus in many ways the successful struggle for the independence of the United States affected the character of American society by altering the status of persons. The freeing of the community led not unnaturally to the freeing of the individual; the raising of colonies to the position of independent states brought with it the promotion of many a man to a higher order in the scale of privilege or consequence. So far at any rate as this aspect of life in America is concerned, it is vain to think of the Revolution as solely a series of political or military events.

THE REVOLUTION
AND THE LAND

It would appear from the satirical remarks of Dickens and others that, eighty years ago, the first question asked of a European visitor to any part of the United States was, "How do you like our institutions?" Our institutions, especially the institutions of democracy, were thought of as the most notable possession or attribute of the United States, and many indeed seem to have regarded them as the source of all our prosperity and prospects of advancement.

But during the past fifty years historians have not been idle, and, though it runs counter to many contemptuous or patronizing declarations that I see in print, to me they seem to have been doing their work with a certain degree of intelligence. In particular, they have been much impressed with the thought that the average man, in all ages, has been more occupied with making a living than with any other one thing. This has led them to doubt whether economic phenomena are not more often the cause than the effect of political institutions and arrangements, and in the case of American History to question closely the view that our political institutions are the source from which all blessings flow.

The doctrine which underlies the present lecture is that political democracy came to the United States as a result of economic democracy, that this nation came to be marked by political institutions of a democratic type because it had, still earlier, come to be characterized in its economic life by democratic arrangements and practices. We do not look to see effects precede causes, and certainly politi-cal democracy came among us somewhat late, certainly long after the Revolution in most states. If we take manhood suffrage as the most convenient symbol of political democracy, we have to say that it was 1840 before manhood suffrage came at all close to being the universal rule of American political life. Long before this, however, America stood committed to economic democracy, which meant, in a country so occupied with agriculture, to the system of landholding which the classical economists called "peasant proprietorship," the system of small holdings where landowner, capitalist or farmer, and laborer are all one, the owner of the land supplying the capital and working the fields with his own labor and that of his family. . . .

In the first place, royal restrictions on the acquisition of land fell into abeyance. The king's proclamation of 1763, forbidding settlement and the patenting of lands beyond the Alleghenies, and those provisions of the Quebec Act of 1774 which in a similar sense restricted westward expansion and the formation of new, interior colonies had, it is true, never been executed with complete rigidity, but they, and the uncertainties of the months preceding the war, had certainly checked many a project of large colonization and many a plan for speculation in land. Now these checks were removed. Moreover, all the vast domains of the Crown fell into the hands of the states, and were at the disposal of the state legislatures, and it was certain that these popular assemblies would dispose of them in some manner that would be agreeable to popular desires. Whether the land law in respect to old holdings should be altered by the Revolution or should remain unchanged, it was certain that in respect to new lands, on which the future hopes of American agriculture and settlement rested, a more democratic system would be installed.

Then there was the matter of the quit-rents, which in most of the colonies, according to the terms on which lands were granted to individual occupants, were to be paid to the crown or to the proprietary of the province. They ranged from a penny an acre to a shilling a hundred acres per annum. It is true that payment was largely evaded, but since the amount received at the time when the Revolution broke out was nearly $100,000, we may count the quit-rent as something of a limitation upon the ready acquisition of land. So at any rate the colonists regarded it, for in making their new constitutions and regulations respecting lands they abolished quit-rents with great emphasis and vigor, and forbade them for the future.

Another encumbrance on land-tenure which the Revolution removed was the provision, by British statute intended to ensure an adequate supply of masts for the royal navy, that no man should cut white-pine trees on his land till the king's surveyor of woods had surveyed it and designated the trees, sometimes many in number, which were to be reserved for the king's use. It is true that the law was not rigorously enforced; it could not be, with such staff as the surveyors had. But John Wentworth, the last royal governor of New Hampshire and the last surveyor of the king's woods in New England, tried diligently to enforce it, and, though he did it tactfully, he found it everywhere exceedingly unpopular. With the coming of the Revolution, the restriction came to an end, and fee simple was fee simple.

In the fourth place, great confiscations of Tory estates were carried out by the state legislatures, generally in the height of the war. New Hampshire confiscated twenty-eight estates, including the large property of its governor, Sir John Wentworth. In Massachusetts a sweeping act confiscated at one blow all the property of all who had fought against the United States or had even retired into places under British authority without permission from the American government. Among the lands confiscated by special mention were those of Sir William Pepperrell, the second baronet of that name, whose vast estate in Maine extended so far along the coast that it was said he could ride all the way from Kittery Point to Saco, a distance of thirty miles, on his own land. In New York, all lands and rents of the crown and all estates of fifty-nine named persons were confiscated, the greatest among them, probably, being that of the Phillipse connection. Probably something like three hundred square miles of the old Phillipse estates were confiscated, bearing a value of several hundred thousand dollars. By 1782 the state of New York had confiscated royalist property in land valued at $2,500,000 in hard money. In all, the state probably received $3,150,000 Spanish dollars for forfeited real estate.

The largest estate confiscated was that of the Penn family, proprietaries of Pennsylvania, which they estimated at nearly a million pounds sterling. The commissioners of the state of Maryland who sold confiscated property in that state took in more than £450,000 sterling. In Georgia the single estate of Sir James Wright was valued at $160,000. The broad lands of the sixth Lord Fairfax, the genial old man in whose service Washington had first practised as a surveyor, and those of Sir John Johnson in the Mohawk country, 50,000 acres, are other examples of Tory confiscation on the grand scale. In one colony and another, hundreds of estates were confiscated. Altogether, it is evident that a great deal of land changed hands, and that the confiscation of Tory estates contributed powerfully to break up the system of large landed properties, since the states usually sold the lands thus acquired in much smaller parcels. Thus the New York law discouraged the sale of such lands in parcels of more than 500 acres. James De Lancey's real estate went to 275 persons, Roger Morris's to 250. A general idea of the extent of the confiscation may be gained from the fact that the British Parliament, after every effort to reduce the claims of the Loyalists, finally compensated them with grants aggregating over three million pounds sterling. To be sure, this was for both real and personal estate, but on the other hand it is to be said that the Loyalists themselves estimated the value of their claims upon Mr. Pitt's government as high as eight million pounds.

These Tory confiscation acts, by the way, had one curious effect upon the development of American institutions. There is no American institution more famous, none that has excited more comment in other countries, largely erroneous comment, to be sure, than the power of American courts to set aside laws for want of conformity to the Constitution. It is often spoken of as a peculiar power of the United States Supreme Court and as a peculiar invention of those who made the Constitution of 1787. In reality it is a power or duty of any court acting under a written constitution, and it was exercised in several instances by state courts before there was a Supreme Court of the United States and before the Constitution of 1787 was framed. It so happens that in most of these cases the law against which this objection was raised was a law regarding Tories. The legislatures were so hot against the Tories and so eager in the pursuit of their spoils that they quite overstepped constitution-

al bounds in their enactments against them. Among the lawyers there grew up the idea, virtually a new idea, that courts might set aside laws if they conflicted with the constitution of the state. The fact is, I suppose, that during this period the legislatures were in the hands of the radical revolutionaries, or extreme Whigs, while the lawyers and judges were more moderate and conservative members of that party. . . .

Social democracy and political democracy progress together in the legislation of the Revolutionary period respecting the suffrage, for before the Revolution the electoral franchise was largely based on land. In the colonial times the right to vote had nowhere been very narrowly restricted, but in all the colonies there had been a property qualification, usually amounting to $150 or $250. In six of the colonies it had been necessary to own real estate, no amount of personal property sufficing. In the northern colonies the real estate usually fixed upon was a freehold that would rent for forty shillings—that old forty-shilling freehold which for three centuries and a half had been the standing qualification for county voters in old England. In a country so wholly given up to agriculture a real-estate qualification excluded few men. In the southern colonies, it was more usual to specify a number of acres, generally fifty. The Virginian law required fifty acres of unoccupied land, or a lot of twenty-five acres with a house upon it, or a town-lot with a house upon it. But what constituted a house? If anyone thinks that our ancestors were innocent of election dodges, he may be interested in the record of one old Virginian election, that of 1762. It appears from the journals of the House of Burgesses that William Skinner had half a lot in Elizabeth City County. On the Saturday before the election he bought a small tight-framed house, ten feet by eight, and had it moved onto the land, with the acknowledged design of thereby qualifying himself to vote, and was to pay for it later. The House allowed his vote. Thomas Payne, being owner of part of a lot, says the testimony in the journal, "purchased of one Mary Almond, for the value of 10s. a small House, about 4 and a Half Feet Pitch, 4 or 5 Feet long, and 2 or 2 and a Half Feet wide, floored or laid with Plank in the Midst of its Height, to put Milkpans, or such Things, on, and that he had the same removed in a Cart, with one Horse, with the Assistance of 7 or 8 Men, and placed on his said Lot, on purpose (as he acknowledges) to qualify himself to vote at that Election." Apparently this was going a little *too* far, and the House ruled his vote out. It then passed a law requiring that the house which was to qualify the voter must be at least twelve feet square, which certainly seems moderate enough.

The Revolution greatly altered these old colonial laws respecting the franchise. Four states, it is true, made no change in their rules, but in all the rest the freehold system was broken down. In New York the value of the freehold required was reduced, and persons who merely rented land or houses were put on a par with those who owned them. In most states, any tax-payer was now allowed to vote, whether he paid taxes on real or on personal estate. In others the amount of money required was lowered. And so it came to pass, by what was primarily a political change, but one that carried the seeds of social changes, that "We the people of the United States" who gave consent to the establishing of the Constitution was a much larger and more democratic body than "We the people of the United States" who acquiesced in the Declaration of Independence, though universal suffrage was yet a long way off.

It has been indicated already with what extensive confiscations of land the course of the Revolution had been marked. Great areas thus fell into the hands of the state governments, and most of them also possessed considerable tracts of wild lands of their own. The use made of such possessions was often such as to promote the advance of agricultural democracy. It is well known that the states were often at their wits' ends for money with which to pay their troops. In such straits an obvious resource in the case of states having a large amount of wild lands was to assign portions of them to their soldiers in lieu of pay. This was done to a very large extent, and the result was that, upon the close of the war, there set in an era of unexampled speculation in American wild lands. Soldiers sold their assignments, and the states made large sales directly, in order to pay their debts. Hence the speculation. The Duke of LaRochefoucauld-Liancourt, an émigré French nobleman who travelled extensively in the United States soon after the Revolution, tells of land near Lancaster, Pennsylvania, bought for $25 an acre, for which $100 was refused five years later. In another passage he speaks of a thousand acres near Canandaigua, New York, bought three years before at a shilling an acre, of which a half had since been sold off at prices ranging from a dollar to three dollars, and even, in some cases, twenty-five dollars. An example of one of the large sales will show, however, how low the prices would sometimes run at the great auctions, especially in the case of lands not situated near any navigable river and hence, under the conditions of transportation then prevailing, not near a market. I choose the example from the narrative of his travels printed by Henry Wansey, a Wiltshire clothier. "Monday. I attended a sale (by auction at the Tontine

125

Coffee House) of some military lands," that is, lands given to the soldiers, "situated in the north part of New York State. Twenty-five acres in the township of Cato," he continues, "were sold at two shillings and eightpence currency" (that is, New York shillings) "per acre; . . . five hundred in Pompey at five shillings and one penny; nine hundred in Tully and Hannibal at three and eightpence; fourteen hundred in Hector and Dryden, at three and eightpence." It will be seen that the classical names which in lavish profusion decorate the map of Cortland and Onondaga counties were already there in 1789—Pompey and Tully, and Fabius and Manlius, and Cincinnatus and Marathon. It has been usual to bestow the credit or discredit of this nomenclature upon General Simeon DeWitt, the surveyor-general of the state. But the late Professor Moses Coit Tyler deemed he had proof that the dreadful deed was done by an office-boy fresh from the study of Lemprière's *Classical Dictionary,* and that the good general must be acquitted of all blame in the matter but that of leaving the selection of names to the unchastened imagination of an office-boy.

However this may be, the lands sold none the less readily, 5,500,000 acres being sold by New York in a single year; and in the end, whatever allowance may be made for speculation, passed ultimately, for the most part, into the hands of small holders.

If the states, impoverished by the war and burdened with debt, found so valuable a resource through sales of state lands, we may well believe that they valued every bit of territory to which they could lay claim. Hence arose a multitude of boundary disputes, opening into several amusing but unedifying quarrels, and fostering discord between states which at that time were none too well disposed toward mutual agreement. Massachusetts found opportunity for quarrel on its western boundary with New York. Pennsylvania and Virginia differed as to the region where Pennsylvania now touches West Virginia. Virginia and North Carolina differed as to their boundary line. South Carolina and Georgia quarrelled about their boundaries at the upper part of the Savannah River, New York and New Hampshire about Vermont, Connecticut and Pennsylvania about the Wyoming country. Far more important than all these disputes was that which raged over the control of the western lands. The political history of this momentous conflict, and of its happy settlement by cessions to the Confederation, is in all the books; but the social consequences of that settlement were surely greater than any others that have been touched upon in this lecture. . . .

NO
Frederick B. Tolles

A RE-EVALUATION
OF THE REVOLUTION
AS A SOCIAL MOVEMENT

Sometimes a single essay, a monograph, or a series of lectures makes historiographical history. It was so in 1893 when Frederick Jackson Turner read his paper on "The Significance of the Frontier in American History." It was so again in 1913 when Charles A. Beard published his *Economic Interpretation of the Constitution.* And it was so in 1925 when J. Franklin Jameson delivered his four lectures at Princeton on "The American Revolution Considered as a Social Movement."

At first glance the comparison with Turner and Beard may seem strained. We are accustomed to think of Jameson as a scholar's scholar, a kind of indispensable historical midwife—curator and editor of manuscripts, director of other men's research, editor of the *American Historical Review*—not as a pathbreaker, an innovator. But this is to do him less than justice. *The American Revolution Considered as a Social Movement* stands as a landmark in recent American historiography, a slender but unmistakable signpost, pointing a new direction for historical research and interpretation. Before Jameson, the American Revolution had been a chapter in political, diplomatic, and military history, a story of Faneuil Hall and Lexington, Independence Hall and Valley Forge, Versailles and Yorktown. After Jameson, it became something different, something greater—a seismic disturbance in American society, a sudden quickening in the American mind.

The American Revolution, like the French, Jameson believed, was accompanied by social and cultural changes of profound significance.

> The stream of revolution, once started, could not be confined within narrow banks, but spread abroad upon the land. Many economic desires, many social aspirations were set free by the political struggle, many aspects of colonial society profoundly altered by the forces thus let loose. The relations of social classes to each other, the institution of slavery, the system of landholding, the course of business, the forms and spirit of the intellectual and religious life, all felt the transforming hand of revolution, all emerged from under it in shapes advanced many degrees nearer to those we know.

Excerpted by special permission from, "A Re-evaluation of the Revolution as a Social Movement," by Frederick B. Tolles, *American Historical Review*, October 1954. Copyright © The American Historical Association.

7. DID THE REVOLUTION CHANGE AMERICAN SOCIETY?

No more than Turner's or Beard's was Jameson's notion wholly new. Just a year earlier, in his massive volume on *The American States during and after the Revolution,* Allan Nevins had devoted fifty pages to the task of demonstrating in impressive detail that "a social and intellectual revolution" occurred between Lexington and Yorktown. Nearly twenty years before, Carl Becker had described the Revolution as a twofold contest: for home-rule on the one hand, for "the democratization of American politics and society" on the other. As far back as 1787, Benjamin Rush had perceived that the American revolution was bigger than the American war, that the real revolution was in "the principles, morals, and manners of our citizens," and that, far from being over, that revolution had only begun.

Jameson's view of the Revolution was not new, but no one hitherto had marshaled the evidence so compactly, conveyed it so lucidly, or argued from it so persuasively. Perceptive historians immediately greeted his little volume as a gem of historical writing—"a truly notable book," Charles A. Beard called it, ". . . cut with a diamond point to a finish, studded with novel illustrative materials, gleaming with new illumination, serenely engaging in style, and sparingly garnished with genial humor."

The influence of this little book with the long title has grown steadily. A year after its publication, the Beards summarized its thesis in their widely read *Rise of American Civilization.* Jameson's emphasis on social factors harmonized perfectly with the intellectual and political climate of the 1930's. In 1940, after the author's death, a second edition appeared, and in 1950 a third—an unusual tribute to a set of academic lectures. With the passage of a quarter-century, the book has achieved the standing of a minor classic. One will find hardly a textbook that does not paraphrase or quote Jameson's words, borrow his illustrations, cite him in its bibliography. The notion of the Revolution as a social upheaval has achieved the final seal of acceptance: it has been taken over by the historical novelists—by such writers as Kenneth Roberts and Howard Fast, to name two rather unlikely bedfellows.

Jameson, one suspects, had no idea he was writing a classic. His aim was simply to challenge American historians by opening new windows on the Revolutionary era, suggesting new directions for future research, throwing out tentative hypotheses for others to test. Over the past quarter-century historians have risen to his challenge with a flood of articles, monographs, academic dissertations, and full-dress histories bearing on one or another of his propositions. But the average textbook-writer, one is tempted to believe, has not got beyond Jameson. The time has come to go back and ask how Jameson's original thesis stands up in the light of all this detailed research; what modifications, if any, must be made; what further extensions, if any, are possible.

Jameson disposed his arguments under four rubrics—the status of persons, the land, industry and commerce, thought and feeling. If we recognize, as he did, that such divisions are purely arbitrary, we may adopt his procedure.

American society, he suggested, was measurably democratized during the Revolution. The upper stratum, the old colonial aristocracy, was largely liquidated—by banishment, voluntary exile, or impoverishment. New groups rose to the surface to take their places. "In most states the strength of the revolutionary party lay most largely in the plain people," and the social changes which they brought about naturally tended "in the direction of levelling democracy." Broadening of the suffrage elevated "whole classes of people . . . in their social status," and the revolutionary philosophy of liberty wrought improvements in the condition of the most debased class in America—the Negro slaves.

Recent studies of individual states and regions seem to suggest that Jameson was too sweeping when he equated colonial aristocrats with Loyalists and implied that this group was erased from American society. In eastern Massachusetts it was perhaps true that "a majority of the old aristocracy" emigrated. But in the central and western part of the state the oldest, most respected families chose the Whig side and remained to perpetuate their local rule in the days of the early Republic. In New Hampshire, except around Portsmouth, society had never been highly stratified, and the Tory emigration bore away few outstanding individuals. In Connecticut, where "the native aristocracy of culture, wealth, religion, and politics" tended to be loyal to the crown, at least half of the Tories never left the state. Others were welcomed back even before the war was over. Within six months of the peace treaty, New Haven was openly extending an invitation to former Loyalists to return, and President Ezra Stiles of Yale College was grumbling about efforts "silently to bring the Tories into an Equality and Supremacy among the Whigs." In New York and Philadelphia, many prominent merchants—perhaps the majority—were Loyalists, or at least neutralists, and they stayed on in such numbers as to give a definite tone to postwar society, politics, and business in these important centers. In Maryland, the "internal" Revolution turns out to have been a struggle between one group of aristocrats—planters, mer-

chants, lawyers—and another; the "plain people" took little part in the conflict and the resultant social shifts were minimal. In Virginia, of course, most of the "F.F.V.'s" were Whigs, and their control of politics was to continue through the days of the "Virginia dynasty." In the North Carolina back country it was the "plain people"— the old Regulators—who were most stubbornly Loyalist. Clearly Jameson's generalizations about the fate of the old aristocracy must be qualified.

What about the new democracy of the Revolutionary period? Unquestionably a sense of dignity and importance came to the common man—the small farmer, the town artisan—as a result of his revolutionary activities and the limited extension of the suffrage. But before we can say with assurance how democratic the new society was, we must answer the prior question: how undemocratic was the old? No one will dispute the fact that provincial society was stratified, that class distinctions existed, that political and social equality were hardly dreamed of. A recent brilliant study of electoral practices in colonial Massachusetts raises, however, some questions. By means of ingenious statistical methods and samplings of contemporary opinion, the author of this study has shown rather convincingly that, in the Bay Colony at least, practically all adult males had the vote. Massachusetts society before 1776, he concludes, was "very close to a complete democracy." And he hints of further revisions to come. "As for the 'internal revolution' in other colonies, " he says, "—perhaps we should take another look. There is more than a hint in the records that what applies to Massachusetts applies without too much change to other colonies as well."

Though the Negro slave received some indirect benefits from the Revolution, the indentured servant, Jameson found, received none. Nor has subsequent research uncovered any important evidence that he overlooked. While he was dwelling on the negative side, Jameson might have mentioned another large dependent class that gained nothing in status as a result of the Revolution. Even before independence was declared, that doughty feminist Abigail Adams was writing to her husband in Congress: "By the way, in the new code of laws which I suppose it will be necessary for you to make, I desire you would remember the ladies and be more generous and favorable to them than your ancestors." Her husband wrote back, as much in earnest as in jest: "Depend on it, we know better than to repeal our masculine systems." It was to be nearly three quarters of a century before the Declaration of Independence would be revised by a group of determined ladies at Seneca Falls to read: "All men and women are created equal." Both negative and positive evidence, then, suggests that the Revolution made less difference in the status of persons in America than Jameson believed.

The doctrine that underlies Jameson's second lecture is, quite explicitly, economic determinism: "political democracy," he says flatly, "came to the United States as a result of economic democracy." The movement for manhood suffrage which reached its fruition in Jacksonian America, he maintains, was rooted in a peculiarly American type of land tenure—the system of small holdings or what he chooses to call "peasant proprietorship." This system the Revolution fixed upon the nation when it swept away the royal restrictions, the archaic manorial laws and usages which had encumbered the land throughout the colonial period. There was, he makes clear, "no violent outbreak," no bloody

massacre of landlords as in France a decade later. Still, "in a quiet, sober, Anglo-Saxon way a great change was effected in the land-system of America between the years 1775 and 1795." Specifically, the changes were of three sorts: the discontinuance of quitrents and of the king's right to mast-trees, the abolition of primogeniture and entail, the confiscation and distribution of the Tory estates.

The importance of the quitrents and the king's "broad arrow" was probably more symbolic than real. Jameson himself admitted this: payment of quitrents, he pointed out, was "largely evaded"; the law giving the king's surveyors the right to reserve the tallest, straightest pine trees for the Royal Navy "was not rigorously enforced." Still, no historian will deny the importance of an emotion-laden symbol, and Jameson insists, quite rightly, that the quitrent and the king's "broad arrow" were symbols of an obsolete and alien feudalism, that until they were done away with, private property was not private property.

There is high authority, of course, for attaching great significance to the abolition of primogeniture and entail in Virginia— the authority of Thomas Jefferson. But these gestures too, it now appears, were more important in the realm of symbol than of economic reality. In point of fact, neither primogeniture nor entail operated to any important degree in Virginia. Recent research has shown that most estates in the Old Dominion were not entailed but could be freely alienated. And primogeniture was mandatory only if the property-owner died intestate. Most Virginia planters were careful to make wills. By their wills they often distributed their property among all their sons, and sometimes even their daughters. So Jefferson, in the words of his most authoritative biographer, "did not destroy the country gentry as a group with the blows of this mighty ax, and there is insufficient reason to believe that he wanted to." What he did was merely to "to remove legal vestiges of Old World aristocracy." The sweeping conclusion reached by a recent student of this problem in Virginia may well apply to other colonies: "No radical change of custom in devising estates resulted from the abolition of primogeniture and entail."

On the confiscation of Loyalist lands much has been written of late years. The evidence has not been canvassed for all the states, but a definite conclusion seems to be emerging: that considerably less diffusion and democratization of land-ownership resulted from the breakup of these estates and their deposition in small parcels than Jameson supposed.

The most intensive study has been centered on the southern counties of New York, where the DeLanceys, the Bayards, the Philipses held sway in colonial times over their vast baronies. When the revolutionary New York government seized the estates and sold them off, some of the land, to be sure, went to former tenants and other landless individuals. But the bulk of it was bought up by wealthy patriots and merely augmented the domains of rival families like the Livingstons, Schuylers, and Roosevelts. "While it is true," concludes the author of this study, "that the disposal of the loyalist estates effected a greater diffusion of ownership, it is questionable whether it went far toward a radical redistribution of landed wealth and a new social and economic order."

The same thing seems to have been true in Maryland, where wealthy Whig planters and speculators bought up a large proportion of the desirable Tory lands in Baltimore and Frederick counties. Nor is the story greatly different in western Massachusetts or New Hampshire. The South

Carolina confiscation law, in the opinion of a contemporary, was actually "so framed that a man who wants land has no chance to get any," for the state required security which only the wealthy landowner could provide.

The case of the North Carolina is instructive. The authority on the Loyalists of that state, noting that the confiscated lands were sold in plots averaging two hundred acres, concludes with Jameson that the confiscations "tended to make the Revolution economic and social as well as political." From his own evidence, however, one could draw the equally justified inference that many a wealthy patriot took advantage of the bargain prices to increase his holdings and consequently his social status. The largest Tory estate was that of the great speculator Henry McCulloh—some 40,000 acres. Of the ninety purchasers of McCulloh's lands thirty-four bought more than one tract. Some acquired as many as ten or fifteen, thereby creating estates as large as 5,000 acres. Robert Raiford purchased parcels from five different Tories and put together an estate of more than a thousand acres. The 3,600 acre estate of Thomas Hooper passed almost intact to John McKinsey. Before a final generalization can be made about the social effects of the confiscations in North Carolina, we need to know more about the previous economic status of the purchasers.

The largest estate to be confiscated in America, as Jameson pointed out, was that of the Penn family. By the Divesting Act of 1779 the Pennsylvania legislature assumed control of twenty-one and a half million acres—all the ungranted lands which by royal charter had belonged to the proprietors. But this proprietary land, from which the Penns had never received any income, was comparable, surely, to the ungranted crown lands which fell into the hands of the other commonwealths. Much more significant is the fact that the private manors, the "proprietary tenths," of the Penns, amounting to more than 500,000 acres, together with the quitrents on them, were specifically "confirmed, ratified and established for ever" in the hands of the Penn family—and this by the most "radical" of all the revolutionary legislatures!

Clearly, there are two ways of reading the evidence concerning the confiscation and sale of Loyalist lands. Jameson, who was arguing a thesis, chose to stress the "democratizing" effects. But there were other social consequences of an opposite tendency—the aggrandizement of certain individuals and families already well entrenched, the opportunities opened for speculation—and we shall not understand all the social results of this great sequestration of lands until we assess these as well.

In particular, until someone has studied the social effects of land speculation in the Revolutionary and post-Revolutionary era as Professor Paul W. Gates has done for a later period, we shall not know whether the operations of the speculators hastened or delayed settlement, encouraged or hindered the system of small holdings. Meanwhile, we may note that Professor Abernethy considers the Virginia land office act of 1779 (drafted, incidentally, by Thomas Jefferson) "a colossal mistake," a blow to economic democracy, and a retarding influence on settlement because it played into the hands of speculators and thus *prevented* the diffusion of land in small holdings. By this act, he says, "democracy was defeated in Virginia at the moment when it might have had its birth."

Land speculation was, of course, a form of business enterprise. And business enterprise, it is now clear, took a sharp spurt as a direct result of Revolutionary conditions. That Jameson should have perceived and stressed this in 1925 is sufficiently remarkable. His chapter on "Industry and Commerce" undoubtedly opened the eyes of many American historians to the economic facts which, as every one now recognizes, are as crucial in the history of a war as the political, diplomatic, and military facts.

Some of the new economic paths which the Revolution opened, turned out to be blind alleys. Postwar interest in the improvement of agriculture, reflected in the sudden popularity of farmers' societies, proved to be short-lived and relatively ineffectual. In some regions the wartime growth of manufacturing, which Jameson noted, was choked off by the postwar flood of cheap British goods, which he neglected to mention.

But in other ways enterprise burgeoned and flourished under wartime and postwar conditions. Opportunities for quick gains in privateering and profiteering, the opening of new markets, the expansion of the credit system, the injection of new supplies of specie into the economy as a result of foreign borrowing, the rise of new business groups around men like Jermiah Wadsworth, William Duer, Robert Morris, the very idea (a new one for Americans) of large-scale business association—all these were constructive economic forces generated by the Revolution. Especially important were the rise of banking and the spread of incorporation. In the words of one economic historian, the Bank of North America, which opened in Philadelphia in 1782, "was identified with the American Revolutionary 'settlement'—as the Bank of England was with that of the 'Glorious Revolution.'"

The same scholar gives us some revealing statistics on the chartering of business corporations: "In contrast with the half-dozen American business charters granted in the entire colonial period, eleven were issued in the United States between 1781 and 1785, twenty-two between 1786 and 1790, and 114 between 1791 and 1795." Economic facts of this order have led one writer to treat the American Revolution as "the triumph of American mercantile capitalism." Whether or not one wishes to adopt this view, it is clear, as Jameson dimly perceived, that the Revolution loosed potent new forces in the American economy. How these forces were related to the social and political democracy which Jameson saw as products of the Revolution remains to be studied.

When he turned from the hard facts of economic history to the impalpable realm of "thought and feeling," Jameson was less at home. Yet even here he opened vistas which a generation of intellectual and cultural historians have explored with profit. The greater part of his final lecture is concerned with the effect of independence on the churches—with disestablishment and the separation of church and state, with the reorganization of the churches on a national basis, with the wartime decline of religious life and the postwar spread of liberal theologies. Subsequent research has added little to Jameson's account of these matters, except to fill in details. What Jameson did—and it was no trifling achievement—was to bring American church history within the purview of American historians—to take, as it were, the first steps toward giving this neglected orphan child a home and a standing within the family of historical disciplines.

Certain of his insights, naturally, have proved more fruitful than others. His *obiter dictum* to the effect that military men can never again play the part in public life that they played after the Revolution falls strangely on our ears, who have known the proconsulate of MacArthur, the foreign ministry of Marshall, the Presidency of Eisenhower. Curiously, Jameson found little evidence of educational advance in the Revolutionary era, except for the founding of new colleges. Had he taken a broader view of education, he might have recognized a number of important developments directly or indirectly related to wartime experience; the improvement of medicine (including dentistry) and of medical education,   the emergency of civil engineering from military engineering; the founding of Judge Tapping Reeve's "law school" at Litchfield, Connecticut, in 1784; the diffusion of scientific knowledge through the revived activity of the American Philosophical Society and the founding of the American Academy of Arts and Sciences; the popularity of pamphleteering as a form of mass education; and—not least important—the informal education, the widening of horizons, that resulted from wartime mobility, from the fact that, for the first time, many Americans rubbed elbows—and minds—not only with Europeans but with other Americans.   The school of intellectual and cultural historians which has sprung up in the last quarter century has made much of the "intellectual democracy" and the "cultural nationalism" which Jameson vaguely perceived as concomitants, in the realm of "thought and feeling," of the American Revolution.

The danger here as elsewhere is that the historian, misled by his enthusiasm for the concept of "revolution," will posit too abrupt a set of changes, will pay too little attention to the evidences of historical continuity. Jameson himself did not altogether avoid this pitfall. For example, he wrote that "Joel Barlow's *Vision of Columbus*, or Presidents Stiles's celebrated election sermon the *The United States Elevated to Glory and Honor,* could not possibly have been written twenty years earlier." If he meant by this that the idea of the United States as an independent nation was not entertained in the 1760's, the statement is obviously correct, though hardly startling. If he meant that before 1775 no American felt or expressed love for the land, pride in its people, confidence in its future, he was just as obviously wrong. For one finds strong feelings of American patriotism in a pre-Revolutionary poem like Freneau and Brackenridge's "The Rising Glory of America," written in 1771, in the sermons of Samuel Davies and Jonathan Mayhew in the 1750's, even in Judge Samuel Sewall's proud paean to his beloved Plum Island, Crane Pond, and Turkey Hill as far back as the last decade of the seventeenth century. Indeed the points at which the supports to Jameson's thesis seem weakest—where for example he argues for sharper changes in the political and social status of individuals than can be justified on the evidence—are precisely those points at which he overlooked or underestimated dynamic forces already present in the society of late colonial America.

Still, a historian who fashions so useful a conceptual tool, who popularizes so fruitful a hypothesis, who enlarges so notably our understanding of a significant era in American history, can be forgiven a few oversights, a few overstatements. Basically, the "Jameson thesis" is still sound, and, what is more important, still vital and suggestive, capable of still further life, still greater usefulness. Jameson, after all, did much more than give us a new approach to the American Revolution. He formulated and cogently applied to a particular period an important general thesis—"the thesis that all the varied activities of men in the same country and period have intimate relations with each other, and that one cannot obtain a satisfactory view of any one of them by considering it apart from the others." For this he deserves homage as one of the founders of American social and cultural history.

POSTSCRIPT

DID THE REVOLUTION SIGNIFICANTLY CHANGE AMERICAN SOCIETY?

The scholarship on Revolutionary America lacks an acceptable synthesis. Changes in eighteenth-century America before 1775 need to be combined with those which developed after the War for Independence. In turn, those changes must be understood in a universal framework which includes all the descriptors which historians have traditionally used to define their work. Actually Jameson's lectures display significant universalism because he surveys political, social, economic and cultural factors in his lectures on the social effects of the Revolution. The flaw in his work is not singularly of causation or effect, but a rigidity in emphasizing postwar changes without acknowledging earlier ones. Jameson's apologizing style remains his defense. He readily admits to an impressionistic interpretation.

Mild as Tolles makes his rebuttal, he nonetheless takes a directly opposite point of view from Jameson. Has Tolles convincingly criticized Jameson's thesis? Is Tolles's reevaluation better argued than the original thesis Jameson presented? Is it possible to find similar flaws in Tolles that he discovers in Jameson? Does one of these scholars provide more evidence than the other? Does one marshal considerably more convincing detail than the other?

Does an analysis of the areas about which Tolles agrees with Jameson reveal the inception of a synthesis? Is it possible that Tolles is correct in implying that the most we can hope for in understanding the American Revolution is to reevaluate it continually, ask questions about it and be satisfied with daring new interpretations even if they lack sufficient supporting detail?

Other important works on the Revolution are Bernard Bailyn, *The Ideological Origins of the American Revolution* (Harvard University Press, 1967); Edmund S. Morgan, *The Birth of the Republic, 1763–1789* (University of Chicago Press, 1956); Herbert Aptheker, *The American Revolution, 1763–1783* (International Publishers, 1960); and Jackson Turner Main, *The Social Structure of Revolutionary America* (Princeton University Press, 1965). R.R. Palmer has placed the American Revolution in the Atlantic context in his two-volume *The Age of the Democratic Revolution* (Princeton University Press, 1959, 1964). For the role of women in the Revolutionary period see Mary Beth Norton, *Liberty's Daughters* (Little, Brown, 1979).

ISSUE 8

DID ECONOMIC SELF-INTEREST MOTIVATE THE WRITING AND RATIFICATION OF THE FEDERAL CONSTITUTION?

YES: Charles A. Beard, from *An Economic Interpretation of the Constitution of the United States* (Macmillan, 1913)

NO: Forrest McDonald, from *We the People* (University of Chicago Press, 1958)

ISSUE SUMMARY

YES: Professor Charles Beard argues that economic interests determined the political structure of the federal government.
NO: Professor Forrest McDonald contradicts Beard with evidence that many delegates voted against policies which would benefit them economically.

One of the great events in modern politics occurred in Philadelphia in 1787. Delegates from almost all of the states assembled there to revise the Articles of Confederation which had governed the country during the past decade. As these politicians struggled through the summer, they produced a new constitution instead of modifying the old one. The Constitution we now live under owes some of its effectiveness to the inadequacies of its predecessor. The failure of the Articles of Confederation to overcome many of the difficulties of creating a strong central government did clarify the task facing the representatives in Philadelphia. The Confederation Congress was unable to regulate trade and lacked the authority to impose taxes. Another major liability hampering the new nation was the distribution of power between the states and the national government. Had the American Revolutionaries over-reacted to Parliament's colonial policies by deliberately creating a weak central government? Did some of them, by 1787, think their initial decision had been a mistake? Certainly the US Constitution provided a more effective government than the Articles of Confederation. It has been one of the most durable republican political systems in the modern world and has served as a model for others. One popular historian, Catherine D. Bowen, has described the writing of the Federal Constitution as the "miracle of Philadelphia."

Thomas Jefferson, who was serving as our minister to Paris in 1787, referred to the assembly of constitution makers as "demi-gods." Historians also eulogized the so-called "Founding Fathers" until Professor Charles A. Beard published *An Economic Interpretation of the Constitution of the United States* in 1913. Professor Beard revolutionized our understanding of the making of the Constitution. He debunked the myth of Jefferson's "demi-gods" by unveiling selfish goals which motivated the men who created our fundamental law in 1787. He approached the study of the Constitution by examining documents ancillary to the law itself: letters, records of the sessions in Philadelphia and, most importantly, *The Federalist Papers.* "In that study," Beard wrote, "I had occasion to read voluminous writings by the Fathers, and I was struck by the emphasis which so many of them placed on economic interests as forces in politics and in the formation of laws and constitutions." Beard's thesis emphasized the following points. He argued that the basic conflict in writing the Constitution as well as ratifying it involved economic issues such as public debts, western lands, real property and personalty (i.e., loans, investment capital, shipping, manufacturing plants). He was not concerned by questions of liberty, freedom or democracy which had been associated with traditional interpretations of the Constitution. Economic self-interest, Beard insisted, motivated the "Founding Fathers." Beard also suggested that the delegates in Philadelphia and particularly those who urged ratification in the state legislatures, the Federalists, held uniform economic views. In short, the political structure of the United States after 1787 was designed to further the economic well-being of the men who wrote the laws. Beard's thesis attracted supporters and, of course, critics. It was not effectively challenged, however, until the late 1950s.

Professor Forrest McDonald directly confronted Beard's arguments and evidence in *We the People* in 1958. In an elaborate counterattack which utilized statistical evidence, McDonald seriously challenged Beard's forty-five-year-old interpretation. He discredited the broad generalizations Beard had relied on and provided evidence which modified, if not negated, Beard's categorical conclusions. Professor McDonald went so far as to supply his readers with four hypotheses as alternative interpretations of the evidence he had compiled. McDonald emphasized the significance of his last hypothesis: "A fourth possible economic interpretation of the making of the Constitution is that it was the expression of the prevailing popular ideology of the socially desirable or normal relationship between government and economy." McDonald, however, did not hide behind this moderate interpretation of the evidence. He locked horns with Beard by unequivocally declaring, ". . . it is impossible to justify Beard's interpretation of the Constitution as 'an economic document' drawn by a 'consolidated economic group whose property interests were immediately at stake.' "

YES Charles A. Beard

AN ECONOMIC INTERPRETATION OF THE CONSTITUTION OF THE UNITED STATES

THE CONSTITUTION AS AN ECONOMIC DOCUMENT

It is difficult for the superficial student of the Constitution, who has read only the commentaries of the legists, to conceive of that instrument as an economic document. It places no property qualifications on voters or officers; it gives no outward recognition of any economic groups in society; it mentions no special privileges to be conferred upon any class. It betrays no feeling, such as vibrates through the French constitution of 1791; its language is cold, formal, and severe.

The true inwardness of the Constitution is not revealed by an examination of its provisions as simple propositions of law; but by a long and careful study of the voluminous correspondence of the period,[1] contemporary newspapers and pamphlets, the records of the debates in the Convention at Philadelphia and in the several state conventions, and particularly, *The Federalist,* which was widely circulated during the struggle over ratification. The correspondence shows the exact character of the evils which the Constitution was intended to remedy; the records of the proceedings in the Philadelphia Convention reveal the successive steps in the building of the framework of the government under the pressure of economic interests; the pamphlets and newspapers disclose the ideas of the contestants over the ratification; and *The Federalist* presents the political science of the new system as conceived by three of the profoundest thinkers of the period, Hamilton, Madison, and Jay.

Doubtless, the most illuminating of these sources on the economic character of the Constitution are the records of the debates in the Convention, which have come down to us in fragmentary form; and a thorough treatment of material forces reflected in the several clauses of the instrument of government created by the grave assembly at Philadelphia would require a rewriting of the history of the proceedings in the light of the great interests represented there.[2] But an entire volume would scarcely suffice to present the results of such a survey, and an undertaking of this character is accordingly impossible here.

The Federalist, on the other hand, presents in a relatively brief and systematic form an economic interpretation of the Constitution by the men best fitted, through an intimate knowledge of the ideals of the framers, to expound the political science of the new government. This wonderful piece of argumentation by Hamilton, Madison, and Jay is in fact the finest study in the economic interpretation of politics which exists in any language; and whoever would understand the Constitution as an economic document need hardly go beyond it. It is true that the tone of the writers is somewhat modified on account of the fact that they are appealing to the voters to ratify the Constitution, but at the same time they are, by the force of circumstances, compelled to convince large economic groups that safety and strength lie in the adoption of the new system.

Indeed, every fundamental appeal in it is to some material and substantial interest. Sometimes it is to the people at large in the name of protection against invading armies and European coalitions. Sometimes it is to the commercial classes whose business is represented as prostrate before the follies of the Confederation. Now it is to creditors seeking relief against paper money and the assaults of the agrarians in general; now it is to the holders of federal securities which are depreciating toward the vanishing point. But above all, it is to the owners of personalty anxious to find a foil against the attacks of levelling democracy, that the authors of The Federalist address their most cogent arguments in favor of ratification. It is true there is much discussion of the details of the new frame-work of government, to which even some friends of reform took exceptions; but Madison and Hamilton both knew that these were incidental matters when compared with the sound basis upon which the superstructure rested.

In reading the pages of this remarkable work as a study in political economy, it is important to bear in mind that the system, which the authors are describing, consisted of two fundamental parts—one positive, the other negative:

I. A government endowed with certain positive powers, but so constructed as to break the force of majority rule and prevent invasions of the property rights of minorities.

II. Restrictions on the state legislatures which had been so vigorous in their attacks on capital.

Under some circumstances, action is the immediate interest of the dominant party; and whenever it desires to make an economic gain through governmental functioning, it must have, of course, a system endowed with the requisite powers.

Examples of this are to be found in protective tariffs, in ship subsidies, in railway land grants, in river and harbor improvements, and so on through the catalogue of so-called "paternalistic" legislation. Of course it may be shown that the "general good" is the ostensible object of any particular act; but the general good is a passive force, and unless we know who are the several individuals that benefit in its name, it has no meaning. When it is so analyzed, immediate and remote beneficiaries are discovered; and the former are usually found to have been the dynamic element in securing the legislation. Take for example, the economic interests of the advocates who appear in tariff hearings at Washington.

On the obverse side, dominant interests quite as often benefit from the prevention of governmental action as from positive assistance. They are able to take care of themselves if let alone within the circle of protection created by the law. Indeed, most owners of property have as much to fear from positive governmental action as from their inability to secure advantageous legislation. Particularly is this true where the field of private property is already extended to cover practically every form of tangible and intangible wealth. This was clearly set forth by Hamilton: "It may perhaps be said that the power of preventing bad laws includes that of preventing good ones. . . . But this objection will have little weight with those who can properly estimate the mischiefs of that inconstancy and mutability in the laws which form the greatest blemish in the character and genius of our governments. They will consider every institution calculated to restrain the excess of law-making, and to keep things in the same state in which they happen to be at any given period, as more likely to do good than harm. . . . The injury which may possibly be done by defeating a few good laws will be amply compensated by the advantage of preventing a number of bad ones."

THE UNDERLYING POLITICAL SCIENCE OF THE CONSTITUTION

Before taking up the economic implications of the structure of the federal government, it is important to ascertain what, in the opinion of The Federalist, is the basis of all government. The most philosophical examination of the foundations of political science is made by Madison in the tenth number. Here he lays down, in no uncertain language, the principle that the first and elemental concern of every government is economic.

1. "The first object of government," he declares, is the protection of "the diversity in the faculties of men, from which the rights of property originate." The chief business of government, from which, perforce, its essential nature must be derived, consists in the control and adjustment of conflicting economic interests. After enumerating the various forms of propertied interests which spring up inevitably in modern society, he adds: "The regulation of these various and interfering interests forms the principal task of modern legislation, and involves the spirit of party and faction in the ordinary operations of the government."

2. What are the chief causes of these conflicting political forces with which the government must concern itself? Madison answers. Of course fanciful and frivolous distinctions have sometimes been the cause of violent conflicts; "but the most common and durable source of factions has been the various and unequal distribution of property. Those who hold and those who are without property have ever formed distinct interests in society. Those who are creditors, and those who are debtors, fall under a like discrimination. A landed interest, a manufacturing interest, a mercantile interest, a moneyed interest,

with many lesser interests grow up of necessity in civilized nations, and divide them into different classes actuated by different sentiments and views."

3. The theories of government which men entertain are emotional reactions to their property interests. "From the protection of different and unequal faculties of acquiring property, the possession of different degrees and kinds of property immediately results; *and from the influence of these on the sentiments and views of the respective proprietors, ensues a division of society into different interests and parties*." Legislatures reflect these interests. "What," he asks, "are the different classes of legislators but advocates and parties to the causes which they determine." These is no help for it. "The causes of faction cannot be removed," and "we well know that neither moral nor religious motives can be relied on as an adequate control."

4. Unequal distribution of property is inevitable, and from it contending factions will rise in the state. The government will reflect them, for they will have their separate principles and "sentiments"; but the supreme danger will arise from the fusion of certain interests into an overbearing majority, which Madison, in another place, prophesied would be the landless proletariat,—an overbearing majority which will make its "rights" paramount, and sacrifice the "rights" of the minority. "To secure the public good," he declares, "and private rights against the danger of such a faction and at the same time preserve the spirit and the form of popular government is then the great object to which our inquiries are directed."

5. How is this to be done? Since the contending classes cannot be eliminated and their interests are bound to be reflected in politics, the only way out lies in mak-

ing it difficult for enough contending interests to fuse into a majority, and in balancing one over against another. The machinery for doing this is created by the new Constitution and by the Union. (*a*) Public views are to be refined and enlarged "by passing them through the medium of a chosen body of citizens." (*b*) The very size of the Union will enable the inclusion of more interests so that the danger of an overbearing majority is not so great. "The smaller the society, the fewer probably will be the distinct parties and interests composing it; the fewer the distinct parties and interests, the more frequently will a majority be found of the same party. . . . Extend the sphere, and you take in a greater variety of parties and interests; you make it less probable that a majority of the whole will have a common motive to invade the rights of other citizens; or if such a common motive exists, it will be more difficult for all who feel it to discover their strength and to act in unison with each other."

Q. E. D., "in the extent and proper structure of the Union, therefore, we behold a republican remedy for the diseases most incident to republican government."[3] . . .

Nevertheless, it may be asked why, if the protection of property rights lay at the basis of the new system, there is in the Constitution no provision for property qualifications for voters or for elected officials and representatives. This is, indeed, peculiar when it is recalled that the constitutional history of England is in a large part a record of conflict over the weight in the government to be enjoyed by definite economic groups, and over the removal of the property qualifications early imposed on members of the House of Commons and on the voters at large. But the explanation of the absence of property qualifications from the Constitution is not difficult.

The members of the Convention were, in general, not opposed to property qualifications as such, either for officers or voters. "Several propositions," says Mr. S. H. Miller, "were made in the federal Convention in regard to property qualifications. A motion was carried instructing the committee to fix upon such qualifications for members of Congress. The committee could not agree upon the amount and reported in favor of leaving the matter to the legislature. Charles Pinckney objected to this plan as giving too much power to the first legislature. . . . Ellsworth objected to a property qualification on account of the difficulty of fixing the amount. If it was made high enough for the South, it would not be applicable to the Eastern States. Franklin was the only speaker who opposed the proposition to require property on principle, saying that 'some of the greatest rogues he was ever acquainted with were the richest rogues.' A resolution was also carried to require a property qualification for the Presidency. Hence it was evident that the lack of all property requirements for office in the United States Constitution was not owing to any opposition of the convention to such qualifications per se."

Propositions to establish property restrictions were defeated, not because they were believed to be inherently opposed to the genius of American government, but for economic reasons—strange as it may seem. These economic reasons were clearly set forth by Madison in the debate over landed qualifications for legislators in July, when he showed, first, that slight property qualifications would not keep out the small farmers whose paper money schemes had been so disastrous to personalty; and, secondly, that landed property qualifications would exclude from Congress the representatives of "those classes of citizens who were not landholders," *i.e.* the personalty interests. This was true, he thought, because the mercantile and manufacturing classes would hardly be willing to turn their personalty into sufficient quantities of landed property to make them eligible for a seat in Congress.

The other members also knew that they had most to fear from the very electors who would be enfranchised under a slight freehold restriction, for the paper money party was everywhere bottomed on the small farming class. As Gorham remarked, the elections at Philadelphia, New York, and Boston, "where the merchants and mechanics vote, are at least as good as those made by freeholders only." The fact emerges, therefore, that the personalty interests reflected in the Convention could, in truth, see no safeguard at all in a freehold qualification against the assaults on vested personalty rights which had been made by the agrarians in every state. And it was obviously impossible to establish a personalty test, had they so desired, for there would have been no chance of securing a ratification of the Constitution at the hands of legislatures chosen by freeholders, or at the hands of conventions selected by them.

A very neat example of this antagonism between realty and personalty in the Convention came out in July 26, when Mason made, and Charles Pinckney supported, a motion imposing landed qualifications on members of Congress and excluding from that body "persons having unsettled accounts with or being indebted to the United States." In bringing up this motion Mason "observed that persons of the latter descriptions had frequently got into the state legislatures in order to promote laws that might shelter their delinquencies; and that this evil had crept into Congress if report was to be regarded."

Gouverneur Morris was on his feet in an instant. If qualifications were to be imposed, they should be laid on electors, not elected persons. The disqualification would fall upon creditors of the United States, for there were but few who owed the government anything. He knew that under this rule very few members of the Convention could get into the new government which they were establishing. "As to persons having unsettled accounts, he believed them to be pretty many. He thought, however, that such a discrimination would be both odious and useless and in many instances unjust and cruel. The delay of settlement had been more the fault of the public than of individuals. What will be done with those patriotic Citizens who have lent money or services or property to their country, without having been yet able to obtain a liquidation of their claims? Are they to be excluded?" On thinking it over, Morris added to his remarks on the subject, saying, "It was a precept of great antiquity as well as of high authority that we should not be righteous overmuch. He thought we ought to be equally on our guard against being wise overmuch. . . . The parliamentary qualifications quoted by Colonel Mason had been disregarded in practice; and was but a scheme of the landed against the monied interest."

Gerry thought that the inconvenience of excluding some worthy creditors and debtors was of less importance than the advantages offered by the resolution, but, after some reflection, he added that "if property be one object of government, provisions for securing it cannot be improper." King sagely remarked that there might be a great danger in imposing a landed qualification, because "it would exclude the monied interest, whose aids may be essential in particular emergencies to the public safety."

Madison had no confidence in the effectiveness of the landed qualification and moved to strike it out, adding, "Landed possessions were no certain evidence of real wealth. Many enjoyed them to a great extent who were more in debt than they were worth. The unjust laws of the states had proceeded more from this class of men than any others. It had often happened that men who had acquired landed property on credit got into the Legislatures with a view of promoting an unjust protection against their Creditors. In the next place, if a small quantity of land should be made the standard, it would be no security; if a large one, it would exclude the proper representatives of those classes of Citizens who were not landholders." For these and other reasons he opposed the landed qualifications and suggested that property qualifications on the voters would be better.

The motion to strike out the "landed" qualifications for legislators was carried by a vote of ten to one; the proposition to strike out the disqualification of persons having unsettled accounts with the United States was carried by a vote of nine to two. Finally the proposition to exclude persons who were indebted to the United States was likewise defeated by a vote of nine to two, after Pinckney had called attention to the fact that "it would exclude persons who had purchased confiscated property and might be some obstacle to the sale of the latter."

Indeed, there was little risk to personalty in thus allowing the Constitution to go to the states for approval without any property qualifications on voters other than those which the state might see fit to impose. Only one branch of new govern-

8. DID SELF-INTEREST MOTIVATE THE CONSTITUTION?

ment, the House of Representatives, was required to be elected by popular vote; and, in case popular choice of presidential electors might be established, a safeguard was secured by the indirect process. Two controlling bodies, the Senate and Supreme Court, were removed altogether from the possibility of popular election except by constitutional amendment. Finally, the conservative members of the Convention were doubly fortified in the fact that nearly all of the state constitutions then in force provided real or personal property qualifications for voters anyway, and radical democratic changes did not seem perilously near.

NOTES

1. A great deal of this valuable material has been printed in the *Documentary History of the Constitution*, Vols. IV and V; a considerable amount has been published in the letters and papers of the eminent men of the period; but an enormous mass still remains in manuscript form. Fortunately, such important papers as those of Washington, Hamilton, Madison, and others are in the Library of Congress; but they are not complete, of course.

2. From this point of view, the old conception of the battle at Philadelphia as a contest between small and large states—as political entities—will have to be severely modified. See Professor Farrand's illuminating paper on the so-called compromises of the Constitution in the *Report of the American Historical Association, 1903*, Vol. I, pp. 73 ff. J.C. Welling, "States' Rights Conflict over the Public Lands," *ibid.* (1888), pp. 184 ff.

3. This view was set forth by Madison in a letter to Jefferson in 1788. "Wherever the real power in a Government lies, there is the danger of oppression. In our Governments the real power lies in the majority of the Community, and the invasion of private rights is *chiefly* to be apprehended, not from acts of Government contrary to the sense of its constituents, but from acts in which the Government is the mere instrument of the major number of the constituents. This is a truth of great importance, but not yet sufficiently attended to, and is probably more strongly impressed upon my mind by facts, and reflections suggested by them, than on yours which has contemplated abuses of power issuing from a very different quarter. Wherever there is an interest and power to do wrong, wrong will generally be done, and not less readily by a powerful and interested party than by a powerful and interested prince." *Documentary History of the Constitution*, Vol. V, p. 88.

NO
Forrest McDonald

A REVALUATION
OF THE BEARD THESIS OF THE
MAKING OF THE CONSTITUTION

Professor Beard interpreted the making of the Constitution as a simple, clear-cut series of events. When all the groups that became Federalists are brought together and analyzed, he asserted, and all the anti-Federalists are brought together and analyzed, the events can be seen as mere manifestations of a fundamentally simple economic conflict. His analysis led him to formulate three basic propositions, one regarding the Philadelphia Convention and two regarding the contest over ratification. [We] may now focus our attention upon these three key propositions of Beard's economic interpretation of the Constitution.

THE PHILADELPHIA CONVENTION

From his analysis of the Philadelphia Convention, Beard concluded that the Constitution was essentially "an economic document drawn with superb skill" by a "consolidated economic group . . . whose property interests were immediately at stake"; that these interests "knew no state boundaries but were truly national in their scope."

From a thorough reconsideration of the Philadelphia Convention, however, the following facts emerge. Fully a fourth of the delegates in the convention had voted in their state legislatures for paper-money and/or debtor-relief laws. These were the very kinds of laws which, according to Beard's thesis, the delegates had convened to prevent. Another fourth of the delegates had important economic interests that were adversely affected, directly and immediately, by the Constitution they helped write. The most common and by far the most important property holdings of the delegates were not, as Beard has asserted, mercantile, manufacturing, and public security investments, but agricultural property. Finally, it is abundantly evident that the delegates, once inside the Convention, behaved as anything but a consolidated economic group.

8. DID SELF-INTEREST MOTIVATE THE CONSTITUTION?

In the light of these and other facts presented [elsewhere], it is impossible to justify Beard's interpretation of the Constitution as "an economic document" drawn by a "consolidated economic group whose property interests were immediately at stake."

THE CONTEST OVER RATIFICATION, FIRST PROPOSITION

Beard asserted that the ultimate test of the validity of an economic interpretation of the Constitution would rest upon a comparative analysis of the economic interests of all the persons voting for and all the persons voting against ratification. He made an analysis of the economic interests of some of the leaders in the movement for ratification and concluded that "in ratification, it became manifest that the line of cleavage for and against the Constitution was between substantial personality interests on the one hand and the small farming and debtor interests on the other."

For the purpose of analyzing this proposition it is necessary to employ Beard's own definitions of interest groups. In the paragraphs that follow, as [elsewhere], the term "men of personalty interests" is used to mean those groups which Beard himself had in mind when he used the term, namely money, public securities, manufacturing and shipping, and western lands held for speculation.

From a thorough reconsideration of the contest over ratification the following facts emerge.

1. In three states (Delaware, New Jersey, and Georgia) the decisions of the ratifying conventions were unanimous, and it is therefore impossible to compare the interests of contending parties. The following analyses of the conventions in these three states may be made, however.

In Delaware almost 77 percent of the delegates were farmers, more than two-thirds of them small farmers with incomes ranging from 75 cents to $5.00 a week. Slightly more than 23 percent of the delegates were professional men—doctors, judges, and lawyers. None of the delegates was a merchant, manufacturer, banker, or speculator in western lands.

In New Jersey 64.1 percent of the delegates were farmers, 23.1 percent were professional men (physicians, lawyers, and college presidents), and only 12.8 percent were men having personalty interests (one merchant, three iron manufacturers, and one capitalist with diversified investments).

In Georgia 50 percent of the delegates were farmers (38.5 percent slave-owning planters and 11.5 percent small farmers), 11.5 percent were frontiersmen whose economic interests were primarily agrarian, 19.2 percent were professional men (lawyers, physicians, and professional officeholders), and only 11.5 percent had personalty interests (all merchants). The interests of 7.7 percent of the delegates were not ascertained.

Beard assumed that ratification in these states was pushed through by a personalty interest groups before agrarian and paper-money groups could organize their forces. The opposite is true. In each of these three states agrarian interests dominated the conventions. In each state there were approximately equal numbers of delegates who had voted earlier for and against paper money.

2. In two states in which the decision was contested (Virginia and North Carolina) the great majority of the delegates on both sides of the question were farmers. In both states the delegates who voted for and the delegates who voted against ratification had substantially the same amounts of the same kinds of property, most com-

monly land and slaves. A large number of the delegates in the Virginia convention had voted on the question of repudiation of debts due British merchants, and the majority of the delegates who had favored such repudiation voted for ratification of the Constitution. Large numbers of delegates in both North Carolina conventions were speculating in western lands. In the first convention a great majority of these land speculators opposed the Constitution; in the second a substantial majority of them favored ratification.

Beard assumed that ratification in these states represented the victory of wealthy planters, especially those who were rich in personalty other than slaves, over the small slaveless farmers and debtors. The opposite is true. In both states the wealthy planters—those with personalty interests as well as those without personalty interests—were divided approximately equally on the issue of ratification. In North Carolina small farmers and debtors were likewise equally divided, and in Virginia the great mass of the small farmers and a large majority of the debtors favored ratification.

3. In four states (Connecticut, Maryland, South Carolina, and New Hampshire) agrarian interests were dominant, but large minorities of delegates had personalty interests.

In Connecticut 57.8 percent of the delegates who favored ratification and 67.5 percent of those who opposed ratification were farmers. Ratification was approved by 76.2 percent of all the delegates, by 81.8 percent of the delegates having personalty interests, and by 73.3 percent of the farmers in the convention. Here, then, four delegates out of five having substantial personalty interests favored the Constitution. On the other hand, three of every four farmers also favored the Constitution.

In Maryland 85.8 percent of the delegates who voted for ratification were farmers, almost all of them wealthy slave-owning planters. The opponents of ratification included from three to six times as large a proportion of merchants, lawyers, and investors in shipping, confiscated estates, and manufacturing as did the delegates who favored ratification. It is to be observed, however, that because the vote in the Maryland ratifying convention was almost unanimous (63 to 11), statistics on the attitudes of the various interest groups would show that every major interest group except manufacturers favored the Constitution. A majority of the areas and of the delegates that had advocated paper money also favored the Constitution.

In South Carolina 59 percent of the delegates who voted for ratification were large slave-owning planters and 10.7 percent were lesser planters and farmers. Of the delegates who voted against ratification, 41.7 percent were large slave-owning planters and 34.2 percent were lesser planters and farmers. Merchants, factors, mariners favored ratification, 70 percent to 30 percent, a margin almost identical to the vote of the entire convention—67 percent for, 33 percent against—and manufacturers, artisans, and mechanics were unanimous in support of the Constitution. On the other hand, 35.7 percent of the delegates who favored ratification were debtors who were in a desperate plight or had borrowed paper money from the state. Only 15.1 percent of those who voted against ratification were debtors or had borrowed paper money from the state. No fewer than 82 percent of the debtors and borrowers of paper money in the convention voted for ratification.

As respects New Hampshire, comparisons are difficult because of the lack of adequate information concerning 28.2

percent of the delegates. Of the delegates whose interests are known, 36.9 percent of those favoring the Constitution and 25 percent of those opposing it were farmers; of the known farmers in the convention 68.7 percent favored ratification. If it is assumed, however, that all the delegates whose interests are not ascertainable were farmers (as in all likelihood most of them were), then 49.1 percent of the delegates favoring ratification were farmers, 54.3 percent of those opposing ratification were farmers, and 52.8 percent of the farmers in the convention voted for ratification. Delegates whose interests were primarily in personalty (merchants, tradesmen, manufacturers, and shipbuilders) voted in favor of ratification, 60.9 percent to 39.1 percent. Delegates from the towns which had voted for and against paper money divided almost equally on the question of ratification: 42 percent of the towns that had voted for paper money and 54 percent of those that had voted against paper sent delegates who voted for the Constitution.

Beard assumed that in these states ratification was the outcome of class struggles between commercial and other personalty groups (Federalists) on the one hand and farmers and advocates of paper money (anti-Federalists) on the other. This generalization is groundless. In each of these states a majority of the men having personalty interests favored ratification, but in each of them a similar majority of the farmers also favored ratification. In one of these states there was no great demand for paper money, in another a large majority of the friends of paper money favored ratification, and in the other two the advocates of paper money were divided almost equally on the question of ratification.

4. In four states (Massachusetts, Pennsylvania, New York, and Rhode Island) men having personalty interests were in a majority in the ratifying conventions.

In Massachusetts, in the popular vote (excluding that of Maine) men whose interests were primarily non-agrarian favored the Constitution by about three to two, and men whose interests were primarily agrarian opposed the Constitution by about 55 percent to 45 percent. In the ratifying convention 80 percent of the merchants and shippers engaged in water-borne commerce, 77 percent of the artisans and mechanics, and 64 percent of the farmers favored ratification. About 83 percent of the retail storekeepers, 85 percent of the manufacturers, and 64 percent of the miscellaneous capitalists opposed ratification. One-fourth of those favoring and one-sixth of those opposing the Constitution were farmers. Of the personalty groups combined, 57.5 percent opposed and 42.5 percent favored ratification. The realty groups combined, including artisans and mechanics, favored ratification by 67 percent to 33 percent.

In Pennsylvania only 34.8 percent of the delegates favoring ratification were farmers, and only 26.1 percent of the opponents were farmers. Almost three-fourths—72.7 percent—of the farmers in the convention favored ratification. The great majority of the delegates on both sides, however, 84.7 percent of those favoring and 91.3 percent of those opposing the Constitution, had substantial investments in one or more of Professor Beard's four forms of personalty.

New York delegates are difficult to classify as farmers because almost all farmers in the convention were also landlords with tenants. Delegates to the state's convention may be classified as elected Federalists, converts from anti-Federalism, delegates who abstained from voting, and anti-Federalists. Of the delegates about whom there is sufficient data on which to generalize, fewer than 20 percent of each group consisted of farmers who had no tenants and who owned none of Beard's four forms of personality.

Rhode Island delegates do not lend themselves to occupational classification because almost everyone in the state normally combined in his own economic activities several kinds of functions. Only 11.8 percent of the delegates favoring ratification and only one of the delegates opposing ratification were found to have no interests except farming. The early opponents of paper money formed the original core of those favoring ratification, yet in the final vote 62 percent of the delegates voting for ratification and 63 percent of those opposing ratification were men who had borrowed money from the state.

Beard's thesis—that the line of cleavage as regards the Constitution was between substantial personalty interests on the one hand and small farming and debtor interests on the other—is entirely incompatible with the facts.

THE CONTEST OVER RATIFICATION, SECOND PROPOSITION

Beard was less certain of the foregoing point, however, than he was of this next one:

Inasmuch as so many leaders in the movement for ratification were large security holders, and inasmuch as securities constituted such a large proportion of personalty, this economic interest must have formed a very considerable dynamic element, if not the preponderating element, in bringing about the adoption of the new system. . . . Some holders of public securities are found among the opponents of the Constitution, but they are not numerous.

This proposition may be analyzed in the same manner that Beard's more general personality-agrarian conclusion was analyzed. To repeat, Beard asserted that public securities were the dynamic element within the dynamic element in the ratification. This assertion is incompatible with the facts. The facts are these:

1. In three states (Delaware, New Jersey, and Georgia) there were no votes against the Constitution in the ratifying conventions, and hence no comparisons can be made. If public securities were the dynamic element in the ratification, however, it would be reasonable to expect that the great majority of delegates in these states which supported the Constitution so unreservedly should have been security holders. But the fact is that in Delaware only one delegate in six owned securities, in New Jersey 34 percent of the delegates, and in Georgia only one delegate.

2. In two states (New Hampshire and North Carolina) the numbers of security holders among the delegates were very small. In New Hampshire only 10.5 percent of those who voted for and only 2.2 percent of those who voted against ratification held securities. In the first North Carolina convention only 2.4 percent of the friends and only 1.1 percent of the opponents of ratification held securities. In the second convention only 2.0 percent of those favoring and only 3.9 percent of those opposing the Constitution were security holders. Superficially these facts tend to substantiate Beard's thesis, for these virtually security-less states were slow to ratify the Constitution. It has been shown, however, that actually the reluctance of these states to adopt the Constitution and their vulnerability to raids on their securities by outsiders were both merely surface manifestations of the same underlying conditions—the isolation, the lack of information, and the lethargy of the

majority of the inhabitants of North Carolina and New Hampshire.

3. In three states (Rhode Island, Maryland, and Virginia) where there were contests and considerable numbers of security holders, the advocates and the opponents of ratification included approximately the same percentages of security holders: in Rhode Island, 50 percent of the advocates and 47 percent of the opponents; in Virginia, 40.5 percent of the advocates and 34.2 percent of the opponents; and in Maryland, 17.4 percent and 27.3 percent respectively. The facts relative to these three states clearly contradict Beard's thesis.

4. In two states (Massachusetts and Connecticut) the advocates of ratification included a considerably larger percentage of holders of securities than did the opponents. In Massachusetts 31 percent of the ratificationists and only 10.1 percent of the anti-ratificationists were security owners, and in Connecticut 36.7 percent and 15 percent respectively. The situations in these two states, and in these two states alone, tend strongly to support Beard's thesis.

5. In three states (Pennsylvania, South Carolina, and New York) a considerably larger percentage of the delegates opposing ratification than of the Federalist delegates held public securities. In Pennsylvania 73.9 percent of the opponents and 50 percent of the supporters of ratification were security owners, in South Carolina 71 and 43 percent respectively, and in New York 63 and 50 percent respectively. The facts pertaining to these states not only fail to harmonize with Beard's thesis but indicate that there the precise opposite of his thesis is true.

In the light of the foregoing facts it is abundantly evident that there are no more grounds for considering the holding of public securities the dynamic element in the ratification than for considering this economic interest the dynamic element in the opposition. There were, indeed, some holders of public securities among the opponents of the Constitution and, contrary to Beard's assertion, they were as numerous as the security holders among the supporters of the Constitution.

On all counts, then, Beard's thesis is entirely incompatible with the facts. Beard's essential error was in attempting to formulate a single set of generalizations that would apply to all the states. Any such effort is necessarily futile, for the various interest groups operated under different conditions in the several states, and their attitudes toward the Constitution varied with the internal conditions in their states.

POSTSCRIPT

DID ECONOMIC SELF-INTEREST MOTIVATE THE WRITING AND RATIFICATION OF THE FEDERAL CONSTITUTION?

Was there a "miracle in Philadelphia" in 1787? Or, was it in Providence in 1790 when Rhode Island became the last state to ratify the Constitution? The vote there tallied 34 to 32, the narrowest margin in all of the thirteen legislatures. As both Beard and McDonald make clear, the writing of the Constitution was only one stage of the process of changing our national government. Ratification, a separate event, merits equal attention. In drawing their conclusions, however, Beard and McDonald each emphasize one of these developments at the expense of the other. Beard thinks the writing of the Constitution along with the Federalist arguments in *The Federalist Papers* takes precedence. McDonald, on the other hand, makes the ratification process in the state legislatures the topic of his conclusion.

There are other important differences between these two opposing historical interpretations. Both professors differ over the kind of historical evidence on which they rely. Beard quoted extensively from literary sources, believing that *The Federalist Papers* accurately reflected the opinions of those who favored ratification. McDonald depended on cliometrics, the use of statistics or quantification in history. Is one of these kinds of historical documentation necessarily more reliable than the other? Do actions better reveal human motives than words? Moreover, are these two types of evidence, along with the interpretations they produce, mutually exclusive? Are there more areas of agreement than McDonald recognized? Is it not possible that the Constitution was written to benefit particular economic interests? Conversely, was it ratified, in most cases, for very different reasons?

Among the books in the extensive historiography of this subject, students will find the following useful. The theme of economic conflict after the Revolution is developed in Merrill Jensen, *The New Nation: A History of the United States During the Confederation, 1781-1789* (Knopf, 1950) and Jackson T. Main, *The Anti-Federalists: Critics of the Constitution, 1781-1788* (University of North Carolina Press, 1961). Another historian who has criticized Beard is Robert E. Brown, *Charles Beard and the Constitution* (Princeton University Press, 1956). Forrest McDonald has also written *E Pluribus Unum: The Formation of the American Republic, 1776-1790* (Houghton-Mifflin, 1965).

ISSUE 9

WAS PRESIDENT JEFFERSON AN OPPONENT OF CIVIL LIBERTIES?

YES: Leonard W. Levy, from *Jefferson and Civil Liberties: The Darker Side* (Harvard University Press, 1963)

NO: Morton Borden, from "Thomas Jefferson," in Morton Borden, ed., *America's Ten Greatest Presidents* (Rand McNally, 1961)

ISSUE SUMMARY

YES: Historian Leonard Levy contends that Jefferson was a messianic nationalist who often violated in practice the lofty theoretical standards of civil liberties which he espoused.
NO: Historian Morton Borden believes that President Jefferson was a moderate and pragmatic politician who placed the nation's best interests above those of the individual states.

"Jefferson still lives," stated John Adams as he died on July 4, 1826, the fiftieth anniversary of Independence Day. Unknown to Adams, Jefferson had passed away a few hours earlier that same day. But Jefferson never really died. He was one of the few heroes of history to become a living legend.

There are two Jeffersons. The first was the true "Renaissance man" who knew a little about everything. "Not a sprig of grass shoots uninteresting to me," he once wrote to his daughter. As a philosopher who spoke to posterity, he waxed eloquent in his letters about civil liberties, the rights of man, states' rights, strict construction of the Constitution and the virtues of the agrarian way of life. Our most intellectual president was also our most practical. He was an architect of the nation's capital, the University of Virginia, and his own home. Visitors to his Monticello plantation are amazed by the elaborate pulley and drainage systems which he devised. A respected member of the Virginia aristocracy who owned about 10,000 acres and from one hundred to two hundred slaves, Jefferson ran his farm in a self-sufficient manner and carefully studied the efficiency of employing slave labor. When he traveled, he recorded everything he observed in detailed journals. The newest inventions—steam engines, thermometers, elevators—fascinated him.

The second Jefferson was the man who has been ranked among the top half-dozen United States presidents in every major poll taken by historians in the last thirty-five years. Does Jefferson deserve such an honor? It depends on how the functions of the presidency are perceived. One role which Jefferson disdained more than any other president in our history is the function of chief of state. So important to the modern presidency, the ceremonial role could have been played by the tall, dignified Virginia aristocrat as well as it was by George Washington, had he so desired. But Jefferson hated formalities. He walked to his inauguration and refused to wear a hat as did the later President, Jimmy Carter. Because he was a widower, he abandoned the practice of holding large, formal parties. He also felt they smacked too much of monarchy. He preferred small, intimate dinners with his intellectual friends and political cronies. A shy, soft-spoken individual who possessed a slight speech impediment, the author of the Declaration of Independence did not campaign for office. He also refused to deliver an annual address to Congress, preferring to send them a well-written message. In short, if one uses modern terminology, Jefferson was not "mediagenic." In 1984, Jefferson might not have even been nominated by his party, much less elected to the office of the presidency.

In the first selection, Leonard Levy levels a further charge against Jefferson. A superficial thinker who held no coherent philosophical views on civil liberties, Jefferson the politician often violated in practice the very principles he espoused in theory. On various occasions, the "sage of Monticello" supported loyalty oaths, urged prosecutions for seditious libel, used the army to enforce laws in time of peace, and endorsed the doctrine that the end justifies the means. Levy's essay is an excellent antidote to those writers who view Jefferson as the prophet of infinite wisdom on questions of freedom.

Few historians accept Levy's view that Jefferson was a messianic nationalist. In the second selection, Professor Morton Borden argues that President Jefferson was a moderate and pragmatic politician who placed the national interests of the country above those of the individual states. His first administration was extremely successful. Abroad he waged a winning war against the Barbary pirates and eliminated the unnecessary bribes previously paid to those rogues. With the stroke of a pen, the purchase of Louisiana from France removed the potential threat to American security posed by Napoleon, eliminated the need for a military alliance with England, and doubled the size of the United States. At home, the public debt was gradually erased, internal taxes reduced or eliminated, and a peaceful transition of power was made from the Federalist to the Republican-Democratic party.

YES

Leonard W. Levy

JEFFERSON AS A LIBERTARIAN: CONCLUSIONS ON THE DARKER SIDE

... Jefferson was not larger than life; he was human and held great power. His mistaken judgments were many, his failings plentiful. Much of Jefferson that passed for wisdom has passed out of date. He was, to be sure, a libertarian, and American civil liberties were deeply in his debt. But he was scarcely the constantly faithful libertarian and rarely, if ever, the courageous one.

The finest moments of American liberty occurred when men defied popular prejudices and defended right and justice at the risk of destroying their own careers. Thus John Adams, at a peak of passionate opposition to the British, defended the hated redcoats against a charge of murder growing out of the Boston Massacre. By contrast Thomas Jefferson never once risked career or reputation to champion free speech, fair trial, or any other libertarian value. On many occasions he was on the wrong side. On others he trimmed his sails and remained silent.

As Secretary of State Jefferson signed the proclamation against the Whiskey Rebels;[1] as Vice President and presiding officer of the Senate, he signed the warrant of arrest for William Duane for a seditious contempt of that august body.[2] Jefferson chose the easy path of lawful performance of his duties instead of conscientious opposition on the ground that liberty and justice were being victimized. In neither case did he speak out *publicly*. He signed in silence and characteristically complained in his private correspondence about the government's abridgments of freedom. His opposition to the Alien and Sedition Acts is famous: what is not so well known is that he never publicly declared his opposition during the period of hysteria. He kept his participation in the Kentucky Resolutions of 1798–99 a secret. In the winter of liberty's danger there was the greatest need for the heated and undisguised voice of dissent to be heard in the land. ...

He was capable of ruthlessness in the exercise of power. As President he behaved as if compensating for his notorious weakness as wartime governor of

Excerpted from *Jefferson and Civil Liberties: The Darker Side*, by Leonard Levy. Copyright ©1963. Reprinted by permission of the author and Harvard University Press.

Virginia, when constitutional scruples and an inclination to shrink from the harsher aspects of politics had made him incapable of bold leadership. Thereafter he acted as if he had disciplined himself to serve in office with energy and decisiveness, at whatever cost. A hard resolution to lead and triumph certainly characterized his presidency.

Often the master politician, he was not averse to the most devious and harsh tactics to achieve his ends. Usually gentle and amiable in his personal relationships, he possessed a streak of wilfulness that sometimes expressed itself in flaring temper, violence, and toughness. His grandson portrayed him as a "bold and fearless" horseman who loved to ride booted with whip in hand. "The only impatience of temper he ever exhibited," recalled Thomas Jefferson Randolph, "was with his horse, which he subdued to his will by a fearless application of the whip, on the slightest manifestation of restiveness."[3] He rode the nation in the same way, booted and spurred during the embargo days, notwithstanding the fact that one of his most memorable utterances announced his belief that mankind had not been born with saddles on their backs to be ridden booted and spurred by those in power over them.[4]

It is revealing that Jefferson arrogated to himself the power to decide personally how much bread, and with what degree of whiteness, the American people could eat during the embargo.[5] He regulated the nation down to its table fare, despite an aversion to centralized government and a dedication to the belief that domestic concerns were a matter of personal or local government. The eye of President Jefferson was so prying, his enemies bitterly joked, that a baby couldn't be born without clearance from a government customs house.

Practices once reprehended by Jefferson as shocking betrayals of natural and constitutional rights suddenly seemed innocent, even necessary and salutary, when the government was in his hands. His accession to power seemed to stimulate a fresh understanding of the existence of public dangers requiring forceful measures that often did not result in a union of principle and practice. When, for example, the party faithful were victims of the Sedition Act, unchecked tyranny was abroad in the land with frightening consequences for the future of liberty. When he was in power the uncontrolled licentiousness and malice of the opposition press took on the hideous features of sedition, deserving of a few exemplary prosecutions to protect the public. Jefferson's presidency, particularly the second term which witnessed the federal sedition prosecutions in Connecticut, the Wilkinson-Burr imbroglio and trials, and the five embargo acts, was an obligato on the arts of political manipulation and severity.

Some of his antilibertarianism can be explained by the ironic fact that he was, in the words of a clear-eyed admirer, a "terrifying idealist, tinged with fanaticism."[6] What other sort of man would impersonally applaud a little bloodletting now and then to fertilize the tree of liberty? Jefferson held his convictions with a fierceness that admitted little room for compromise—if he was in a position of power to deny it—and no room for self-doubt. Unduly sensitive to criticism by others, he wore a hair shirt— often a dangerous attire for a politician— which covered a spirit rarely capable of objective disinterestedness.

Jefferson had the mentality and passion of a true believer, certain that he was absolutely right, a marked contrast to the skepticism of modern libertarians such as Justice Oliver Wendell Holmes or Judge Learned Hand. Holmes believed that the first mark of a civilized man was the capacity to doubt his own first principles, while Hand remarked that the spirit of liberty was the spirit which was not too sure that it was right. Jefferson was a product of the eighteenth century which regarded truths as immutable and self-evident. Yet philosophic truths concerning the nature of man or the first principles of government were not on a footing with practical legislation or executive policies. Jefferson had read Locke and the British empiricists as well as the Deists, scientists, and French *philosophies*. He might reasonably have been somewhat more skeptical of the rightness of his own favorite theories that he translated into national policy; he might have been less cocksure, less ready to subscribe to the proposition that certitude was the test of certainty.

In politics, particularly, where the art of the possible is often the highest value, making compromise a necessity, the capacity to doubt one's own convictions is indispensable.[7] The poorest compromise is almost invariably better than the best dictation which leaves little if any scope of freedom to the losing side and corrupts the spirit of those in power. In his old age Jefferson observed wisely: "A government held together by the bands of reason only, requires much compromise of opinion; that things even salutary should not be crammed down the throats of dissenting brethren, especially when they may be put into a form to be willingly swallowed, and that a good deal of indulgence is necessary to strengthen habits of harmony and fraternity."[8] The observation was not an abstract one. Jefferson was arguing at the time in behalf of a constitutional amendment that would authorize the national government—which by then he was denominating the "foreign" department in contrast to the states that composed the

"domestic" department—to build roads and canals.[9] He had an utterly exquisite constitutional conscience when he was not in power.

Jefferson's only constitutional qualms during his presidency concerned what he believed to be his questionable authority to purchase Louisiana. He never doubted for a moment the rightness of his behavior during the Burr and embargo episodes. The intensity of his convictions and his incapacity for self-criticism propelled him onward, more resolute than ever in the face of outside criticism. The certainty that he was right, combined with his terrifying idealism, led him to risk the fate of the nation on the chance that an experiment in commercial sanctions might prove a substitute for war. Opposition only goaded him to redouble his efforts to prove himself right. He behaved as if a prisoner of his ideas, or, to put the thought less charitably, as a doctrinaire "tinged with fanaticism."

The self-skeptic, the practical politician, and the democrat conduct themselves otherwise. Any one of them in a position of power tends to operate with an understanding of the necessity of compromise and the obnoxiousness, not to mention the immorality or political stupidity, of cramming legislation "down the throats of dissenting brethren." Legislation, as William James once observed about democracy generally, is a business in which something is done, followed by a pause to see who hollers; then the hollering is relieved as best it can be until someone else hollers. Jefferson, however, was faintly doctrinaire. Exhilarated by the experience of putting an idea in motion and backing it by force, he could not back down or admit that he had been wrong. What counted most was the attainment of his objective, the validation of his conviction, not its impact on those who, failing to appreciate his idealism or personal stake, hollered long and loud. He reacted not by relieving their hollering but by a stretch of the rack that increased their protests and his own power to override them.

Jefferson tended to stretch his political powers as he stretched his mind in intellectual matters, leaving his conscience behind—and sometimes his good sense. His voluminous correspondence showed no hint that he suffered from uncertainty or was tormented by his conscience when he so readily used the army to enforce the embargo and recklessly disregarded the injunctions of the Fourth Amendment. Lincoln in the greatest of all crises in American history had a supreme moral objective as well as a political one to sustain him; but he was constantly racked by self-doubt. The exercise of power, not always constitutionally justifiable, exacted of him a price that included melancholy and an agonized soul. In moments of despair he could doubt that Providence was with him and even that his position was indeed the morally superior one.

The contrast with Jefferson was towering. Thwarted by the courts in Burr's case, Jefferson doubted not himself but the loyalty of the judges. Evasions of the embargo filled him with astonishment not that his policy could have such a result but that the people could be so rankly fraudulent and corrupt. Rumors of resistance were matched by his impulse to crush it by force. There was no inner struggle in Jefferson; the tragedy of his antilibertarianism lacked poignancy. He was oblivious of the tragedy itself, symbolized by that moment of enormity when he approved of the use of any means, even if odious and arbitrary, to achieve his end.

Vanity, the enemy of self-doubt also played its role in fashioning his darker side. His *amour-propre* prevented him from

checking an illiberal act once begun or from admitting his error after the event. Witness his conduct of the Burr prosecutions and the way in which he was driven to defend Wilkinson. His persistent defense of his role in the case of Josiah Philips bears testimony to the same trait. When caught in a flagrancy as when it was revealed that he had hired the journalistic prostitute Callendar to poison the reputations of political opponents, or when he was accused of permitting the sedition prosecutions in Connecticut, he denied the truth. In deceiving others, as John Quincy Adams said, he deceived himself. In deceiving himself he denied himself insight into his abridgments of liberty, though he was acutely perceptive of abridgments by others.

Perhaps the chief explanation of his darker side was his conviction that the great American experiment in self-government and liberty was in nearly constant danger. He completely identified with that experiment, to the point that an attack on him or on the wisdom of his policies quickly became transmuted in his mind as a threat to the security of the tender democratic plant.

During the Revolution, coercive loyalty oaths and proscription of Tory opinions seemed a cheap price to pay when independence was the goal and the outcome was in doubt. The Alien and Sedition Acts, following the enactment of Hamilton's economic policies, forever convinced Jefferson that his political opponents were unalterably committed to the destruction of public liberty in America. In the flush of victory, at that splendid moment of the First Inaugural, he admitted the Federalists into the camp of loyal Americans, but not for long. If the scurrilousness of the Federalists press did not convince him that his magnanimous judgment had been mistaken, opposition to the purchase of Louisiana, coupled to threats of secession, proved his belief that popular government in America was imperiled. Burr's conspiracy brought the ugly menace to a head, justifying drastic countermeasures.

Open defiance of the embargo once again threw the Union's future info grave doubt. That defiance seemed to sabotage majority rule and the only hope of avoiding a war that might end the democratic experiment. In time of such acute crisis, when insurrection existed on a widespread basis and treason itself again loomed, the methods of Draco were tempting. The behavior of the Essex Junto during the War of 1812 reconfirmed Jefferson's worst fears. In the postwar period, from his hilltop at Monticello, he imagined that a monarchistic, clerical cabal had re-formed under a new party guise, employing doctrines of nationalistic consolidation to destroy public liberty.

Over the years he constantly sensed a conspiracy against republicanism. He had a feeling of being besieged by the enemies of freedom who would use it to subvert it. The face of the enemy changed—now that of a Tory; later that of a monarchist, a political priest, an Essex Juntoman, a Quid, or a Burrite; still later that of a judicial sapper-and-miner, an American-system consolidationist, or a Richmond lawyer. The face of the enemy or his name might change, but not his tory principles nor his subversive goal.

To the experiment of democracy in America, as Jefferson called it, he was committed heart, mind, and soul. Believing that experiment to be in grave jeopardy throughout most of his public life, he was capable of ruthlessness in defeating its enemies. His own goal was free men in a free society, but he did not always use freedom's instruments to attain it. He sometimes confused the goal with self-vindication or the triumph of his party. On other occasions instability and a lack of faith were revealed by his doubts of the opposition's loyalty. They were prone, he believed, to betray the principles of the Revolution as expressed in the Declaration of Independence. On still other occasions his eagerness to make America safe for democracy made him forgetful of Franklin's wise aphorism that they who seek safety at the expense of liberty deserve neither liberty nor safety.

The terrible complexities of any major issue, such as Burr's conspiracy or the embargo, particularly as seen from the White House, also help to explain Jefferson's conduct. The strain and responsibilities of the highest office did not stimulate the taking of bold risks on the side of liberty when it seemed to be pitted against national security. Moreover, problems had a way of presenting themselves in a form that mixed conflicting political considerations and obscured clear-cut decisions on libertarian merits. To a mind that was keenly alerted against the conspiracies of Federalist boogeymen and sensed a union between self, party, and nation, the virtue of an independent judiciary became the vice of judicial interference with majority rule; fair trial and a strict interpretation of treason became obstacles to the preservation of the Union; academic freedom became a guise for the dissemination of pernicious doctrines.

Jefferson's darker side derived in part, too, from the fact that he had no systematic and consistent philosophy of freedom. He was neither a seminal nor a profound thinker. Part of his genius consisted of his ability to give imperishable expression to old principles and to the deepest yearnings of his fellow citizens. Style, as much as substance, accounted for his staying power.

He once defended himself against the accusation that there was not a single fresh idea in the Declaration of Independence by replying that the objective was not to find new principles or arguments never before thought of. It was, rather,

> to place before mankind the common sense of the subject, in terms so plain and firm as to command their assent... Neither aiming at originality of principle or sentiment, nor yet copied from any particular and previous writing, it was intended to be an expression of the American mind, and to give to that expression the proper tone and spirit called for by the occasion. All its authority rests then on the harmonizing sentiments of the day.[10]

As a distinguished admirer has written, "Jefferson's seminal achievement was to institutionalize familiar eighteenth-century ideas. He made abstract notions about freedom a dominating faith and thereby the dynamic element in the strivings of men." Moreover he had the superlative talent of organizing a party that might realize his ideals by infusing the new nation with a sense of its special democratic destiny. But his failure to develop a theory of liberty existed and more than likely influenced his antilibertarian thought and action.

In the thousands of pages of his published works there is a notable scarcity of extended treatments on a single subject. Insatiably curious, he knew a little about nearly everything under the sun and a great deal more about law and politics than any man of his time. But in all his writings, over a period of fifty years of high productivity, there is not a single sustained analysis of liberty. He was pithy, felicitous, repetitive, and ever absorbed by the subject, but never wrote a book or even a tract on the meaning of liberty, its dimensions, limitations, and history.

That he made no contribution of this kind is not per se a criticism, for the brief preambles to the Declaration of Independence and the Virginia Statute of Religious Freedom are worth all the books that have been written on liberty. He had not, however, thought through the tough and perplexing problems posed by liberty: the conditions for its survival and promotion; the types of liberty and conflicts between them; the validity of various legal tests for measuring the scope of liberty or its permissible area of operation; and the competing claims of other values. ...

A philosopher of freedom without a philosophy of freedom, Jefferson was ill-equipped, by his ritualistic affirmations of nebulous and transcendental truths, to confront the problem posed by General Wilkinson's conduct in New Orleans, or the circulation of Hume's history of England in the colleges, or the savage distortions of the opposition press. He reacted expedientially on an *ad hoc* basis and too often hastily. Then his *amourpropre* prevented his candid acknowledgment of a mistaken judgment that demeaned the libertarian values he symbolized to the nation.

Regret and remorse are conspicuously absent from Jefferson's writings, as is reflective reconsideration of a problem. Something in his make-up, more than likely a stupendous ego, inhibited second thoughts. Whether he would deny the plain facts or stubbornly reiterate his original position, he failed to work out fresh guide lines for future conduct. Restatement, not re-evaluation, marked his thinking, and beneath an eloquently turned phrase there lurked a weary, problem-begging cliché. That it was commonplace rarely deprived it of its profundity as a libertarian principle. The "self-evident truths" of the Declaration of Independence will continue to survive all scorn of being "glittering generalities." They tend, however, to overarch real cases.

Jefferson, for example, might declare in his Second Inaugural Address, "If there be any among us who would wish to dissolve this Union or to change its republican form, let them stand undisturbed as monuments of the safety with which error of opinion may be tolerated where reason is left free to combat it." The principle was so broad that it failed to have pertinence for him when he learned that a few "political Priests" and "Federal printers," who had been confident that no federal court would take cognizance of their seditious calumnies, were being criminally prosecuted for their libels against him and his Administration. His awareness of the general distinction between preparation and attempt, or between conspiracy to commit treason and overt acts of treason, escaped application in the case of the Burrites, though not in the case of the Whiskey Rebels. A commitment to the large principle of intellectual liberty had no carry-over when the possibility arose that a "Richmond lawyer" might be appointed professor of law at the University of Virginia.

Maxims of liberty—"glittering generalities"—were frail props for a sound, realistic libertarianism. A mind filled with maxims will falter when put to the test of experience. A mind filled with maxims contents itself with the resonant quality of a noble utterance. Such a mind, although libertarian, cannot produce a libertarian analysis like Madison's *Report* of 1799–1800 on the Alien and Sedition Acts, or Wortman's *Treatise Concerning Political Enquiry.* Jefferson's only tracts and books were *A Summary View of the Rights of British America,* which was a protest against British encroachments on colonial freedom at the eve of the Revolution; *Notes on the State of Virginia,* a guidebook and utilitarian history; the *Manual of Parliamentary Practice;* his *Autobiography* and *The Anas,* which comprise his memoirs; *The Life and Morals of Jesus of Nazareth;* and the philological work, *Essay on Anglo-Saxon.* Despite his interest in freedom, its meaning did not interest him as a subject for even an essay. . . .

Though contributing little to any breakthroughs in libertarian thought, except in the important realm of freedom of religion, Jefferson more than any was responsible for the public sensitivity to libertarian considerations. If the quality of the new nation was measured by the ideals and aspirations that animated it, Jefferson had erred only slightly in confusing his own reputation with that of the democratic experiment. Notwithstanding the reciprocal scurrilities and suspicions of the opposed parties, or more importantly their conflicting interests, Americans were indeed all Federalists, all Republicans. They were equally attached to the "experiment in freedom" and the "empire of liberty." Anyone who depreciates the national commitment to libertarian values, which were bottomed on an extraordinary legal and political sophistication, deprives himself of an understanding of the times—and of the impact of Thomas Jefferson upon it. Jefferson cannot lightly be excused because he lived in an earlier time.

That Jefferson's libertarianism was considerably less than perfect or that his practice flagged behind his faith does not one whit diminish the achievements by which he is best remembered and should be. That he did not always adhere to his libertarian principles does not erode their enduring rightness. It proves only that Jefferson often set the highest standard of freedom for himself and posterity to be measured against. His legacy was the idea that as an indispensable condition for the development of free men in a free society, the state must be bitted and bridled by a Bill of Rights which should be construed in the most generous terms, its protections not to be the playthings of momentary majorities or of those in power.

NOTES

1. Rich, *Presidents and Civil Disorder*, p. 5.
2. James Morton Smith, *Freedom's Fetters: The Alien and Sedition Laws and American Civil Liberties* (Ithaca, N.Y., 1956), pp. 297–298, 299–300.
3. "My Grandfather, Mr. Jefferson," in Rosenberger, ed., *Jefferson Reader*, pp. 65–66.
4. Jefferson to Roger C. Weightman, June 24, 1826, in Lipscomb, XVI, 182.
5. See Jefferson to Gallatin, Sept. 9, 1808, in Lipscomb, XII, 161. See also, in *ibid.*, pp. 86, 95–96, 103, 111, 128, 130, 145–146, 169.
6. Dixon Wecter, "Thomas Jefferson, The Gentle Radical," in Rosenberger, ed., *Jefferson Reader*, p. 312, reprinting an essay from Wecter's *The Hero in America: A Chronicle of Hero-Worship* (New York, 1941).
7. Jefferson himself expressed a similar opinion in a letter to William Duane, the eminent Republican publisher. In the course of the letter Jefferson discoursed on the need for sensitivity to the possibility that one's own political judgments may be wrong when in conflict with those of the majority of one's party. He spoke of his own fallibility, the spirit of compromise, and the attribute of self-distrust. But the purpose of the letter was to bring Duane back to the Republican fold. He had been running editorials criticizing Madison's Administration, and Jefferson's remarks were calculated to discourage Duane from expressing independent judgment. The entire lecture on self-distrust and compromise was a tactical device to restore party unity by ridding the Republican press of dissent. Jefferson was scarcely admitting that he was or had ever been wrong; he was trying to convince Duane that he was wrong. See Jefferson to Duane, April 30, 1811, in Lipscomb, XIII, 47–52.
8. Jefferson to Edward Livingston, April 4, 1824, in *ibid.*, XVI, 25.
9. *Ibid.* See also Jefferson to William B. Giles, Dec. 26, 1825, in *ibid.*, p. 148.
10. Jefferson to Henry Lee, May 8, 1825, in *ibid.*, p. 118.

NO

Morton Borden

THOMAS JEFFERSON

For twelve years the Constitution worked, after a fashion. From its inception the new document had been subjected to severe trials and divisive strains. A rebellion in Pennsylvania, a naval war with France, a demand for states' rights from Virginia and Kentucky, and various Western schemes of disunion—all had been surmounted. Had it not been for the great prestige of George Washington and the practical moderation of John Adams, America's second attempt at a federal union might have failed like the first. Partisan passions had run high in the 1790's, and any single factor on which men disagreed—Hamilton's financial plans or the French Revolution or the Sedition Act—might easily have caused a stoppage of the nation's political machinery.

The two-party system emerged during this decade, and on each important issue public opinion seemed to oscillate between Federalist and Democratic-Republican. Perhaps this was to be expected of a young nation politically adolescent. Year by year Americans were becoming more politically alert and active; if there was little room for middle ground between these two factions, yet opinions were hardly fixed and irrevocable. The culmination of partisan controversy and the test of respective strengths took place in the monumental election of 1800.

Jefferson was feared, honestly feared, by almost all Federalists. Were he to win the election, so they predicted, all the hard constructive gains of those twelve years would be dissipated. Power would be returned to the individual states; commerce would suffer; judicial power would be lessened; and the wonderful financial system of Hamilton would be dismantled and destroyed. Jefferson was an atheist, and he would attack the churches. Jefferson was a hypocrite, an aristocrat posing as democrat, appealing to the baser motives of human beings in order to obtain votes. Jefferson was a revolutionary, a Francophile and, after ruining the Army and Navy under the guise of economy measures, might very well involve the nation in a war with England. In short, it was doubtful if the Constitution could continue its successful course under such a president.

Excerpted from "Thomas Jefferson," in *America's Ten Greatest Presidents,* Morton Borden, ed. Copyright ©1961 by Morton Borden. Reprinted by permission of Rand McNally & Co. and the author.

In like manner the Republicans feared another Federalist victory. To be sure, John Adams had split with Hamilton and had earned the enmity of the Essex Junto. But would he not continue Hamilton's "moneyed system"? Did not Adams share the guilt of every Federalist for the despicable Alien and Sedition Acts? Was it not true that "His Rotundity" so admired the British system that he was really a monarchist at heart? Republicans were not engaging in idle chatter, nor were they speaking solely for effect, when they predicted many dire consequences if Adams were elected. A typical rumor had Adams uniting "his house to that of his majesty of Britain" and "the bridegroom was to be king of America."

Throughout the country popular interest in the election was intense, an intensity sustained over months of balloting. When the Republicans carried New York City, Alexander Hamilton seriously suggested that the results be voided. And when the breach between Adams and Hamilton became public knowledge, Republicans nodded knowingly and quoted the maxim: "When thieves fall out, honest men come by their own."

The Federalists were narrowly defeated. But the decision was complicated by a result which many had predicted: a tied electoral vote between the two Republican candidates, Aaron Burr and Thomas Jefferson. (Indeed, the Twelfth Amendment was adopted in 1804 to avoid any such recurrence.) A choice between the two would be made by the House of Representatives. At this moment, February, 1801, the Constitution seemed on the verge of collapse. Federalist members of the lower house united in support of Burr; Republicans were just as adamant for Jefferson. After thirty-five ballots, neither side had yet obtained the necessary majority. The issue seemed hopelessly deadlocked. What would happen on March 4, inauguration day?

One representative from Maryland, sick with a high fever, was literally carried into Congress on a stretcher to maintain the tied vote of his state. The Republican governor of Pennsylvania, Thomas McKean, threatened to march on Washington with troops if the Federalists persisted in thwarting the will of the people. Hamilton was powerless; his advice that Jefferson was the lesser evil went unheeded. So great was their hatred of the Virginian that most Federalists in Congress would have opposed him regardless of the consequences. After all, they reasoned, Jefferson would dismantle the Federal government anyway. In the end, however, patriotism and common sense prevailed. For the choice was no longer Jefferson or Burr, but Jefferson or no president at all. A few Federalists, led by James A. Bayard of Delaware, could not accept the logic of their party, and threw the election to Jefferson.

What a shock it was, then, to read Jefferson's carefully chosen words in his inaugural address:

> But every difference of opinion is not a difference of principle. We have called by different names brethren of the same principle. We are all republicans—we are all federalists. If there be any among us who would wish to dissolve this Union or to change its republican form, let them stand undisturbed as monuments of the safety with which error of opinion may be tolerated where reason is left free to combat it. I know, indeed, that some honest men fear that a republican government cannot be strong; that this government is not strong enough. But would the honest patriot, in the full tide of successful experiment, abandon a government which has so far kept us free and firm, on the theoretic and visionary fear that this

163

government, the world's best hope, may by possibility want energy to preserve itself? I trust not. I believe this, on the contrary, the strongest government on earth. I believe it is the only one where every man, at the call of the laws, would fly to the standard of the law, and would meet invasions of the public order as his own personal concern. Sometimes it is said that man cannot be trusted with the government of himself. Can he, then, be trusted with the government of others? Or have we found angels in the form of kings to govern him? Let history answer this question.

The words were greeted with applause— and confusion. It was obvious that Jefferson wanted to salve the wounds of bitter factionalism. While many Federalists remained distrustful and some even regarded it as hypocritical, most men approved the tone of their new president's message.

But what did Jefferson mean? Were there no economic principles at stake in his conflicts with Hamilton? Were there no political and constitutional principles implicit in the polar views of the respective parties? And, in the last analysis, did not these differences reflect a fundamental philosophical quarrel over the nature of human beings? Was not the election of 1800 indeed a revolution? If not, then what is the meaning of Jeffersonianism?

For two terms Jefferson tried, as best he could, to apply the standards of his inaugural address. Naturally, the Alien and Sedition Acts were allowed to lapse. The new secretary of the treasury, Albert Gallatin, was instructed to devise an easily understood program to erase the public debt gradually. Internal taxes were either abolished or reduced. Frugality and economy were emphasized to an extreme. Elegant and costly social functions were replaced by simple and informal receptions. The expense of maintaining ambassadors

at the courts of Portugal, Holland, and Prussia was erased by withdrawing these missions. The Army and Navy were pared down to skeleton size. To be sure, Jefferson had to reverse himself on the matter of patronage for subordinate Government posts. Originally he planned to keep these replacements to a minimum, certainly not to permit an individual's partisan opinions to be a basis for dismissal unless the man manifestly used his office for partisan purposes. This position was politically untenable, according to Jefferson's lieutenants, and they pressed him to accept a moderate number of removals. Indeed, Jefferson's handling of patronage is symbolic of what Hamilton once called his "ineradicable duplicity."

The Federalist leaders cried out in anguish at every one of these policy changes. The lowering of the nation's military strength would increase the danger of invasion. It was a rather risky gamble to assume that peace could be maintained while European war was an almost constant factor, and the United States was the major neutral carrier. The abolition of the excises, especially on distilled spirits, would force the Government to rely on tariffs, an unpredictable source of revenue depending on the wind and waves. It was charged that several foreign ambassadors were offended by Jefferson's rather affected and ultrademocratic social simplicity. Most important, the ultimate payment of the public debt would reduce national power.

This time, however, the people did not respond to the Federalist lament of impending anarchy. After all, commerce prospered throughout most of Jefferson's administration. Somehow the churches remained standing. No blood baths took place. The Bank of the United States still operated. Peace was maintained. Certainly, some Federalist judges were under attack, but the judicial power passed through this ordeal to emerge unscathed and even enhanced. Every economic indicator—urban growth, westward expansion, agricultural production, the construction of canals, turnpikes and bridges—continued to rise, undisturbed by the political bickering in Washington.

At first the Federalists were confident that they would regain power. Alexander Hamilton's elaborate scheme for an organization to espouse Christianity and the Constitution, as the "principal engine" to restore Federalist power, was rejected out of hand. He was told that "our adversaries will soon demonstrate to the world the soundness of our doctrines and the imbecility and folly of their own." But hope changed to despair as the people no longer responded; no "vibration of opinion" took place as in the 1790's. Federalism was the party of the past, an antiquated and dying philosophy. "I will fatten my pigs, and prune my trees; nor will I any longer . . . trouble to govern this country," wrote Fisher Ames: "You federalists are only lookers-on." Jefferson swept the election of 1804, capturing every state except Connecticut and Delaware from the Federalist candidate, Charles C. Pinckney. "Federalism is dead," wrote Jefferson a few years later, "without even the hope of a day of resurrection. The quondam leaders indeed retain their rancour and principles; but their followers are amalgamated with us in sentiment, if not in name."

It is the fashion of some historians to explain the Federalist demise and Republican ascendancy in terms of a great change in Jefferson. A radical natural law philosopher when he fought as minority leader, he became a first-rate utilitarian politician as president. The Virginian became an American. Revolutionary theory was cast aside when Jefferson faced the prosaic problem of having to run the country. He began to adopt some of the techniques and policies of the Federalists. Indeed, it is often observed that Jefferson "outfederalized the Federalists."

There is much to be said for this view. After all, less than three months after he assumed the presidency, Jefferson dispatched a naval squadron to the Mediterranean on a warlike mission, without asking the permission of Congress. Two members of his Cabinet, Levi Lincoln and Albert Gallatin, thought the action unconstitutional, and so advised the President. Almost from the moment of its birth the young nation had paid tribute, as did every European power, rather than risk a war with the Barbary pirates. But Jefferson could not abide such bribery. No constitutional scruples could delay for a moment his determination to force the issue. Later, Congress declared war, and in four years Barbary power was shattered. The United States under Jefferson accomplished an object that England, France, Spain, Portugal, and Holland had desired for more than a century—unfettered commerce in the Mediterranean. Here, then, in this episode, is a totally different Jefferson—not an exponent of states' rights and strict interpretation of the Constitution, but an American nationalist of the first order. . . .

In still other ways Jefferson's presidency was marked by Federalist policies which encouraged the growth of central power. Internal improvements loomed large in Jefferson's mind. While many turnpikes and canals were financed by private and state capital, he realized that Federal support would be necessary, especially in the western part of the nation. With the use of Federal money obtained from the sale of public lands, and (later) aided by direct congressional appropriations, the groundwork for the famous Cumberland road was established during Jefferson's administration. He enthusiastically supported Gallatin's plan to spend twenty million dollars of Federal funds on a network of national roads and canals. Other more pressing problems intervened, however, and it was left to later administrations to finance these local and interstate programs. If Hamilton had pressed for internal improvements in the 1790's (he suggested them in the *Report on Manufactures*), Jefferson probably would have raised constitutional objections.

Finally, is not Jefferson's change of tack further reflected in the political history of that era? Over the span of a few years it seemed as if each party had somehow reversed directions. In 1798–99 Jefferson and Madison penned the Virginia and Kentucky Resolutions as an answer to the Federalists' infamous Alien and Sedition Acts. In 1808–9 more radical but comparable rumblings of dissatisfaction emanated from some New England Federalists over Jefferson's Embargo Act. For the embargo, says one of Jefferson's biographers, was "the most arbitrary, inquisitorial, and confiscatory measure formulated in American legislation up to the period of the Civil War." Further, both parties splintered during Jefferson's administration. Many moderate Federalists, like John Quincy Adams, found themselves in closer harmony with Administration policy than with Essex Junto beliefs. And Jefferson's actions alienated old comrades, like John Randolph, Jr., whose supporters were called the Tertium Quids. It is interesting to note that there is no historical consensus of why, when, how, or what precipitated the break between Randolph and Jefferson. Randolph is always referred to as brilliant but erratic; and whatever immediate reason is alleged, the cause somehow has to do with Randolph's personality and Jefferson's betrayal of the true doctrines.

It is part of Jefferson's greatness that he could inspire a myth and project an image. But one must not confuse myth and reality, shadow and substance. Thomas Jefferson as he was, and Thomas Jefferson as people perceived him, are quite different. While both concepts of course, are of equal value in understanding our past, it is always the historian's task to make the distinction. Too often, in Jefferson's case, this has not been done. Too often the biographers have described the myth—have taken at face value the popular view of Jefferson and his enemies, contained in the vitriolic newspaper articles and pamphlets, the passionate debates and fiery speeches of that period—and missed or misconstrued the reality.

This is understandable. Even the principals inevitably became involved and helped to propagate the exaggerated images of the 1790's and thus misunderstood one another's aims and motives. Jefferson, according to his grandson, never considered Federalist fulminations "as abusing him; they had never known him. They had created an imaginary being clothed with odious attributes, to whom they gave his name; and it was against that creature of their imaginations they had levelled their anathemas." John Adams, reminiscing in a letter to Jefferson, wrote: "Both parties have excited artificial terrors and if I were summoned as a witness to say upon oath, which party had excited . . . the most terror, and which had really felt the most, I could not give a more sincere answer, than in the vulgar style 'Put them in a bag and shake them, and then see which comes out first.'"

On March 4, 1801, following a decade of verbal violence, many Americans were surprised to hear that "We are all republicans—we are all federalists." Some historians act as if they, too, are surprised. These historians then describe Jefferson's administration as if some great change took place in his thinking, and conclude that he "outfederalized the Federalists." This is a specious view, predicated on an ultraradical Jefferson of the 1790's in constant debate with an ultraconservative Hamilton. Certainly Jefferson as president had to change. Certainly at times he had to modify, compromise, and amend his previous views. To conclude, however, that he outfederalized the Federalists is to miss the enormous consistency of Jefferson's beliefs and practices.

Jefferson was ever a national patriot second to none, not even to Hamilton. He always conceived of the United States as a unique experiment, destined for greatness so long as a sharp line isolated American civilization from European infection. Thus he strongly advised our youth to receive their education at home rather than in European schools, lest they absorb ideas and traits he considered "alarming to me as an American." From "Notes on Virginia" to his advice at the time of Monroe's doctrine, Jefferson thought of America first. It matters not that Hamilton was the better prophet; Jefferson was the better American. The French minister Adet once reported: "Although Jefferson is the friend of liberty . . . although he is an admirer of the efforts we have made to cast off our shackles. . . . Jefferson, I say, is an American, and as such, he cannot sincerely be our friend. An American is the born enemy of all the peoples of Europe."

Jefferson's nature was always more practical than theoretical, more common-sensical than philosophical. Certainly the essence of his Declaration of Independence is a Lockean justification of revolution; but, said Jefferson, "It was . . . an expression of

the American mind," meant "to place before mankind the common sense of the subject." Jefferson always preferred precision to "metaphysical subtleties." The Kentucky and Virginia Resolutions can be understood only as a specific rebuttal of the Sedition Act. "I can never fear that things will go far wrong," wrote Jefferson, "where common sense has fair play."

One must also remember that Hamilton's power lessened considerably in the last four years of Federalist rule. He had a strong coterie of admirers, but the vast body of Federalists sided with John Adams. Despite all Hamilton did to insure Adams' defeat, and despite the split in Federalist ranks, the fact that Jefferson's victory in 1801 was won by a narrow margin indicated Federalist approval of Adams' actions. Certainly the people at that time—Jefferson and Adams included—regarded 1801 as the year of revolution. But if historians must have a revolution, perhaps Adams' split with the Hamiltonians is a better date. "The mid-position which Adams desired to achieve," writes Manning Dauer, "was adopted, in the main, by Jefferson and his successors."

To be sure, the two men disagreed on many matters of basic importance. Jefferson placed his faith in the free election of a virtuous and talented natural aristocracy; Adams did not. Within the constitutional balance, Jefferson emphasized the power of the lower house; Adams would give greater weight to the executive and judiciary. Jefferson, as a general rule, favored a strict interpretation of the Constitution; Adams did not fear broad construction. Both believed that human beings enjoyed inalienable rights, but only Jefferson had faith in man's perfectability. Jefferson could say, "I like a little rebellion now and then. It is like a storm in the atmosphere"; Adams had grown more conservative since 1776.

9. WAS PRESIDENT JEFFERSON AN OPPONENT OF CIVIL LIBERTIES?

Jefferson always defended and befriended Thomas Paine; Adams found Edmund Burke's position on the French Revolution more palatable.

Yet, the sages of Quincy and Monticello were both moderate and practical men. Despite the obvious and basic contrasts, both Adams and Jefferson stood side by side on certain essentials: to avoid war, to quiet factionalism, to preserve republican government. Their warm friendship, renewed from 1812 to 1826 in a remarkable and masterful correspondence, was based on frankness, honesty, and respect. "About facts," Jefferson wrote, "you and I cannot differ, because truth is our mutual guide; And if any opinions you may express should be different from mine, I shall receive them with the liberality and indulgence which I ask for my own." Jefferson and Adams represent, respectively, the quintessence of the very best in American liberalism and conservatism. Their indestructible link, then, was "a keen sense of national consciousness," a realization that America's destiny was unique. This is the meaning of Jefferson's words: "We are all republicans—we are all federalists."

POSTSCRIPT

WAS PRESIDENT JEFFERSON AN OPPONENT OF CIVIL LIBERTIES?

Both Professors Levy and Borden reject the notion that Jefferson was a hypocrite who outfederalized the Federalists by reversing his states rightist and strict constructionist approaches to the Constitution when he was president. After all, no person who spends forty years of his life as a public figure, as Jefferson did, should be expected to be philosophically wedded to an unchanging set of principles. But Borden seems to approve of Jefferson's pragmatic, common-sense, and moderate approach to politics. Rejecting many of the differences between Federalists and Republicans as mere political rhetoric, Borden views Jefferson as a national patriot. Jefferson became a proponent of strong executive power as president, says Borden, because he believed such measures as the Louisiana Purchase and the embargo furthered the nation's best interests.

Professor Levy agrees with Borden that Jefferson was a staunch believer in the uniqueness of the American democratic experiment. But Levy concentrates on the darker side of the "sage of Monticello." Because he believed that the European powers and the Federalist opponents were constantly conspiring against the American republic, Jefferson thought it was necessary for the national government to take stern measures against these enemies of liberty. Hence, much of Jefferson's second administration was filled with federal sedition prosecutions against opposition newspaper editors in Connecticut, the trial of former Vice-President Aaron Burr, and the passage of the five embargo acts against foreign trade. Why did Jefferson resort to such extreme measures? Because, says Levy, he was a philosopher of liberty without a philosophy of liberty. A superficial thinker who believed certain truths were self-evident, Jefferson, Levy argues, never really thought through the problems of maintaining liberty when it conflicted in the real world with the competing claims of other values.

Leonard Levy's *Jefferson and Civil Liberties: The Darker Side* (Belknap, 1963) is one of the few modern critical biographies of Jefferson. Forrest McDonald's *Thomas Jefferson* (Kansas, 1976) is another. No student should miss McDonald's concise critical summary of Washington's and Jefferson's precedent-setting impact on the American presidency in "A Mirror for Presidents," *Commentary* (December, 1976). Sympathetic treatments of Jefferson can be found in Dumas Malone's magisterial *Jefferson and His Time,* 6 volumes (Little, Brown, 1948-1981) and Merrill Peterson's, *Thomas Jefferson and the New Nation: A Biography* (Oxford, 1970). Henry C. Dethloff's, ed., *Thomas Jefferson and American Democracy* (Heath, 1971), is the best reader about our most intellectual chief executive.

ISSUE 10

DID WOMEN ACHIEVE GREATER AUTONOMY IN THE NEW NATION?

YES: Nancy Woloch, from *Women and the American Experience* (Alfred A. Knopf, 1984)

NO: Gerda Lerner, from "The Lady and the Mill Girl: Changes in the Status of Women in the Age of Jackson," *American Studies,* Volume 10, No. 1, Spring 1961

ISSUE SUMMARY

YES: Professor Woloch perceives autonomy and authority in the domestic life of middle-class wives.
NO: Historian Lerner considers a spectrum of women's roles, emphasizing the problems of female industrial workers.

In colonial America and during the War for Independence women learned skills, worked at occupations, and specialized in professions necessary to meet the needs of the times. Women practiced law, pounded iron as blacksmiths, barbered, trapped furs and tanned leather, made guns, built ships, worked silver, and edited and printed newspapers. Individual women marked niches for themselves in the American pantheon. Betsy Ross, in addition to her legendary task of designing and sewing the first Stars and Stripes, managed a very profitable upholstery firm. Mary McCauley, known as "Molly Pitcher," started off the day on June 28, 1778, serving water to thirsty minutemen but spent the afternoon trading shots with Redcoats. Phillis Wheatley served time as a slave but her genius vanquished racial as well as sexual stereotypes; her poems found admirers in Boston, London and Paris. Abigail Adams's letters immortalized both her private and public opinions. She served with her diplomat husband in Europe and witnessed the beginnings of the federal government as the United States capital moved from New York to Philadelphia, and finally to Washington.

Social and economic changes after 1783 altered the economic status of women. Increased urbanization, the accumulation of wealth and the imitation of European bourgeois values and habits combined to eliminate the androgynous workplace where previously women could display their skills alongside men. Perhaps a diminished concern over survival proffered changes in behavior also. With the onset of industrialization, work which had been performed in homes was being transferred to factories, and women usually worked only for a limited time, until they married. Residence and workplace were no longer one; the roles of wife, mother and worker could no longer be easily juggled.

Most historians interpret the War for Independence as a negative influence on women's status. The opinions of foreign visitors, however, were mixed. Alexis de Tocqueville, acknowledged as the most acute of the early-nineteenth-century observers of the United States, uncovered an interesting dichotomy. "In America," he wrote, "the independence of woman is irrevocably lost in the bonds of matrimony. If an unmarried woman is less constrained there than elsewhere, a wife is subjected to stricter obligations." The Frenchman was astonished because "Long before an American girl arrives at the marriageable age, her emancipation from maternal control begins; she has scarcely ceased to be a child when she already thinks for herself, speaks with freedom and acts on her own impulse."

Class distinctions separated American women into different groups. Very different sources of family income—agriculture versus commerce or the professions—further complicate any generalizations. Geographical influences determined women's behavior as much as social standing. The sectional divisions of North, South and West which historians use to explain the alignment of general attitudes in the United States must also be considered. The kind of household added still another dimension. Contrast the modest rural cottage where the housewife prepared almost all foodstuffs and much of the clothing on the premises, with the lifestyle of the mistress of a plantation whose concerns were similar but whose duties were largely supervisory, and then with the urban wife whose environment provided the opportunity to purchase most necessities if she wished instead of making them.

In the first selection, Woloch described the world of the early-nineteenth-century lady in favorable terms. "Within her own domestic space, however, she had gained both a new degree of autonomy and a new degree of authority over others," she concluded. Lerner characterized this same time period as bringing "an actual deterioration in the economic opportunities open to women, a relative deterioration in their political status and a rising level of expectation and frustration in a privileged elite group of educated women."

YES   Nancy Woloch

THE HOME AND THE WORLD

When the *Ladies Magazine* first appeared in 1828, a transformation in domestic life was well under way, at least in the commercial, urbanizing Northeast. During colonial days, when most families lived on farms, the household was a productive unit. All family members engaged in work to sustain it, work that was done in or near the home. As part of the family labor force, women and children were subordinate to paternal authority. But during the early nineteenth century, as a market economy developed, old patterns of life started to vanish. Men who once would have been farmers or craftsmen were now working outside the home to earn the income that supported it. The home was no longer a center of production, nor did family members work together for family sustenance. Within the emerging middle class, "home" became a private enclave, a retreat from the "world" and a refuge from commercial life. And within the home, women assumed a distinctive role.

The middle-class wife, like the *Ladies Magazine* reader of 1828, remained at home while her income-earning husband went to work outside it, in office or store, business or profession. While the man ventured forth into the world, the woman at home gained an independent realm of her own, one that was no longer constantly under male domination. Domestic life was now under female control. Nor was the wife tied down to wheel and loom, hearth and dairy. Once home manufacture was transferred to workplace, the woman at home was responsible primarily for housekeeping, child rearing, and moral and religious life. Within her own domestic space, however, she had gained both a new degree of autonomy and a new degree of authority over others.

The doctrine of sphere, as expounded in the *Ladies Magazine*, *Godey's Lady's Book*, and countless other publications, celebrated the new status of the middle-class woman, along with her distinctive vocation, values, and character. It also described an unspoken bargain between middle-class women and men. While men were still heads of families, their real domain was now in the world—a world of business, professions, politics, and money making. Family status depended on their earned income and public roles. Women were expected to devote themselves entirely to private life, to the "chaste circle of the fireside," and to maintain an alternate world with separate values. But their roles at home also helped to define family status. Moreover, within the home, they had gained new clout and respect. The bargain was based on mutual gain. If men had the opportunity to rise in the world, women had the opportunity to rise in the home.

The middle-class woman's role was of course a dependent one. Her authority expanded only as the family's productive functions contracted, and those functions contracted only when family income went up. Rising income was at the center of woman's sphere. Only with substantial support could a married woman adopt the nonproductive role once reserved for the very wealthy or the antieconomic attitudes propounded by the *Ladies Magazine*. In reality, few women could sever themselves completely from either home production or physical work. Middle-class women and those who aspired to that status remained active contributors to the family economy. Most women, moreover, were only remote beneficiaries of the middle-class bargain. In rural areas, on farms in New England, in the South, and in the Midwest, traditional ways of life persisted. Household production continued, women and children were still part of the family labor force, and paternal authority as head of that labor force remained in effect, if not entirely intact. A woman's clout did not increase if a family was poor, or if she was not attached to a dependable, income-producing man. In many cases, the perquisites of woman's sphere—influence, autonomy, and au-thority—were little more than shared aspirations.

Nor were women of any class able to ignore worldly concerns. Within the growing middle class, woman's sphere was as precarious an ideal as its counterpart for men—the opportunity to rise in the world. The early-nineteenth-century family was likely to be in both financial and geographical motion. Income rose or fell according to personal fate and twists and turns of the economy such as the depression that diminished *Ladies Magazine* subscriptions in 1834. Buffeted by panics or elevated by good fortune, Americans faced the possibility of downward mobility at every turn. The "vicissitudes" were particularly precarious for women, who had little ability to determine family finances. When a husband died or a father failed in business, consequences could be dire. Shifts in family fortune, moreover, were usually linked to shifts in locale, to constant waves of internal migration—from rural areas to towns and cities, or from crowded areas to vacant land. Hardly insulated by sphere, early-nineteenth-century women were continually adapting to new homes, communities, associations, and economic situations.

But in important ways, woman's sphere was also a reality with which many women could identify, because their everyday patterns of life and work were becoming increasingly different from those of men. Even on the family farm, that most traditional of settings, men were now attuned to the market economy while women's responsibilities remained tied to the household economy. In towns and cities, differences between male and female work patterns were even more marked. During colonial times, as historian Nancy Cott points out, the work of both men and women was closely tied to the land. It was seasonal, discontinuous, and task-oriented. But during the early nineteenth century, as the economy changed and as wage labor replaced family labor, male work patterns became oriented to time, not task. Whatever a man did for a living—laborer, businessman, tradesman, or clerk—he now had a clearly defined working day. His work, accordingly, became separated from the rest of life. Household work, however, remained in a time warp of task orientation. Women's work day expanded and contracted to fit the jobs at hand, whether the washing of clothes, baking of bread, or care of children—activities that all merged into life. In short, women's work and homebound world remained premodern, whereas men's was changing. A distinctive rhythm of labor and life style also defined woman's sphere.

Finally, women of all regions and all social levels could hope to benefit from the new importance now attributed to their shared vocation. In traditional society, household work and child-care had never drawn much acclaim. During the early nineteenth century, however, they were found to have social significance, to contribute to the well-being of society at large. Women's sphere was in fact a new social space, one that had not been recognized before. On the one hand, it was an enclosed, limited, private space. On the other, it was an improvement over having no space at all. Woman's sphere, according to popular literature, encompassed a now important social institution, the home. It linked all women together in a valuable vocation—domesticity and child rearing. It fostered a positive consciousness of gender, one that had not existed in the colonial era. And it necessitated a redefinition of female charac-

ter, one appropriate to the middle-class woman's elevated domestic status.

During the early nineteenth century, the home took on new significance, material and emotional. By mid-century, the middle-class home had become a substantial place, with pantries and drawing rooms, mirrors and pianos, and at least some of the items featured in *Godey's Lady's Book*—upholstered sofas, elaborate furniture, carpets, and draperies. Its center was no longer the hearth, where colonial women did much of their work, but the parlor, where the family assembled. Since middle-class Americans had not only far more possessions but rising standards of neatness and cleanliness, "housework" quickly replaced "housewifery." Even with hired help, the middle-class woman was hardly idle, since home maintenance and management was now a more elaborate procedure.

The middle-class home was also viewed as an emotional space, a refuge from the competitive world, and a source of stability and order in a society that seemed to be losing both. And it was now under feminine sway. Increasingly, the home was idealized as a bastion of feminine values, of piety and morality, affection and self-sacrifice—commodities that were in short supply outside it. Literature directed at women, especially, lost no opportunity to define the home as a feminine fief. "The family state . . . is the aptest earthly illustration of the heavenly kingdom and woman is its chief minister," educator Catharine Beecher declared in her *Treatise on Domestic Economy* in the 1840s. "The duties of the woman are as sacred and important as any ordained by man." By midcentury, the home was depicted as an insulated, privatized, feminized shrine. "Our homes—what is their corner-stone but the virtue of a woman, and on what does social well-being rest but in our homes?" asked *Godey's Lady's Book* in 1856.

> Must we not trace all other blessings of civilized life to the doors of our private dwellings? Are not our hearthstones guarded by holy forms, conjugal, filial and parental love, the corner-stone of church and state, more sacred than either, more necessary than both? Let our temples crumble and capitals of state be levelled with the dust, but spare our homes! Man did not invent, and he cannot improve or abrogate them. A private shelter to cover . . . two hearts dearer to each other than all in the world; high walls to exclude the profane eyes of every human being; seclusion enough for the children to feel that mother is a holy and peculiar name—this is home. . . . Here the church and state must come for their origin and support. Oh! spare our homes.

While the middle-class home expanded in size and significance, the family itself was getting smaller. Americans were having fewer children. In 1800, the national birth rate had been the highest in the world; but during the next few decades it rapidly fell, a process that would continue for the rest of the century. The mother of 7.04 in 1800 became the mother of 5.92 in 1850 and 3.56 by 1900. Although the decline was national, it was uneven. During the early nineteenth century, large families were still the rule in most agricultural regions, along the newly settled frontier and among immigrants and blacks. Rural fertility, in fact, was also falling, but urban fertility was consistently lower. The most precipitous drop was among the new middle class in towns and cities.

But as the family began to shrink, the value attached to motherhood rose. Though such mounting significance had already been suggested in post-Revolutionary rhetoric, during the early nineteenth century it increased dramatically. Once household production waned, child raising became the family's central focus and purpose. In the middle-class home, children were no longer family workers but rather *what* the family produced. More time was devoted to their upbringing, more resources to their education, more effort to instilling the values and traits that would keep them in the middle class. The increased importance of child rearing contributed to an authority shift in the family. Paternal power dropped a notch as maternal affection became the main psychological force at home. The mother was now the primary child rearer, the crucial dispenser of values and former of character. She could "generate those moral tendencies which cover the whole of existence," as a minister wrote in the *Ladies Magazine*. "Her character is felt throughout the intricate workings of society." By the 1830s, when the publishing industry began an era of rapid expansion, the mother's significance was celebrated on all sides.

Innumerable tracts and stories—like those in the *Ladies Magazine*—paid tribute to the mother of Washington. In prints and etchings, a new iconography of motherhood developed. Magazines featured scenes of mothers at home, surrounded by children, in affectionate poses. In literature directed at women, motherhood was celebrated as the ultimate opportunity for self-sacrifice and, simultaneously, the ultimate role of female power. "How entire and perfect is this dominion over the unformed character of your infant," *Ladies Magazine* author Lydia Sigourney exuded in her *Letters to Mothers* (1838). No opportunity was lost to celebrate the social utility of motherhood. It was mothers, as Lydia Maria Child declared in her popular *Mother's Book*

175

(1831) "on whose intelligence and discretion the safety and prosperity of our nation so much depend."

Nor was the expansion of maternal influence just rhetorical. By midcentury, it began to be recognized in the law. Northern states started to alter the tradition of paternal custody in cases of separation and divorce. Courts began to consider the "needs" of young children and "parental fitness," as well as to award custody to the "innocent party." Women did not gain equal custody rights, to say nothing of preference, until the end of the century. But adulation of motherhood was not without some legal ramifications, at least in the North. In the antebellum South, where patriarchy remained intact, legal encroachments on paternal power were rejected.

While celebrations of woman's sphere stressed the significance of domestic roles and maternal influence, they also suggested a new and positive consciousness of gender. The polarity of spheres that segregated middle-class men and women was not without an emotional bonus. Since women shared a common vocation, values, and attitudes appropriate to the home, not the world, they did have more in common with one another than with men, as Sarah Hale contended in the *Ladies Magazine*. And they profited from long-term, intense relationships with other women—relationships that continued for decades, despite marriage and geographical separation, often taking the form of lengthy visits and correspondence. Such correspondence, as historian Carroll Smith Rosenberg contends, reveals that "Women's sphere had an essential dignity and integrity that grew out of women's shared experiences and mutual affection." Within their self-contained female world— noncompetitive, empathetic, and sup-

portive—women valued one another and thereby gained a sense of security and self-esteem. "Women, who had little status and power in the larger world of male concerns, possessed status and power in the lives of other women."

Historians disagree as to whether an intimate mother-daughter relationship lay at the heart of this female world, or whether the peer relationship was more important. In either case, early-nineteenth-century middle-class women assumed centrality in one another's lives, depended emotionally on one another, and appreciated their same-sex connections and friendships. The role of friendship as an outlet for shared "sentiments" was reflected in the New England letters and diaries analyzed by historian Nancy Cott. Men, in these documents, were usually remote, distant figures, often without names. Or they might be referred to, with muted sarcasm, as "the Lords of Creation," an expression favored by Sarah Hale in the *Ladies Magazine*. But affection among women was explicit. Friendship provided an opportunity to exchange "reciprocal views and feelings," wrote Eliza Chaplin to Laura Lovell in 1820. "To you I unfold my whole heart without apology." "I do not believe that men can ever feel so pure an enthusiasm for women as we can feel for one another," *Ladies Magazine* author Catharine Sedgwick revealed to her diary in 1834. "Ours is nearest to the love of angels."

The positive consciousness of gender suggested by personal documents reflected and supported a new assessment of female character. According to the doctrine of sphere, character traits, like social roles, were now divided between men and women. Men were expected to be competitive, assertive, individualistic, and materialistic so as to be able to make their way in the world. The woman at home needed a compensatory set of character traits. Dependent and affectionate, she was also pious, pure, gentle, nurturant, benevolent, and sacrificing. Such "softer" virtues had been filtering in throughout the eighteenth century, especially in advice tracts destined for the upwardly mobile. But during the early nineteenth century, the softer virtues became accepted as innate. Women, moreover, compared to men, were believed to have a firmer grip on religion and morals, a virtual monopoly on piety and purity, a positive sense of moral superiority. In traditional society, women were not assumed to be superior to men in any way. Now, piety and purity provided some leverage. They also involved a new set of bargains between women and men.

PIETY AND PURITY

During the early nineteenth century, ministers provided a vital bolster to the doctrine of woman's sphere. They opposed those forces antithetical to women's interests—materialism, immorality, intemperance, and licentiousness. They helped to formulate a new definition of female character. Christian virtues—such as humility, submission, piety, and charity—were now, they suggested, primarily female virtues. Most important, ministers confirmed female moral superiority. Women might be the weaker members of society, but they were now assured that they exceeded men in spiritual fervor and moral strength.

Religion was also one of the few activities beyond the home in which women might participate without abdicating their sphere. Their participation in the churches was in fact vital. Women formed the majority of congregants. Accordingly, female piety, and even activism, were heartily encouraged by their ministers. "We look to you, ladies, to raise the standard of character in our own sex," announced New England clergyman Joseph Buckminster in an 1810 sermon. "We look to you for the continuance of domestick purity, for the revival of domestick religion, for the increase of our charities, and the support of what remains of religion in our private habits and publick institutions." Under such circumstances, a mutually dependent relationship developed between Protestant clerics and their middle-class female parishioners. Both saw themselves as outsiders in a society devoted to the pursuit of wealth, as allies who strove for morality in a competitive world. It was no accident that women's publications such as the *Ladies Magazine* counted on ministers for articles exalting the character of women. Ministers in turn depended on women for their loyal support.

Despite clegymen's persistent fears that their authority was diminishing, religion was not on the wane. Protestantism flourished during the early nineteenth century. The Second Great Awakening of the first quarter of the century was surpassed by the great evangelical crusades of the second. Presbyterians and Congregationalists attracted members in New England, fiery waves of revivals swept over New York state, westerners flocked to camp meetings on the frontier, and Baptists and Methodists made gains nationwide. According to some estimates, formal church membership tripled. Throughout all this fervor, women remained prominent. Their affinity for piety became evident in a spate of revivals at the start of the century. The Second Great Awakening marked the beginning of the new alliance between women and ministers as well as of their unstated bargain: clerical endorsement of female moral superiority in exchange for women's support and activism.

Female converts outnumbered male converts three to two in the Second Great Awakening in New England, and women formed the bulk of congregations thereafter. They played an equally prominent role in revival-swept western New York. By 1814, for instance, women outnumbered men in the churches and religious societies of bustling Utica, and they could be relied on to urge the conversion of family members. A mother's conversion, ministers learned, could lead to those of her children and husband; a daughter's conversion might soon create a pious family. The most zealous activists of these early revivals, significantly, were women of the new middle class—the wives and daughters of men who worked outside the home. Church membership became a boost to upward mobility. But female religiosity also moved down the social scale, to wives of artisans and farmers, just as it spread to other regions. On the midwestern frontier, it was women who could be counted on to form congregations, join religious societies, and demand Sabbath observance. Piety had become female property. When Englishwoman Frances Trollope investigated American society in the 1830s, she claimed that she had never seen a country "where religion had so strong a hold upon the women, or a slighter hold upon the men."

If religion had a hold on women, however, they in turn had a hold on the clergy. Through weight of numbers, women gained a genuine influence in Protestant churches that they lacked elsewhere. They contributed, for instance, to a softening of doctrine: the old idea of infant damnation had little appeal to American mothers. Ministers, accordingly, granted that Christian nurture could outweigh original sin.

Discarding predestination as an axiom, ministers now suggested that mothers, not God, were responsible for their children's souls. The "feminization" of religion and of child rearing went hand in hand. Ministers bolstered the authority not only of the pious mother but of any pious woman, even the once insignificant daughter. Evangelical magazines, for instance, celebrated female influence in tales of dying daughters who, to the end, sought the conversion of relatives and friends. Social weakness, even fatal illness, was no obstacle to spiritual strength.

While ministers accorded women a new degree of influence, religious commitment offered other advantages. It also provided a community of peers outside the home, among like-minded women in church-related associations. The passivity of the convert, once she was united with her sisters, could be transformed into activist zeal. Early-nineteenth-century women provided the constituency for a multitude of societies formed under clerical auspices. They joined Bible and tract societies, which distributed pious literature, and Sabbath school unions, such as those endorsed in the *Ladies Magazine,* and missionary societies, which raised funds for pious endeavors. They formed charitable associations to aid the indigent and maternal associations to foster Christian motherhood. Through voluntary religious groups, women gained one another's company, new routes to participation in the world, and clerical approval. "While the pious female . . . does not aspire after things too great for her," a minister told a women's charitable society in 1815, "she discovers that there is wide field opened for the exercise of all her active powers."

In many ways, the evangelical Protestant experience was loaded with potential for women. Conversion encouraged introspection and self-attention. Cooperative efforts in church groups inspired a conscious sense of sisterhood and mutual interest. And clerical assurance of moral superiority supported a new degree of authority over others. But religious activism also had built-in limitations; clerical support meant clerical control. In the heat of revivals, as female piety assumed new significance, ministers warned women to avoid leadership roles as, for example, revivalists. Their piety was to be limited to the private role of personal persuasion; "influence" was contingent on acceptance of limits. As long as a woman kept to her "proper place," a tract society pamphlet explained in 1823, she might exert "almost any degree of influence she pleases." This was part of the implicit bargain between clergymen and women parishioners. It was also a fundamental tenet espoused by Sarah Hale in the *Ladies Magazine*.

If piety became a vital component of female character, so did purity, a word with several meanings. One was passionlessness, or lack of sexual feeling. According to the doctrine of sphere, the sexes were distinguished by features that were not merely different but opposite. Lust and carnality were male characteristics, or liabilities. Women, less physical, more spiritual, and morally superior, were indeed closer to "angels." This was of course a new development. In traditional society, women, like men, were assumed to be sexual beings. Since weaker of will, they were often assumed to be even more lustful, licentious, and insatiable than men. But early in the nineteenth century, around the time of the Second Great Awakening, purity became a female bargaining point. Like piety, it was now a prerequisite for influence. Sermons often warned that if purity gave way, all of the perquisites of sphere were lost. "Let her lay aside delicacy," a

minister held in 1837, "and her influence over our sex is gone."

Though ministers were the first authorities to endorse the female virtue of purity, they were not the only ones. By mid-century, the medical profession also confirmed that passionlessness was an innate and commendable female characteristic. "The majority of women (happily for them)," physician William Acton stated in a much-quoted medical treatise, "are not much troubled with sexual feeling of any kind." There were dissenting opinions within the profession. But in medical manuals aimed at the upwardly mobile middle class, midcentury physicians usually emphasized the debilitating effects of sexual indulgence, recommended infrequent intercourse, opposed contraception, and confirmed female asexuality. They also assured women that their physical health, and social roles, were determined by their reproductive organs. Doctors explained that the uterus was linked to the female nervous system, and that any malfunction affected the entire body, causing a gamut of ailments—headaches, backaches, indigestion, insomnia, and nervous disorders. Women's unusual physiology, indeed, determined her emotions, character, and vocation. "Mentally, socially, spiritually, [woman] is more interior than a man," a Philadelphia physician concluded in the 1860s. "The house, the chamber, the closet, are the centers of her social life and power."

Like other components of woman's sphere, purity encompassed both sanctions and benefits. The sanctions were stressed in the advice literature directed at middle-class women. Etiquette manuals, for instance, counseled prudent behavior that would serve to deter male advances. "Sit not with another in a space that is too narrow," warned the *Young Ladies Friend*.

179

Magazine fiction offered tales about girls who lacked discretion, were consequently victimized by male predators, and ended up ruined, impoverished, ostracized, or dead. Such proscriptions were related to significant changes in courtship customs, since incidence of premarital pregnancy sharply declined—from a high of almost 30 percent of first births in the late eighteenth century to a new low of under 10 percent in the mid-nineteenth century. This precipitous drop, historians contend, suggests the acceptance by both young men and women of a new ideology of sexual restraint. Convictions about female purity imposed limitations not only on women but men as well.

Purity was also a code word for a new degree of female sexual control within marriage. During the early nineteenth century, when the fertility of white women began its precipitous decline, the shrinking family became a hallmark of the new middle class. It may also have been a result of the new clout of wives within middle-class homes. Now imbued with moral superiority, wives gained a right of refusal, an escape from "submission," and power to limit the frequency of sexual relations. They also gained more control over the number of children they had. Available methods of family limitation (beyond folk remedies and patent medicines) were abstinence, as recommended in medical literature, and withdrawal, which was condemned; abortion was also a possible last resort, at least until later in the century when it was outlawed. Although abstinence was not the sole effective means of curbing births, it probably was in widespread use. And female purity was probably an ideal on which middle-class men and women agreed, an asset for the family that wanted to rise in the world—a family in which children were no longer

economic assets but, rather, liabilities. In the early nineteenth century, sexual restraint appeared to both serve family goals and enhance women's autonomy within the home.

Convictions about female purity also affected women's relation to the medical profession. Connections between women and doctors were hardly as clear-cut as the unstated bargain between women and ministers. Physicians were a far newer source of authority. Medicine became a recognized profession only after the turn of the century. By the 1820s, all states except three had laws requiring medical practitioners to be licensed, and most licensing laws required graduation from medical college. As a result, women were excluded from medical practice, and midwifery, once a female monopoly, began a slow decline. In rural areas and on the frontier, midwives continued to deliver babies, and also among the urban poor. The rural midwife, indeed, remained in business into the twentieth century. But the urbanizing East set the trend for the future. During the early nineteenth century, middle-class mothers in towns and cities turned to physicians. No longer a public female ritual, childbirth became a private event with two main participants, a woman and a male professional.

The physician's new role in childbirth brought both loss and gain. The entourage of women relatives and friends who had once played a supportive part gradually vanished. But middle-class women seemed to appreciate the use of the forceps (the physician's prerogative) as the means of a faster delivery with less suffering. Mothers, indeed, became the doctor's prime constituency, since a successful obstetric practice paved the way for a profitable family practice. Moreover, with the rise of the medical profession, female ill health assumed new visibility.

Middle-class women of the early nineteenth century were distinguished by their debilitating illnesses—nervousness, anemia, hysteria, headaches, backaches. The marked rise in female illness, much of it never diagnosed, may have been connected to physical causes—such as the spread of venereal disease—or psychological ones. Women's dependent status could have had debilitating effects on their health. Sickness might also have had a positive function, providing reprieve from domestic work. In any case, physical fragility became a female liability. When Catharine Beecher surveyed women's health across the nation in the 1850s, she concluded that sick women outnumbered the healthy three to one. Reporting from one Illinois town, Beecher gave her version of the terrible state of women's health.

> Mrs. H. an invalid. Mrs. G. scrufula. Mrs. W. liver complaint. Mrs. S. pelvic disorders. Mrs. B. pelvic deseases very badly. Mrs. B. not healthy. Mrs. T. very feeble. Mrs. G. cancer. Mrs. N. liver complaint. Do not know one healthy woman in the place.

If all the facts and details of women's diseases were known, Catharine Beecher claimed, "It would send a groan of terror and horror over the land."

Even when chronically ill, however, women did not completely trust their doctors. The professionalization of medicine did not ensure its competence. At midcentury, as historian Regina Morantz explains, medicine was in a state of crisis. "Heroic" medicine—bleeding and enormous doses of dangerous substances—was being discarded, but it had not yet been replaced by anything better. Not only were well-trained doctors unlikely to be very effective, but few were well trained. During the 1830s, any profit-minded doctor could open a medical college and, however lax its standards, produce hundreds of graduates to be licensed. Women had especial reason to be wary. Since female complaints of all sorts were believed to stem from uterine malfunction, the woman patient might well be subjected to "local treatment"—a procedure involving uterine cauterization, injection of solutions, even the insertion of leeches. Not surprisingly, "local treatment" seemed a dire assault on female purity. And not surprisingly, middle-class women sought alternatives.

One set of alternatives were nonmedical remedies or fads—Grahamism (diet reform), water cures. animal magnetism, or phrenology. The *Ladies Magazine,* for instance, ran many features on phrenology, complete with huge charts of the human skull. Middle-class women also took refuge at spas, joined ladies' physiological societies, where health and medicine were discussed and accepted the views of health reformers. The latter usually favored preventive measures that would preclude the need to resort to physicians at all—such as exercise, fresh air, baths, and cereals. Similar measures were endorsed in the medical columns of *Godey's Lady's Book,* written by doctors. Women also turned to irregular practitioners—unlicensed dispensers of remedies and advice, who might well be women. Dr. Harriot Hunt, for instance, went into practice in Boston with her sister in the 1830s, after an apprenticeship with other irregulars. Opposed to the "heroic" methods of the licensed profession, which rejected her, she prescribed homeopathic, preventive measures and became interested in the psychological causes of women's ailments. An even less regular practitioner, Mary Gove Nichols, once a contributor to the *Ladies Magazine,* became a water cure therapist and health reformer, catering, like

Hunt, to a female clientele. Although not committed to the female passionlessness, these leading irregulars were committed to the protection of women from male depravity.

Another response to the professionalization of medicine was explained in *Godey's Lady's Book.* Women, wrote Sarah Hale, should be allowed to enter the medical profession in order to minister to women and children. Her argument for women doctors was based on the sanctity of sphere. Propriety and morality dictated that women should be examined by women. The woman physician, moreover, would raise the moral tone of the profession and open to women new avenues for practicing their altruism, benevolence, and sympathy. Through the entry of women into medicine, woman's sphere would be not destroyed but preserved. Hale lent especial support to Elizabeth Blackwell, the

first woman medical college graduate and licensed woman physician. Like Hunt and Nichols, Blackwell was hardly a subscriber to the doctrine of female asexuality. She was, however, a crusader against prostitution and obscenity, and a supporter of the moral purity movement.

The doctrine of woman's sphere, and its redefinition of female character, could therefore be used as a bargaining tool. Piety, purity, and moral superiority could be mobilized to increase women's authority at home and demand more influence outside it. The doctrine of sphere could also be used to bolster other demands, such as that for "advanced" education. Although only a small proportion of Americans had any education beyond the primary level, an increasing number of them were women. Sending a daughter to an academy or seminary was now a perquisite of the expanding middle class.

NO

Gerda Lerner

THE LADY AND THE MILL GIRL: CHANGES IN THE STATUS OF WOMEN IN THE AGE OF JACKSON

The period 1800-1840 is one in which decisive changes occurred in the status of American women. It has remained surprisingly unexplored. With the exception of a recent, unpublished dissertation by Keith Melder and the distinctive work of Elisabeth Dexter, there is a dearth of descriptive material and an almost total absence of interpretation. Yet the period offers essential clues to an understanding of later institutional developments, particularly the shape and nature of the woman's rights movement. This analysis will consider the economic, political, and social status of women and examine the changes in each area. It will also attempt an interpretation of the ideological shifts which occurred in American society concerning the "proper" role for women.

Periodization always offers difficulties. It seemed useful here, for purposes of comparison, to group women's status before 1800 roughly under the "colonial" heading and ignore the transitional and possible atypical shifts which occurred during the American Revolution and the early period of nationhood. Also, regional differences were largely ignored. The South was left out of consideration entirely because its industrial development occurred later.

The status of colonial women has been well studied and described and can briefly be summarized for comparison with the later period. Throughout the colonial period there was a marked shortage of women, which varied with the regions and always was greatest in the frontier areas. This (from the point of view of women) favorable sex ratio enhanced their status and position. The Puritan world view regarded idleness as sin; life in an underdeveloped country made it absolutely necessary that each member of the community perform an economic function. Thus work for women, married or single, was not only approved, it was regarded as a civic duty. Puritan town councils expected single girls, widows, and unattached women to be self-supporting and for a long time provided needy spinsters with parcels of land. There was no social sanction against married women working; on the contrary, wives were expected to help their husbands in their trade and won social approval for doing extra work in or out of the home. Needy children, girls as well as boys, were indentured or apprenticed and were expected to work for their keep.

The vast majority of women worked within their homes, where their labor produced most articles needed for the family. The entire colonial production of cloth and clothing and in part that of shoes was in the hands of women. In addition to these occupations, women were found in many different kinds of employment. They were butchers, silversmiths, gunsmiths, upholsterers. They ran mills, plantations, tan yards, shipyards, and every kind of shop, tavern and boarding house. They were gate keepers, jail keepers, sextons, journalists, printers, "doctoresses," apothecaries, midwives, nurses, and teachers. Women acquired their skills the same way as did the men, through apprenticeship training, frequently within their own families.

Absence of a dowry, ease of marriage and remarriage, and a more lenient attitude of the law with regard to women's property rights were manifestations of the improved position of wives in the colonies. Under British common law, marriage destroyed a woman's contractual capacity; she could not sign a contract even with the consent of her husband. But colonial authorities were more lenient toward the wife's property rights by protecting her dower rights in her husband's property, granting her personal clothing, and upholding pre-nuptial contracts between husband and wife. In the absence of the husband, colonial courts granted women "femme sole" rights, which enabled them to conduct their husband's business, sign contracts, and sue. The relative social freedom of women and the esteem in which they were held was commented upon by most early foreign travelers in America.

But economic, legal, and social status tells only part of the story. Colonial society as a whole was hierarchical, and rank and standing in society depended on the position of the men. Women did not play a determining role in the ranking pattern; they took their position in society through the men of their own family or the men they married. In other words, they participated in the hierarchy only as daughters and wives, not as individuals. Similarly, their occupations were, by and large, merely auxiliary, designed to contribute to family income, enhance their husbands' business or continue it in case of widowhood. The self-supporting spinsters were certainly the exception. The underlying assumption of colonial society was that women ought to occupy an inferior and subordinate position. The settlers had brought this assumption with them from Europe; it was reflected in their legal concepts, their willingness to exclude women from political life, their discriminatory educational practices. What is remarkable is the extent to which this felt inferiority of women was constantly challenged and modified under the impact of environment, frontier conditions, and favorable sex ratio.

By 1840 all of American society had changed. The Revolution had substituted an egalitarian ideology for the hierarchical concepts of colonial life. Privilege based on ability rather than inherited status, upward mobility for all groups of society, and unlimited opportunities for individual self-fulfillment had become ideological goals, if not always realities. For men, that is; women were, by tacit consensus, excluded from the new democracy. Indeed, their actual situation had in many respects deteriorated. While, as wives, they had benefitted from increasing wealth, urbanization, and industrialization, their role as economic producers and as political members of society differed sharply from that of men. Women's work outside of the home no longer met with social approval; on the contrary, with two notable exceptions, it was condemned. Many business and professional occupations formerly open to women were now closed, many others restricted as to training and advancement. The entry of large numbers of women into low status, low pay, and low skill industrial work had fixed such work by definition as "woman's work." Women's political status, while legally unchanged, had deteriorated relative to the advances made by men. At the same time the genteel lady of fashion had become a model of American femininity, and the definition of "woman's proper sphere" seemed narrower and more confined than ever.

Within the scope of this essay only a few of these changes can be more fully explained. The professionalization of medicine and its impact on women may serve as a typical example of what occurred in all the professions.

In colonial America there were no medical schools, no medical journals, few hospitals, and few laws pertaining to the practice of the healing arts. Clergymen and governors, barbers, quacks, apprentices, and women practiced medicine. Most practitioners acquired their credentials by reading Paracelsus and Galen and serving an apprenticeship with an established practitioner. Among the semi-trained "physics," surgeons, and healers, the occasional "doctoress" was fully accepted and frequently well rewarded. County records of all the colonies contain references to the work of the female physicians. There was even a female Army surgeon, a Mrs. Allyn, who served during King Philip's war. Plantation records mention by name several slave women who were granted special privileges because of their useful service as midwives and "doctoresses."

The period of the professionalization of American medicine dates from 1765, when Dr. William Shippen began his lectures on midwifery in Philadelphia. The founding of medical faculties in several colleges, the standardization of training requirements, and the proliferation of medical societies intensified during the last quarter of the 18th century. The American Revolution dramatized the need for trained medical personnel, afforded firsthand battlefield experience to a number of surgeons and brought increasing numbers of semi-trained practitioners in contact with the handful of European-trained surgeons working in the military hospitals. This was an experience from which women were excluded. The resulting interest in improved medical training, the gradual appearance of graduates of medical colleges, and the efforts of medical societies led to licensing legislation. In 1801 Maryland required all medical practitioners to be licensed; in 1806 New York enacted a similar law, followed by all but three states. This trend was reversed in the 1830s and 40s when most states repealed their licensure requirements. This was due to pressure from eclectic, homeopathic practitioners, the public's dissatisfaction with the "heroic medicine" then practiced by licensed physicians, and to the distrust of state regulation, which was widespread during the Age of Jackson. Licensure as prime proof of qualification for the practice of medicine was reinstituted in the 1870s.

In the middle of the 19th century it was not so much a license of an M.D. which marked the professional physician as it was graduation from an approved medical college, admission to hospital practice and to a network of referrals through other physicians. In 1800 there were four medical schools, in 1850, forty-two. Almost all of them excluded women from admission. Not surprisingly, women turned to eclectic schools for training. Harriot Hunt, a Boston physician, was trained by apprenticeship with a husband and wife team of homeopathic physicians. After more than twenty years of practice she attempted to enter Harvard Medical school and was repeatedly rebuffed. Elizabeth Blackwell received her M.D. from Geneva (New York) Medical College, an eclectic school. Sarah Adamson found all regular medical schools closed against her and earned an M.D. in 1851 from Central College at Syracuse, an eclectic institution. Clemence Lozier graduated from the same school two years later and went on to found the New York Medical College and Hospital for women in 1862, a homeopathic institution which was later absorbed into the Flower-Fifth Avenue Hospital.

Another way in which professionalization worked to the detriment of women can be seen in the cases of Drs. Elizabeth and Emily Blackwell, Marie Zakrzewska, and Ann Preston, who despite their M.D.s and excellent training were denied access to hospitals, were refused recognition by county medical societies, and were denied customary referrals by male colleagues. Their experiences were similar to those of most of the pioneer women physicians. Such discrimination caused the formation of alternate institutions for the training of women physicians and for hospitals in which they might treat their patients. The point here is not so much that any one aspect of the process of professionalization excluded women but that the process, which took place over the span of almost a century, proceeded in such a way as to institutionalize an exclusion of women,

which had earlier been accomplished irregularly, inconsistently, and mostly by means of social pressure. The end result was an *absolute* lowering of status for all women in the medical profession and a *relative* loss. As the professional status of all physicians advanced, the status differential between male and female practitioners was more obviously disadvantageous and underscored women's marginality. Their vital exclusion from the most prestigious and lucrative branches of the profession and their concentration in specializations relating to women and children made such disadvantaging more obvious by the end of the 19th century.

This process of pre-emption of knowledge, of institutionalization of the profession, and of legitimation of its claims by law and public acceptance is standard for the professionalization of the sciences, as George Daniels has pointed out. It inevitably results in the elimination of fringe elements from the profession. It is interesting to note that women had been pushed out of the medical profession in 16th-century Europe by a similar process. Once the public had come to accept licensing and college training as guarantees of up-to-date practice, the outsider, no mater how well qualified by years of experience, stood no chance in the competition. Women were the casualties of medical professionalization.

In the field of midwifery the results were similar, but the process was more complicated. Women had held a virtual monopoly in the profession in colonial America. In 1646 a man was prosecuted in Maine for practicing as a midwife. There are many records of well-trained midwives with diplomas from European institutions working in the colonies. In most of the colonies midwives were licensed, registered, and required to pass an examination before a board. When Dr. Shippen announced his pioneering lectures on midwifery, he did it to "combat the widespread popular prejudice against the man-midwife" and because he considered most midwives ignorant and improperly trained.

Yet he invited "those women who love virtue enough, to own their Ignorance, and apply for instruction" to attend his lectures, offering as an inducement the assurance that female pupils would be taught privately. It is not known if any midwives availed themselves of the opportunity.

Technological advances, as well as scientific, worked against the interests of female midwives. In 16th-century Europe the invention and use of obstetrical forceps had for three generations been the well-kept secret of the Chamberlen family and had greatly enhanced their medical practice. Hugh Chamberlen was forced by circumstances to sell the secret to the Medical College in Amsterdam, which in turn transmitted the precious knowledge to licensed physicians only. By the time the use of the instrument became widespread, it had become associated with male physicians and male midwives. Similarly in America, introduction of the obstetrical forceps was associated with the practice of male midwives and served to their advantage. By the end of the 18th century a number of male physicians advertised their practice of midwifery. Shortly thereafter female midwives also resorted to advertising, probably in an effort to meet the competition. By the early 19th century male physicians had virtually monopolized the practice of midwifery on the Eastern seaboard. True to the generally delayed economic development in the Western frontier regions, female midwives continued to work on the frontier until a much later period. It is interesting to note that the concepts of "propriety" shifted with the

prevalent practice. In 17th-century Maine the attempt of a man to act as a midwife was considered outrageous and illegal; in mid-19th-century America the suggestion that women should train as midwives and physicians was considered equally outrageous and improper.

Professionalization, similar to that in medicine with the elimination of women from the upgraded profession, occurred in the field of law. Before 1750, when law suits were commonly brought to the courts by the plaintiffs themselves or by deputies without specialized legal training, women as well as men could and did act as "attorneys-in-fact." When the law became a paid profession and trained lawyers took over litigation, women disappeared from the court scene for over a century.

A similar process of shrinking opportunities for women developed in business and in the retail trades. There were fewer female storekeepers and business women in the 1830s than there had been in colonial days. There was also a noticeable shift in the kind of merchandise handled by them. Where previously women could be found running almost every kind of retail shop, after 1830 they were mostly found in businesses which served women only.

The only fields in which professionalization did not result in the elimination of women from the upgraded profession were nursing and teaching. Both were characterized by a severe shortage of labor. Nursing lies outside the field of this inquiry, since it did not become an organized profession until after the Civil War. Before then, it was regarded peculiarly as a woman's occupation, although some of the hospitals and the Army during wars employed male nurses. These bore the stigma of low skill, low status, and low pay. Generally, nursing was regarded as simply an extension of the unpaid services performed by the housewife—a characteristic attitude that haunts the profession to this day.

Education seems, at first glance, to offer an entirely opposite pattern from that of the other professions. In colonial days women had taught "Dame schools" and grade schools during summer sessions. Gradually, as educational opportunities for girls expanded, they advanced just a step ahead of their students. Professionalization of teaching occurred between 1820 and 1860, a period marked by a sharp increase in the number of women teachers. The spread of female seminaries, academies, and normal schools provided new opportunities for the training and employment of female teachers.

This trend, which runs counter to that found in the other professions, can be accounted for by the fact that women filled a desperate need created by the challenge of the common schools, the ever-increasing size of the student body, and the westward growth of the nation. America was committed to educating its children in public schools, but it was insistent on doing so as cheaply as possible. Women were available in great numbers, and they were willing to work cheaply. The result was another ideological adaptation: in the very period when the gospel of the home as woman's proper sphere was preached most loudly, it was discovered that women were the natural teachers of youth, could do the job better than men, and were to be preferred for such employment. This was always provided, of course, that they would work at the proper wage differential—30 to 50 percent of the wages paid male teachers was considered appropriate. The result was that in 1888 in the country as a whole 63 percent of all teachers were women, while the figure for the cities only was 90.04 percent.

It appeared in the teaching field, as it would in industry, that role expectations were adaptable provided the inferior status group filled a social need. The inconsistent and peculiar patterns of employment of black labor in the present-day market bear out the validity of this generalization.

There was another field in which the labor of women was appreciated and which they were urged to enter—industry. From Alexander Hamilton to Matthew Carey and Tench Coxe, advocates of industrialization sang the praises of the working girl and advanced arguments in favor of her employment. The social benefits of female labor particularly stressed were those bestowed upon her family, who now no longer had to support her. Working girls were "thus happily preserved from idleness and its attendant vices and crimes," and the whole community benefitted from their increased purchasing power.

American industrialization, which occurred in an underdeveloped economy with a shortage of labor, depended on the labor of women and children. Men were occupied with agricultural work and were not available or were unwilling to enter the factories. This accounts for the special features of the early development of the New England textile industry: the relatively high wages, the respectability of the job and relatively high status of the mill girls, the patriarchal character of the model factory towns, and the temporary mobility of women workers from farm to factory and back again to farm. All this was characteristic only of a limited area and of a period of about two decades. By the late 1830s the romance had worn off: immigration had supplied a strongly competitive, permanent work force willing to work for subsistence wages; early efforts at trade union organization had been shattered, and mechanization had turned semi-skilled factory labor into unskilled labor. The process led to the replacement of the New England-born farm girls by immigrants in the mills and was accompanied by a loss of status and respectability for female workers.

The lack of organized social services during periods of depression drove ever greater numbers of women into the labor market. At first, inside the factories distinctions between men's and women's jobs were blurred. Men and women were assigned to machinery on the basis of local need. But as more women entered industry the limited number of occupations open to them tended to increase competition among them, thus lowering pay standards. Generally, women regarded their work as temporary and hesitated to invest in apprenticeship training, because they expected to marry and raise families. Thus they remained untrained, casual labor and were soon, by custom, relegated to the lowest paid, least skilled jobs. Long hours, overwork, and poor working conditions would characterize women's work in industry for almost a century.

Another result of industrialization was in increasing differences in life styles between women of different classes. When female occupations, such as carding, spinning, and weaving, were transferred from home to factory, the poorer women followed their traditional work and became industrial workers. The women of the middle and upper classes could use their newly gained time for leisure pursuits: they became ladies. And a small but significant group among them chose to prepare themselves for professional careers by advanced education. This group would prove to be the most vocal and troublesome in the near feature.

As class distinctions sharpened, social attitudes toward women became polarized.

The image of "the lady" was elevated to the accepted ideal of femininity toward which all women would strive. In this formulation of values, lower-class women were simply ignored. The actual lady was, of course, nothing new on the American scene; she had been present ever since colonial days. What was new in the 1830s was the cult of the lady, her elevation to a status symbol. The advancing prosperity of the early 19th century made it possible for middle-class women to aspire to the status formerly reserved for upper-class women. The "cult of true womanhood" of the 1830s became a vehicle for such aspirations. Mass circulation newspapers and magazines made it possible to teach every woman how to elevate the status of her family by setting "proper" standards of behavior, dress, and literary tastes. *Godey's Lady's Book* and innumerable gift books and tracts of the period all preach the same gospel of "true womanhood"—piety, purity, domesticity. Those unable to reach the goal of becoming ladies were to be satisfied with the lesser goal—acceptance of their "proper place" in the home.

It is no accident that the slogan "woman's place is in the home" took on a certain aggressiveness and shrillness precisely at the time when increasing numbers of poorer women *left* their homes to become factory workers. Working women were not a fit subject for the concern of publishers and mass media writers. Idleness, once a disgrace in the eyes of society, had become a status symbol. Thorstein Veblen, one of the earliest and sharpest commentators on the subject, observed that it had become almost the sole social function of the lady "to put in evidence her economic unit's ability to pay." She was "a means of conspicuously unproductive expenditure," devoted to displaying her husband's wealth. Just as the cult of white womanhood in the

South served to preserve a labor and social system based on race distinctions, so did the cult of the lady in an egalitarian society serve as a means of preserving class distinctions. Where class distinctions were not so great, as on the frontier, the position of women was closer to what it had been in colonial days; their economic contribution was more highly valued, their opportunities were less restricted, and their positive participation in community life was taken for granted.

In the urbanized and industrialized Northeast the life experience of middle-class women was different in almost every respect from that of the lower-class women. But there was one thing the society lady and the mill girl had in common—they were equally disfranchised and isolated from the vital centers of power. Yet the political status of women had not actually deteriorated. With very few exceptions women had neither voted nor stood for office during the colonial period. Yet the spread of the franchise to ever wider groups of white males during the Jacksonian age, the removal of property restrictions, the increasing numbers of immigrants who acquired access to the franchise, made the gap between these new enfranchised voters and the disfranchised women more obvious. Quite naturally, educated and propertied women felt this deprivation more keenly. Their own career expectations had been encouraged by widening educational opportunities; their consciousness of their own abilities and of their potential for power had been enhanced by their activities in the reform movements of the 1830s; the general spirit of upward mobility and venturesome entrepreneurship that pervaded the Jacksonian era was infectious. But in the late 1840s a sense of acute frustration enveloped these educated and highly spirited women. Their rising expectations had met with frustration, their hopes had been shattered; they were bitterly conscious of a relative lowering of status and a loss of position. This sense of frustration led them to action; it was one of the main factors in the rise of the woman's rights movement.

The women, who at the first woman's rights convention at Seneca Falls, New York, in 1848 declared boldly and with considerable exaggeration that "the history of mankind is a history of repeated injuries and usurpations on the part of man toward woman, having in direct object the establishment of an absolute tyranny over her," did not speak for the truly exploited and abused working woman. As a matter of fact, they were largely ignorant of her condition and, with the notable exception of Susan B. Anthony, indifferent to her fate. But they judged from the realities of their own life experience. Like most revolutionaries, they were not the most downtrodden but rather the most status-deprived group. Their frustrations and traditional isolation from political power funneled their discontent into fairly utopian declarations and immature organizational means. They would learn better in the long, hard decades of practical struggle. Yet it is their initial emphasis on the legal and political "disabilities" of women which has provided the framework for most of the historical work on women.* For almost a hundred years sympathetic historians have told the story of women in America by deriving from the position of middle-class women a generalization concerning all American women. To avoid distortion, any valid generalization concerning American women after the 1830s should reflect a recognition of class stratification.

*To the date of the first printing of this article (1969).

For lower-class women the changes brought by industrialization were actually advantageous, offering income and advancement opportunities, however limited, and a chance for participation in the ranks of organized labor.** They, by and large, tended to join men in their struggle for economic advancement and became increasingly concerned with economic gains and protective labor legislation. Middle- and upper-class women, on the other hand, reacted to actual and fancied status deprivation by increasing militancy and the formation of organizations for woman's rights, by which they meant especially legal and property rights.

The four decades preceding the Seneca Falls Convention were decisive in the history of American women. They brought an actual deterioration in the economic opportunities open to women, a relative deterioration in their political status, and a rising level of expectation and subsequent frustration in a privileged elite group of educated women. It was in these decades that the values and beliefs that clustered around the assertion "Woman's place is in the home" changed from being descriptive of an existing reality to becoming an ideology. "The cult of true womanhood" extolled woman's predominance in the domestic sphere, while it tried to justify women's exclusion from the public domain, from equal education, and from participation in the political process by claims to tradition, universality, and a history dating back to antiquity, or at least to the *Mayflower*. In a century of modernization and industrialization, women alone were to remain unchanging, embodying in their behavior and attitudes the longing of men and women caught in rapid social change for a mythical archaic past of agrarian

family self-sufficiency. In pre-industrial America the home was indeed the workplace for both men and women, although the self-sufficiency of the American yeoman, whose economic well-being depended on a network of international trade and mercantilism, was even then more apparent than real. In the 19th and 20th centuries, the home was turned into the realm of woman, while the workplace became the public domain of men. The ideology of "woman's sphere" sought to upgrade women's domestic function by elaborating the role of mother, turning the domestic drudge into a "homemaker" and charging her with elevating her family's status by her exercise of consumer functions and by her display of her own and her family's social graces. These prescribed roles never were a reality. In the 1950s Betty Friedan would describe this ideology and rename it "the feminine mystique," but it was no other than the myth of "woman's proper sphere" created in the 1840s and updated by consumerism and the misunderstood dicta of Freudian psychology.

The decades 1800–1840 also provide the clues to an understanding of the institutional shape of the later women's organizations. These would be led by middle-class women whose self-image, life experience, and ideology had largely been fashioned and influenced by these early, transitional years. The concerns of middle-class women—property rights, the franchise, and moral uplift—would dominate the woman's rights movement. But side by side with it, and at times co-operating with it, would grow a number of organizations serving the needs of working women.

American women were the largest disfranchised group in the nation's history, and they retained this position longer than any other group. Although they found

---

** In 1979, I would not agree with this optimistic generalization.

ways of making their influence felt continuously, not only as individuals but as organized groups, power eluded them. The mill girl and the lady, both born in the age of Jackson, would not gain access to power until they learned to cooperate, each for her own separate interests. It would take almost six decades before they would find common ground. The issue around which they finally would unite and push their movement to victory was the "impractical and utopian" demand raised at Seneca Falls—the means to power in American society—female suffrage.

POSTSCRIPT

DID WOMEN ACHIEVE GREATER AUTONOMY IN THE NEW NATION?

"The frustration in a privileged elite group of educated women" found an outlet of sorts in the reform efforts which began in the Age of Jackson. Causes such as the abolition of slavery and the banishment of alcohol attracted numerous female participants and offered women opportunities to exercise their leadership abilities. Several outstanding women later turned their attention from temperance and racial injustice to the benefit of their own sex. Lucretia Mott, Sarah and Angelina Grimké, Susan B. Anthony and Elizabeth Cady Stanton organized their sisters to pursue the rights of women with female suffrage as one of the main objectives.

The minimal amount of overlapping in Woloch and Lerner symptomizes the vitality of women's studies. Old generalizations are being subjected to scrutiny by researchers with access to previously untapped materials, often with radically different approaches to standard topics. Perhaps the history of American women presently lacks the full substructure of scholarship necessary to create meaningful generalizations. Does that preclude an intelligent person from drawing tentative conclusions? Is it possible to pencil in some guidelines, to create a framework? Can't we learn by asking questions about what we don't know?

There is a large and growing historiography of American women. Mary Beth Norton's *Liberty's Daughters: The Revolutionary Experience of American Women* (Little, Brown, 1979) offers a consciously different interpretation of an old subject. Page Smith's *Daughters of the Promised Land: Women in American History* (Little, Brown, 1972) has a more conventional approach. Mary P. Ryan's *Womanhood in America: From Colonial Times to the Present* (New Viewpoints, 1975) and Lois W. Banner's *Women in Modern America: A Brief History* (Harcourt, Brace, Jovanovich, 1974) are widely used as textbooks. Individual women may be researched in *Notable American Women: A Biographical Dictionary,* four volumes (Harvard University Press, 1971, 1980). Elaine Partnow's two-volume *The Quotable Woman* (Pinnacle Books, 1977) has witty and insightful passages from the writings of women who were born after 1800.

PART 3
ANTEBELLUM
AMERICA

Pressures and trends that began building in the early years of the American nation continued to gather momentum until conflict was to become almost inevitable. America had to respond to challenges from members of society who felt alienated from or forgotten by the new nation. The ideals of human rights and democratic participation that guided the founding of the nation had been applied only to selected segments of the population. Changes in the nature of the voting population and the way in which Americans viewed their place in the world had dramatic implications for the future. The level and quality of participation in the "American experiment" by disenfranchised or disaffected members of the society and the world became an important issue for America.

Did the Election of 1828 Represent a Democratic Revolt of the People?

Was American Foreign Policy in the Early Nineteenth Century Imperialistic?

Did Antebellum Reform Have a Great Impact on the Nation?

Did Slavery Destroy the Black Family?

Did the Frontier Determine the Course of American History?

ISSUE 11

DID THE ELECTION OF 1828 REPRESENT A DEMOCRATIC REVOLT OF THE PEOPLE?

YES: Robert V. Remini, "Election of 1828," in Arthur M. Schlesinger, Jr., ed., *The Coming to Power: Critical Presidential Elections in American History* (Chelsea House Publishers, 1971, 1972)

NO: Richard P. McCormick, "New Perspectives on Jacksonian Politics," *The American Historical Review,* January, 1960

ISSUE SUMMARY

YES: Professor Robert V. Remini argues that the 1828 presidential election symbolized the people's arrival at political responsibility and began a genuine, nationally organized, two-party system that came of age in the 1830s.
NO: Historian Richard P. McCormick maintains that voting statistics demonstrate that a genuine political revolution did not take place until the presidential elections of 1840, when fairly well-balanced political parties had been organized in virtually every state.

According to the conventional wisdom, Andrew Jackson's election to the presidency in 1828 began the era of the common man in which the mass of voters, no longer restrained from voting by property requirements, rose up and threw the elite leaders out of our nation's capital. While recent historians are not quite sure what constituted Jacksonian democracy or who supported it, and they question whether there ever existed such an era of egalitarianism, American history textbooks still include the obligatory chapter on the age of Jackson.

There are several reasons the old-fashioned view of this period still prevails. In spite of the new scholarly interest in social history, it is still easier to generalize about political events. Consequently, most texts continue to devote the major portion of their pages to detailed examinations of the successes and failures of various presidential administrations. Whether Jackson was more significant than other presidents is difficult to assess because "Old Hickory's" forceful personality, compounded with his use of strong executive authority, engendered constant controversy in his eight years in office.

Another reason the traditional concept of Jacksonian democracy has not been abandoned is because critics of the progressive interpretation have not been able to come up with an acceptable alternative view. Culminating with Arthur Schlesinger, Jr.'s, Pulitzer Prize-winning and beautifully written *The Age of Jackson* (Little, Brown, 1945), the progressive historians viewed Jackson's election in 1828 as the triumph of the common man in politics. Oversimplified as this interpretation may be, there is little doubt that a major change was taking place in our political system during these years. The death of both Thomas Jefferson and John Adams on July 4, 1826, the fiftieth anniversary of our Declaration of Independence from England, signified the end of the revolutionary generation's control over American politics. The first six presidents had been leaders or descendants of leaders in the revolutionary movement. At the Constitutional Convention in 1787, most of the time was spent discussing the powers of the presidency. Because of the recent experience with the British king, the Founding Fathers were fearful of strong executive authority. Therefore, the presidency was entrusted only to those individuals whose loyalty remained unquestioned. Jackson was the first president of the United States who did not come from either Virginia or Massachusetts. Though Jackson was only a teenager at the time of the American Revolution, his career was similar to those of the early Founding Fathers. Like Washington and Jefferson, Jackson became a living legend before he was fifty years old. His exploits as an Indian fighter and the military hero of the Battle of New Orleans in the War of 1812 were more important than his western background in making him presidential material.

During the past two decades, a number of historians have studied the effects of our presidential elections on the development and maintenance of our two party system. Borrowing concepts and analytical techniques from political scientists and sociologists, the "new political" historians have demonstrated the effectiveness of our parties in selecting candidates, running campaigns, developing legislation, and legitimizing conflicts within our democratic system. By 1815, the first-party system of competition between the Federalists and the Republican-Democrats had broken down, in part because the Federalists had refused to become a legitimate opposition party. A second-party system developed during the Jackson era between Old Hickory's Democratic party and his Whig opponents. It lasted until the 1850s when the slavery issue led to the formation of a new system of party competition between Republicans and Democrats.

The following selections disagree on the significance of the 1828 presidential race as a critical election in the development of the second party system. Professor Robert Remini argues that the 1828 presidential election symbolized the people's arrival at full political responsibility and began a genuine, nationally organized, two party system that matured in the 1830s. But historian Richard McCormick revises the traditional interpretation. His analysis of the voting statistics demonstrates that a genuine political revolution did not take place until the presidential election of 1840 when fairly well-balanced parties had been organized in virtually every state.

YES

Robert V. Remini

JACKSON, CALHOUN AND LIBERTY

. . . Jackson's appearance on the national scene in larger-than-life size was indeed fortuitous. He arrived just as the country was undergoing profound economic and political changes, when a new generation of men was coming forward to seize leadership from an older social and political elite. These men saw in Jackson a symbol of their own ambitions; they also saw in him a living example of the self-made man. Surely if an orphan boy from the backwoods could make good, there was no reason why they too could not aspire to wealth and social status by relying on their own talents to get what they wanted.

Furthermore, this was an age of developing professionalism in all fields—including politics. In the 1820's, men were hard at work perfecting the techniques of winning elections. They built machines to manage the popular vote; they believed in organization; and they were determined to rule. As sharp-nosed professionals, like Van Buren, they were quick to sense the response the General's popularity produced among the "rising" classes of Americans and to realize that association with Jackson might be crucial to their future position in politics, both nationally and locally. Small wonder, then, that Van Buren decided in the winter of 1826-27 to move into the Jackson camp and to bring with him as many of the Old Republicans as he could influence. "If Gen Jackson & his friends will put his election on old party grounds," Van Buren wrote to one Radical, "preserve the old systems, avoid if not condemn the practices of the last campaign we can by adding his personal popularity to the yet remaining force of old party feeling, not only succeed in electing him but our success when achieved will be worth something."

Since Jackson had resigned his Senate seat after his House defeat and was therefore not in Washington, Van Buren went to Vice-President Calhoun, who was now openly allied to the General, and offered him Radical support for the election of Jackson in 1828. Van Buren promised to swing over the Richmond Junto, the Virginia political machine, through his influence with Thomas Ritchie, editor of the Richmond *Enquirer* and a leader of the Junto. He also

Excerpted from "Election of 1828," by Robert Remini, in *The Coming to Power,* Arthur Schlesinger, Jr., ed. Copyright ©1971, 1972. Reprinted by permission of McGraw-Hill Book Co., publishers.

promised to tour the South and do everything possible to bring the entire Old Republican faction into the new coalition, even to the extent of seeing Crawford and winning his support. During their conversation about this alliance, Calhoun and Van Buren also discussed the possibility of holding a national nominating convention to replace the outmoded caucus system, but nothing definite was decided at this time.

In a subsequent letter to Ritchie, Van Buren clearly stated that his concern for the political scene went further than a single election. He urged the Radicals to join him in this new coalition, not simply to defeat Adams but to achieve "what is of still greater importance, the substantial reorganization of the Old Republican party." He called for a revival of the two-party system and for a renewal of Jefferson's old North-South alliance, between what he termed the "planters of the South and the plain Republicans of the North." For Van Buren, like many other politicians of the day, recognized that the political system of the 1820's had failed to respond to a changing society and that unless something were done right away it might collapse altogether.

Because of the efforts of many men to restructure the system, the election of 1828 witnessed the reemergence of the two-party system in American politics. The Jackson-Calhoun-Van Buren coalition eventually became known as the "Democratic" Republican party, or simply the Democratic party, while the Adams-Clay combination was called the "National" Republican party. With respect to party principles—not that they were much discussed in the campaign of 1828—the Democrats tended, when prodded, to restate the doctrines of Jefferson, particularly those emphasizing the rights of the states and the importance of the ordinary citizen. The National Republicans, on the other hand, affirmed the need for a strong central government in advancing the material well-being of the nation. Although there continued to be personal factions and cliques operating within the system, and while party organization did not advance in every state with equal rapidity, still in 1828 there was the beginning of a genuine, nationally organized, two-party system, a system that came of age in the 1830's. . . .

Balloting in the election extended from September to November. In most states, voting occurred over a period of several days. The states did not provide an official ballot; instead, the parties printed their own ballots, distributing them to friends and employing high-pressure party hacks at the polls to get the voter to accept the ticket. It was not unusual for a person to be accosted by several hawkers at once and threatened with bodily harm unless he accepted the proffered ballot.

The procedures for voting varied considerably throughout the twenty-four states. Delaware and South Carolina were the only states whose legislatures chose the electors. In all other states, they were chosen from a general or district ticket by an electorate that was roughly equivalent—except in Louisiana, Virginia, and Rhode Island—to the adult, white male population. Maryland, Maine, Illinois, Tennessee, and New York were the states using the district system, which meant that their electoral votes could be split between the candidates on a proportional basis. In all other states where the general ticket was employed, the candidate with the highest popular vote received all the electoral votes. Only Rhode Island and Virginia continued to restrict suffrage with property qualifications, and Louisiana maintained tax payments as a voting requirement.

When the election ended and the ballots were counted, it was clear that Jackson had won a stupendous victory. Out of a total of 1,155,022 popular votes cast, John Quincy Adams received 507,730; Andrew Jackson won 647,292 or just a little better than 56 per cent of the entire vote. This was an extraordinary achievement by Jackson, a veritable landslide. In percentages it was unequalled in any presidential election during the nineteenth century. And his total represented substantial support from all sections of the country, including New England.

The total popular vote in the election represented an increase of nearly eight hundred thousand over the previous election in 1824. In Pennsylvania alone, the number rose from forty-seven thousand to 152,000 four years later. There were several reasons for this spectacular rise. In the first place, the two-party system had been reestablished, if unevenly, and where in 1824 there were several candidates running for the Presidency there were only two in 1828. Second, there was considerable interest in the election generated to a large extent by an exciting, if not scurrilous, campaign initiated by both the Democratic and National Republican parties. Third, there was a concerted effort on the part of many politicians to get out the vote at election time; and finally, four states, representing a considerable electorate, changed their laws and transferred the selection of electors from the legislature to the people.

In the Electoral College, Jackson's victory was even more impressive. He won a total of 178 electoral votes to 83 for Adams. He swept everything south of the Potomac River and west of New Jersey. Adams carried New England (except for a single electoral vote in Maine), Delaware, New Jersey, and most of Maryland. Adams and Jackson shared New York, with the General taking 20 of the state's 36 electoral votes. All the remaining states went to Old Hickory. The election was relatively close in New Hampshire, New York, New Jersey, Maryland, Kentucky, Louisiana, Ohio, and Indiana. In the final analysis, what made the difference in virtually every one of these states was superior party organization.

In the Vice-Presidential race, Calhoun won an easy reelection over Richard Rush, but received 7 fewer electoral votes than Jackson, because Georgia, which resented Calhoun's treatment of William H. Crawford when they sat in Monroe's Cabinet together, awarded 7 votes to Senator William C. Smith of South Carolina.

Aside from the importance of party in producing Jackson's triumph there was also his own popularity and charisma. He was a living, authentic legend, the victor of New Orleans, the man who won over the British the greatest feat of arms in American history. Moreover, there was a dignity and bearing about him that bespoke leadership and authority. He was "presidential-looking," more so than any other public figure of the day. He inspired confidence among the largest mass of voters despite his lack of education and his reputation as an untamed westerner. In that sense Jackson himself was the essential issue in the campaign, just as he would be again in 1832, and the people in "vast numbers" crowded to his side.

Recently, however, some historians have questioned the vastness of the 1828 victory. Comparing the statistics of this election with previous state elections and future presidential elections, one historian has raised serious doubts as to whether the people poured out to the polls to express their confidence in Jackson. Perhaps it is possible to make meaningful comparisons between a presidential election and a state election for local officers held at different times or two presidential elections separated by a dozen or more years. And perhaps not. But in any event the fact remains that no matter how the statistics are analyzed or interpreted the people themselves who lived at the time believed that Jackson's election represented a great surge of popular support for the General. They believed that the ordinary citizen, the so-called "common man," who were farmers, workers, frontiersmen, and the like, had seized the opportunity to express their political opinion by voting for Jackson. And what is believed by the electorate is frequently more important than the objective reality. Many Democratic politicians, of course, saw the contest as one between "farmers & mechanics of the country" on one hand and the "rich and well born" on the other, "between the *aristocracy* and democracy of America." Thus when they read the returns from such states as Pennsylvania, Virginia, North Carolina, Ohio, and elsewhere they were astounded by the figures and therefore convinced of the truth of their own propaganda.

Not only did the Democrats see the election as a victory produced by the "vast numbers" of American people, but the National Republicans thought so too. That is what is even more astonishing. "Well," sighed one of them, "a great revolution has taken place.... This is what I all along feared but to a much greater extent." "It was the howl of raving Democracy," wrote another, "that tiped /sic/ Pennsylvania & New York & Ohio—and this will be kept up here after to promote the ends of the /Democratic party./" "All our efforts," said one of Clay's friends, "have not withstood the Torrent." Hezekiah Niles in his newspaper credited Jackson's "triumphant victory" to the "ardor of thousands." And Edward Everett of Massachusetts, one of

Adams' most dedicated supporters in Congress, explained to his brother that the General won "by a majority of more than *two* to *one,* an event astounding to the friends of the Administration and unexpected by the General himself and his friends.... /They/ are embarrassed with the vastness of their triumph and the numbers of their party."

Generations of historians, therefore, have interpreted Jackson's election in 1828 as the beginning of the "rise of the common man" in American history. Of course, such an easy and sweeping generalization does not take into consideration the fact that the "common man" had been rising for generations, and had made notable political advances long before Jackson appeared on the scene. Yet this election seemed to symbolize the people's arrival to political responsibility. Whether or not this was objectively true hardly mattered; what mattered was an expressed sense of participation in the electoral process experienced by ordinary citizens and that because of it a true "man of the people" had at last been elected President of the United States.

The notion of a popular "uprising" in Jackson's favor was strengthened by the scenes that occurred during his inauguration as President on March 4, 1829. Some twenty thousand people from all parts of the country converged on Washington to witness the triumph of their candidate. It was "like the inundation of the northern barbarians into Rome," wrote one, "save that the tumultuous tide came in from a different point of the compass." Daniel Webster was dumbfounded at the scene. "I never saw such a crowd here before," he said. "Persons have come five hundred miles to see General Jackson, *and they really seem to think that the country is rescued from some dreadful danger.*"...

11. DID THE ELECTION OF 1823 REPRESENT A DEMOCRATIC REVOLT?

When the ceremony ended, the throng rushed through the streets and avenues to get to the White House, where a reception was scheduled to permit the people to meet their new President. But what was planned as a function of proper decorum turned into a wild mêlée. The mob poured through the White House looking for Jackson and the refreshments that had been promised them. They were "scrambling, fighting, romping" from one room to the next. "The President," wrote Mrs. Samuel H. Smith, "after having been *literally* nearly pressed to death & almost suffocated & torn to pieces by the people in their eagerness to shake hands with Old Hickory, had retreated through the back way or south front & had escaped to his lodgings at Gadsby's." It was a "regular Saturnalia," said one congressman who watched the scene. The mob "broke in, in thousands . . . in one uninterrupted stream of mud and filth." The danger to the White House—to say nothing of life and limb—grew so great that the liquor was taken outside to the garden to draw the crowd from the house. Men jumped through the windows in their haste to reach the alcohol, thus instantly easing the pressure inside the mansion. So began the Administration of the "people's President," an Administration baptized by the screams and shouts of a wildly enthusiastic public.

The election of 1828 was in some respects the first modern presidential election. Democrats launched a national campaign of song, slogan, and shouting to attract the largest possible number of votes. It was the first campaign which witnessed a concerted effort to manipulate the electorate on a mass scale. Hereafter the major parties sought presidential candidates with wide popular appeal—frequently war heroes—then backed them with an engine of ballyhoo in order to create the numbers which would provide success. In the 1828 election, barbecues, parades, tree plantings, and the like were extensively used as part of the popular entertainment. Such techniques had been employed in previous elections but not on such a lavish scale. When they proved so effective by virtue of Jackson's extraordinary victory they became standard techniques in subsequent elections, receiving their biggest display in 1840.

But Jackson's impressive showing was not so much the result of the campaign ballyhoo as it was the organization that provided it, plus the General's widespread popularity based on his military exploits. The organization in time became an elaborate party machine through which the ordinary citizen could control the operation of Government and shape public policy. But the major importance of Jackson's election was the conscious and concerted effort of many politicians to organize an effective popular majority. In the process, the two-party system slowly reemerged after a hiatus of nearly sixteen years. So ended the political disorder of the Era of Good Feelings. A new party system had begun.

NO
Richard P. McCormick

NEW PERSPECTIVES ON
JACKSONIAN POLITICS

. . . The historical phenomenon that we have come to call Jacksonian democracy has long engaged the attention of American political historians, and never more insistently than in the past decade. From the time of Parton and Bancroft to the present day scholars have recognized that a profoundly significant change took place in the climate of politics simultaneously with the appearance of Andrew Jackson on the presidential scene. They have sensed that a full understanding of the nature of that change might enable them to dissolve some of the mysteries that envelop the operation of the American democratic process. With such a challenging goal before them, they have pursued their investigations with uncommon intensity and with a keen awareness of the contemporary relevance of their findings. . . .

That a "new democracy, ignorant, impulsive, irrational" entered the arena of politics in the Jackson era has become one of the few unchallenged "facts" in an otherwise controversial field. Differences of opinion occur only when attempts are made to account for the remarkable increase in the size of the active electorate. The commonest explanations have emphasized the assertion by the common man of his newly won political privileges, the democratic influences that arose out of the western frontier, or the magnetic attractiveness of Jackson as a candidate capable of appealing with singular effectiveness to the backwoods hunter, the plain farmer, the urban workingman, and the southern planter.

Probably because the image of "mighty democratic uprising" has been so universally agreed upon, there has been virtually no effort made to describe precisely the dimensions of the "uprising." Inquiry into this aspect of Jacksonian democracy has been discouraged by a common misconception regarding voter behavior before 1824. As the authors of one of our most recent and best textbooks put it: "In the years from the beginning of the government to 1824, a period for which we have no reliable election statistics, only small numbers of citizens seemed to have bothered to go to the polls." Actually, abundant data on pre-1824 elections is available, and it indicates a far higher rate of voting than has been realized. Only be taking this data into consideration can voting behavior after 1824 be placed in proper perspective.

The question of whether there was indeed a "mighty democratic uprising" during the Jackson era is certainly crucial in any analysis of the political character of Jacksonian democracy. More broadly, however, we need to know the degree to which potential voters participated in elections before, during, and after the period of Jackson's presidency as well as the conditions that apparently influenced the rate of voting. Only when such factors have been analyzed can we arrive at firm conclusions with respect to the dimensions of the political changes that we associate with Jacksonian democracy. Obviously in studying voter participation we are dealing with but one aspect of a large problem, and the limitations imposed by such a restrictive focus should be apparent.

In measuring the magnitude of the vote in the Jackson elections it is hardly significant to use the total popular vote cast throughout the nation. A comparison of the total vote cast in 1812, for example, when in eight of the seventeen states electors were chosen by the legislature, with the vote in 1832, when every state except South Carolina chose its electors by popular vote, has limited meaning. Neither is it revealing to compare the total vote in 1824 with that in 1832 without taking into consideration the population increase during the interval. The shift from the legislative choice of electors to their election by popular vote, together with the steady population growth, obviously swelled the presidential vote. But the problem to be investigated is whether the Jackson elections brought voters to the polls in such enlarged or unprecedented proportions as

to indicate that a "new democracy" had burst upon the political scene.

The most practicable method for measuring the degree to which voters participated in elections over a period of time is to relate the number of votes cast to the number of potential voters. Although there is no way of calculating precisely how many eligible voters there were in any state at a given time, the evidence at hand demonstrates that with the exception of Rhode Island, Virginia, and Louisiana the potential electorate after 1824 was roughly equivalent to the adult white male population. A meaningful way of expressing the rate of voter participation, then, is to state it in terms of the percentage of the adult white males actually voting. This index can be employed to measure the variations that occurred in voter participation over a period of time and in both national and state elections. Consequently a basis is provided for comparing the rate of voting in the Jackson elections with other presidential elections before and after his regime as well as with state elections.

Using this approach it is possible, first of all, to ascertain whether or not voter participation rose markedly in the three presidential elections in which Jackson was a candidate. Did voter participation in these elections so far exceed the peak participation in the pre-1824 elections as to suggest that a mighty democratic uprising was taking place? . . .

In the 1824 election not a single one of the eighteen states in which the electors were chosen by popular vote attained the percentage of voter participation that had been reached before 1824. Prior to that critical election, fifteen of those eighteen states had recorded votes in excess of 50 per cent of their adult white male population, but in 1824 only two states—Maryland and Alabama—exceeded this modest mark.

The average rate of voter participation in the election was 26.5 per cent. This hardly fits the image of the "roaring flood of the new democracy... foaming perilously near the crest...."

There would seem to be persuasive evidence that in 1828 the common man flocked to the polls in unprecedented numbers, for the proportion of adult white males voting soared to 56.3 per cent, more than double the 1824 figure. But this outpouring shrinks in magnitude when we observe that in only six of the twenty-two states involved were new highs in voter participation established. In three of these—Maryland, Virginia, and Louisiana—the recorded gain was inconsiderable, and in a fourth—New York—the bulk of the increase might be attributed to changes that had been made in suffrage qualifications as recently as 1821 and 1826. Six states went over the 70 per cent mark, whereas ten had bettered that performance before 1824. Instead of a "mighty democratic uprising" there was in 1828 a voter turnout that approached—but in only a few instances matched or exceeded—the maximum levels that had been attained before the Jackson era.

The advance that was registered in 1828 did not carry forward to 1832. Despite the fact that Jackson was probably at the peak of his personal popularity, that he was engaged in a campaign that was presumably to decide issues of great magnitude, and that in the opinion of some authorities a "well-developed two-party system on a national scale" had been established, there was a slight decline in voter participation. The average for the twenty-three states participating in the presidential contest was 54.9 per cent. In fifteen states a smaller percentage of the adult white males went to the polls in 1832 than in 1828. Only five states bettered their pre-1824 highs. Again the conclusion would be that it was essentially the pre-1824 electorate—diminished in most states and augmented in a few—that voted in 1832. Thus, after three Jackson elections, sixteen states had not achieved the proportions of voter participation that they had reached before 1824. The "new democracy" had not yet made its appearance....

When an examination is made of voting in other than presidential elections prior to 1824, the inaccuracy of the impression that "only small numbers of citizens" went to the polls becomes apparent. Because of the almost automatic succession of the members of the "Virginia dynasty" and the early deterioration of the national two-party system that had seemed to be developing around 1800, presidential elections did not arouse voter interest as much as did those for governor, state legislators, or even members of Congress. In such elections at the state level the "common man" was stimulated by local factors to cast his vote, and he frequently responded in higher proportions than he did to the later stimulus provided by Jackson.

The average voter participation for all states in 1828 was 56.3 per cent. Before 1824 fifteen of the twenty-two states had surpassed that percentage. Among other things, this means that the 1828 election failed to bring to the polls the proportion of the electorate that had voted on occasion in previous elections. There was, in other words, a high potential vote that was frequently realized in state elections but which did not materialize in presidential elections. The unsupported assumption that the common man was either apathetic or debarred from voting by suffrage barriers before 1824 is untenable in the light of this evidence....

Down to this point the voter turnout in the Jackson elections has been compared with that in elections held prior to 1824. Now it becomes appropriate to inquire whether during the period 1824 through 1832 voters turned out in greater proportions for the three presidential contests than they did for the contemporary state elections. If, indeed, this "new democracy" bore some special relationship to Andrew Jackson or to his policies, it might be anticipated that interest in the elections in which he was the central figure would stimulate greater voter participation than gubernatorial contests, in which he was at most a remote factor.

Actually, the election returns show fairly conclusively that throughout the eight-year period the electorate continued to participate more extensively in state elections than in those involving the presidency. Between 1824 and 1832 there were fifty regular gubernatorial elections in the states that chose their electors by popular vote. In only sixteen of these fifty instances did the vote for President surpass the corresponding vote for governor. In Rhode Island, Delaware, Tennessee, Kentucky, Illinois, Mississippi, Missouri, and Georgia the vote for governor consistently exceeded that for President. Only in Connecticut was the reverse true. Viewed from this perspective, too, the remarkable feature of the vote in the Jackson elections is not its immensity but rather its smallness.

Finally, the Jackson elections may be compared with subsequent presidential elections. Once Jackson had retired to the Hermitage, and figures of less dramatic proportions took up the contest for the presidency, did voter participation rise or fall? This question can be answered by observing the percentage of adult white males who voted in each state in the presidential elections of 1836 through 1844. ... Voter participation in the 1836 election remained near the level that had

been established in 1828 and 1832, with 55.2 per cent of the adult white males voting. Only five states registered percentages in excess of their pre-1824 highs. But in 1840 the "new democracy" made its appearance with explosive suddenness.

In a surge to the polls that has rarely, if ever, been exceeded in any presidential election, four out of five (78.0 per cent) of the adult white males cast their votes for Harrison or Van Buren. This new electorate was greater than that of the Jackson period by more than 40 per cent. In all but five states—Vermont, Massachusetts, Rhode Island, Kentucky, and Alabama—the peaks of voter participation reached before 1824 were passed. Fourteen of the twenty-five states involved set record highs for voting that were not to be broken throughout the remainder of the ante bellum period. Now, at last, the common man—or at least the man who previously had not been sufficiently aroused to vote in presidential elections—cast his weight into the political balance. This "Tippecanoe democracy," if such a label is permissible, was of a different order of magnitude from the Jacksonian democracy. The elections in which Jackson figured brought to the polls only those men who were accustomed to voting in state or national elections, except in a very few states. The Tippecanoe canvass witnessed an extraordinary expansion of the size of the presidential electorate far beyond previous dimensions. It was in 1840, then, that the "roaring flood of the new democracy" reached its crest. And it engulfed the Jacksonians.

The flood receded only slightly in 1844, when 74.9 per cent of the estimated potential electorate went to the polls. Indeed, nine states attained their record highs for the period. In 1848 and 1852 there was a general downward trend in voter participation, followed by a modest upswing in

1856 and 1860. But the level of voter activity remained well above that of the Jackson elections. The conclusion to be drawn is that the "mighty democratic uprising" came after the period of Jackson's presidency. . . .

There remains to be considered the factor of Jackson's personal popularity. Did Jackson, the popular hero, attract voters to the polls in unprecedented proportions? The comparisons that have already been made between the Jackson elections and other elections—state and national—before, during, and after his presidency would suggest a negative answer to the question. Granted that a majority of the voters in 1828 favored Jackson, it is not evident that his partisans stormed the polls any more enthusiastically than did the Adams men. Of the six highest states in voter participation in 1828, three favored Adams and three were for Jackson, which could be interpreted to mean that the convinced Adams supporters turned out no less zealously for their man than did the ardent Jacksonians. When Van Buren replaced Jackson in 1836, the voting average increased slightly over 1832. And, as has been demonstrated, the real manifestation of the "new democracy" came not in 1828 but in 1840.

The most satisfactory explanation for the increase in voter participation between 1824 and 1828 is a simple and obvious one. During the long reign of the Virginia dynasty, interest in presidential elections dwindled. In 1816 and 1820 there had been no contest. The somewhat fortuitous termination of the Virginia succession in 1824 and the failure of the congressional caucus to solve the problem of leadership succession threw the choice of a President upon the electorate. But popular interest was dampened by the confusion of choice presented by the multiplicity of candidates,

by the disintegration of the old national parties, by the fact that in most states one or another of the candidates was so overwhelmingly popular as to forestall any semblance of a contest, and possibly by the realization that the election would ultimately be decided by the House of Representatives. By 1828 the situation had altered. There were but two candidates in the field, each of whom had substantial sectional backing. A clear-cut contest impended, and the voters became sufficiently aroused to go to the polls in moderate numbers.

One final question remains. Why was the vote in the Jackson elections relatively low when compared with previous and contemporary state elections and with presidential votes after 1804? The answer, in brief, is that in most states either Jackson or his opponent had such a one-sided advantage that the result was a foregone conclusion. Consequently there was little incentive for the voters to go to the polls.

This factor can be evaluated in fairly specific quantitative terms. If the percentage of the total vote secured by each candidate in each state in the election of 1828 is calculated, the difference between the percentages can be used as an index of the closeness, or one-sidedness, of the contest. In Illinois, for example, Jackson received 67 per cent of the total vote and Adams, 33; the difference—thirty-four points—represents the margin between the candidates. The average difference between the candidates, taking all the states together, was thirty-six points. Expressed another way this would mean that in the average state the winning candidate received more than twice the vote of the loser. Actually, this was the case in thirteen of the twenty-two states. . . . Such a wide margin virtually placed these states in the "no contest" category. . . .

When Jacksonian democracy is viewed

11. DID THE ELECTION OF 1823 REPRESENT A DEMOCRATIC REVOLT?

from the perspectives employed in this analysis, its political dimensions in so far as they relate to the behavior of the electorate can be described with some precision. None of the Jackson elections involved a "mighty democratic uprising" in the sense that voters were drawn to the polls in unprecedented proportions. When compared with the peak participation recorded for each state before 1824, or with contemporaneous gubernatorial elections, or most particularly with the vast outpouring of the electorate in 1840, voter participation in the Jackson elections was unimpressive. The key to the relatively low presidential vote would seem to be the extreme political imbalance that existed in most states as between the Jacksonians and their opponents. Associated with this imbalance was the immature development of national parties in connection with the Jackson elections. As balanced, organized parties subsequently made their appearance from state to state, and voters were stimulated by the prospect of a genuine contest, a marked rise in voter participation occurred. Such conditions did not prevail generally across the nation until 1840, and then at last the "mighty democratic uprising" took place.

POSTSCRIPT

DID THE ELECTION OF 1828 REPRESENT A DEMOCRATIC REVOLT OF THE PEOPLE?

The two essays in this issue discuss the presidential election of 1828 from different approaches. Professor Robert Remini of the University of Illinois at Chicago Circle has recently completed a sympathetic and detailed three-volume biography of *Andrew Jackson* (New York, 1977, 1984). Included in his writings is an earlier account of *The Election of Andrew Jackson* (Philadelphia, 1963). The portion of his essay which is reprinted here is an example of good, solid narrative history sprinkled with interpretations. Though a full-fledged, two party system was not yet in effect in all parts of the country, Remini demonstrates that a well-organized coalition of supporters for Andrew Jackson existed in Congress and a number of states in various sections of the country. Often holding different ideological perspectives, these politicians united around one common goal: the election of Andrew Jackson to the presidency. Remini's description of the staged rallies, the name calling, the fudging of the issues, and the importance of organization over ideology, bears strong resemblance to our most recent presidential campaign.

Professor Richard McCormick, a veteran analyzer of nineteenth-century politics, views the 1828 election through the lens of quantitative history. He uses statistics to break down a number of generalizations about the significance of Jackson's election. The Rutgers University professor discounts the removal of property qualifications for voting, the influence of the western states, and the charisma of Jackson as the major reasons why twice as many voters turned out in the 1828 presidential race than they did four years earlier. He argues that in spite of such statistics, a higher percentage of voters had turned out for earlier gubernatorial and legislative elections in most states than for the 1828 presidential election. In McCormick's view, the key election was 1840, not 1828. Why? Because by this time, the two parties—Whigs and Democrats—were equally balanced in all sections of the country, and voters turn out in larger numbers when they perceive a closely contested presidential race.

McCormick's article raises a number of questions. Is he comparing apples and oranges, as Remini seems to imply? Using McCormick's data, is it possible for other historians to reach different conclusions? How does one explain a fifty-percent increase in voter turnout between 1824 and 1828?

For more information, see Richard P. McCormick's, "Political Development and the Second Party System" as well as the other essays in William Nisbet Chambers' and Walter Dean Burnham's, eds., *The American Party Systems: Stages of Political Development* (New York, 1967).

ISSUE 12

WAS AMERICAN FOREIGN POLICY IN THE EARLY NINETEENTH CENTURY IMPERIALISTIC?

YES: T.D. Allman, from "The Doctrine That Never Was," *Harpers,* January, 1984

NO: Robert H. Ferrell, from "Manifest Destiny," *American Diplomacy,* (W.W. Norton, 1959)

ISSUE SUMMARY

YES: Journalist T.D. Allman argues that President Monroe's original policy of nonintervention in Latin America was subverted by later presidents to justify military intervention by the United States there.
NO: Diplomatic historian Robert Ferrell believes that although the American government waged an aggressive war in Mexico, it was inevitable that the United States would obtain Texas, New Mexico, and California.

The American government in the early 1800s greatly benefitted from the fact that European nations generally considered what was going on in North America of secondary importance to what was happening in their own countries. In 1801, President Jefferson became alarmed when he learned that France had acquired the Louisiana territory from Spain. He realized that our western states might revolt if the government did not control the city of New Orleans as a seaport for shipping their goods. Jefferson dispatched his negotiators to buy the port. He pulled off the real-estate coup of the nineteenth century when his diplomats caught Napoleon in a moment of despair. With a stroke of the pen, the Louisiana Purchase of 1803 nearly doubled the size of the country for $15 million. The exact northern, western, and southeastern boundaries were not clearly defined. "But," as diplomatic historian Thomas Bailey has pointed out, "the American negotiators knew that they had bought the western half of perhaps the most valuable river valley on the face of the globe, stretching between the Rockies and the Mississippi, and bounded somewhere on the north by British North America."

After England fought an indecisive war with the United States in the years 1812-1815, she realized that it was to her advantage to maintain peaceful relations with her former colony. In 1817, the Great Lakes which bordered on the United States and Canada were mutually disarmed. Over the next half century, the principle of demilitarization was extended to the land, resulting in an undefended frontier line which stretched for more than 3,000 miles. The Convention of 1818 clarified the northern boundary of the Louisiana Purchase and ran a line along the forty-ninth parallel from Lake of the Woods in Minnesota to the Rocky Mountains. Beyond that point there was to be a ten-year joint occupancy in the Oregon Territory. In 1819, Spain sold Florida to the United States after Secretary of State John Quincy Adams sent a note telling the Spanish government to keep the Indians on their side of the border or else to get out of Florida. A few years later, the Spanish Empire crumbled in the New World and a series of Latin American republics emerged.

Afraid that the European powers might attack the newly independent Latin American republics and that Russia might expand south into the Oregon Territory, Secretary of State John Quincy Adams convinced President James Monroe to reject a British suggestion for a joint declaration and to issue instead a unilateral policy statement. The Monroe Doctrine, as it was called by a later generation, had three parts. First, it closed the western hemisphere to any future colonization. Second, it forbade "any interposition" by the European monarchs which would "extend their system to any portion of this hemisphere as dangerous to our peace and safety." And third, the United States pledged to abstain from any involvement in the political affairs of Europe. Viewed in the context of 1823, it is clear that President Monroe was merely restating the principles of unilateralism and nonintervention. Both of these were at the heart of American isolationism.

While President Monroe renounced the possibility of American intervention in European affairs, he made no such disclaimer toward Latin America as was originally suggested by Great Britain. It would be difficult to colonize in South America. But the transportation revolution, the land hunger which created political turmoil in Texas, and the need for ports on the Pacific to increase our trade in the Pacific encouraged the acquisition of new lands contiguous to the southwestern boundaries. Newspaper and magazine writers referred to the "manifest destiny" of Americans to spread democracy, freedom, and American settlers across the North American continent with the exception of Canada which was in Great Britain's possession.

In the first selection, journalist T.D. Allman outlines his belief that President Polk as well as twentieth-century presidents distorted President Monroe's original policy of nonintervention in Latin America in order to rationalize expansionist military incursions by the United States in the area. Diplomatic historian Robert Ferrell justifies the United States government's expansionist policies in the 1840s in terms of the ideology of Manifest Destiny. Although the American government waged an aggressive war against Mexico, Ferrell argues that it was inevitable for the United States to possess Texas, New Mexico, and California.

YES

T. D. Allman

THE DOCTRINE THAT NEVER WAS

At stake was more than some Caribbean island. America itself, one elder statesman informed the president, faced a crucial test "in the great struggle between liberty and despotism." Would the Russians and their allies be permitted to take over Latin America? Or would we Americans stop them?

The president, for the moment, kept his own counsel, but the intelligence community had made its judgment. The Caribbean was only the beginning. The "general expectation," the president's chief military adviser warned, was that the Russians and their surrogates were plotting to "employ force against South America" as well. We must fight for the hemisphere's freedom, one House leader urged the secretary of state, even if it meant "a war for it against all Europe."

But the secretary of state turned out to be a dove. The Russian menace, he argued, was more an American fantasy than a political reality. He suggested that the United States pursue détente with the Russians while letting the Latin Americans work out their own problems in their own ways.

A sense of crisis gripped Washington. Would the president stand up for America? Or would he let aggression be its own reward? Finally the president made his decision, and informed Congress.

The year might have been 1983, the president Ronald Reagan. But it was 1823. The elder statesman was James Madison. The military adviser was Secretary of War John Calhoun. Henry Clay was the hawk in Congress; John Quincy Adams was the secretary of state.

The president was James Monroe. And we all know what Monroe did. Or do we?

The Monroe Doctrine, 160 years later, is more and more with us. "The first major foreign policy statement by an American president," Richard Nixon said in 1981, as Central America once again made headlines, "was the Monroe Doctrine. We cannot allow the Soviet Union to get a further foothold in Latin

America. Cuba and Nicaragua is enough."

President Reagan and his followers evidently agree. Over the past three years the Monroe Doctrine has enjoyed a notable revival. In 1982 Senator Steven Symms of Idaho proposed a resolution committing the United States to stopping Marxism-Leninism in the Western Hemisphere by "whatever means may be necessary, . . . including use of arms." A few senators fretted that the Symms measure would be a new Tonkin Gulf resolution. But the resolution's backers did not see it that way. The Senate was only "reinstituting the 1823 Monroe Doctrine to protect the Western Hemisphere," a Symms spokesman explained. The new "Monroe Doctrine" passed both houses by an overwhelming vote.

The Monroe Doctrine, according to some of Reagan's supporters, not only empowers the president to make war in Latin America; it forbids the United States to make peace. Negotiating with "communists" in the Western Hemisphere "is a direct contradiction of the Monroe Doctrine," Howard Phillips, national director of the Conservative Caucus, announced last July. But is the Monroe Doctrine sufficient to protect the freedom of the Americas? In April William Safire urged the president "to update the Monroe Doctrine." Defending countries like El Salvador was not enough, he argued. The U.S. should go on the offensive against "the subverting countries." Safire called for a "Reagan Corollary" to the Monroe Doctrine. Now, with the invasion of Grenada, supporters of the Monroe Doctrine have their Reagan Corollary. By what right do we Americans violate the sovereignty of others? Is there any difference between the Reagan Corollary and the Brezhnev Doctrine?

Neither the president nor his supporters, it seems fair to say, sense any moral or legal contradiction between "saving" El Salvador and subverting Nicaragua—between defending the hemisphere and invading a hemispheric neighbor. For many Americans these actions embody a return to the values of a safer, surer time—the reassertion of principles going back to the Founding Fathers. Senator Jesse Helms caught this mood well when he called for "reinstituting" the Monroe Doctrine. "It's time America starts acting like America again," he declared.

President Monroe never proclaimed a Monroe Doctrine. Instead he rejected the calls for alarms and war, and adopted Adams's proposal for negotiations with Russia and strict U.S. nonintervention in Latin American affairs. In fact, Monroe's policy in almost all respects was the opposite of what we imagine the Monroe Doctrine to be. Far from hurling defiance at the emperor of Russia and his fellow members of the Holy Alliance, Monroe informed Congress of "the great value" he and his cabinet "invariably attached to the friendship of the Emperor" and their "solicitude to cultivate the best understanding with his government." Monroe did not tell the Europeans they had no business being involved in the Western Hemisphere. Instead he explicitly recognized Russia's "rights and interests" in Alaska, and propounded a doctrine of U.S. respect for the colonial rights of other European powers as well. "With the existing colonies or dependencies of any European power," he pledged, "we have not interfered and shall not interfere."

Why did President Monroe proclaim no Monroe Doctrine? One reason is that no great Russian-led conspiracy to crush freedom in the New World existed, and both Monroe and Adams knew it. Russia wanted only an amicable settlement of the Alaska boundary, not new colonies in the New World. Indeed, by the time Monroe sent his message to Congress, all the principal European powers—Great Britain, France, Austria, and Russia—had abjured future colonization in the Americas. They all also either opposed, or refused to support, any attempt by Spain to regain its lost empire. "The story that the president prevented a terrible danger," observes Dexter Perkins, the premier historian of the Monroe Doctrine, "is legend and nothing more."

Monroe had another reason for not proclaiming a Monroe Doctrine. The real threat to the United States at that time came neither from Russia and its allies nor from Latin America. It was Great Britain whose power and ambition threatened U.S. interests. Both the U.S. and Britain claimed the Oregon Country, a vast territory stretching from California north to Alaska. If the British checked our ambitions there the way they had checked our ambitions in Canada, the United States, whose borders then stopped at the Rocky Mountains, would be denied a Pacific coastline. Preventing future British colonization in North America, not averting future European colonization in Latin America, was the overwhelming U.S. strategic concern in 1823.

It was fear of being co-opted by the British, not fear of the Holy Alliance, that led President Monroe to write his message to Congress. A few months earlier Britain had urged the United States to join it in opposing any European attempts to recolonize the Americas. The British wanted the two countries to pledge to respect Latin America's territorial integrity and to avoid military intervention there. France, the member of the Holy Alliance thought most likely to attack Latin America, accepted the British proposal without hesitation. But in Washington it created alarm—not because of what it meant for the independence of Latin America, but because of what it implied for the independence of the United States.

Monroe opposed any U.S. action that "would have the appearance of taking a position subordinate to that of Great Britain." Adams was equally against any scheme that might make America look like "a cockboat in the wake of the British man-of-war." Rather than let Britain seize the initiative, the United States issued its own declaration on Latin American independence. Though this declaration was later generally regarded as one of the key provisions of the Monroe Doctrine, it was nothing of the kind. Monroe's statement fell far short of the commitment to Latin American independence the British and French had already made. He made no pledge that the United States would either respect or defend the independence of Latin America. He did, however, inform the Europeans, in the interests of maintaining "the amicable relations existing between the United States and those powers," that his administration would not view with "indifference" any "interposition" in Latin American countries recognized by the United States.

This was no New World declaration of independence. Monroe proclaimed no unalienable right of self-determination; in fact the rhetoric of our Declaration of Independence is entirely absent from his message. And Monroe's statement, mild as it was, contained an even bigger irony. Because it was limited to Latin American nations whose independence the United States "acknowledged," it excluded such countries as Brazil, Peru, and Haiti, whose independence the United States had not recognized. Monroe and Adams, it should be emphasized, were fervent anticolonialists. Why, then, was Monroe's statement so limited?

The answer lies in Monroe's desire to

avoid, not launch, an American crusade against Europe on behalf of hemispheric liberty. He wanted to end fifty years of U.S. embroilment in Europe's wars and rivalries, and get on with the business of consolidating the independence—and expanding the territory—of the United States. His message strongly reaffirmed the U.S. policy of nonalignment and nonintervention set out by President Washington in his Farewell Address. Monroe also made it quite clear to the British that, even though he was recognizing Russia's ownership of Alaska, he had no intention of letting Oregon slip from America's grasp. He asserted:

> as a principle in which the rights and interests of the United States are involved, that the American Continents, by the free and independent condition which they have assumed and maintain, are henceforth not to be considered as subjects for future colonization by any European Power.

This was hardly the Monroe Doctrine forever justifying—indeed ordaining—U.S. military intervention in Latin America. Monroe and Adams adamantly opposed foreign military intervention, including U.S. military intervention, as a matter of principle. They were determined to avoid U.S. involvement in the quarrels of both Europe and Latin America. The "purpose" of Monroe's message, as Adams put it, was to avow American principles "while disclaiming all intention of attempting to propagate them by force." Furthermore, this particular section of the message was quite separate from his discussion of Latin America. As Monroe himself put it, his statement dealt with "the North West Coast of this Continent." Far from proclaiming a Latin America doctrine, Monroe was serving notice that the United States did not intend to be left out of any territorial settlement in North America.

"[W]e should emphasize the fact," Perkins writes in *A History of the Monroe Doctrine*, "that there is no evidence that Monroe was in any degree aware that he was enunciating maxims which should govern in perpetuo, or at least for a long time to come, the foreign policy of the United States. The language of the message related to a specific situation." The Europeans, the Latin Americans, and even Monroe and his immediate successors completely forgot about the statement soon after it was made. Even when real threats arose to the independence of the New World, U.S. policy remained one of "indifference."

Only one example need be cited. In 1833 Britain, reneging on its earlier pledge, seized the Malvinas Islands from Argentina. How did the United States react to this flagrant act of "future colonization"? The United States did nothing. A decade after Monroe's message had been sent to Congress, no one in Washington had any idea there was such a thing as a Monroe Doctrine. And so the scene was set, 149 years later, for the Falkland Islands war.

If Monroe did not proclaim the Monroe Doctrine, who did? Though not even he presumed to use the word "doctrine," the honor belongs to President James Knox Polk—conqueror of Mexico and real founder of our national doctrine of continual violation of the sovereignty of our Latin American neighbors.

The year was 1845 and, like some later presidents, Polk had a hidden agenda. He wanted to launch a war against Mexico in order to seize California, but great obstacles stood in his way. He had won the presidency on a pledge to gain for the United States Texas and the "whole territory of Oregon," not California. Yet Texas had been annexed before he took office, and Britain was too strong to challenge. So Polk, a generation after Monroe's injunction against "future colonization," was obliged to accept a negotiated settlement that left half of Oregon—the present Canadian province of British Columbia—under British colonial rule.

Polk had hoped Mexico would go to war with the United States over Texas, and thus provide an excuse for seizing California. But he soon faced the same dilemma some of his successors would. What does one do with an aggressor who refuses to attack? In a rehearsal for the Tonkin Gulf resolution, Polk used naval patrols and raids into Mexican territory to provoke a Mexican "attack." For more than a year he also mounted a concerted disinformation campaign designed to convince Congress and the public that U.S. rights in Texas were threatened by Mexico. Finally, Polk's spurious contention that the Mexicans had "shed American blood on American soil" stampeded Congress into a declaration of war.

Still, how could a war to defend Texas justify the conquest of California?

The "principle avowed by Mr. Monroe," Polk claimed, made it not only proper, but necessary. The British, the president said, were conspiring to seize California for themselves. What better way to prevent "future colonization" there than to seize it for ourselves? No British conspiracy existed then, just as no Holy Alliance conspiracy had existed in 1823. But the substance of the Monroe Doctrine had been established. Thereafter, U.S. presidents would attack the weak in Latin America on the grounds of defending them against conspiracies by powerful Europeans.

The phrase "Monroe Doctrine" did not come into popular use until the 1850s. Having taken half of Mexico, many Americans also wanted Central America, the site of the prospective interocean canal, as well. "Let no technical impediment be thrown in the way of our Americanizing Central America," declaimed the representative from Missouri, in one of the earliest formulations of both the Roosevelt and the Reagan corollaries. "Humanity, philanthropy, and Christianity demand that it shall be done at no distant day."

But what could justify such intervention? Theodore Roosevelt ultimately provided the same answer that, in one variant or another, our presidents have given us, not just for invasions of countries like Grenada or for destabilization campaigns against countries like Nicaragua, but for intervention in countries like Vietnam and Cambodia as well. "[A]dherence of the United States to the Monroe Doctrine," Roosevelt informed Congress, entitled the president to "the exercise of an international police power." America's commitment to "civilization," he added, gave it a special right to intervene in countries guilty of "wrongdoing or impotence."

In fulfillment of the Roosevelt Corollary, dozens of countries, and not just in Latin America, would experience U.S. invasion and military occupation. Only two examples need be cited.

In Nicaragua and the Philippines, U.S. forces fought protracted counterinsurgency wars in order both to stop "outside aggression" and to confer democracy on the threatened countries. Many Americans supported these wars, but not everyone was convinced of their justice. "We talk of civilizing lower races," observed William Graham Sumner, "but we have never done it yet. We have exterminated them." "If you want war," he added, "nurture a doctrine." The United States won its wars against Aguinaldo in the Philippines and Sandino in Nicaragua, and both nations were occupied by U.S. forces for decades.

But there was no triumph of liberty—only the Somozas followed by the Sandinistas in Nicaragua, and the eventual establishment of the Marcos dictatorship in Manila.

"President Monroe, in his famous message to Congress," the secretary of state reminded his audience, "denounced the expansionist and despotic system of Czarist Russia and its allies." Would Americans be unequal to the proud legacy of President Monroe now that the Russian conspiracy threatened the world?

It might have been one of President Reagan's aides speaking. But it was John Foster Dulles. The year was 1954, and the United States was about to overthrow democracy in Guatemala in order, as President Eisenhower explained, to stop a Soviet "beachhead" from being established in the Western Hemisphere. Already the Eisenhower administration had restored the Shah to power in Iran, setting up one more domino fated to fall later. Soon it was to establish Diem in Saigon. But for the moment the United States was busy injecting, in the name of Monroe and liberty, the poison that still festers in Central America today.

These actions were not unusual. Since the end of World War II a quality of the fantastic has run through the conduct of U.S. foreign policy. Successive administrations have acted out the same fantasy in Cambodia, in Iran, and all over Latin America—the fantasy that invading a foreign nation can liberate it, and that imposing a government of our choice on foreign peoples can make them free. But most of all the U.S. has acted out a fantasy about itself—the Monroe fantasy that once upon a time our presidents, by proclaiming doctrines, could make whole hemispheres conform to our notions of what they should be; and that if Americans only proclaim, and enforce, enough doctrines now, then the whole world will become safe for democracy.

It started soon after World War II with the Truman Doctrine, which, as Henry Steele Commager notes, "was widely hailed as... a worldwide equivalent of the Monroe Doctrine." Since then we have had the Eisenhower, Nixon, and Carter doctrines. Yet, none of these doctrines have had much success in conferring liberty on others. "Cambodia," President Nixon declared in 1970, "is the Nixon Doctrine in its purest form." And in the gruesome fate of that nation we have the most extreme example of what our doctrines have produced—carnage, destruction, terror, mass death.

What might Monroe and his contemporaries have made of all these doctrines? They would have denounced the Reagan Corollary and its variants not just as a threat to the liberties of others, but as a violation of American principles that threatened America's own freedoms as well. Monroe and his colleagues opposed such military interventions because they had quite literal notions of both independence and freedom. They believed that the independence of Latin America meant freedom from "interposition" not only by the Europeans, but by us. Adams's proudest boast was that the United States, "without a single exception, respected the independence of other nations [and] abstained from interference in the concerns of others, even when the conflict has been for principles to which she clings."

But most of all they feared what American violations of the liberties of others would do to the cause of liberty in the United States. America's "glory is not *dominion*, but *liberty*," Adams declared on the Fourth of July, 1821. If Americans cared to preserve their liberties, he added, they should not go "abroad in search of monsters to destroy." America's commitment to "freedom and independence" would then be replaced by "the murky radiance of dominion and power." "The fundamental maxims of her policy," he warned, "would insensibly change from *liberty* to *force.*"

Adams never forsook his principles, even when the Monroe Doctrine epoch of conquest had become established. In 1848, the former president and secretary of state, still considered the primary author of the Monroe Doctrine, collapsed and died on the floor of the House of Representatives after protesting the war President Polk claimed was justified by "the principle avowed by Mr. Monroe."

Monroe opposed expansion at Mexico's expense for the same reason he very probably would have opposed the Vietnam War. Like Lyndon Johnson later, Polk called his war an attempt "to extend the area of liberty." But Monroe feared that this kind of expansion would create divisions within the United States—a veritable crisis of American liberty—that no president could control. Monroe was right. Polk got his war. But, like Johnson and Nixon, he got it at the cost of a first-class constitutional crisis at home. For as the facts came out, Congress and the public began to realize that Polk had committed aggression against the Constitution, not just Mexico.

"Allow a president to invade a neighboring nation whenever he deems it necessary," declared Abraham Lincoln, then a freshman congressman, "... and you allow him to make war at pleasure. Study to see if you can fix any limit to his power in this respect after you give him so much as you propose." In the end, the fundamental question raised by Polk's war was the same question raised by the war in Southeast Asia. But the attack on Mexico produced an American domestic crisis that makes Watergate seem trivial. Conquering Cali-

fornia was easy enough. But who could overcome the American divisions the Mexican war created? The answer was that no one could. The question of whether slavery was to be permitted in the newly seized lands divided the United States more deeply than any other issue, either before or since.

Samuel Eliot Morison's epitaph for our first Monroe Doctrine war to "extend the area of freedom" by force is also the epitaph for what remains the most horrible event in American history. Had there been "no Mexican War," he points out, "there would have been no Civil War, at least not in 1861."

John Calhoun, like John Quincy Adams, lived long enough to see the Monroe message turned into the Monroe Doctrine. Even though he had opposed Adams's approach in 1823, Calhoun was outraged at Polk's misrepresentation of Monroe's declaration, as he made clear on a number of occasions, most notably when Polk, having conquered California, turned his attentions to Central America. Predictably, the president discerned a foreign conspiracy there. Equally predictably, Polk had decided that the Monroe declaration of 1823 empowered him to intervene in the supposedly threatened territory, which in this case was the Yucatán.

"Declarations are not policy," Calhoun protested, "and cannot become settled policy." The president "tells you that these declarations have become the settled policy of this country." But decisions of war and peace, he reminded the nation, under the Constitution "belong to us—to Congress." As for U.S. military intervention, he went on, "There is nothing said of it [in the Monroe statement]; and with great propriety it was omitted." Polk was attempting to go "infinitely and dangerously beyond Mr. Monroe's declaration."

Like Adams and Monroe himself, Calhoun recognized the real danger of a Monroe Doctrine approach: it allowed the president to turn U.S. policy from a matter of constitutional deliberation into a matter of executive privilege. To let presidential doctrine decide national policy was not merely to undermine the Constitution. It was to empower presidents like Polk "to make us a party to all their wars," Calhoun predicted, "and hence I say, if this broad interpretation be given to these declarations, we shall forever be involved in wars."

President Reagan has conquered Grenada; but what does his historically unprecedented control of press coverage of the invasion imply for the First Amendment? He is fighting an undeclared war against Nicaragua. But what does this CIA operation imply for constitutional warmaking powers?

Grenada has a population of less than 120,000, and a gross national product of $60 million a year. During the uproar over the invasion, another statistic caught my attention. In five years, U.S. military expenditures have doubled; we are now spending a quarter of a trillion dollars annually to defend "freedom." It certainly is to be hoped that the Marines will bring democ-

racy to the little island. But what price will we Americans wind up paying for these attempts "to extend the area of liberty" by force?

On December 2, 1823, the very day Monroe's policy of nonintervention was announced to Congress, Henry Clay and John Quincy Adams discussed the same issues the Reagan Corollary raises today. Adams told Clay that he viewed a "war for South American independence...in a different light from you—as necessarily placing high interests of different portions of the Union in conflict with each other, and thereby endangering the Union itself."

"Not a successful war," replied Clay. "But a successful war, to be sure, creates a military influence and power, which I consider the greatest danger of war."

Two hundred years after our independence from Britain, our past is to us what the monarchy has become to the British. It long ago lost the power to govern our actions, and its illusory glitter often blinds us to the realites of both the world and our place in it. But like Bagehot's constitutional monarch, the past, if we are willing to listen, still has the power to warn.

NO

Robert Hugh Ferrell

MANIFEST DESTINY

In the history of American diplomacy few ideas have been more important than "manifest destiny"—the belief of the people of the United States that the North American continent, despite prior claims by France, Spain, Russia, Great Britain, and Mexico, was destined to become American territory. This mystic conviction translated itself into reality in the years from the beginning of the nineteenth century to the end of the Civil War. It was the presiding force behind the Mexican War of 1846–1848, the subject of the present chapter. French claims to North America vanished with the Louisiana Purchase of 1803. Spanish claims received settlement in the Adams-Onís Transcontinental Treaty of 1819, after which Spain's lands contiguous to the United States passed under control of the new government of Mexico. Russia's claims to Pacific territory withdrew northward to Alaska in a Russian-American agreement of 1824. British claims to Oregon territory disappeared in a treaty signed in 1846. And by 1848 Mexico's claims to Texas, New Mexico, and California were no more. "Away, away with all those cobweb tissues of rights of discovery, exploration, settlement, continuity, etc.," cried the New York editor, John L. O'Sullivan, who in the year 1845 coined the phrase "manifest destiny." It was, O'Sullivan claimed, "the right of our manifest destiny to overspread and to possess the whole of the continent which Providence has given us for the development of the great experiment in liberty and federative self-government entrusted to us."

Some exponents of manifest destiny believed that the United States should not confine its territorial ambitions to the continent of North America. According to one writer "Its floor shall be as a hemisphere, its roof the firmament of the star-studded heavens, and its congregation an Union of many Republics, comprising hundreds of happy millions... governed by God's natural and moral law of equality." Such hopes, of course, were never to be realized, and manifest destiny in its more practical vision limited itself to North America.

"Manifest Destiny," adapted from *American Diplomacy, A History* by Robert H. Ferrell, with the permission of the author and the publisher, W.W. Norton & Company, Inc. Copyright ©1959 by W.W. Norton & Company, Inc.

Two questions might arise at this point, the first of which can be stated as follows: Was manifest destiny nothing but imperialism, an American brand of a well-known nineteenth-century European practice? The nineteenth century was the age of imperialism in Europe, and although European nations undertook their vast colonial conquests in the latter part of the century, whereas the United States pursued its manifest destiny and continental ambition in earlier years, still it might well seem that there was little difference between imperialism and manifest destiny.

In actual fact there was a considerable difference. Manifest destiny was not imperialism if the latter term is properly defined as "rule over alien peoples." There were few Indians in the American West, hardly any at all if compared to the millions of inhabitants of Africa and the hundreds of millions of Asians. It is true that American policy toward the Indians frequently adhered to the frontier maxim that the only good Indians were dead Indians, and it is true that new diseases brought by the settlers decimated the Indians. But in view of the few Indians in the United States one must say that only in an extremely legalistic sense was the American nation imperialist during the early nineteenth century.

A second question in connection with manifest destiny concerns specifically the Mexican War. Was not this war, one of the most important chapters in American territorial expansion, a war of aggression—did not Americans pick a quarrel in 1846 with a weak and divided Mexico for the purpose of despoiling the Mexicans of New Mexico and California, and could not one therefore say that manifest destiny, at least as avowed in 1846–1848, was only an excuse for a war of conquest? . . .

MEXICO AND THE TEXAS REVOLUTION

At the turn of the nineteenth century the lands of Mexico belonged to Spain, and it was only after some years of uncertainty during the Napoleonic wars, after reconquest of Mexico by Spain at the end of the wars, that Mexico in 1821 became an independent nation. Twenty-five years of independence followed before the government in Mexico City had to face war with the United States.

The tasks of the Mexican government in its early years were, by any standard, large. The lands of Mexico began in Central America at the border of Guatemala. Mexican territory reached eastward through Yucatan, northward through the isthmus of Tehuantepec to spread like a gigantic fan across twelve hundred miles of virgin territory from the Sabine River in the east to California in the west. Over these distances the government in Mexico City had to exert its authority, distances that in the early nineteenth century rendered them much more remote from the Mexican capital than mid-twentieth century Fairbanks or Honolulu from Washington, D.C. The task of administering the territory of Mexico from the capital in Mexico City was therefore almost impossible. The northern Mexican provinces of Texas, New Mexico, and California were distinctly separated by geography from the populous region about Mexico City, and were oriented economically to the United States. From the Nueces River to the Rio Grande was a desert tract. South of the Rio Grande for hundreds of miles there was almost no cultivation. Westward for hundreds of miles stretched sheer wilderness and desert.

Was there any chance that with time Mexico might have peopled its northern empire? Not unless time were reckoned in terms of several decades, perhaps a century or more, and even this might not have sufficed. Some six million Indians and half-castes lived in Mexico—no one knows, of course, just what the population really was—and controlling this ignorant and poverty-stricken mass were only some 60,000 Spanish-speaking and Spanish-descended persons who were the government officials and landholders and priests and army officers. Nearly all of the 60,000 Spanish lived in the area now embraced within the republic of Mexico. They had little desire to migrate to the northern provinces, Texas and New Mexico and California. They remained in their comfortable towns and ranches, and only a trickle of people from Mexico proper entered the upper territories. This trickle could do little when the Yankee flood began coming across the Sabine shortly after signature of the Transcontinental Treaty in 1819.

One cannot stress sufficiently the point that Texas and the other northern territories of Mexico were virtually empty lands, lacking Mexican settlers, and because of distance lacking almost any control from Mexico City.

Mexican establishments in California, like those in Texas, were pitiful in their poverty and unimportance. If in Texas there were only about three thousand Mexicans of Spanish origin in the 1830's, there were little more than four thousand in California, a mere handful consisting chiefly of priests and monks about the missions, soldiers employed to keep the Indians submissive, and a few large land-owners and cattle raisers. In California the area of Mexican control never extended north of San Francisco, nor inland beyond the coastal area. The first Mexican settlers had come at about the time of the American revolution, and few settlers followed them.

Certainly there could be no comparison between the Mexican attempt to settle California and the effort by Englishmen a hundred and fifty years earlier to settle the province of New England, for in the Great Migration of 1630–1642 some 16,000 Englishmen from the Old World came there, to say nothing of simultaneous English migrations to other parts of America.

Aside from the difficulty of holding the northern territories there was the more serious problem of the debility and incompetence of the Mexican government. The revolution against Spain had broken out in 1810, and the Mexicans triumphed conclusively over the forces of their mother country in 1821. In the next year a military adventurer, Agustín de Iturbide, made himself emperor of Mexico with the title of Augustus I. After a short time he fell from power, went abroad, returned, and was shot. The Mexicans in 1824 established a federal constitution on the United States model, and this constitution managed to stay in effect for five years, after which another military leader, Bustamante, subverted it and took office for three years. He was displaced by Antonio López de Santa Anna, the prince of Mexican adventurers, who was in and out of power several times in the next two decades. There was no peace in Mexico before 1877 when General Porfirio Díaz took the reins of government and held them with absolute authority until 1911, after which came a new time of trouble for government in Mexico.

It was nominally the effort of Santa Anna in 1835 to centralize the Mexican government that led to a revolt in Texas in 1835–1836, but behind the constitutional issue lay the weakness of Mexican control in Texas, the thinness of Mexican settlement, and—above all—the fact that in the fifteen years preceding the Texas revolution some thirty thousand Americans had moved into the Mexican province.

Land hunger had drawn American settlers to Texas during the years after the first group arrived in 1821 under the guidance of the *empresario* Stephen F. Austin. Austin had contracted with the Mexican government for many thousands of acres of land in return for bringing in families of settlers. The families paid about ten cents an acre for their land, with liberal arrangements of credit, at a time when inferior land was selling in the United States for $1.25 cash. The United States government, following a financial panic in 1819, had tightened its land policy, and the Bank of the United States, then the principal bank of credit in the country, had drastically reduced its loans and raised its rates of interest, so that settlers seeking cheap lands were driven by force of circumstance to accept the propositions of such men as Stephen Austin. Few of these early American settlers in Texas stopped to inquire as to the type of government they would encounter in their new country. Even the demand of Mexican authorities that they become converts to Catholicism did not disturb their consciences, and they accepted the forms of Catholicism as easily as they accepted other Mexican laws exercised through the Texas organs of the Mexican government—always provided that government, law, and religion did not interfere with their wholehearted search for cheap land.

Naturally the carefree attitude and abandon with which settlers moved into Texas changed when, after a few years, prosperity permitted leisure for thought and consideration. What in early days had proved acceptable began to irk. Especially the effects of frontier religious revivals must be considered, for as Methodist and Baptist preachers took up superinten-

dence over the souls of American frontiersmen, there came advice from the new ministers that it was blasphemous for the settlers to participate in any way in the forms of the Catholic Church. By the latter 1820's, when signs of civilization were appearing at every hand and settlers were becoming annoyed by increased numbers of Mexican government officials, a new spirit of discontent swept the scattered communities of Texas. Settlers remembered their old allegiance to the United States. When General Andrew Jackson took office as president of the United States in 1829, a wave of enthusiasm and hope rose in the American West. No frontier settlement, even in Mexican Texas, could forget that the "Ginral" was a man of the people. Meanwhile life kept improving. "Within four miles of me," wrote one Texan settler in the mid-1830's, "there are more than one thousand inhabitants, chiefly new emigrants, and within the same distance we have four small stores, two blacksmith shops and two schools. We have a dancing frolic every week and preaching allmost [sic] every Sunday."

In a bare decade and a half more settlers came to Texas than in centuries of Spanish administration. This was the inescapable statistic of the Texas situation by the time of the Texas revolution. By the early 1830's the American settlers outnumbered the Spanish-Mexican population by ten to one. Mexican administrators in Mexico City and in Texas took alarm. The Americans had been fairly happy under the short-lived constitution of 1824, the easy requirements of which were laxly enforced. The processes of Mexican government had not touched them to any important extent. But when the government of Santa Anna sought in 1835 to tighten the administration in Texas, trouble began, which might have been foreseen from the moment the first American immigrants entered Texas in 1821. It was not foreseen, and by 1835 time had run out on Mexican claims to Texas. There followed during the winter and early spring of 1835–1836 the chief events of the Texas revolution.

Some settlers in Texas had risen in November 1835 and in an unorganized but effective fashion had expelled the few Mexican soldiers and administrators then present on Texas soil. To quell this rebellion, Santa Anna led a large army of 3,000 men into Texas and began his assault with the famous attack on the Alamo. There the rapacious Mexican leader isolated 188 Americans under Colonel William B. Travis and raised from the cathedral the black flag of No Quarter. For seven or eight days the Texans held out, issuing a defiant call for help to "all Americans in the world." But no help arrived, and the Mexican troops closed in on the defenders and slaughtered them to the last man. The Alamo, to indulge in an understatement, incited Texans to fury. "Thermopylae had her messenger of defeat—the Alama had none," roared General Edward Burleson when he heard the news of the tragedy. Foolishly Santa Anna followed up this slaughter by an even larger carnival at Goliad, where he shot down more than 300 American prisoners in cold blood. News of these massacres spread terror among thousands of the Texas settlers, and as Santa Anna advanced there began a wild flight to the border of the United States, the Sabine River. A long, suffering procession of refugees, women and children and Negro slaves, struggled to reach American territory. The exodus took place in cold weather, with incessant rain. Fortunately Santa Anna shortly thereafter met his downfall when General Sam Houston caught him encamped in a trap. Houston had only to attack. This the Texan leader

vigorously did, to the embarrassment of the Head of the Mexican State, who at the crucial moment was taking a siesta. With the Battle of San Jacinto on April 21, 1836, the capture of Santa Anna and dispersal of his army, Texas became independent....

The Texan revolution of 1835–1836 made no change in American policy. Andrew Jackson, consummate politician that he was, refused during his second administration to sponsor admission of Texas to the union. Desiring annexation, he refrained from making political capital of it, for fear that the Texas question if propelled into politics would reopen the slavery question, uneasily adjourned by the Compromise of 1820. Northern congressional leaders were certain that Texas upon admission to the union would be a slave state, and this would raise the inconvenient issue of balance of slave versus free states in the Senate, which then was exactly even, thirteen slave and thirteen free. Especially they thought of what might happen if Texas upon annexation should split itself into five or ten slave states, for this would ruin any hope of maintaining the sectional balance. Jackson was aware of Northern feeling on this matter. The most obtuse statesman—which Jackson assuredly was not—could hardly remain ignorant of the rising feeling between North and South. Jackson moved gingerly and with complete impartiality of action, if not of feeling, when the Texans in 1836 declared their independence.... Giving as excuse for his inaction the existence of a treaty between his country and Mexico, and the proprieties of international intercourse, Jackson had in mind the delicate political situation in the United States.

With the refusal of the Jackson administration to annex Texas after San Jacinto, relations between the two sovereign

English-speaking states of North America settled down to a brief and quiet interlude. Jackson recognized Texan independence eleven months after San Jacinto, four months longer than the American government had waited to recognize Mexico after its successful revolution against Spain in 1821. The Mexicans nonetheless protested American recognition of Texas, and refused themselves to recognize Texan independence, a policy in which they persisted to the bitter end. Events continued in this course—Texan independence, American recognition, Mexican nonrecognition—until President John Tyler in 1844 sponsored in the Senate a treaty of annexation, and failing in that effort resorted early in 1845 to a joint resolution of annexation. . . .

To no avail were the antislavery arguments against annexation. The feeling of manifest destiny was too strong and too popular in 1845, antislavery sentiment not yet strong enough. Tyler's joint resolution passed Congress with a whoop. "You might as well attempt to turn the current of the Mississippi," Old Hickory declared in a letter given to the press at the crucial political moment, "as to turn the democracy from the annexation of Texas to the United States . . . obtain it the U. States must—peaceably if we can, but forcibly if we must."

All but forgotten in the uproar were the pretensions of the Mexican government. Texas, Mexican diplomats had been claiming, was still part of Mexico, and annexation by the United States would be tantamount to a declaration of war. Upon passage of the joint resolution of March 1, 1845, the Mexican minister in Washington asked for and received his passports.

THE MEXICAN WAR

A year elapsed after the annexation of Texas before the war with Mexico began. There followed after Tyler's resolution of March 1845 a period of maneuvering and uncertainty during which President Polk waited to see what the Mexicans would do. The president was not averse to war. Still, he did not wish war if he could get its fruits without any fighting. He therefore sent a representative to Mexico City, John Slidell, in the hope of obtaining Mexican recognition of a Texas boundary at the Rio Grande, in exchange for which the United States would assume payment of claims of its nationals against the Mexican government. (Because Mexico had been in turmoil for thirty years and more, many Americans had found their properties confiscated and sometimes their lives endangered by the various revolutionary troubles; these claims had been settled by a mixed claims commission for approximately two million dollars, but the Mexicans had refused to pay the claims.) This was Slidell's minimum proposal: recognition of the Rio Grande boundary in return for American assumption of the claims payments. In addition the emissary was empowered to purchase New Mexico and California for $25,000,000. Polk would have gone as high as $40,000,000. He especially desired California with its fine harbor of San Francisco.

The president's representative, Slidell, unfortunately for Mexico, met with rebuff. Before Slidell's journey to Mexico City Polk had received a statement in writing from the Mexican foreign minister to the effect that an American commissioner would find a friendly reception. The Mexican government upon Slidell's arrival refused to treat with him, on the technicality that his credentials were those of a minister plenipotentiary rather than a special *ad hoc* representative. What happened was that the Mexican government of the moment, led by General Mariano Paredes, was in imminent peril of being thrown from office, and could not face the hostility of popular opinion in the capital city, should it undertake to negotiate with the Americans. The Mexican people—when one spoke of a "people" of Mexico in the nineteenth century he meant little more than the literate inhabitants of the capital—were determined that annexation of Texas would be tantamount to war.

Whatever sort of government was in control, it was a fatuous act in 1846 to turn down an overture from the government of the United States. Mexico was in the position of refusing to sell territories that she could not keep anyway. Napoleon in 1803, seeing that he could not hold Louisiana, had sold it. There were no Napoleons in Mexico in 1846 but only factional politicians who found momentary power too sweet to relinquish, be the responsibilities of their decisions ever so serious for the future of their country.

And so John Slidell went away, and President Polk, tired of the irresolution of his adversary, disposed American troops under Brigadier General Zachary ("Old Zach") Taylor in the disputed border area of Texas between the Nueces River and the Rio Grande. The local Mexican commander on April 25, 1846 surprised a company of American soldiers, killing or wounding sixteen and capturing the remainder, and the war was on. This even before news had reached the Mexican commander that the government in Mexico City had declared a "defensive war" against the United States. In Washington, Polk was preparing a war message to Congress when the welcome news arrived of the Mexican attack. War, Polk then could assert, had been forced upon the United States by act of Mexico. Congress declared on May 13, 1846 that "by the act of the Republic of Mexico, a state of war exists between the Government and the United States."

That this war with Mexico in the mid-nineteenth century was not a popular conflict soon became obvious to everyone. The war with Mexico of 1846–1848 never evoked the popularity that surrounded the first or second World Wars or the war with Spain in 1898. Not merely was there grumbling and disgruntledness in New England, but outright speeches against the war by such Western opponents as Congressman Abraham Lincoln of Illinois. The issue on which opposition arose was, of course, the extension of slavery. Northern opposition to the war found expression everywhere from pulpits, rostrums, and "stump" platforms. No sooner had the war begun than it received a name indicating its alleged origin—President Polk's War. . . .

President Polk in taking the country to war against Mexico did not, incidentally, act from proslavery motives. Polk was dismayed at the debates over the slavery issue, and became embittered after the war began by the reintroduction into Congress in January 1847 of the Wilmot Proviso to prevent the expansion of slavery into new territory. Slavery as an institution, the president always maintained, had no connection with the war or the peace. "Its introduction in connection with the Mexican War," he recorded in his diary, "is not only mischievous but wicked." Although a citizen of Tennessee and a slaveholder, like his predecessor Andrew Jackson, he had in mind first and foremost the territory and Pacific ports of California, and only after this goal was achieved would he concern himself over the slavery question. Economic interests, but of a territorial sort, moved Polk in his actions, peaceful and otherwise, toward Mexico. . . .

The Treaty of Guadalupe Hidalgo was concluded on February 2, 1848, and had a most interesting background. It was signed by Trist after his commission had expired. President Polk through Secretary of State James Buchanan had annulled Trist's commission, fearing that to have a negotiator accompanying Scott's army would seem to the Mexicans like a sign of American weakness. But Trist at this point began to fear that without an immediate peace there might develop a sentiment in the United States for taking all of Mexico. The Mexican government had been reconstituted through the efforts of General Scott, whose troops were billeted comfortably in the Mexican capital. The abject defeat of the Mexicans was so obvious that, as Trist knew, it might well encourage the more ambitious apostles of manifest destiny to stretch the American eagle's wings all the way to Guatemala. . . . Trist negotiated his treaty at the little village of Guadalupe Hidalgo just outside Mexico City and sent the treaty off to Washington to see what Polk would do with it.

Polk was furious. The president, an able, conscientious, sincere man, was intensely suspicious of political plots during his administration—and he saw a plot in Trist's treaty.

Polk, it seems altogether fair to say, had begun the Mexican War not out of partisan but for national reasons. The president believed that his country's future demanded a border of Texas at the Rio Grande, and in addition he wanted to acquire New Mexico and especially California. This was a broadly national purpose, but as Whig opposition to the war became more vehement Polk found that matters of politics plagued his every move, that he had to be circumspect in his every act to fend off the Whigs and keep the war going to a victorious conclusion. He managed to do this, but only with difficulty, and one of his worst problems in the conduct of the war was that the two

leading military commanders, Generals Taylor and Scott, were both Whigs and likely to profit personally from the war by being nominated on the Whig ticket for the presidency. . . .

Trist's treaty, despite the improprieties of its conclusion, was not unwelcome, for Polk's agent had secured New Mexico and California plus Mexican acceptance of the Texan boundary at the Rio Grande, and the United States was to pay $15,000,000 and assume the adjusted claims of its citizens against the Mexican government. These terms, Polk realized, were virtually the maximum that Slidell had been empowered to negotiate in the abortive mission of 1846, and despite his intense disgust with Trist for acting without commission the president sent the treaty to the Senate, which gave its advice and consent on March 10, 1848. After ratification by Mexico, Polk proclaimed the treaty in effect on the anniversary of American independence, July 4, 1848. By this stroke of war, following upon the stroke of diplomacy which had gained Texas in 1845, the United States had added altogether (including Texas) 1,200,000 square miles to its domain, an increase of more than sixty-six per cent.

What could one say about manifest destiny, as it had found fulfillment in the events of 1845–1848? The peaceful process by which the United States of America had been expanding across the enormously valuable North American continent had been punctuated by a short and sharp and altogether victorious war. At the time, people were asking whether political leaders from the Southern portion of the United States had not forced the war with Mexico for the enlargement of their slave domains, for the miserable purpose of obtaining "more pens to cram slaves in." This fear, so far as concerned the reasoning of President Polk himself and probably many of his supporters, was unfounded. Even so, in the twentieth century when war led to the near-destruction of Western civilization, many people were again going to ask if the Mexican War were not an unjust war of aggression. Was, then, the Mexican War a conflict that for this latter reason should have been avoided? Should not the United States in 1846–1848 have trusted to its diplomacy and restrained its pursuit of manifest destiny, if that were possible?

The answer to this question is not easy. No American today would like to give up the territories secured from Mexico. Those expanses so varied in their riches gave us first gold, then oil, now uranium, and have increased enormously the power of the United States. If one may be permitted the luxury of reading the present into the past—assuredly a most unhistorical operation—he can easily see that at a time in the mid-twentieth century when the power of the United States and the Union of Soviet Socialist Republics is so neatly balanced, any large subtraction from American power might have changed the course of history. This is no fanciful notion, pleasantly speculated upon in these pages, but an idea that bears some considerable possibilities for thought. What might have happened if the United States during the second World War had not had enough economic and military strength to throw the victory to the Allies? Or for that matter, what might have happened in the gray spring of 1918 when the German offensive came within an ace of success, if the morale of Allied troops had not been bucked up by the prospect, soon to be realized, of two million American soldiers in France? If the nation had stopped at the Sabine River, if such statesmen as John Tyler and James K. Polk had taken Mexican complaints and protests as insuperable obstacles to realization of manifest destiny, the American people might today find their personal and public circumstances altogether unenviable. . . .

POSTSCRIPT

WAS AMERICAN FOREIGN POLICY IN THE EARLY NINETEENTH CENTURY IMPERIALISTIC?

Professor Ferrell presents an interesting defense of the United States policy of Manifest Destiny toward Mexico in the 1840s. Admitting that the United States created conditions which pushed Mexico into starting the war, Ferrell nevertheless justifies the goals of the war which were the acquisition of Texas, New Mexico, and California. Not everyone will agree with Professor Ferrell's acceptance of the ideology of Manifest Destiny.

Some books, like Richard W. Van Alstyne's, *The Rising American Empire* (Quadrangle, 1965), and William A. Williams's, *The Tragedy of American Diplomacy* (Delta, 1962), would criticize the narrow definition of imperialism which Ferrell employs. These radical historians believe that America created an economic empire during its earliest years as a nation which has continued into the present day. They argue for a broader definition of imperialism and go beyond Allman's criticisms of the Monroe Doctrine. Even though the United States never exerted political control over Latin America, nevertheless, the radical historians argue that the United States has been the major imperialistic power in the area because of its extraordinary economic influence.

Journalist T.D. Allman views our "unmanifest destiny" toward Latin America through the lens of our current foreign policy. As justified as many of his criticisms are concerning our historical interventions in this area, the implication is that our policy choices lay between the two extremes of armed intervention or complete non-involvement. Are there no other options? A good starting point to answer this question is Dexter Perkins's *A History of the Monroe Doctrine* (Little, Brown, 1941). For a critical but more temperate view than Allman, see Gaddis Smith's "The Legacy of Monroe's Doctrine," *The New York Times Magazine* (September 9, 1984).

ISSUE 13

DID ANTEBELLUM REFORM HAVE A GREAT IMPACT ON THE NATION?

YES: Arthur M. Schlesinger, Sr., from *The American as Reformer* (Harvard University Press, 1950)

NO: Ronald G. Walters, *American Reformers, 1815–1860* (Hill and Wang, 1978)

ISSUE SUMMARY

YES: Professor Arthur M. Schlesinger, Sr., considers antebellum reform one of the most important periods of change in United States history.
NO: Professor Ronald Walters blames the reformers and their organizations for the failure to achieve significant change in antebellum America.

"What is man born for but to be a Reformer, a Remaker of what man has made," Ralph Waldo Emerson insisted in a lecture before a Boston audience in January 1841. By that time, the reform impulse in nineteenth-century America had been attacking social problems for over a decade. Emerson defined a reformer as "a renouncer of lies; a restorer of truth and good." With these words, the "Sage of Concord" as Emerson was known, articulated the thoughts of countless others caught up in a multifarious crusade which had the perfection of society as its goal.

Antebellum reformers directed their major efforts at abolition (the destruction of slavery) and temperance (the eradication of alcoholism by prohibiting the drinking of spirits). Other important issues revolved around women's rights, the treatment of prisoners and the insane, working conditions, and a more healthy society through sound nutrition. Those reformers, less attracted to reforming society than to replacing it, established Utopian communes as an alternative way of living.

The origins of the reform impulse stretch back to colonial America. It is no exaggeration to argue that the very inception of English colonial life is an example of the reforming zeal. Not only did the Pilgrims institute religious reform, but they also sought to establish the perfect society. Quakers in Philadelphia in 1709 provided a home so that the insane could be removed from prisons, where they had been lumped together with criminals. In 1775 the first abolition organization began meeting, also in Philadelphia. In a more specific way, Margaret Brent appeared before the Maryland Assembly in 1639 and demanded the right to vote. These various manifestations of reform stem, in part, from the opportunities inherent in a pluralistic society. One of the major characteristics of pluralism is the right to organize and join voluntary associations. Freedom to organize, freedom of speech and the demand for equality form the matrix in which the search for the perfect society was conducted.

In part, reform in nineteenth-century America meant eliminating social injustice imported from the Old World. Imprisonment for indebtedness was one of these remnants. Kentucky abolished this crime in 1821 and many other states followed suit. In 1835 Bostonians founded the Society for the Prevention of Pauperism. By 1834 construction workers in eastern cities had reduced their working hours to ten per day. By 1860 most American workers enjoyed this right. Other reforms focused on changing human nature, risky as that business might be. The drive for temperance attacked a universal problem—alcoholism. The more extreme advocates wanted to stop the drinking of spirits altogether. The most adamant included coffee on their list of prohibited beverages. By 1826 a national temperance organization existed. A decade later, taking "The Pledge" became a symbol of teetotaling or refusing to drink alcohol. Clearly the greatest injustice in the United States was slavery. In 1833 local abolitionist groups in New York and Massachusetts merged their efforts and the movement picked up steam until their goal was partially accomplished thirty years later with the Emancipation Proclamation. The Utopian movement blossomed from 1820 to 1860. Some of these groups were organized around secular values, others were devoted to religious principles. They offered a choice to people who rejected a society characterized by urbanism, industrialization and the cash nexus. As the colonial reforming impulse signaled the health of the pluralistic society in British North America, so antebellum reform had its side effects also. The principal one of these was the opportunity for women to participate in them. No matter what the issue was, American women joined, organized, petitioned, and spoke out. In 1848 the first women's rights convention was held in Seneca Falls, New York. The concern for women's rights came to the reform movement late. It raised questions of sexual equality, which, like temperance (in the sense of drunk drivers), prisoners' rights, and conditions in asylums for the insane are still in question today.

Professor Schlesinger writes, "A hundred years afterwards, Emerson's words sound as if they had been uttered of our own age." Professor Walters contradicts him with "It is one of the minor tragedies of antebellum reform that no one noticed its death and few mourned its passing."

YES
Arthur M. Schlesinger

THE AMERICAN AS REFORMER

THE HISTORICAL CLIMATE OF REFORM

"I wish to offer to your consideration some thoughts on the particular and general relations of man as a reformer." Ralph Waldo Emerson thus opened a famous address in 1841 on the first great upsurge of social reform in United States history. At the time American society along the seaboard was two centuries old. The people had subdued the savages, reshaped their physical environment, won political independence, established representative institutions, founded towns and cities, developed agriculture and trade, entered upon manufacturing. The country had attained a provisional maturity, and despite the more primitive conditions on the western frontier, thinking men were taking stock of the achievements and conducting what the speaker called a "general inquisition into abuses." And so, as Emerson went on to say, "In the history of the world the doctrine of Reform had never such scope as at the present hour." It seemed to him that every human institution was being questioned—"Christianity, the laws, commerce, schools, the farm, the laboratory"—and that not a "town, statute, rite, calling, man, or woman, but is threatened by the new spirit."

A hundred years afterward, Emerson's words sound as if they had been uttered of our own age, though whether the spirit of reform be deemed a threat or promise is a matter of personal opinion, and Emerson's other remarks attest that he himself regarded it as vital to social health. Between his time and ours of course much has happened. Cycles of reform and repose have come and gone until by a giant turn of the wheel the American people again find themselves in a period when in the history of the world the doctrine of reform had never such scope as at the present hour. In venturing to treat Emerson's theme a century later I need hardly say that I do so without Emerson's intuitive wisdom and philosophic acumen. Instead, I bring to it the poorer gifts of the historical scholar, those of the foot soldier rather than of the air pilot.

I can only hope that the longer span of national experience since his day, plus the historian's special approach, will add something, however slight, to an understanding of the conditions and nature of the reform impulse in the United States.

The reform urge has obviously not been an American monopoly, nor has the nation ever been immune to struggles for human betterment elsewhere. In particular there has been a like-mindedness with England. The colonists were deeply indebted to the mother country for their notions of individual liberty and free institutions, as well as for that "salutary neglect"—Burke's phrase—which enabled them to develop these conceptions yet farther. Even after Independence this kinship continued, as it has to the present time. Ideologically America has never been isolated from Europe nor Europe from America, and the cross-fertilization of ideals and practices has yielded mutual benefit.

The United States, however, until very recent times has nearly always set the pace for the Old World in reform zeal. The outstanding exception has been in solutions for the social maladjustments arising from industrialization, where Britain as the older country faced these problems in acute form before America was hardly aware of them. The English, for example, led in factory legislation, the mitigation of child labor and the legalizing of trade-unions. Another but less conclusive instance in a different field was England's earlier abolition of Negro servitude. The two governments, obeying a common impulse, acted simultaneously in 1807 to outlaw the African slave trade; then Britain ended human bondage throughout the Empire in 1833, whereas the United States waited until 1865. This delay was not due to any lack

of will on the part of American humanitarians, however, but to the fact that the circumstances in the two lands were so very different. In England's case the institution existed some thousands of miles away. Moreover, Parliament had full power to deal with it, and the colonies affected were in a static or decaying economic condition. In America, on the other hand, slavery not only existed at home, but it was anchored in state and local law and was recognized by the Federal Constitution. It was also bound up, directly or indirectly, with the material welfare of a large part of the nation. Nonetheless Britain's action inspired the immediate formation of the American Anti-Slavery Society and so threw the American movement into higher gear.

In the case of most other social innovations, however, America has stood at the forefront. Thus (white) manhood suffrage was attained in the United States by the middle of the nineteenth century but not in England until the early twentieth. In like manner America outstripped the older country in regard to liberty of the press, the separation of church and state, the abolition of barbarous punishments, restraints on the liquor traffic, public education and prison reform, not to mention other achievements.

The basic reason for the generally faster pace of reform may be found in two conditions. In the first place, men were not burdened to the same extent by the weight of tradition. Less energy had to be used in tearing down the old and revered, more was left for building anew, and the large measure of self-government enjoyed even by the colonists simplified the process. As Emerson put it on one occasion,

> America was opened after the feudal mischief was spent, and so the people made a good start. . . . No inquisition

233

here, no kings, no nobles, no dominant church. . . . We began with freedom, and are defended from shocks now for a century by the facility with which through popular assemblies every necessary measure of reform can instantly be carried.

The second factor was the kind of people who emigrated to America, not only the original settlers but also their successors, the far greater number of immigrants. Early or late, these transplanted Europeans were men who rebelled against conditions as they found them in their homelands—against a class society, against religious, political and economic oppression—and, unlike their more docile neighbors, they carried their rebellion to the point of going to a distant continent where life was strange, dangers abounded and new careers must be sought. The departure of such folk slowed down the impetus to change at home, just as it tended to quicken it in the adopted country.

Given these two circumstances, the surprising thing is that the tempo of reform in America was not far more precipitate. As Anthony Trollope observed with particular reference to the Revolutionary era, "this new people, when they had it in their power to change all their laws, to throw themselves upon any Utopian theory that the folly of a wild philanthropy could devise, . . . did not do so." He attributed this caution to their inherited English practicality, but there was more to it than that. By starting life in a new state they acquired a new state of mind. Those who had fled from religious bigotry could now worship as they wished, those who had suffered political discrimination were generally free to vote and run for office, while all could make an easier living and attain a greater human dignity. To revise an old proverb, nothing sobers like success. The owner of property, however eager to improve society, has a personal investment in orderly change, and under conditions of self-government a legislative body is, as Emerson remarked in the essay just quoted, "a standing insurrection, and escapes the violence of accumulated grievance."

In other words, virtually every newcomer to America underwent a sea change. No matter how desperate his lot had been in Europe, he quickly displayed what impatient extremists despise as a middle-class attitude toward reform. Being even surer of the future than of the present, he could not love innovation for its own sake, or be willing to risk all existing good in a general overturn. Hence he threw his weight on the side of piecemeal progress.

This temper has continued to dominate the American mind. Despite the growing industrialization and maldistribution of wealth of the last seventy-five years, despite the one third of the nation "ill-housed, ill-clad, ill-nourished," a Gallup poll a few years ago indicated that about nine out of every ten people still regard themselves as belonging to the great middle class. This means, in contrast to most European countries, that there is no large self-conscious group which feels so inferior or so handicapped as not to be able to better itself by constitutional methods. . . .

Whence has American reform derived its abiding vitality? Many rivulets have contributed to the stream, some with constant flow and others intermittently. None, however, has been more potent than religion. As Edmund Burke observed, "All Protestantism, even the most cold and passive, is a sort of dissent," but the men who settled the colonies represented "the dissidence of dissent and the Protestantism of the Protestant religion."

Did this fact, however, always denote a general open-mindedness toward human rights and hopes? The Puritans, it has often been pointed out, though demanding freedom of conscience for themselves in England, denied it to others upon going to Massachusetts. But that is not the whole story. The core of Puritanism, once the theological husks are peeled away, was intense moral zeal both for one's own salvation and for that of the community. This attitude, as in the instance noted, could engender intolerance, but by the same token it could also engender intolerance of intolerance; and the history of the Puritan spirit as a social force in America shows that the disposition to challenge vested injustice was the more significant aspect.

Roger Williams and Anne Hutchinson are outstanding early examples. The New England clergymen who preached defiance of England as the Revolution approached exhibited the same quality in the political field. A Tory called them "Mr. Otis's black Regiment" who "like their Predecessors of 1641 . . . have been unceasingly sounding the Yell of Rebellion in the Ears of an ignorant & deluded people." In like manner a later generation of the strain abetted most of the humanitarian crusades of Emerson's period, earning Bronson Alcott's affectionate encomium of being "the Lord's chore boys." With equal ardor laymen of Puritan stock were at the same time promoting the public-school movement in New England and the newly settled West, thus enriching significantly the concept of democracy.

A similar concern for the public welfare galvanized most of the other religious groups. They too strove to comfort the afflicted and afflict the comfortable. In answer to protests against such activities a church-gathering in Peterboro, New York, resolved,

> That the correctness of this opinion turns wholly on the character of the politics which are preached: for whilst it is clearly wrong to preach anti-Bible or unrighteous politics on the Sabbath or on any other day, nothing can be clearer than that no day is too holy to be used in preaching the politics which are inculcated in the Bible.

The Quakers in particular wielded an influence out of proportion to their numbers.

To be sure, the more breathless reformers sometimes rebuked the churches for faintheartedness, notably in the case of antislavery which created special difficulties by splitting the national bodies along sectional lines. It is also true that the foes of reform, no less than the friends, resorted to the Bible for vindication. Not only the defenders of slavery but the opponents of temperance, of women's rights and of the peace movement managed to dig up scriptural authority. This, however, was something like the homage which vice pays to virtue, for the advantage rested inevitably with those who interpreted God as love, not as greed or oppression. Even the censorious William Lloyd Garrison was impressed when the two great popular churches, the Methodist and the Baptist, anticipated the political disruption of the Union by separating into Northern and Southern branches in 1844-1845 over a question involving slavery.

If America has been less ostensibly religious in more recent times, the teachings of Jesus have nevertheless continued as vitally to fuel humanitarian enterprises. Churchgoers have been at the van of all such undertakings, and the clergy by espousing the 'social gospel' have opened minds to new human needs and persistently pricked the popular conscience. In short, religion, in America at least, has not been the opiate of the masses.

Even in politics liberal movements have turned constantly to Holy Writ for inspiration. William Jennings Bryan in the greatest convention speech in American history denounced the business magnates who would press down upon the brow of labor a "crown of thorns" and "crucify mankind upon a cross of gold." Theodore Roosevelt, defying the reactionary leaders of the Republican party, declared he stood at Armageddon and battled for the Lord. Woodrow Wilson, a religionist in the Scottish Covenanter tradition, always kept his Bible by his bedside. And the latest surge of political reform, the New Deal, took as its slogan "the more abundant life." President Truman merely voiced a common opinion when he declared in a recent address, our "belief in the dignity and the freedom of man" is "derived from the word of God, and its roots are deep in our spiritual foundations."

This belief, however, had independent support in the doctrines derived from Europe's Age of Enlightenment. These eighteenth-century avowals of human excellence and man's boundless capacity for progress found instant and permanent lodgment in America, where they confirmed common observation as well as the more enlightened religious teachings. Incorporated in the Preamble of the Declaration of Independence, they not only served their immediate purpose, but resounded back to the Old World, where they still reverberate. At home the Preamble was more a great editorial than a factual report, as none knew better than its slaveholding author Thomas Jefferson, but it proved an incomparable rallying cry for reformers then as it has ever since.

If all men are created equal, demanded the abolitionists in their day, why are black men held in bondage? If all are created equal, cried the feminists in their time, why are women denied their rights? If human beings are equally entitled to life, liberty and the pursuit of happiness, asked others in their turn, how justify the plight of the distressed farmers, under-privileged children, the hungry poor, the innocent victims of war? Not many years ago Roger Baldwin of the American Civil Liberties Union was arrested for attempting to read the Declaration of Independence in front of the City Hall during a labor outbreak in Paterson, New Jersey. However benighted the policeman's action may seem, he and his superiors should at least be given credit for recognizing the great manifesto as an irrefutable challenge to a repressive *status quo*.

That indeed has been its historic function. No one has stated the case more tellingly in our own generation than a citizen of foreign birth.

> If I ask an American [writes Mary Antin] what is the fundamental American law, and he does not answer me promptly, "That which is contained in the Declaration of Independence," I put him down for a poor citizen. . . . What the Mosaic Law is to the Jews, the Declaration is to the American people. It affords us a starting-point in history and defines our mission among nations. . . . Up to the moment of our declaration of independence, our struggle with our English rulers did not differ from other popular struggles against despotic governments. Again and again we respectfully petitioned for redress of specific grievances, as the governed, from time immemorial, have petitioned their governors. But one day we abandoned our suit for petty damages, and instituted a suit for the recovery of our entire human heritage of freedom; and by basing our claim on the fundamental principles of the brotherhood of man and the sovereignty of the masses, we assumed championship of the oppressed against their oppressors, wherever found. . . . The American confession of faith, therefore, is a recital of the doctrines of liberty and equality.

It is true that the sober findings of science and scholarship since 1776 have shaken the foundations of the natural-rights philosophy on which the Declaration was based, but the aspiration to realize the dream it held forth has nevertheless continued as strong as ever. As President Truman put it in his State of the Union message in January 1950, "At every point in our history, these ideals have served to correct our failures and shortcomings, to spur us on to greater efforts, and to keep clearly before us the primary purpose of our existence as a nation. . . . These principles give meaning to all that we do."

Thus two basic sets of ideas or ideals, the one stemming from the Christian religion and the other from the Declaration of Independence, have sustained and refreshed the reform impulse. But great national crises, though less constant in effect, have also played a role. One may sympathize with Benjamin Franklin's view that there never was a good war or a bad peace and still recognize that the Revolutionary War—thanks partly to the lapse of British control—brought about such human gains in various states as a more democratic redistribution of land, the separation of church and state, the abrogation of primogeniture and entail and the first restraints on slavery and the slave trade. In like fashion the Civil War wrote into the Constitution the greatest of all American reforms, the total abolition of slavery. This showing, of course, can in no sense justify the spiritual and material costs of war.

Probably most of these advances would have come sooner or later in any event, and the Civil War, moreover, actually set back such burgeoning reforms as temperance, women's rights and international peace. Besides, the moral letdown following an armed conflict often militates against social progress, as notably in the 1920's. Yet war, within such limits, has actually contributed to human betterment.

The peacetime crises known as depressions have exerted a more positive influence. In periods of general social dislocation, injustices long endured become intolerable, and men in their despair may even seek a passport to Utopia. The hard times following the Panic of 1837, for example, hurried many states into abolishing lotteries and imprisonment for debt, helped remove the restrictions on wives as to property rights, and generated forty or more short-lived collectivist communities. Similarly, the economic slump dating from 1873 speeded the movement for railroad regulation and for 'cheap money,' raised the Knights of Labor to national importance, and begot the Socialist Labor party as well as Henry George's panacea of the single tax. One need only recall the Great Depression of 1929, however, to realize to what extent a general economic collapse accelerates reform. It may appear unfortunate that so much of our social thinking has been done in abnormal times, but often the mind functions most clearly when action is imperative. . . .

NO

Ronald G. Walters

AMERICAN REFORMERS 1815-1860

PATTERNS AND CHANGES

Several things came together to produce antebellum reform, including important changes in what Americans believed. By 1814—the year the War of 1812 ended—a combination of theological and economic developments led many men and women to assume that the world did not have to be the way it was and that individual efforts mattered. Such notions are not terribly ancient; nor are they universal among human societies. They were, however, articles of faith for middle-class nineteenth-century Americans, with their confidence in progress and human will. The religious revivalism of the 1820s encouraged this optimistic and activist spirit by teaching that good deeds were the mark of godliness and that the millennium was near. Other significant new ideas, attitudes, and systems of thought jostled around in the public press and likewise encouraged reform. Some of these beliefs were scientific, a few were daring, many were foolish, and all helped nineteenth-century people think of novel solutions to ancient evils, as well as discover sins their ancestors never imagined.

Although antebellum reform emerged out of that cultural ferment, the real moving force behind it was a broad transformation of American society after 1814. Historians and economists grope for the correct term to describe what happened—"takeoff," "industrialization," and "modernization" have all been used. Scholars also endlessly debate how and why such dramatic changes occurred. But the changes themselves touched the farthest corners of economic, social, and political life. They created the material conditions reform movements needed in order to exist and they jarred thousands of people into thinking about what had to be done to ensure the future glory of America and Americans. . . .

Changes in the nature of politics had almost as much significance for antebellum reform as did the economic transformation of the United States. If nothing else served to indicate that there was political turmoil between 1815 and 1860, the ebb and flow of partisan organizations would tell the story. The War of 1812 was the deathblow to the Federalist Party, which had once claimed George Washington, John Adams, and Alexander Hamilton among its leaders. Even before 1812 it had virtually been reduced to a New England remnant, thanks to the rise of Thomas Jefferson and his supporters, called Republicans or Democratic-Republicans. For several years after the war, most national political conflict took place among Democratic-Republicans rather than between two distinct, well-identified parties. That began to change after 1824 when John Quincy Adams, one of four Democratic-Republican presidential candidates, defeated Andrew Jackson. By 1828, when Jackson triumphed over Adams, the factions were becoming more sharply defined. Jackson, now under the label Democratic, had a superb ability both to unite his supporters and to create enemies. By the time he left office, his protégé and successor, Martin Van Buren, was confronted with a well-organized opposition, the Whig Party. Whigs and Democrats fought it out on fairly equal terms for more than a decade, but after 1848 the former disintegrated over the issue of slavery. The Democrats held together—often tenuously—until 1860, when they, too, split apart. After 1854, however, they faced a formidable challenge from the Republican Party, whose candidate, Abraham Lincoln, captured the presidency in 1860. This brief catalogue of political flux, complicated though it may seem, leaves out such ephemeral smaller parties as the Anti-

Masonic, Liberty, Free Soil, and Know-Nothing, some of them having made respectable showings in local, state, and even national elections.

Reformers disagreed among themselves on political questions and could be found in every one of the major and minor parties, although more in the Whig and Republican than in the Democratic. Their numbers even included many men and women who rejected parties altogether. It was partisan conflict, rather than any particular political organization, that most influenced their actions.

A new style of political warfare began to emerge after 1800, as politicians learned how to court an expanding electorate. By 1810 a majority of states had lowered franchise requirements to the point where most adult white males could vote. When Jackson made his first run for the presidency in 1824, only three states restricted suffrage for white men in any meaningful way and in many areas even recent immigrants found it easy to cast ballots. This may have been democracy, but it also permitted anyone, including the worst sort of rascals, to help select the nation's leaders. Reformers complained that a degraded and sinful majority, manipulated by political machines, had more of a voice in the nation's affairs than they, the godly minority, did.

Politicians disgusted reformers by seeking the electorate's lowest common denominator. No promise was too extreme, no spectacle too extravagant, if it got votes. The political system, reformers thought, rewarded those who appealed to the rabble and who pretended to be common folk rather than appear superior in morality and intellect. The results were horrifying to right-minded men and women: high offices bestowed on the likes of Andrew Jackson, a duelist who married a divorcee, or Richard M. Johnson, Van Buren's Vice-President, who lived in sin with a black mistress. All around them reformers saw a frightful decline from the days of the Founding Fathers, when great men walked the earth and when wisdom and virtue had a place in government.

Yet reformers could not, and did not, entirely reject politics. The Jacksonian political system itself made their propaganda effective by creating a close link between "public opinion" and governmental action. Many reform crusades, moreover, were designed to have political consequences. If everything worked according to plan, temperance, Sunday schools, and public education, for instance, would produce a morally responsible electorate. In far more direct ways reformers engaged in political action. Evangelical Protestants lobbied Congress in 1828 to stop postal employees from working on Sunday (an effort to improve public morality); and in the next decade abolitionists mounted a petition campaign urging Congress to take stands against slavery. A faction within their movement began to run its own candidates for office in 1840. Temperance workers likewise became involved in political campaigns, winning significant victories in the 1850s and making alcohol a major issue for the next eighty years. Quite obviously there were times when reformers went beyond the powers of persuasion and sought to use the government to make people behave. In the process they dipped their toes, and sometimes a great deal more, into the muddy waters of democratic electioneering, despite their contempt for its mindless excesses.

The ambivalence reformers had toward politics is revealing, even if it was not absolute. America was becoming a strange and different place in the antebellum period and partisan warfare symbolized the change just as surely as did territorial expansion, alterations in family patterns, and the appearance of immigrants, cities, and factories. But politicians held out no promise of leading the transformation of the United States in a virtuous fashion; that task fell to reformers, almost by default. . . .

How reform helped people to respond to a changing world varied with the particular crusade. At one extreme there were causes such as health reform and temperance, which were primarily significant for assisting people in achieving self-mastery and individual dignity. At the other extreme were antislavery and school reform, which acted more as explanations of what had to be done to society. Communitarianism played both roles. But important as the nature of a reform was, the position it held in a person's life depended greatly on whether one was a leader or a follower.

Leaders found a career that had not existed two or three generations earlier. Before 1800 very few people had been able to give themselves over entirely to moral or social causes. Full-time gadflies like Tom Paine were rare and most of them in the eighteenth century were religious itinerants, like the great Quaker abolitionist, John Woolman. Before the 1820s, reform more commonly was a sideline for men, and some, women, who had social position, or at least gainful employment. The archetype of such a reformer was Ben Franklin, who included good deeds among his other activities. Only with the technological and social changes of the nineteenth century did it become possible for large numbers of Americans to make a livelihood out of agitation. To be sure, some leaders of antebellum reform did hold other jobs, as clergymen and even in business, like Arthur and Lewis Tappan. But many either rejected conventional occupations (including a fair proportion of onetime or would-be ministers) or else kept halfheartedly at other work while giving much income and emotional energy to a cause. A life such as William Lloyd Garrison's, which for thirty-five years consisted primarily of editing a reform newspaper, would have been unthinkable in Franklin's day.

Reform was a demanding profession, with poverty and violence among its dangers; but it had its rewards. For women it was virtually the only way to have public influence; to men it offered a kind of moral authority that law, politics, business, and (in some circles) the ministry no longer had. The greatest satisfactions, however, were personal, as reformers often acknowledged. Reform, they declared, transformed them in much the same manner as a religious conversion would have. Lydia Maria Child described it well. In the 1830s and already a successful author, she met Garrison, who "got hold of the strings of my conscience and pulled me into reforms." The encounter changed "the whole pattern of my life-web." Mrs. Child would have seasons of doubt and unhappiness afterward, but she found a meaning in antislavery she had not discovered in religion or writing fiction. For her and hundreds of her colleagues, reform was more than just another job. It was an important part of one's self.

Most people involved in reform were not leaders. They were obscure men with regular employment, single women, or women with family responsibilities. They drifted out of reform after a few years, or at most stayed on the periphery of it throughout their adulthood. Although their participation, dues, and consumption of propaganda kept reforms alive, they made little mark in the historical record. There were hundreds of thousands of

such people engaged in various causes, and the experiences of one of them, Henry Cummins, may have been more typical than were those of a celebrity like William Lloyd Garrison. A teenager in Eugene, Oregon, in the 1850s, Cummins described himself as "reformatory all round." His commitment to health reform gave him pride and self-discipline—as an eighteen-year-old he noted with satisfaction that "the cravings of my appetite, on account of my rigid abstemiousness, are fast subsiding." (It is not entirely clear which appetite he meant: the previous month he read Dr. Russell Trall's *Home Treatment for Sexual Abuses.*) Important though control of his bodily urges was, Cummins gained most from the social network his enthusiasms spun for him. From what was then a small town, distant from the cultural centers of the land, he corresponded with friends throughout Oregon on reform matters and inquired about the possibilities of going East to study phrenology or the water cure. Cummins was dedicated to reforms for years, but many of his acquaintances passed through them as a brief stage in life. "Most of the young men who commence the study of Phrenology, in Oregon," a friend noted, "have finely [finally] turned out Preachers or Merchants or drunkards." (That correspondent gave himself two more years as a phrenological lecturer, after which he planned to "study medison," which he thought "will not take me long with my knowledge.")

Antebellum reform was not entirely a movement of lonely youth, but much of its significance among the rank and file does appear to have come from the self-control, intellectual stimulation, and social contacts it provided young people like Cummins. (The surviving minutes of some small-town temperance societies deal less with the evils of drink than with costumes, rituals, and meetings with members of the opposite sex.) It does not demean reform to say that it did a great deal for reformers. It was no small blessing for individuals to have been able to put their lives in order and do some good in the process. A reform commitment inevitably depends on a peculiar resonance between the situation of the reformer and a broader problem.

Antebellum reform had its place in history, just as it did in the lives of individuals. In some respects it looked backward to traditions long predating it. The obvious instances were its evangelical Protestant imagery and its use of the rhetoric of the American Revolution. Less apparent debts to the past were the belief in conspiracies and an insistence that freedom was the right of human beings to buy and sell in the marketplace with a minimum of interference—both of them habits of mind going back to the eighteenth century and beyond. The latter view could be radical when directed against restrictive laws and entrenched privilege, as it was during the American Revolution. But by the end of the nineteenth century it became conservative dogma, ending up as little more than a rationale for allowing Americans to exploit their land and each other without having the government do anything about it. Yet such a definition of freedom still had much of its egalitarian thrust when it appeared in antebellum reform. A few people (communitarians, most notably) did challenge it and attempted to substitute an ethic of cooperation and harmony. The idea of laissez-faire, nonetheless, predominated among reformers and gave a critical edge to their analyses of tyranny, particularly to the abolitionist argument that the slave rightfully owned his or her labor.

Despite the significance of what was old

in antebellum reform, many things were new about it. The prospect of making a career out of reform was one of them. Another was the matter of how people believed problems ought to be solved. Eighteenth-century reformers generally took human betterment—the limited amount of it they thought possible—to be something for members of the elite to determine and implement. It was the responsibility of those with moral and financial advantages to do their part to ameliorate suffering. That was to be done without any expectation that the millennium was at hand or that social relationships would be changed in the least. Antebellum reformers saw things differently. Some men and women, consistent with their evangelical Protestantism, insisted that change could be total, for people and for society, and that it began with the individual, no matter how lowly. Making a sinner's heart yearn for good behavior, not imposing morality by force or giving charity, was the task of reform. Reformers, of course, were not of a single mind about that. Temperance advocates were especially committed to legislating morality and there were others who swam against the individualistic and voluntaristic currents of antebellum reform. The most important of them developed quite innovative forms of coercion—schools, asylums, and assorted institutions to uplift and cure mankind. But antebellum Americans broke with their eighteenth-century predecessors whichever course they chose, whether they tried to improve humanity through conversion or confinement.

And yet the greatest transformation of American reform lay ahead, after 1860, really after the 1870s. Signs of change began to appear as early as the 1850s, when many reformers lowered their goals and lost some of the evangelical fervor of the

1830s and early 1840s. The trend continued, at an accelerated pace after the Civil War, until by the 1870s a prominent faction of Northeastern reform, consisting in part of ex-abolitionists and their children, dropped its horizon to the point where it would have been satisfied with little more than civil service laws, honest elections, and free trade. That was less ambitious than wanting to save the world.

Some of the gloomier mood came from the bitter sectional conflict of the late 1840s and the 1850s and the Civil War. The majority of reformers were above the Mason-Dixon line and most were drawn to the Northern cause, willing to subordinate their programs and swallow their doubts in order to help it triumph. They had, moreover, to reconsider their belief that the individual could be a force in history. Despite acts of heroism, humans seemed irrelevant when huge organizations delivered men and material to the front lines and cared for the sick and wounded. It was a massive army rather than sanctified hearts that won the war.

It was not just the war that took the fire out of antebellum reformers. A bit of the change came about because of what had *not* been accomplished in decades of agitation. Sinners were harder to reach than anyone imagined; drunkards stayed drunkards, the insane were not made sane, and so it went. Reformers had been far too optimistic about what propaganda and moral suasion could do. If nothing else, fatigue and a lack of results began dampening enthusiasm by 1860.

When success did come, it proved to have as much a chastening effect as failure. The destruction of slavery in 1865 deprived reformers of their most emotionally compelling issue. Few white Americans could bring to the cause of civil rights for blacks the same passion they invested in antislavery. Certainly some abolitionists kept faith in racial justice down to the end of the nineteenth century, and most crusades persisted after 1860—temperance and woman's rights actually reached peaks much later. When people worked for causes after 1860, however, their objectives usually were more modest than those of antebellum reformers and their emotional pitch was lower. As hopes for humanity declined, so did participation in reform. Political corruption in the 1870s simply provided more reasons for morally sensitive people to retreat in disgust from social involvement: the most meaningful of wars ended with elected officials wallowing in the public trough. Perhaps human nature was fatally flawed and mankind was indeed beyond redemption in this world.

By the 1890s yet other styles of reform began to emerge, types more familiar to us, although they may also be passing. Their story is too complicated to tell except in outline, as further reminder that modes of changing the world change like everything else. Since the late nineteenth century, reform has largely been secular and (often) committed to science as a guide to managing human affairs. Only in rare instances has a religious tone been as prominent as it was in the early nineteenth century. But where God retreated, the state advanced. Beginning with the Populists of the 1880s, reformers have called upon the government to solve problems with a casualness that would have appalled their early-nineteenth-century counterparts. There was no precedent in antebellum reform for the zeal of Progressives and New Dealers to construct regulatory agencies to oversee social and economic matters. This bureaucratic impulse was directed toward setting fair terms for competition in the marketplace and protecting Americans from the worst hazards of the day. In desiring to do that, rather than striving to create a perfect world, latter-day reformers expected less than antebellum ones had. They were, nonetheless, more perceptive for recognizing that solutions to the evils of modern life have more to do with industries and cities than with the sinful hearts of individuals. . . .

A MATTER OF TIME

Reformers may not be the best judges of their own place in the universe. True enough, antebellum crusaders assessed their social origins fairly well (they characterized themselves as hardworking Christians of modest means, neither very rich nor very poor). On non-sociological matters, however, they seem to have been less astute. Like most American reformers, they often envisioned themselves as part of some grand procession stretching across the centuries—soldiers in the long march of Protestantism, Reason, Progress, or Democracy. At other moments they (again like later reformers) regarded themselves as outsiders whose critical distance from their society enabled them to see its flaws. In both instances the basic assumption was that they were special people, either quite detached from their time and place or else having a peculiar position within it. There is truth to that notion and it is frequently echoed by historians. Certainly commitment to a cause does separate people from the apathetic or hostile majority. One of the attractions of antebellum reform clearly was the way its organizations and meetings provided moralistic men and women with little islands of righteousness amid what they thought was a vast churning ocean of depravity, acquisitiveness, and disorder.

Yet there are flaws to the idea that reformers and radicals are greatly different from their non-reformist peers. Whatever illusions crusaders may have about their uniqueness, they are products of a milieu. Antebellum reform could not have existed without contemporary developments in printing and transportation. It also reflected, sometimes indirectly, widespread concerns about family life, cultural diversity, economic opportunities, vice, and political turmoil. Above all, it provided men and women with one out of many possible means for comprehending, coping with, shaping, and occasionally ignoring the larger nineteenth-century processes of urbanization, industrialization, population growth, and immigration.

But it is not enough to root antebellum reform in economic, demographic, social, and technological changes. To leave it there is to miss the importance of style, by which I mean the way reformers perceived problems, strategies, tactics, and solutions. That is where culture enters the picture—it inevitably limits the number of responses people can make to a social situation and it determines the particular configuration of ideas, emotions, attitudes, insights, and blind spots characteristic of reformers and radicals in a given age. The style of antebellum reform, in its initial stages, was very much that of evangelical Protestantism, with a leavening of rhetoric from the American Revolution and a dash of economic and scientific thought, especially in communitarianism and labor reform. In the 1820s and 1830s reformers usually thought they were attacking sins, not social problems, and they urged individual repentance rather than legislation and coercion.

By the 1840s that had begun to change, understandably so because reform is never homogeneous or static (unless it has a rigid core of ideology, something American social movements generally lack). Moral commitments can lead in several directions and they tend to be modified by events, successes, failures, and even by boredom. In the case of antebellum reformers, dissatisfaction with religion and churches prompted exploration of such "sciences" as health reform, phrenology, and spiritualism (which often merely dressed Protestant pieties in one-theological language). The ineffectiveness of voluntarism and moral suasion pushed reformers into advocating diverse forms of governmental action, including temperance laws and construction of asylums to turn deviants into model citizens. A mode of reform which, in the 1830s, sought to transform the world, was itself greatly transformed by 1860.

Occasionally scholars argue about whether certain American "movements" (antebellum crusades among them) were backward-looking or forward-looking. The answer for pre-Civil War reform is that it was both. It attempted to preserve and extend ancient virtues—orderliness, plain living, freedom from external restraints, and so on; but it also made some shifts in emphasis and added such newer goals as strict self-control. (The latter was advocated in nearly every cause from antislavery to the Graham diet, phrenology, and asylum-building.) If reformers could not entirely accept the behavior of their contemporaries, they nonetheless could not entirely reject the values and accomplishments of the social order then emerging in the United States. Like most of their contemporaries, they were simultaneously awed and made uneasy by the rising glory of the United States and by humankind's marvelous mechanical and electrical inventions. Only some less popular causes—communitarianism, feminism, non-

resistance, and labor reform—came close to posing a threat to an urbanizing, commercial, and industrial society. The chief effect of other crusades—notably temperance, phrenology, and asylum- or school-building—was to encourage people to adjust to, rather than resist, the brave new world of the nineteenth century.

Most antebellum reformers were, at heart, trying to adapt old and respectable verities, plus a few new ones, to an age of cities, steampower, rowdy politics, and get-rich-quick schemes. To their way of thinking, that did not require stopping progress in its tracks. Proper morality, they assumed, would ensure that God's (or nature's) plan would continue to unfold as it was supposed to. For them, reform explained what was wrong with individuals and the nation, what might go wrong in the future, and how to avoid it without sacrificing the historic mission of Americans to increase and be prosperous.

It is one of the minor tragedies of antebellum reform that no one noticed its death and few mourned its passing. The old millennialism and the ability to believe in several causes simultaneously began to slip quietly away in the 1850s. By the 1870s they were all but gone.

Perhaps the analogy is wrong. Eras do not die, like living creatures; they merge and blend into each other. Antebellum reforms did set the tone for much of what was to come afterward: the search for scientific (or at least secular) modes of social thought, the quest for equality for women and black people, the professionalization of reform, and much more. But the future belonged to new sorts of people: to those who accepted the human body as a positive good; to those who could tolerate diversity and believed that morality was not absolute; to those who had faith in improvement and adjustment rather than in the millennium; to those who saw economic and urban problems as economic and urban problems, not moral failures; to those who believed that human beings are not masters of their destiny and that social change does not depend on overcoming the sinfulness of the human heart. Above all, the future of reform belonged to institution users—to men and women who thought of bureaus, agencies, and the government generally as instruments of social policy.

I have in mind, of course, the strand of liberalism stretching from Progressivism through the New Deal to the "Great Society" of the 1960s: it was at once more practical than antebellum reform and less radical. It seldom sought to transform America; more often, it tried to make the system run better. Except in rare radical moments (there were some in the 1960s), hope for a new heaven on earth, commitment to reform as a style of life, and repudiation of sin and governmental coercion—characteristics of some of the greatest of antebellum reformers—were ground up by the machinery of modern times.

POSTSCRIPT

DID ANTEBELLUM REFORM
HAVE A GREAT IMPACT ON THE NATION?

How do we measure the effectiveness of reformers and their organizations? Indeed, is it possible to do so? Professors Schlesinger and Walters have relied on historical comparisons to measure the impact of early nineteenth-century reform. Schlesinger surveyed American history from colonial times until 1950 in his lectures and concluded that the antebellum period was one of the two most significant periods of change in the history of the United States. Walters confines his subject to the era of antebellum reform itself, 1815–1960, but does make comparisons with later reform movements such as Progressivism, the New Deal and the Great Society. In his view, nineteenth-century reformers were not as successful as their twentieth-century counterparts.

Schlesinger emphasizes continuity by pointing out the colonial origins of the characteristics of American reform such as religion, the sea change immigrants who came here experienced, their rebellious nature and the concepts of the Declaration of Independence. Intense periods of change wax and wane, according to Schlesinger, but there existed a reform spirit in America with similar characteristics in 1950 and 1620.

Walters opposes this attempt at a unifying interpretation by arguing discontinuity between reform in the nineteenth and twentieth centuries. He ignores the colonial origins and finds no universal characteristics throughout our history. In fact, he paints the antebellum reformers as peculiar to themselves and concludes that their unique characteristics caused the failure of their efforts to improve society. The protagonists in Walters's book have clay feet.

Historians have written extensively on nineteenth-century reform. Alice F. Tyler's, *Freedom's Ferment: Phases of American Social History to 1860* (University of Minnesota Press, 1944) remains a standard introduction. Clifford S. Griffin discusses temperance in *Their Brother's Keeper: Moral Stewardship in the United States, 1800-1865* (Rutgers University Press, 1960). Merton L. Dillon surveys the abolition movement in *The Abolitionists: The Growth of a Dissenting Minority* (North Illinois University Press, 1974). For women's rights, see Ellen C. DuBois, *Feminism and Suffrage: The Emergence of an Independent Women's Movement in America, 1848-1869* (Cornell University Press, 1978). Michael Fellman's *The Unbounded Frame: Freedom and Community in Nineteenth-Century Utopianism* (Greenwood Press, 1973) is a recent introduction to the subject of alternative living.

ISSUE 14

DID SLAVERY DESTROY THE BLACK FAMILY?

YES: Stanley M. Elkins, from *Slavery: A Problem in American Institutional and Economic Life,* Third Edition (University of Chicago Press, 1976)

NO: Eugene D. Genovese, *Roll Jordan Roll: The World the Slaves Made* (Random House, 1974)

ISSUE SUMMARY

YES: History professor Elkins maintains slavery was a closed system of total control which turned the culturally uprooted African slaves into passive and childlike Samboes.
NO: Professor Genovese argues that slaves developed their own system of family and cultural values within the southern paternalistic and pre-capitalistic slave society.

Until recently, historians debated the slavery issue with the same arguments used over a century ago by the abolitionists and plantation owners. The South may have lost its slaves in the Civil War but, up to the 1950s, it had been winning the textbook war. Slavery had been viewed as a paternalistic institution which civilized and Christianized the heathen African who, though bought and sold by his masters, was better off than many free northern workers; he was, at least, cared for in his non-working hours and old age by his masters. The prodigious research of Georgia-born Professor Ulrich B. Phillips and his followers who mined the records of the large plantation owners, gave a picture of slavery which reflected the views of those slave masters. Because Phillips considered blacks intellectually inferior to whites, his books seem woefully outdated to the American student today.

The climate of opinion changed after World War II; Hitler made the concept of "race" a dirty word which no respected biologist or social scientist would use. Assuming that "the slaves were merely ordinary human beings and that innately Negroes were, after all, only white men with black skins. . . ," Professor Kenneth Stampp wrote a history of slavery from a northern white liberal, or abolitionist, point of view. *The Peculiar Institution* (Vintage, 1956) utilized many of the same sources as Phillips's books but came to radically different conclusions; slavery was here considered an inhuman institution, plantation owners brutal masters, and slaves were seen as cogs in a highly profitable labor system.

To many historians, it appeared that Professors Phillips and Stampp were merely re-fighting the issues of the Civil War. In 1959 Stanley Elkins wrote his path-breaking book *Slavery* (Chicago, 1959), which tried to break through the deadlock by discussing what the "peculiar institution" looked like from the point of view of the slaves themselves. Because of the paucity of traditional written sources like letters, diaries, and autobiographies (most slaves were illiterate), Elkins used two other approaches to probe for the personality of the slave: theoretical knowledge drawn from modern psychology, and an analogy drawn from the literature on concentration camps. In the section reprinted here, Elkins adopts psychological models which demonstrate how the slave so completely changed his behavior that he became the passive, infantile, irresponsible Sambo so often portrayed in the traditional literature of the South. According to Freudian theory, the slaves adopted the values of the superego (in this case the plantation owner); role psychology explains why slaves adopted such passive behavior and rarely attempted to run away, much less create a rebellion. (Since all slaves lived in a repressed environment, all avenues of communication began and ended with the master.)

The Elkins thesis dominated writings on slavery during the 1960s. Because the civil rights and black movements peaked during this period, there was a great deal of anxiety and anger expended by liberals and radicals who preferred to recollect the heroic activities of Nat Turner and Harriet Tubman rather than those of "Uncle Sambo" and "Mammy." Most scholars debated Elkins on his own terms, however, and either disagreed with, or modified many of his controversial conclusions. But Elkins had succeeded in breaking through many of the old categories for discussing slavery and forced historians to view slavery with insights still used by social scientists today.

Eugene Genovese agreed with Elkins that it was important to view slavery through the eyes of the slave owners themselves. But like many writers in the 1970s, Genovese disagreed with Elkins about the use of traditional sources to uncover slave culture. In his many books and articles, Genovese combined a search through the plantation records with a careful reading of slave autobiographies and the controversial records of the former slave interviews recorded in the 1930s by writers working for the federal Works Progress Administration (WPA). As a Marxist who defended Ulrich Phillips's conception of the plantation as a pre-capitalist feudal institution, Genovese's later writings reflected less concern for the economic aspects and more for the cultural interactions of blacks and whites in the antebellum South.

In these selections Stanley Elkins describes slavery as a closed system of total control run by a perverted patriarchy which turned the culturally uprooted African slaves into passive and childlike Sambos. Professor Eugene Genovese argues that southern slavery existed in a pre-capitalistic society dominated by a paternalistic ruling class of white slaveholders who ruled over their white and slave families. Under this system of paternalism, cultural bonds were forged between master and slave which recognized the slaves' humanity and enabled them to develop their own system of family and cultural values.

YES

Stanley M. Elkins

SLAVERY AND NEGRO PERSONALITY

PERSONALITY TYPES AND STEREOTYPES

... It will be assumed that there were elements in the very structure of the plantation system—its "closed" character—that could sustain infantilism as a normal feature of behavior. These elements, having less to do with "cruelty" per se than simply with the sanctions of authority, were effective and pervasive enough to require that such infantilism be characterized as something much more basic than mere "accommodations." It will be assumed that the sanctions of the system were in themselves sufficient to produce a recognizable personality type.

It should be understood that to identify a social type in this sense is still to generalize on a fairly crude level—and to insist for a limited purpose on the legitimacy of such generalizing is by no means to deny that, on more refined levels, a great profusion of individual types might have been observed in slave society. Nor need it be claimed that the "Sambo" type, even in the relatively crude sense employed here, was a universal type. It was, however, a plantation type, and a plantation existence embraced well over half the slave population. Two kinds of material will be used in the effort to picture the mechanisms whereby this adjustment to absolute power—an adjustment whose end product included infantile features of behavior—may have been effected. One is drawn from the theoretical knowledge presently available in social psychology, and the other, in the form of an analogy, is derived from some of the data that have come out of the German concentration camps. It is recognized in most theory that social behavior is regulated in some general way by adjustment to symbols of authority—however diversely "authority" may be defined either in theory or in culture itself—and that such adjustment is closely related to the very formation of personality. A corollary would be, of course, that the more diverse those symbols of authority may be, the greater is the permissible variety of adjustment to them—and the wider the margin of individuality, consequently, in the development of the self. The question here has to do with the wideness or narrowness of that margin on the antebellum plantation.

The other body of material, involving an experience undergone by several

Excerpted from *Slavery: A Problem in American Institutional and Intellectual Life*, PP. 86-87, 125-139. Copyright ©1959, 1968, 1976, The University of Chicago. Footnotes have been omitted.

million men and women in the concentration camps of our own time, contains certain items of relevance to the problem here being considered. The experience was analogous to that of slavery and was one in which wide-scale instances of infantilization were observed. The material is sufficiently detailed, and sufficiently documented by men who not only took part in the experience itself but who were versed in the use of psychological theory for analyzing it, that the advantages of drawing upon such data for purposes of analogy seem to outweigh the possible risks. . . .

The application of the model to the concentration camp should be simple and obvious. What was expected of the man entering the role of camp prisoner was laid down for him upon arrival:

> Here you are not in a penitentiary or prison but in a place of instruction. Order and discipline are here the highest law. If you ever want to see freedom again, you must submit to a severe training. . . . But woe to those who do not obey our iron discipline. Our methods are thorough! Here there is no compromise and no mercy. The slightest resistance will be ruthlessly suppressed. Here we sweep with an iron broom!

Expectation and performance must coincide exactly; the lines were to be read literally; the missing of a single cue meant extinction. The role was pervasive; it vetoed any other role and smashed all prior ones. "Role clarity"—the clarity here was blinding; its definition was burned into the prisoner by every detail of his existence:

> In normal life the adult enjoys a certain measure of independence; within the limits set by society he has a considerable measure of liberty. Nobody orders him when and what to eat, where to take up his residence or what to wear, neither to take his rest on Sunday nor when to have his bath, nor when to go to bed. He is not beaten during his work, he need not ask permission to go to the W.C., he is not continually kept on the run, he does not feel that the work he is doing is silly or childish, he is not confined behind barbed wire, he is not counted twice a day or more, he is not left unprotected against the actions of his fellow citizens, he looks after his family and the education of his children.
>
> How altogether different was the life of the concentration-camp prisoner! What to do during each part of the day was arranged for him, and decisions were made about him from which there was no appeal. He was impotent and suffered from bedwetting, and because of his chronic diarrhea he soiled his underwear. . . . The dependence of the prisoner on the SS . . . may be compared to the dependence of children on their parents. . . .

The impact of this role, coinciding as it does in a hundred ways with that of the child, has already been observed. Its rewards were brutally simple—life rather than death; its punishments were automatic. By the survivors it was—it had to be—a role *well played.*

Nor was it simple, upon liberation, to shed the role. Many of the inmates, to be sure, did have prior roles which they could resume, former significant others to whom they might reorient themselves, a repressed superego which might once more be resurrected. To this extent they were not "lost souls." But to the extent that their entire personalities, their total selves, had been involved in this experience, to the extent that old arrangements had been disrupted, that society itself had been overturned while they had been away, a "return" was fraught with innumerable obstacles.

It is hoped that the very hideousness of a special example of slavery has not disqualified it as a test for certain features of a far milder and more benevolent form of slavery. But it should still be possible to say, with regard to the individuals who lived as slaves within the respective systems, that just as on one level there is every difference between a wretched childhood and a care-free one, there are, for other purposes, limited features which the one may be said to have shared with the other.

Both were closed systems from which all standards based on prior connections had been effectively detached. A working adjustment to either system required a childlike conformity, a limited choice of "significant others." Cruelty per se cannot be considered the primary key to this; of far greater importance was the simple "closed-ness" of the system, in which all lines of authority descended from the master and in which alternative social bases that might have supported alternative standards were systematically suppressed. The individual, consequently, for his very psychic security, had to picture his master in some way as the "good father," even when, as in the concentration camp, it made no sense at all. But why should it not have made sense for many a simple plantation Negro whose master did exhibit, in all the ways that could be expected, the features of the good father who was really "good"? If the concentration camp could produce in two or three years the results that it did, one wonders how much more pervasive must have been those attitudes, expectations, and values which had, certainly, their benevolent side and which were accepted and transmitted over generations.

For the Negro child, in particular, the plantation offered no really satisfactory father-image other than the master. The "real" father was virtually without authority over his child, since discipline, parental responsibility, and control of rewards and punishments all rested in other hands; the slave father could not even protect the mother of his children except by appealing directly to the master. Indeed, the mother's own role loomed far larger for the slave child than did that of the father. She controlled those few activities—household care, preparation of food, and rearing of children—that were left to the slave family. For that matter, the very etiquette of plantation life removed even the honorific attributes of fatherhood from the Negro male, who was addressed as "boy"—until, when the vigorous years of his prime were past, he was allowed to assume the title of "uncle."

From the master's viewpoint, slaves had been defined in law as property, and the master's power over his property must be absolute. But then this property was still human property. These slaves might never be quite as human as *he* was, but still there were certain standards that could be laid down for their behavior: obedience, fidelity, humility, docility, cheerfulness, and so on. Industry and diligence would of course be demanded, but a final element in the master's situation would undoubtedly qualify that expectation. Absolute power for him meant absolute dependency for the slave—the dependency not of the developing child but of the perpetual child. For the master, the role most aptly fitting such a relationship would naturally be that of the father. As a father he could be either harsh or kind, as he chose, but as a *wise* father he would have, we may suspect, a sense of the limits of his situation. He must be ready to cope with *all* the qualities of the child, exasperating as well as ingratiating. He might conceivably have to expect in this child—besides his loyalty, docility, humility, cheerfulness, and (under supervision) his diligence—such additional qualities as irresponsibility, playfulness, silliness, laziness, and (quite possibly) tendencies to lying and stealing. Should the entire prediction prove accurate, the result would be something resembling "Sambo."

The social and psychological sanctions of role-playing may in the last analysis prove to be the most satisfactory of the several approaches to Sambo, for, without doubt, of all the roles in American life that of Sambo was by far the most pervasive. The outlines of the role might be sketched in by crude necessity, but what of the finer shades? The sanctions against overstepping it were bleak enough, but the rewards— the sweet applause, as it were, for performing it with sincerity and feeling—were something to be appreciated on quite another level. The law, untuned to the deeper harmonies, could command the player to be present for the occasion, and the whip might even warn against his missing the grosser cues, but could those things really insure the performance that melted all hearts? Yet there was many and many a performance, and the audiences (whose standards were high) appear to have been for the most part well pleased. They were actually viewing their own masterpiece. Much labor had been lavished upon this chef d'oeuvre, the most genial resources of Southern society had been available for the work; touch after touch had been applied throughout the years, and the result—embodied not in the unfeeling law but in the richest layers of Southern lore—had been the product of an exquisitely rounded collective creativity. And indeed, in a sense that somehow transcended the merely ironic, it was a labor of love. "I love the simple and unadulterated slave, with his geniality, his mirth, his swagger, and his nonsense," wrote Edward Pollard. "I love to look upon his countenance shining with content and grease; I love to study his affectionate

heart; I love to mark that peculiarity in him, which beneath all his buffoonery exhibits him as a creature of the tenderest sensibilities, mingling his joys and his sorrows with those of his master's home." Love, even on those terms, was surely no inconsequential reward.

But what were the terms? The Negro was to be a child forever. "The Negro . . . in his true nature, is always a boy, let him be ever so old. . . ." "He is . . . a dependent upon the white race; dependent for guidance and direction even to the procurement of his most indispensable necessaries. Apart from this protection he has the helplessness of a child—without foresight, without faculty of contrivance, without thrift of any kind." Not only was he a child; he was a happy child. Few Southern writers failed to describe with obvious fondness the bubbling gaiety of a plantation holiday or the perpetual good humor that seemed to mark the Negro character, the good humor of an everlasting childhood.

The role, of course, must have been rather harder for the earliest generations of slaves to learn. "Accommodation," according to John Dollard, "involves the renunciation of protest or aggression against undesirable conditions of life and the organization of the character so that protest does not appear, but acceptance does. It may come to pass in the end that the unwelcome force is idealized, that one identifies with it and takes it into the personality; it sometimes even happens that what is at first resented and feared is finally loved."

Might the process, on the other hand, be reversed? It is hard to imagine its being reversed overnight. The same role might still be played in the years after slavery— we are told that it was—and yet it was played to more vulgar audiences with cruder standards, who paid much less for what they saw. The lines might be repeated more and more mechanically, with less and less conviction; the incentives to perfection could become hazy and blurred, and the excellent old piece could degenerate over time into low farce. There could come a point, conceivably, with the old zest gone, that it was no longer worth the candle. The day might come at last when it dawned on a man's full waking consciousness that he had really grown up, that he was, after all, only playing a part.

MECHANISMS OF RESISTANCE TO ABSOLUTE POWER

One might say a great deal more than has been said here about mass behavior and mass manifestations of personality, and the picture would still amount to little more than a grotesque cartoon of humanity were not some recognition given to the ineffable difference made in any social system by men and women possessing what is recognized, anywhere and at any time, simply as character. With that, one arrives at something too qualitatively fine to come very much within the crude categories of the present discussion; but although it is impossible to generalize with any proper justice about the incidence of "character" in its moral, irreducible, individual sense, it may still be possible to conclude with a note or two on the social conditions, the breadth or narrowness of their compass, within which character can find expression.

Why should it be, [turning] to Latin America, that there one finds no Sambo, no social tradition, that is, in which slaves were defined by virtually complete consensus as children incapable of being trusted with the full privileges of freedom and adulthood? There, the system surely had its brutalities. The slaves arriving there from Africa had also undergone the capture, the sale, the Middle Passage. They too had been uprooted from a prior culture, from a life very different from the one in which they now found themselves. There, however, the system was not closed.

Here again the concentration camp, paradoxically enough, can be instructive. There were in the camps a very small minority of the survivors who had undergone an experience different in crucial ways from that of the others, an experience which protected them from the full impact of the closed system. These people, mainly by virtue of wretched little jobs in the camp administration which offered them a minute measure of privilege, were able to carry on "underground" activities. In a practical sense the actual operations of such "undergrounds" as were possible may seem to us unheroic and limited; stealing blankets; "organizing" a few bandages, a little medicine, from the camp hospital; black market arrangements with a guard for a bit of extra food and protection for oneself and one's comrades; the circulation of news; and other such apparently trifling activities. But for the psychological balance of those involved, such activities were vital; they made possible a fundamentally different adjustment to the camp. To a prisoner so engaged, there were others who mattered, who gave real point to his existence—the SS was no longer the *only* one. Conversely, the role of the child was not the only one he played. He could take initiative; he could give as well as receive protection; he did things which had meaning in adult terms. He had, in short, alternative roles; this was a fact which made such a prisoner's transition from his old life to that of the camp less agonizing and destructive; those very prisoners, moreover, appear to have been the ones who could, upon liberation, resume normal lives most easily. It is, in fact, these people—not those of the ranks—who have described the camps to us.

It was just such a difference—indeed, a much greater one—that separated the typical slave in Latin America from the typical slave in the United States. Though he too had experienced the Middle Passage, he was entering a society where alternatives were significantly more diverse than those awaiting his kinsman in North America. Concerned in some sense with his status were distinct and at certain points competing institutions. This involved multiple and often competing "significant others." His master was, of course, clearly the chief one—but not the only one. There could, in fact, be a considerable number: the friar who boarded his ship to examine his conscience, the confessor, the priest who made the rounds and who might report irregularities in treatment to the *procurador;* the zealous Jesuit quick to resent a master's intrusion upon such sacred matters as marriage and worship (a resentment of no small consequence to the master); the local magistrate, with his eye on the king's official protector of slaves, who would find himself in trouble were the laws too widely evaded; the king's informer who received one-third of the fines. For the slave the result was a certain latitude; the lines did not all converge on one man; the slave's personality, accordingly, did not have to focus on a single role. He was, true enough primarily a slave. Yet he might in fact perform multiple roles. He could be a husband and a father (for the American slave these roles had virtually no meaning); open to him also were such activities as artisan, peddler, petty merchant, truck gardener (the law reserved to him the necessary time and a share of the proceeds, but such arrangements were against the law for Sambo); he could be a communi-

cant in the church, a member of a religious fraternity (roles guaranteed by the most powerful institution in Latin America—comparable privileges in the American South depended on a master's pleasure). These roles were all legitimized and protected *outside* the plantation; they offered a diversity of channels for the development of personality. Not only did the individual have multiple roles open to him as a slave, but the very nature of these roles made possible a certain range of aspirations should he some day become free. He could have a fantasy-life not limited to catfish and watermelons; it was within his conception to become a priest, an independent farmer, a successful merchant, a military officer. The slave could actually—to an extent quite unthinkable in the United States—conceive of himself *as a rebel.* Bloody slave revolts, actual wars, took place in Latin America; nothing on this order occurred in the United States. But even without a rebellion, society here had a network of customary arrangements, rooted in antiquity, which made possible at many points a smooth transition of status from slave to free and which provided much social space for the exfoliation of individual character.

To the typical slave on the ante-bellum plantation in the United States, society of course offered no such alternatives. But that is hardly to say that something of an "underground"—something rather more, indeed, than an underground—could not exist in Southern slave society. And there were those in it who hardly fitted the picture of "Sambo."

The American slave system, compared with that of Latin America, was closed and circumscribed, but, like all social systems, its arrangements were less perfect in practice than they appeared to be in theory. It was possible for significant numbers of slaves, in varying degrees, to escape the full impact of the system and its coercions upon personality. The house servant, the urban mechanic, the slave who arranged his own employment and paid his master a stipulated sum each week, were all figuratively members of the "underground." Even among those working on large plantations, the skilled craftsman or the responsible slave foreman had a measure of independence not shared by his simpler brethren. Even the single slave family owned by a small farmer had a status much closer to that of house servants than to that of plantation labor gang. For all such people there was a margin of space denied to the majority; the system's authority-structure claimed their bodies but not quite their souls.

Out of such groups an individual as complex and as highly developed as William Johnson, the Natchez barber, might emerge. Johnson's diary reveals a personality that one recognizes instantly as a type—but a type whose values came from a sector of society very different from that which formed Sambo. Johnson is the young man on the make, the ambitious free-enterpriser of American legend. He began life as a slave, was manumitted at the age of eleven, and rose from a poor apprentice barber to become one of the wealthiest and most influential Negroes in ante-bellum Mississippi. He was respected by white and black alike, and counted among his friends some of the leading public men of the state.

It is of great interest to note that although the danger of slave revolts (like Communist conspiracies in our own day) was much overrated by touchy Southerners; the revolts that actually did occur were in no instance planned by plantation laborers but rather by Negroes whose qualities of leadership were developed well outside the full coercions of the plantation authority-system. Gabriel, who led the revolt of 1800, was a blacksmith who lived a few miles outside Richmond; Denmark Vesey, leading spirit of the 1822 plot at Charleston, was a freed Negro artisan who had been born in Africa and served several years aboard a slavetrading vessel; and Nat Turner, the Virginia slave who fomented the massacre of 1831, was a literate preacher of recognized intelligence. Of the plots that have been convincingly substantiated (whether they came to anything or not), the majority originated in urban centers.

For a time during Reconstruction, a Negro elite of sorts did emerge in the South. Many of its members were Northern Negroes, but the Southern ex-slaves who also comprised it seem in general to have emerged from the categories just indicated. Vernon Wharton, writing of Mississippi, says:

> A large portion of the minor Negro leaders were preachers, lawyers, or teachers from the free states or from Canada. Their education and their independent attitude gained for them immediate favor and leadership. Of the natives who became their rivals, the majority had been urban slaves, blacksmiths, carpenters, clerks, or waiters in hotels and boarding houses; a few of them had been favored body-servants of affluent whites.

The William Johnsons and Denmark Veseys have been accorded, though belatedly, their due honor. They are, indeed, all too easily identified, thanks to the system that enabled them as individuals to be so conspicuous and so exceptional and, as members of a group, so few.

NO
Eugene D. Genovese

THE WORLD OF THE SLAVES

According to the slaveholders, slave men had little sense of responsibility toward their families and abused them so mercilessly that Ole Massa constantly had to intervene to protect the women and children. Skeptics might wonder how these allegedly emasculated men so easily dominated the strong-willed and physically powerful women of the matriarchal legend, but the slaveholders never troubled themselves about such inconsistencies.

"Negroes are by nature tyrannical in their dispositions," Robert Collins of Macon, Ga., announced, "and, if allowed, the stronger will abuse the weaker; husbands will often abuse their wives and mothers their children." Thus, he concluded, masters and overseers must protect the peace of the quarters and punish aggressors.

Life in the quarters, like lower-class life generally, sometimes exploded in violence. Court records, plantation papers and ex-slave accounts reveal evidence of wife-beating but do not remotely sustain the pretension that without white interference the quarters would have rung with the groans of abused womanhood. Too many black men did not believe in beating their wives, and too many black women, made physically strong by hard field work, were not about to be beaten. So, why should slaveholders, who thought nothing of stripping a woman naked and whipping her till she bled, express so much concern? The pontificating of the ideologues might be dismissed as politically serviceable rubbish, but the concern of the slaveholders who wrote in agricultural journals primarily for each other's eyes and who penned private instructions for overseers demands explanation.

The slaveholders needed order and feared that domestic abuse would undermine the morale of the labor force. By asserting himself as the protector of black women and domestic peace, the slaveholder asserted himself as *paterfamilias* and reinforced his claims to being sole father of a "family, black and white." In this light, the efforts of the drivers or plantation preachers or other

Excerpted from "The World of the Slaves," "Slave Men, Slave Families," "Don't Mess with Mammy," and "Some Chose Freedom," as reprinted in the *Washington Post*, October 27, 1974. Copyright ©1974. Reprinted by permission of Random House, Inc. publishers.

prestigious slaves to restrain abusive husbands represented an attempt by the quarters to rule themselves.

The slaveholders intuitively grasped something else. A black man whose authority in the house rested on his use of force may have picked the worst way to assert himself, but in a world in which so much conspired to reduce men to "guests in the house" and to emasculate them, even this kind of assertion, however unmanly by external standards, held some positive meaning.

Defending Their Own

The slave women did not often welcome Ole Massa's protection. They preferred to take care of themselves or, when they needed help, to turn to their fathers, brothers or friends. As any policeman in a lower-class neighborhood, white or black, knows, a woman who is getting the worst of a street fight with her man and who is screaming for help usually wants relief from the blows; she does not want her man subjected to an outsider's righteous indignation and may well join him in repelling an attack.

When Ellen Botts' mother—the much-respected Mammy of a sugar plantation—showed up with a lump on her head inflicted by her hot-tempered husband, she told her master that she had had an accident. She would deal with her husband herself and certainly did not want to see him whipped. When James Redpath asked a slave woman in South Carolina if slave women expected to leave their husbands when they fell out, he got the contemptuous answer meddlers in other people's love lives ought to expect: "Oh, no, not allus; we sometimes quarrel in de daytime and make all up at night."

The slaveholders, in their tender concern for black women who suffered abuse from their husbands, remained curiously silent about those who fell back on their husbands' protection. Laura Bell's father won her mother's hand by volunteering to take a whipping in her place. Most slaveholders had the sense to prohibit such gallantry, but no few black men braved their wrath by interposing themselves between their wives or daughters and the white man who sought to harm them. Not only husbands but male friends killed, beat or drove off overseers for whipping their women.

Black women fell victims to white lust, but many escaped because the whites knew they had black men who would rather die than stand idly by. In some cases black men protected their women and got off with a whipping or no punishment at all; in other cases they sacrificed their lives.

Even short of death, the pride of assertive manliness could reach fearful proportions. An overseer tried to rape Josiah Henson's mother but was overpowered by his father. Yielding to his wife's pleas and the overseer's promise of no reprisal, the enraged slave desisted from killing him. The overseer broke his promise. Henson's father suffered 100 lashes and had an ear nailed to the whipping post and then severed.

"Previous to this affair my father, from all I can learn, had been a good-humored and light-hearted man, the ringleader in all fun at corn-huskings and Christmas buffoonery. His banjo was the life of the farm, and all night long at a merry-making would he play on it while the other Negroes danced. But from this hour he became utterly changed. Sullen, morose, and dogged, nothing could be done with him."

Threats of being sold south had no effect on him. The thoughts running through his mind as he came to prefer separation from the wife he loved to enduring life there must remain a matter of speculation. His master sold him to Alabama, and he was never heard from again.

Resisting Oppression

The slaveholders deprived black men of the role of provider; refused to dignify their marriages or legitimize their issue; compelled them to submit to physical abuse in the presence of their women and children; made them choose between remaining silent while their wives and daughters were raped or seduced and risking death; and threatened them with separation from their family at any moment.

Many men caved in under the onslaught and became irresponsible husbands and indifferent fathers. The women who had to contend with such men sometimes showed stubborn cheerfulness and sometimes raging bitterness; they raised the children, maintained order at home, and rotated men in and out of bed. Enough men and women fell into this pattern to give rise to the legends of the matriarchy, the emasculated but brutal male, and the fatherless children.

Many men and women resisted the "infantilization," "emasculation" and "dehumanization" inherent in the system's aggression against the slave family. How many? No one will ever know. At issue is the quality of human relationships, which cannot be measured. But there exists as much evidence of resistance and of a struggle for a decent family life as of demoralization. A brutal social system broke the spirit of many and rendered others less responsible than human beings ought to be. But enough men came out of this test of fire whole, if necessarily scarred, to demonstrate that the slaves had powerful inner resources. A terrible system of human oppression took a heavy toll of its victims, but their collective accomplishment in resisting the system constitutes a heroic story. That resistance provided black people with solid norms for family life and role differentiation, even if circumstances caused a dangerously high lapse from those norms. The slaves from their own experience had come to value a two-parent, male-centered household, no matter how much difficulty they had in realizing the ideal.

The role of the male slave as husband and father therefore requires a fresh look. If many men lived up to their assigned irresponsibility, others, probably a majority, overcame all obstacles and provided a positive male image for their wives and children. An ex-slave recalled his boyhood:

"I loved my father. He was such a good man. He was a good carpenter and could do anything. My mother just rejoiced in him. Whenever he sat down to talk she just sat and looked and listened. She would never cross him for anything. If they went to church together she always waited for him to interpret what the preacher had said or what he taught was the will of God. I was small but I noticed all of these things. I sometimes think I learned more in my early childhood about how to live than I have learned since."

Protective fathers appeared in the lullabies slave mothers sang to their children:

Kink head, wherefore you skeered?
Old snake crawled off, 'cause he's a-
feared.
Pappy will smite him on de back
With a great big club—Ker whack! Ker
whack!

Many ex-slaves recalled their fathers as stern disciplinarians, and the slaveholders' complaints about fathers' abusing their children may be read as supporting evidence. Other slave men left their children a memory of kindness and affection that remained through life. Will Adams' father, a foreman on a Texas plantation, came in exhausted after a long day's work but never failed to take his son out of bed and to play with him for hours. The spirituals and other slave songs reflected the importance of the father in the lives of the children; many of them sang of the re-unification of the family in heaven and of the father's return.

Middle-Class Norms

Men knew that they might have to part from their wives and children, but that knowledge did not engender indifference so much as a certain stoical submission to that which had to be endured. Under painful conditions, many did their best even while others succumbed. Mingo White's father, upon being sold, did nothing unusual when he charged a male friend with responsibility for looking after his son. A principle of stewardship had arisen in the quarters. Even in the absence of a father, some male would likely step in to help raise a boy to manhood. When the war ended, men crisscrossed the South to reclaim their families and to assert authority over their children.

Slave children usually did have an image of a strong black man before them. Critical scholars have made the mistake of measuring the slave family by middle-class norms; naturally, they have found it wanting.

Even when a slave boy was growing up without a father in the house, he had as a model a tough, resourceful driver, a skilled mechanic or two, and older field hands with some time for the children of the quarters. Some of those men devoted themselves to playing surrogate father to all the children. They told them stories, taught them to fish and trap animals, and instructed them in the ways of survival in a hostile white world.

The norm in the quarters called for adults to look after children, whether blood relatives or not. Every plantation had some

men who played this role. Under the worst of circumstances, one or two would have been enough; usually, however, there were a number. And there were the preachers. To the extent that the slaves heard their preachers, the children saw before them influential black men whose eloquence and moral force commanded the respect of the adults.

The slave children, like the ghetto children of later decades, saw a pattern of behavior that implied clear sexual differentiation and a notion of masculinity with its own strengths and weaknesses.

DON'T MESS WITH MAMMY

The daughters of the Confederacy suggested in 1923 that Congress set aside a site in Washington for a suitable memorial to the antebellum plantation Mammy. The good ladies had picked their symbol carefully, for no figure stands out so prominently in the moonlight-and-magnolias legend of the Old South. The hostile reaction of so many blacks confirmed the judgment. As the old regime has come under increasingly critical scrutiny, Mammy has had a steadily worsening press. She remains the most elusive and important black presence in the Big House. To understand her is to move toward understanding the tragedy of plantation paternalism.

First, the white legend, Lewis H. Blair, attacking racial segregation in 1889, wrote:

"Most of us above 30 years of age had our mammy, and generally she was the first to receive us from the doctor's hands, and was the first to proclaim, with heart bursting with pride, the arrival of a fine baby. Up to the age of 10 we saw as much of the mammy as of the mother, perhaps more, and we loved her quite as well. The mammy first taught us to lisp and to walk, played with us and told us wonderful stories, taught us who made us and who redeemed us, dried our tears and soothed our bursting hearts, and saved us many a well-deserved whipping . . ."

Word Had Force of Law

Mammy comes through the black sources in much the same way, but only so far. Lindey Faucette of North Carolina remembered her grandmother, Mammie Beckie, who "toted de keys," whose word had the force of law with Marse John and Mis' Annie, and who slept in the bed with her mistress when the master's law practice kept him in town all night. Alice Sewell of Alabama especially recalled the plantation Mammy's comforting the relatives of deceased slaves, arranging for the burial, and leading the funeral services. Ellen Botts of Louisiana noted: "All de niggers have to stoop to Aunt Rachel like they curtsy to Missy." And Adeline Johnson, who had served as a Mammy in South Carolina, spoke in her old age in accents that would have warmed the hearts of those Daughters of the Confederacy:

"I hope and prays to git to hebben. Whether I's white or black when I git dere, I'll be satisfied to see my Savior dat my old marster worshipped and my husband preached 'bout. I wants to be in hebben wid all my white folks, just to wait on them and love them and serve them, sorta lak I did in slavery time. Dat will be 'nough hebben for Adeline."

Who were these Mammies? What did they actually do? Primarily, the Mammy raised the white children and ran the Big House either as the mistress' executive officer or her de facto superior. Her power extended over black and white so long as she exercised restraint, and she was not to be crossed.

She carried herself like a surrogate mistress—neatly attired, barking orders, conscious of her dignity, full of self-respect. She played the diplomat and settled the interminable disputes that arose among the house servants; when diplomacy failed, she resorted to her whip and restored order. She served as confidante to the children, the mistress, and even the master. She expected to be consulted on the love affairs and marriages of the white children and might even be consulted on the business affairs of the plantation. She presided over the dignity of the whole plantation and taught the courtesies to the white children as well as to those black children destined to work in the Big House. On the small and medium-sized plantations she had to carry much of the house work herself, and her relationship to the field slaves drew closer.

In general, she gave the whites the perfect slave—a loyal, faithful, contented, efficient, conscientious member of the family who always knew her place; and she gave the slaves a white-approved standard of black behavior. She also had to be a tough, worldly-wise, enormously resourceful woman; that is, she had to develop all the strength of character not usually attributed to an Aunt Jane.

Mammy supposedly paid more attention to the white children than to her own. Even W. E. B. Du Bois, who was rarely taken in by appearances and legends, thought so. He described the Mammy as "one of the most pitiful of the world's Christs. . . . She was an embodied Sorrow, an anomaly crucified on the cross of her own neglected children for the sake of the children of masters who bought and sold her as they bought and sold cattle."

The Mammy typically took her responsibilities to the white family as a matter of high personal honor and in so doing undoubtedly could not give her own children as much love and attention as they deserved. House nannies, white and black, free and slave, have often fallen into this trap. But the idea that the Mammies actually loved the white children more than their own rests on nothing more than wishful white perceptions. That they loved the white children they themselves raised—hardly astonishing for warm, sensitive, generous women—in no way proves that they loved their own children the less. Rather, their position in the Big House, including their close attention to the white children sometimes at the expense of their own, constituted the firmest protection they could have acquired for themselves and their immediate families. Mammies did not often have to worry about being sold or about having their husbands or children sold. The sacrifices they made for the whites earned them genuine affection in return, which provided a guarantee of protection, safety, and privilege for their own children:

Barrier Against Abuse

The relationship between the Mammies and their white folks exhibited that reciprocity so characteristic of paternalism. "Of course," a planter in Virginia told a northern reporter in 1865, "if a servant has the charge of one of my little ones, and I see the child grow fond of her, and that she loves the child, I cannot but feel kindly towards her." Of course, Mom Genia Woodbury, who had been a slave in South Carolina, acknowledged that when white folks treat you kindly, you develop kind feelings toward their children.

The devotion of the white children, who regularly sought her as their protector, confidante, and substitute mother, established a considerable barrier against the abuse of Mammy or her family. "We would not hesitate about coming to see you," Laura S. Tibbetts of Louisiana wrote her sister-in-law, "if I could bring my servants, but I could not bring my baby without assistance. She is a great deal fonder of her Mammy than she is of me. She nurses her and it would be a great trial to go without her."

The immunity that Mammy secured for herself did not fully cover husband and children, but it went far enough to shield them from the worst. Mammy distraught, hurt, or angry was not to be borne. More than one overseer learned to his cost to walk gingerly around her and hers. Ma Eppes of Alabama said that an overseer had whipped the plantation Mammy when the mistress was away:

"When Miss Sarah comed back and found it out she was the maddest white lady I ever seed. She sent for the overseer and she say, 'Allen, what you mean by whipping Mammy? You know I don't allow you to touch my house servants... I'd rather see them marks on my old shoulders than to see 'em on Mammy's. They wouldn't hurt me no worse.' Then she say, 'Allen, take your family and git offen my place. Don't you let sundown catch you here.' So he left. He wasn't nothing but white trash nohow."

Another overseer made the incredible mistake of asking his employer for permission to punish Mammy. The reply: "What! What! Why I would as soon think of punishing my own mother! Why man you'd have four of the biggest men in Mississippi down on you if you even dare suggest such a thing, and she knows it! All you can do is to knuckle down to Mammy."

The plantation Mammy was not, as is so easily assumed, some "white man's nigger," some pathetic appendage to the powerful whites of the Big House. Her strength of character, iron will and impressive self-discipline belie any glib generalizations.

•

She did not reject her people in order to identify with stronger whites, but she did place herself in a relationship to her own people that reinforced the paternalist social order. Thus, she carried herself with courage, compassion, dignity and self-respect and might have provided a black model for these qualities among people who needed one, had not the constricting circumstances of her own development cut her off, in essential respects, from playing that role. Her tragedy lay not in her abandonment of her own people but in her inability to offer her individual power and beauty to black people on terms they could accept without themselves sliding further into a system of paternalistic dependency.

SOME CHOSE FREEDOM

The boldest slaves struck the hardest blow an individual could against the regime: they escaped to freedom. During the 1850s about a thousand slaves a year ran away to the North, Canada, and Mexico. Increased vigilance by the slaveholders and their police apparatus may have reduced the number from 1,011 in 1850 to 803 in 1860 as the census reports insist, but even so, the economic drain and political irritation remained serious.

The slaves in the border states, especially the extreme northern tier, had a much better chance to escape than did those in Mississippi or Alabama. But even in Texas, Arkansas and Louisiana, slaveholders had to exercise vigilance, for many slaves went over the Mexican border or escaped to friendly Indians.

Who ran away? Any slave might slip into the woods for a few days, but those whose departure rated an advertisement and organized chase—those who headed for freedom in the North, the Southern cities, or the swamps—fell into a pattern.

At least 80 per cent were men between the ages of 16 and 35. At least one-third of the runaways belonged to the ranks of the skilled and privileged slaves—those with some education and with some knowledge of the outside world—and women occupied these ranks only as house servants.

The whip provided the single biggest provocation to running away. Many slaves ran in anticipation of a whipping or other severe punishment, and others in anger after having suffered it. In some cases—too many—slaves ran not simply from a particular whipping but from the torments regularly inflicted by cruel or sadistic masters or overseers.

A large if underdetermined number of slaves ran away to rejoin loved ones from whom they had been forcibly parted. Newspaper advertisements frequently contained such words as "He is no doubt trying to reach his wife." Slaveholders had great trouble with newly purchased slaves who immediately left to try to find parents or children as well as wives. In some instances the slaves had unexpected success when their masters, touched by the evidence of devotion and courage, reunited the family by resale.

In many more cases family ties prevented slaves from running away or kept them close to home when they did run. Frederick Law Olmsted reported from the lower Mississippi Valley that planters kept a sharp eye on mothers, for few slaves would leave permanently if they had to leave their mothers behind to face the master's wrath.

"The Thousand Obstacles"
Among the deterrents to making the long run to free states none loomed larger than the fear of the unknown. Most knew only the immediate area and often only a narrow strip of that. Even many skilled and relatively sophisticated slaves lacked an

elementary knowledge of geography and had no means of transportation.

If most slaves feared to think about flight to the North, many feared even to think of short-term flight to the nearby woods or swamps. The slaves faced particularly difficult conditions in the swampy areas alongside the great plantation districts of Louisiana and the eastern low country. Solomon Northrup, a slave on a Louisiana cotton plantation in the 1840s, wrote:

"No man who has never been placed in such a situation can comprehend the thousand obstacles thrown in the way of the fleeing slave. Every white man's hand is raised against him—the patrollers are watching for him—the hounds are ready to follow on his track, and the nature of the country is such as renders it impossible to pass through it with any safety."

And yet, large numbers of slaves did brave the elements, the dogs, and the patrols; did swallow their fears; and did take to the woods. No plantation of any size totally avoided the runaway problem. Everywhere, the slavesholders had to build a certain loss of labor-time and a certain amount of irritation into their yearly calculations.

Slaves from one plantation assisted runaways from other plantations under certain circumstances. The slaves from neighboring plantations often knew each other well. They met for prayer meetings, corn shuckings, Christmas, and other holiday barbecues; often formed close attachments; and sometimes extended their idea of a plantation family to at least some of these friends and acquaintances. Within this wider circle, the slaves would readily help each other if they shunned those they regarded as strangers. But even strangers might find succor if they were fleeing the plantations of slaveholders known to be cruel.

Those who fled to freedom made an inestimable contribution to the people they left behind, which must be weighed against their participation in a safety-valve effect. These were slaves who, short of taking the path of insurrection, most clearly repudiated the regime; who dramatically chose freedom at the highest risk; who never let others forget that there was an alternative to their condition.

POSTSCRIPT

DID SLAVERY DESTROY THE BLACK FAMILY?

Anne Lane has edited a collection of historical essays in *The Debate Over Slavery* (Illinois, 1971) which critiques every aspect of Elkins's path-breaking book. There is disagreement over the question whether Latin American slavery was less harsh than North American slavery. Comparative historical studies yielded mixed results. Elkins believes that Spanish law and the Catholic church mitigated the harshness of the institution. Genovese, to the contrary, maintains that Latin American governmental officials were often corrupt and did not enforce the law while many Catholic priests were more interested in saving the souls of the masters rather than the slaves.

There was also controversy concerning the Sambo-image of the typical slave. Elkins's work relied on applying theoretical models to a study of slavery but contained no original research into primary sources. Those writers like Genovese who have delved into the WPA slave narratives and records of the plantation owners have uncovered a much more complicated picture of the slave. Some deny slaves ever internalized the personality of Sambo. Others argue that the slaves adopted two personalities: Sambo who appeared before the white slave masters and a second individual who revealed his true self to his contemporaries in the slave quarters. The student who has carefully read Genovese's account of the slave Mammy will perceive a many-sided individual.

The middle of the 1970s witnessed an explosion of books on slavery. Robert Fogel and Stanley Enterman's *Time on the Cross* (Little, Brown, 1974) relied on a computerized analysis of available statistical data to claim, as did Ulrich B. Phillips, that slaves received cradle-to-grave social services. This work received a great deal of public notoriety though historians later panned many of its statistics under the equation "garbage in, garbage out." Eugene D. Genovese's *Roll Jordan Roll* (Vintage, 1976) remains the best comprehensive treatment of slavery, while Herbert G. Gutman demolishes numerous stereotypes about the slave family in his overwhelming *The Black Family in Slavery and Freedom 1750-1925* (Vintage, 1977). No student should pass up Alex Haley's *Roots* (Doubleday, 1976). Part fact, part fiction, this one book and its subsequent television series has done more than all the works written by historians to destroy the romantic picture of slavery as portrayed in earlier histories, novels, and motion pictures.

ISSUE 15

DID THE FRONTIER DETERMINE THE COURSE OF AMERICAN HISTORY?

YES: Frederick J. Turner, from *The Frontier in American History* (Holt and Co., 1920, 1947)

NO: George W. Pierson, from "The Frontier and American Institutions: A Criticism of the Turner Thesis," in *The New England Quarterly,* June 1942

ISSUE SUMMARY

YES: Professor Frederick Turner considers American History synonymous with the history of the frontier.
NO: Professor George Pierson enumerates the shortcomings of Turner's attempt to force all of American history into a mold.

Not only historians but also novelists and film makers have influenced our images of the American frontier. The novels of James Fenimore Cooper (1789–1851) outlined much of the social mythology of the West in his Leatherstocking Tales such as *The Pathfinder, The Pioneers* and *The Last of the Mohicans.* By the time (1893) the historians descended on the subject of the West in full force, the leader of the advance, Frederick Jackson Turner, made it plain that the frontier had disappeared. Turner meant that unsettled land, in the sense Europeans and then Americans had come to think of the New World, had vanished. Turner's scholarship, and especially that of his countless disciples, proved that the frontier as a historical concept was anything but dead. It is ironically touching, as well as appropriate, that Turner read his seminal paper on the significance of the frontier at the quadricentennial festivities for Columbus's initial voyage. When film makers discovered the frontier themes which had first appeared in literature and history, they overproduced westerns with the consequence that frontier myths turned into clichés and occasionally were parodied in films like *Cat Ballou* and *Blazing Saddles.* Is it possible to ignore these oversimplifications, and their reincarnations on television, in an attempt to understand Turner's frontier thesis in its original format?

Turner surveys an impressive range of topics to give his thesis a panoramic appearance. No frontier experience seems to have been neglected. While attempting to convince us that the frontier can no longer be ignored as a major historical subject, however, Turner has also opened himself up to the charge that he has overemphasized the West's impact on the nation. One of Turner's major critics, Professor Pierson, notes not only this exaggeration but also omissions. Turner's ideas about history reflect a strong Positivist influence, meaning material aspects of history are emphasized at the expense of ones which are not measurable such as culture. According to Pierson, Turner also neglects themes such as industrialization and commerce which are crucial to a materialistic interpretation of modern history. Pierson seems to have uncovered a major flaw when he points out the insularity of Turner's ethnocentrism despite his familiarity with German historiography and Italian economic thought. Pierson argues, as does Hayes in Issue One, that if the frontier thesis has any merit, it will bear the weight of historical comparison. The existence of the frontier should explain not only the development of the United States but also that of New Spain, later Mexico, and New France. Hayes insists in Issue One that the frontier experience was a part of European history and not at all unique to the United States. Perhaps the most damning point Pierson makes is Turner's failure to develop his ideas or to revise them substantially over time. Turner, he says, was preoccupied with discovering ways in which his thesis could encapsulate the American experience and, consequently, did not attempt to provide details to accompany his generalizations. He hints that Turner's frontier thesis was a pronouncement to be accepted because of the intrinsic truth its author thought it displayed. Turner left the substantiation of his thesis to others, principally his graduate students.

"Up to our own day, American history has been in a large degree the history of the colonization of the Great West. The existence of an area of free land, its continuous recession, and the advance of American settlement westward, explain American development," Turner boldly asserted in 1893. "Steadily the frontier of settlement advanced and carried with it individualism, democracy, and nationalism, and powerfully affected the East and the Old World," he concluded. Pierson, some fifty years later, attacked his generalization with, "In what it proposes, the frontier hypothesis needs painstaking revision. By what it fails to mention, the theory today disqualifies itself as an adequate guide to American development."

YES
Frederick Jackson Turner

THE FRONTIER
IN AMERICAN HISTORY

THE SIGNIFICANCE OF THE FRONTIER IN AMERICAN HISTORY

In a recent bulletin of the Superintendent of the Census for 1890 appear these significant words: "Up to and including 1880 the country had a frontier of settlement, but at present the unsettled area has been so broken into by isolated bodies of settlement that there can hardly be said to be a frontier line. In the discussion of its extent, its westward movement, etc., it can not, therefore, any longer have a place in the census reports." This brief official statement marks the closing of a great historic movement. Up to our own day American history has been in a large degree the history of the colonization of the Great West. The existence of an area of free land, its continuous recession, and the advance of American settlement westward, explain American development.

Behind institutions, behind constitutional forms and modifications, lie the vital forces that call these organs into life and shape them to meet changing conditions. The peculiarity of American institutions is, the fact that they have been compelled to adapt themselves to the changes of an expanding people— to the changes involved in crossing a continent, in winning a wilderness, and in developing at each area of this progress out of the primitive economic and political conditions of the frontier into the complexity of city life. Said Calhoun in 1817, "We are great, and rapidly—I was about to say fearfully— growing!" So saying, he touched the distinguishing feature of American life. All peoples show development; the germ theory of politics has been suffi-

ciently emphasized. In the case of most nations, however, the development has occurred in a limited area; and if the nation
has expanded, it has met other growing
peoples whom it has conquered. But in
the case of the United States we have a
different phenomenon. Limiting our attention to the Atlantic coast, we have the
familiar phenomenon of the evolution of
institutions in a limited area, such as the
rise of representative government; the
differentiation of simple colonial governments into complex organs; the progress
from primitive industrial society, without
division of labor, up to manufacturing civilization. But we have in addition to this a
recurrence of the process of evolution in
each western area reached in the process
of expansion. Thus American development has exhibited not merely advance
along a single line, but a return to primitive conditions on a continually advancing frontier line, and a new development
for that area. American social development has been continually beginning over
again on the frontier. This perennial re-
birth, this fluidity of American life, this
expansion westward with its new opportunities, its continuous touch with the simplicity of primitive society, furnish the
forces dominating American character.
The true point of view in the history of this
nation is not the Atlantic coast, it is the
Great West. Even the slavery struggle,
which is made so exclusive an object of
attention by writers like Professor von
Holst, occupies its important place in
American history because of its relation to
westward expansion.

In this advance, the frontier is the outer edge of the wave—the meeting point
between savagery and civilization. Much
has been written about the frontier from
the point of view of border warfare and
the chase, but as a field for the serious

study of the economist and the historian
it has been neglected.

The American frontier is sharply distinguished from the European frontier—a fortified boundary line running through dense
populations. The most significant thing
about the American frontier is, that it lies
at the hither edge of free land. In the census reports it is treated as the margin of
that settlement which has a density of two
or more to the square mile. The term is
an elastic one, and for our purposes does
not need sharp definition. We shall consider the whole frontier belt, including the
Indian country and the outer margin of the
"settled area" of the census reports. This
paper will make no attempt to treat the
subject exhaustively; its aim is simply to
call attention to the frontier as a fertile field
for investigation, and to suggest some of
the problems which arise in connection
with it. . . .

In the course of the seventeenth century the frontier was advanced up the atlantic river courses, just beyond the "fall
line," and the tidewater region became the
settled area. In the first half of the eighteenth century another advance occurred.
Traders followed the Delaware and the
Shawnese Indians to the Ohio as early as
the end of the first quarter of the century.
Gov. Spotswood, of Virginia, made an ex-
pedition in 1714 across the Blue Ridge.
The end of the first quarter of the century
saw the advance of the Scotch-Irish and
the Palatine Germans up the Shenandoah
Valley into the western part of Virginia,
and along the Piedmont region of the
Carolinas. The Germans in New York
pushed the frontier of settlement up the
Mohawk to German Flats. In Pennsylvania
the town of Bedford indicates the line of
settlement. Settlements soon began on the
New River, or the Great Kanawha, and on

269

the sources of the Yadkin and French Broad. The King attempted to arrest the advance by his proclamation of 1763, forbidding settlements beyond the sources of the rivers flowing into the Atlantic; but in vain. In the period of the Revolution the frontier crossed the Alleghenies into Kentucky and Tennessee, and the upper waters of the Ohio were settled. When the first census was taken in 1790, the continuous settled area was bounded by a line which ran near the coast of Maine, and included New England except a portion of Vermont and New Hampshire, New York along the Hudson and up the Mohawk about Schenectady, eastern and southern Pennsylvania, Virginia well across the Shenandoah Valley, and the Carolinas and eastern Georgia. Beyond this region of continuous settlement were the small settled areas of Kentucky and Tennessee, and the Ohio, with the mountains intervening between them and the Atlantic area, thus giving a new and important character to the frontier. The isolation of the region increased its peculiarly American tendencies, and the need of transportation facilities to connect with the East called out important schemes of internal improvement, which will be noted farther on. The "West," as a self-conscious section, began to evolve.

From decade to decade distinct advances of the frontier occurred. By the census of 1820 the settled area included Ohio, southern Indiana and Illinois, southeastern Missouri, and about one-half of Louisiana. This settled area had surrounded Indian areas, and the management of these tribes became an object of political concern. The frontier region of the time lay along the Great Lakes, where Astor's American Fur Company operated in the Indian trade, and beyond the Mississippi, where Indian traders extended their activi-ty even to the Rocky Mountains; Florida also furnished frontier conditions. The Mississippi River region was the scene of typical frontier settlements.

The rising steam navigation on western waters, the opening of the Erie Canal, and the westward extension of cotton culture added five frontier states to the Union in this period. Grund, writing in 1836, declares: "It appears then that the universal disposition of Americans to emigrate to the western wilderness, in order to enlarge their dominion over inanimate nature, is the actual result of an expansive power which is inherent in them, and which by continually agitating all classes of society is constantly throwing a large portion of the whole population on the extreme confines of the State, in order to gain space for its development. Hardly is a new State or Territory formed before the same principle manifests itself again and gives rise to a further emigration; and so is it destined to go on until a physical barrier must finally obstruct its progress."

In the middle of this century the line indicated by the present eastern boundary of Indian Territory, Nebraska, and Kansas marked the frontier of the Indian country. Minnesota and Wisconsin still exhibited frontier conditions, but the distinctive frontier of the period is found in California, where the gold discoveries had sent a sudden tide of adventurous miners, and in Oregon, and the settlements in Utah. As the frontier had leaped over the Alleghenies, so now it skipped the Great Plains and the Rocky Mountains; and in the same way that the advance of the frontiersmen beyond the Alleghenies had caused the rise of important questions of transportation and internal improvement, so now the settlers beyond the Rocky Mountains needed means of communication with the East, and in the furnishing of these arose the settlement of the Great Plains and the development of still another kind of frontier life. Railroads, fostered by land grants, sent an increasing tide of immigrants into the Far West. The United States Army fought a series of Indian wars in Minnesota, Dakota, and the Indian Territory.

By 1880 the settled area had been pushed into northern Michigan, Wisconsin, and Minnesota, along the Dakota rivers, and in the Black Hills region, and was ascending the rivers of Kansas and Nebraska. The development of mines in Colorado had drawn isolated frontier settlements into that region, and Montana and Idaho were receiving settlers. The frontier was found in these mining camps and the ranches of the Great Plains. The superintendent of the census for 1890 reports, as previously stated, that the settlements of the West lie so scattered over the region that there can no longer be said to be a frontier line. . . .

Having now roughly outlined the various kinds of frontiers, and their modes of advance, chiefly from the point of view of the frontier itself, we may next inquire what were the influences on the East and on the Old World. A rapid enumeration of some of the more noteworthy effects is all that I have time for.

First, we note that the frontier promoted the formation of a composite nationality for the American people. The coast was preponderantly English, but the later tides of continental immigration flowed across to the free lands. This was the case from the early colonial days. The Scotch-Irish and the Palatine Germans, or "Pennsylvania Dutch," furnished the dominant element in the stock of the colonial frontier. With these peoples were also the freed indented servants, or redemptioners, who at the expiration of their time of service passed to the frontier. Governor Spotswood of Virginia writes in 1717, "The inhabitants of our frontiers are composed generally of such as have been transported hither as servants, and, being out of their time, settle themselves where land is to be taken up and that will produce the necessarys of life with little labour." Very generally these redemptioners were of non-English stock. In the crucible of the frontier the immigrants were Americanized, liberated, and fused into a mixed race, English in neither nationality nor characteristics. The process has gone on from the early days to our own. Burke and other writers in the middle of the eighteenth century believed that Pennsylvania was "threatened with the danger of being wholly foreign in language, manners, and perhaps even inclinations." The German and Scotch-Irish elements in the frontier of the South were only less great. In the middle of the present century the German element in Wisconsin was already so considerable that leading publicists looked to the creation of a German state out of the commonwealth by concentrating their colonization. Such examples teach us to beware of misinterpreting the fact that there is a common English speech in America into a belief that the stock is also English.

In another way the advance of the frontier decreased our dependence on England. The coast, particularly of the South, lacked diversified industries, and was dependent on England for the bulk of its supplies. In the South there was even a dependence on the Northern colonies for articles of food. Governor Glenn, of South Carolina, writes in the middle of the eighteenth century: "Our trade with New York and Philadelphia was of this sort, draining us of all the little money and bills we could gather from other places for their bread, flour, beer, hams, bacon, and other things of their produce, all which, except beer, our new townships begin to supply us with, which are settled with very industrious and thriving Germans. This no doubt diminishes the number of shipping and the appearance of our trade, but it is far from being a detriment to us." Before long the frontier created a demand for merchants. As it retreated from the coast it became less and less possible for England to bring her supplies directly to the consumer's wharfs, and carry away staple crops, and staple crops began to give way to diversified agriculture for a time. The effect of this phase of the frontier action upon the northern section is perceived when we realize how the advance of the frontier aroused seaboard cities like Boston, New York, and Baltimore, to engage in rivalry for what Washington called "the extensive and valuable trade of a rising empire."

The legislation which most developed the powers of the national government, and played the largest part in its activity, was conditioned on the frontier. Writers have discussed the subjects of tariff, land, and internal improvement, as subsidiary to the slavery question. But when American history comes to be rightly viewed it will be seen that the slavery question is an incident. In the period from the end of the first half of the present century to the close of the Civil War slavery rose to primary, but far from exclusive, importance. But this does not justify Dr. von Holst (to take an example) in treating our constitutional history in its formative period down to 1828 in a single volume, giving six volumes chiefly to the history of slavery from 1828 to 1861, under the title "Constitutional History of the United States." The growth of nationalism and the evolution of American political institutions were dependent

on the advance of the frontier. Even so recent a writer as Rhodes, in his "History of the United States since the Compromise of 1850," has treated the legislation called out by the western advance as incidental to the slavery struggle.

This is a wrong perspective. The pioneer needed the goods of the coast, and so the grand series of internal improvement and railroad legislation began, with potent nationalizing effects. Over internal improvements occurred great debates, in which grave constitutional questions were discussed. Sectional groupings appear in the votes, profoundly significant for the historian. Loose construction increased as the nation marched westward. But the West was not content with bringing the farm to the factory. Under the lead of Clay—"Harry of the West"—protective tariffs were passed, with the cry of bringing the factory to the farm. The disposition of the public lands was a third important subject of national legislation influenced by the frontier.

The public domain has been a force of profound importance in the nationalization and development of the government. The effects of the struggle of the landed and the landless States, and of the Ordinance of 1787, need no discussion. Administratively the frontier called out some of the highest and most vitalizing activities of the general government. The purchase of Louisiana was perhaps the constitutional turning point in the history of the Republic, inasmuch as it afforded both a new area for national legislation and the occasion of the downfall of the policy of strict construction. But the purchase of Louisiana was called out by frontier needs and demands. As frontier States accrued to the Union the national power grew. In a speech on the dedication of the Calhoun monument Mr. Lamar explained: "In 1789 the States were the creators of the Federal Government; in 1861 the Federal Government was the creator of a large majority of the States." . . .

It was this nationalizing tendency of the West that transformed the democracy of Jefferson into the national republicanism of Monroe and the democracy of Andrew Jackson. The West of the War of 1812, the West of Clay, and Benton and Harrison, and Andrew Jackson, shut off by the Middle States and the Mountains from the coast sections, had a solidarity of its own with national tendencies. On the tide of the Father of Waters, North and South met and mingled into a nation. Interstate migration went steadily on—a process of cross-fertilization of ideas and institutions. The fierce struggle of the sections over slavery on the western frontier does not diminish the truth of this statement; it proves the truth of it. Slavery was a sectional trait that would not down, but in the West it could not remain sectional. It was the greatest of frontiersmen who declared: "I believe this Government can not endure permanently half slave and half free. It will become all of one thing or all of the other." Nothing works for nationalism like intercourse within the nation. Mobility of population is death to localism, and the western frontier worked irresistibly in unsettling population. The effect reached back from the frontier and affected profoundly the Atlantic coast and even the Old World.

But the most important effect of the frontier has been in the promotion of democracy here and in Europe. As has been indicated, the frontier is productive of individualism. Complex society is precipitated by the wilderness into a kind of primitive organization based on the family. The tendency is anti-social. It produces antipathy to control, and particularly to any direct control. The tax-gatherer is viewed as a representative of oppression. Prof. Osgood, in an able article, has pointed out that the frontier conditions prevalent in the colonies are important factors in the explanation of the American Revolution, where individual liberty was sometimes confused with absence of all effective government. The same conditions aid in explaining the difficulty of instituting a strong government in the period of the confederacy. The frontier individualism has from the beginning promoted democracy.

The frontier States that came into the union in the first quarter of a century of its existence came in with democratic suffrage provisions, and had reactive effects of the highest importance upon the older States whose peoples were being attracted there. An extension of the franchise became essential. It was *western* New York that forced an extension of suffrage in the constitutional convention of that State in 1821; and it was *western* Virginia that compelled the tide-water region to put a more liberal suffrage provision in the constitution framed in 1830, and to give to the frontier region a more nearly proportionate representation with the tide-water aristocracy. The rise of democracy as an effective force in the nation came in with western preponderance under Jackson and William Henry Harrison, and it meant the triumph of the frontier—with all of its good and with all of its evil elements. An interesting illustration of the tone of frontier democracy in 1830 comes from the same debates in the Virginia convention already referred to. A representative from western Virginia declared:

> But, sir, it is not the increase of population in the West which this gentleman ought to fear. It is the energy which the mountain breeze and western habits impart to those emigrants. They are regenerated, politically I mean, sir. They soon become

working politicians; and the difference, sir, between a *talking* and a *working* politician is immense. The Old Dominion has long been celebrated for producing great orators; the ablest metaphysicians in policy; men that can split hairs in all abstruse questions of political economy. But at home, or when they return from Congress, they have negroes to fan them asleep. But a Pennsylvania, a New York, an Ohio, or a western Virginia statesman, though far inferior in logic, metaphysics, and rhetoric to an old Virginia statesman, has this advantage, that when he returns home he takes off his coat and takes hold of the plow. This gives him bone and muscle, sir, and preserves his republican principles pure and uncontaminated.

So long as free land exists, the opportunity for a competency exists, and economic power secures political power. But the democracy born of free land, strong in selfishness and individualism, intolerant of administrative experience and education, and pressing individual liberty beyond its proper bounds, has its dangers as well as its benefits. Individualism in America has allowed a laxity in regard to governmental affairs which has rendered possible the spoils system and all manifest evils that follow from the lack of a highly developed civic spirit. In this connection may be noted also the influence of frontier conditions in permitting lax business honor, inflated paper currency and wild-cat banking. The colonial and revolutionary frontier was the region whence emanated many of the worst forms of an evil currency. The West in the War of 1812 repeated the phenomenon on the frontier of that day, while the speculation and wild-cat banking of the period of the crisis of 1837 occurred on the new frontier belt of the next tier of States. Thus each one of the periods of lax financial integrity coincides with periods when a new set of frontier communities had arisen, and coincides in area with these successive frontiers, for the most part. The recent Populist agitation is a case in point. Many a State that now declines any connection with the tenets of the Populists, itself adhered to such ideas in an earlier stage of the development of the State. A primitive society can hardly be expected to show the intelligent appreciation of the complexity of business interests in a developed society. The continual recurrence of these areas of paper-money agitation is another evidence that the frontier can be isolated and studied as a factor in American history of the highest importance.

The East has always feared the result of an unregulated advance of the frontier, and has tried to check and guide it. The English authorities would have checked settlement at the headwaters of the Atlantic tributaries and allowed the "savages to enjoy their deserts in quiet lest the peltry trade should decrease." This called out Burke's splendid protest:

> If you stopped your grants, what would be the consequence? The people would occupy without grants. They have already so occupied in many places. You can not station garrisons in every part of these deserts. If you drive the people from one place, they will carry on their annual tillage and remove with their flocks and herds to another. Many of the people in the back settlements are already little attached to particular situations. Already they have topped the Appalachian Mountains. From thence they behold before them an immense plain, one vast, rich, level meadow; a square of five hundred miles. Over this they would wander without a possibility of restraint; they would change their manners with their habits of life; would soon forget a government by which they were disowned; would become hordes of English Tartars; and, pouring down upon your unfortified frontiers a fierce and irresistible cavalry, become masters of your governors and your counselors, your col-

lectors and comptrollers, and of all the slaves that adhered to them. Such would, and in no long time must, be the effect of attempting to forbid as a crime and to suppress as an evil the command and blessing of Providence, "Increase and multiply." Such would be the happy result of an endeavor to keep as a lair of wild beasts that earth which God, by an express charter, has given to the children of men.

But the English Government was not alone in its desire to limit the advance of the frontier and guide its destinies. Tidewater Virginia and South Carolina gerrymandered those colonies to insure the dominance of the coast in their legislatures. Washington desired to settle a State at a time in the Northwest; Jefferson would reserve from settlement the territory of his Louisiana Purchase north of the thirty-second parallel, in order to offer it to the Indians in exchange for their settlements east of the Mississippi. "When we shall be full on this side," he writes, "we may lay off a range of States on the western bank from the head to the mouth, and so range after range, advancing compactly as we multiply." Madison went so far as to argue to the French minister that the United States had no interest in seeing population extend itself on the right bank of the Mississippi, but should rather fear it. When the Oregon question was under debate, in 1824, Smyth, of Virginia, would draw an unchangeable line for the limits of the United States at the outer limit of two tiers of States beyond the Mississippi, complaining that the seaboard States were being drained of the flower of their population by the bringing of too much land into market. Even Thomas Benton, the man of widest views of the destiny of the West, at this stage of his career declared that along the ridge of the Rocky mountains, "the western limits of the Republic should be drawn, and the statue

of the fabled god Terminus should be raised upon its highest peak, never to be thrown down." But the attempts to limit the boundaries, to restrict land sales and settlement, and to deprive the West of its share of political power were all in vain. Steadily the frontier of settlement advanced and carried with it individualism, democracy, and nationalism, and powerfully affected the East and the Old World.

The most effective efforts of the East to regulate the frontier came through its educational and religious activity, exerted by interstate migration and by organized societies. Speaking in 1835, Dr. Lyman Beecher declared: "It is equally plain that the religious and political destiny of our nation is to be decided in the West," and he pointed out that the population of the West "is assembled from all the States of the Union and from all the nations of Europe, and is rushing in like the waters of the flood, demanding for its moral preservation the immediate and universal action of those institutions which discipline the mind and arm the conscience and the heart. And so various are the opinions and habits, and so recent and imperfect is the acquaintance, and so sparse are the settlements of the West, that no homogeneous public sentiment can be formed to legislate immediately into being the requisite institutions. And yet they are all needed immediately in their utmost perfection and power. A nation is being 'born in a day.' . . . But what will become of the West, if her prosperity rushes up to such a majesty of power, while those great institutions linger which are necessary to form the mind and the conscience and the heart of that vast world. It must not be permitted. . . . Let no man at the East quiet himself and dream of liberty, whatever may become of the West . . . Her destiny is our destiny."

With the appeal to the conscience of New England, he adds appeals to her fears lest other religious sects anticipate her own. The New England preacher and school-teacher left their mark on the West. The dread of Western emancipation from New England's political and economic control was paralleled by her fears lest the West cut loose from her religion. Commenting in 1850 on reports that settlement was rapidly extending northward in Wisconsin, the editor of the Home Missionary writes: "We scarcely know whether to rejoice or mourn over this extension of our settlements. While we sympathize in whatever tends to increase the physical resources and prosperity of our country, we can not forget that with all these dispersions into remote and still remoter corners of the land the supply of the means of grace is becoming relatively less and less." Acting in accordance with such ideas, home missions were established and Western colleges were erected. As seaboard cities like Philadelphia, New York, and Baltimore strove for the mastery of Western trade, so the various denominations strove for the possession of the West. Thus an intellectual stream from New England sources fertilized the West. Other sections sent their missionaries; but the real struggle was between sects. The contest for power and the expansive tendency furnished to the various sects by the existence of a moving frontier must have had important results on the character of religious organization in the United States. The multiplication of rival churches in the little frontier towns had deep and lasting social effects. The religious aspects of the frontier make a chapter in our history which needs study.

From the conditions of frontier life came intellectual traits of profound importance.

The works of travelers along each frontier from colonial days onward describe certain common traits, and these traits have, while softening down, still persisted as survivals in the place of their origin, even when a higher social organization succeeded. The result is that to the frontier the American intellect owes its striking characteristics. That coarseness and strength combined with acuteness and inquisitiveness; that practical inventive turn of mind, quick to find expedients; that masterful grasp of material things, lacking in the artistic but powerful to effect great ends; that restless, nervous energy; that dominant individualism, working for good and for evil, and withal that buoyancy and exuberance which comes with freedom—these are traits of the frontier, or traits called out elsewhere because of the existence of the frontier. Since the days when the fleet of Columbus sailed into the waters of the New World, America has been another name for opportunity, and the people of the United States have taken their tone from the incessant expansion which has not only been open but has even been forced upon them. He would be a rash prophet who should assert that the expansive character of American life has now entirely ceased. Movement has been its dominant fact, and, unless this training has no effect upon a people, the American energy will continually demand a wider field for its exercise. But never again will such gifts of free land offer themselves. For a moment, at the frontier, the bonds of custom are broken and unrestraint is triumphant. There is not *tabula rasa*. The stubborn American environment is there with its imperious summons to accept its conditions; the inherited ways of doing things are also there; and yet, in spite of environment, and in spite of custom, each frontier did indeed furnish a new field of opportunity, a gate of escape from the bondage of the past; and freshness, and confidence, and scorn of older society, impatience of its restraints and its ideas, and indifference to its lessons, have accompanied the frontier. What the Mediterranean Sea was to the Greeks, breaking the bond of custom, offering new experiences, calling out new institutions and activities, that, and more, the ever retreating frontier has been to the United States directly, and to the nations of Europe more remotely. And now, four centuries from the discovery of America, at the end of a hundred years of life under the Constitution, the frontier has gone and with its going has closed the first period of American history.

NO

George Wilson Pierson

THE FRONTIER AND AMERICAN INSTITUTIONS A CRITICISM OF THE TURNER THEORY

How much of Frederick Jackson Turner's frontier hypothesis is reliable and useful today? This problem has begun to trouble economists, sociologists, geographers, and most of all the teachers of graduate students in the field of American history.

For how shall we account for the industrial revolution by the frontier? Do American music and architecture come from the woods? Did American cattle? Were our religions born of the contemplation of untamed nature? Has science, poetry, or even democracy, its cradle in the wilderness? Did literature grow fertile with innovation in the open spaces? Above all what happens to intellectual history if the environment be all?

The predicament of the scholar, who has been living in a comfortable frontier philosophy, is beginning to attract some attention. Nor may we comfort ourselves with the assurance that ours is a purely academic debate. For frontier legends of one kind or another have now so permeated American thought as to threaten drastic consequences. Have not our most influential journalists and statesmen for some time been ringing *pessimistic* changes on the theme of "lost frontier," "lost safety-valve," "lost opportunity"? Such convictions can lead to legislation. In Congress the underlying issue could shortly be: was there but one economic frontier, was it really a "safety-valve," and are both now gone? The cultural historian meanwhile asks: is it true that the frontier was "the line of most rapid and effective Americanization?" More particularly, since we are now trying to define and safeguard the "American way of life," what share did the "frontier" have in its creation, and to what cultural influences must we henceforth look for its preservation?

No matter how phrased, these questions are fundamental. They suggest a serious re-study of our premises. And the place to begin, the present writer has concluded, is with Professor Turner's own theories in the matter: that is, with his celebrated and influential essays on the significance of the American frontier.

My proposal is, therefore, first to re-examine, and then overhaul, what Professor Turner wrote on the relation of the frontier to American institutions. For his brilliant papers have been the Bible, and today still constitute the central inspiration, of an extraordinary and widely-held faith. That such an investigation may lead us to question, or in particulars abandon entirely, the doctrine once taught us by a beloved man is unfortunately only too obvious. But that this autopsy is necessary is the argument of the considerations advanced above, and the theme of much that follows.

How was it then—according to the essays—that the frontier affected American institutions? What really was Turner's theory in this matter—and what examples did he give to support his theory? Finally, is this part of his doctrine a reasonable and useful guide to students of American history today? . . .

THE PRACTICAL RESULTS FOR SOCIAL INSTITUTIONS

Let us examine next the specific proofs or illustrations advanced by Turner in the demonstration of his hypothesis. What examples did he give in his essays; what signs of frontier influence on American institutions are we advised to see? . . .

Most important of all by far, of course, the frontier made us national and made us democratic. The nationalizing influence of the frontier could hardly, it seemed to Turner, be exaggerated. It enforced unity and encouraged patriotism in many obvious and tangible ways. The menace of the Indians and the French made the frontier a consolidating agent, suggested the Albany Congress of 1754, and led to the building of forts and the creation of a national army. Again, the frontier was

geographically more unified than the seaboard. Thus, toward the end of the Colonial Period, the Piedmont frontier "stretched along the western border like a cord of union"; while later the Mississippi Valley transfixed the barrier set up by the slavery dispute. In the third place, the mobility of population and the ease of interior communication prevented the development of provincialism. In the fourth place, the empty frontier regions became the melting-pot of European stocks, and even the New Englander tended to lose "the acuteness of his sectionalism" on the way through New York and Pennsylvania to the West. Again, "the economic and social characteristics of the frontier worked against sectionalism"; the Middle-Western frontier developed special needs; hostility to class and regional privilege fostered a co-operative point of view; and the abuses of the railroads and Eastern monopolies led to appeals for protection to the national government. Inevitably the frontier regions were soon trying to realize their interests in legislation. "Loose construction advanced as the nation marched westward."

By this last, Turner meant to suggest that the frontier was responsible for much nationalistic legislation by the Federal Government, particularly in the economic field. Furthermore, such enactments automatically increased the strength of the Union and its government for general purposes thereafter. To quote Turner's proposition again, "the legislation which most developed the powers of the national government, and played the largest part in its activity, was conditioned on the frontier." "The pioneer needed the goods of the coast, and so the grand series of internal improvement and railroad legislation began, with potent nationalizing effects." "The public domain has been a force of profound importance in the nationalization and development of the government." "Administratively the frontier called out some of the highest and most vitalizing activities of the general government." Such repetition of thought . . . gives a fair idea of the emphasis and conviction with which Turner kept returning to this favorite idea of his about the nationalizing influence of the frontier. Yet this last example or proof of frontier influence presents such curious internal inconsistencies that the commentator cannot forbear to pause a moment.

What Turner was thinking of, and cited again and again, was the tariff, banking, and internal improvement legislation of the period of Henry Clay on the one hand—and on the other, the Western protest movements, with their proposals for the control and reform of big business by national legislation, in the era after the Civil War.

As to the first, it is well known that Clay found supporters for his "American system" in the Ohio Valley, but is it necessary to infer that genuine frontiersmen supported the idea of the tariff or were in favor of the National Bank? The pioneers may have voted for Clay on other grounds, and in any case they appear to have voted at least as heavily for Andrew Jackson, whose opinions on the tariff were nebulous and whose views on the bank were almost unprintable. A similar fate overtakes the case for internal improvements, that is, for the theory that the frontier led the central government into the building of roads and canals. What Jackson did to the Maysville Bill is familiar to us all. And what had happened to J. Q. Adams's really national program is surely no secret. As a matter of fact, in another connection, but without realizing that he was destroying his own argument, Turner stated the case exactly. He quoted Adams as confessing "My own

system of administration, which was to make the national domain the inexhaustible fund for progressive and unceasing internal improvement, has failed." Then Turner gave the reason. "The reason is obvious; a system of administration was not what the West demanded; it wanted land." That is to say, the West wanted land far more than it wanted the federal government to go into any grand series of internal improvements. How had Turner been led into his error? The answer seems to be: he had equated the West and the continent with "frontier"; and the more densely settled this area became, the more it, as frontier, would demand internal improvements. The futility of this equation for any purposes of exact thinking is perhaps beginning to be clear.

As for the Granger and Populist and Progressive crusades, which were in part pioneer Western and which did have nationalistic implications, the difficulty is this: what had happened to the ineradicably self-reliant, *laissez-faire* individualism of the Kansas frontiersmen to make them throw up their hands? And whence came the inspiration and the very shape of the reforms they advocated?

It would seem that Turner's evidence in the matter of internal improvements, and the nationalizing effect of the frontier on economic legislation, needs further study.

But that "the most important effect of the frontier has been in the promotion of democracy here and in Europe," Turner was positive. He said so in his first great essay and he stuck to the point right through to the end. The argument ran approximately as follows: the forest, the dangers, the lonely helplessness of life in the American wilderness, made the frontiersmen individualistic and self-reliant. At the same time, the deliberate abandonment of European societies and the separation from the more densely settled communities of the seaboard, together with the difficulties of the journey and the confusion of races and types in the new settlements, tended to destroy old social disciplines, old class arrangements, old privileges and superiorities. Finally, and most important of all, the extraordinary wealth of the continent, particularly the opportunity represented by the free land, gave everyone a chance to become as wealthy and self-respecting as his neighbor. Hence, the creation of a race of optimists and democrats. From democrats and from the frontier surroundings, of course, came democratic institutions.

To review Turner's presentation of this argument would require many pages, but a few quotations may be useful in establishing the poetic and dogmatic flavor of his pronouncements as stated in these famous essays. "The frontier individualism has from the beginning promoted democracy." "Liberty and equality flourished in the frontier periods of the Middle West as perhaps never before in history." "The Mississippi Valley has been the especial home of democracy." More particularly "American democracy came from the forest." In translation, the word "forest" could mean many things, but generally the ingredients seem to be one part hardship, three parts free land. "Most important of all has been the fact that an area of free land has continually lain on the western border." These free lands were the "gate of escape." They "promoted individualism, economic equality, freedom to rise, democracy." "In a word, then, free lands meant free opportunities. Their existence has differentiated the American democracy from the democracies which have preceded it." Finally, in 1914, twenty-one years after his first optimistic rebellion against the germ theory of American development, Turner put his thoughts into their most challenging and controversial form:

> American democracy was born of no theorist's dream; it was not carried in the *Sarah Constant* to Virginia, nor in the *Mayflower* to Plymouth. It came out of the American forest, and it gained new strength each time it touched a new frontier. Not the constitution, but free land and an abundance of natural resources open to a fit people, made the democratic type of society in America for three centuries while it occupied its empire.

If this was so, what democratic institutions in particular did the American forest produce? Apparently most of those that had gained repute since 1775. First, of course, came the reforms of the Revolution and the Jeffersonian period: the abolition of entail and primogeniture, the disestablishment of the churches, the demands for public education and the abolition of slavery. "Jefferson was the first prophet of American democracy, and when we analyze the essential features of his gospel, it is clear that the Western influence was the dominant element." From the Mississippi Valley in the thirties came manhood suffrage and all the reforms of Jacksonian democracy, including that for the elimination of imprisonment for debt. In the forties and fifties came new state constitutions with provisions for an elective judiciary. Finally, after the Civil War, the Mississippi Valley and the Plains gave birth to the Granger and Greenback movements, and to the Populist crusade. Bryan Democracy and the Republicanism of Theodore Roosevelt "were Mississippi Valley ideals in action."

The reader will recall that Benjamin F. Wright and a number of others have long since perceived and stated the surprising poverty of at least certain frontier areas in democracy and in political invention. Yet a few additional queries may legitimately be raised at this point. For instance, are we really prepared to ascribe the platform of the Populists and the reforms of Progressivism to the frontier? Does not the history of social legislation in England and on the Continent indicate a quite different explanation? Again, it would appear that the woman suffrage idea originated in Europe and found but slim support in the Ohio Valley. The direct dependence of our belated Civil Service legislation on the earlier English movement will be apparent to anyone who cares to investigate that subject. As for manhood suffrage, whatever may have been the contributions of the wilderness frontier, is it not hard to believe that the American democrat sprang, as it were, full-armed, ballot in hand, out of the Western woods? Surely one cannot today dismiss the long evolution of Parliament, the history of Colonial legislatures, the methods of the New England town meeting, the self-government of Congregational churches, and the voting habits of trading-company stockholders without a thought. This leads to another disconcerting observation. Turner nowhere seriously credits Anglo-American Protestantism (what Tocqueville so discerningly called our "republican religion") with democratic tendencies. One is left to infer that such equalitarian and humanitarian interests as American Christianity has displayed must have derived from the experience of conquering the West.

Thus, to conclude our exposition of the Turner hypothesis, the West's "steady influence toward democracy" was not without its influence on the East, and on Europe. It was not until the early nineteenth century, and then "largely by reason of the drainage of population to the West, and the stir in the air raised by the Western winds of Jacksonian democracy,

that most of the older States reconstructed their constitutions on a more democratic basis. From the Mississippi Valley . . . came the inspiration for this era of change." The possibility that their citizens might escape to practically free land "compelled the coastwise States to liberalize the franchise; and it prevented the formation of a dominant class, whether based on property or on custom." As for Europe, what it derived from the frontier is less clear. The frontier is asserted to have turned both pioneer and Easterner away from Europe, and to have been the goal of peasant and artisan, the mecca for Europe's idealists and social reformers, through three hundred years.

"The men of the Mississippi Valley compelled the men of the East to think in American terms instead of European." When cities and sections turned their energies to the interior, "a genuine American culture began."

GENERAL CRITICISM

Turner's theoretical system, with proof and illustration, has now been developed and quoted at sufficient length to enable us to proceed to the next step: an attempt at an overall criticism.

First, then, let me say emphatically that it would seem small-minded to forget or to depreciate the inspiration that these essays originally offered to historians. Nor does it seem that we, of half a century later, have yet heard arguments that would warrant us in discarding the celebrated hypothesis entirely, out of hand. Too much of Turner's interpretation still seems reasonable, and corresponding to fact. Even in so condensed an analysis as has just been offered, the poetic insights and the masterful grasp of an understanding mind are hardly to be disguised. No blanket repudiation is therefore here to be proposed.

On the other hand, Turner himself did make a number of flat-footed and dogmatic statements, did put forward some highly questionable interpretations, did on occasion guess and not verify, did exaggerate—and stick for more than twenty years to the exaggerations. Hence it would seem that, however badly the master may have been served by his students and continuers in other particulars, these followers have been made the scapegoats a little too hastily. For they have not alone been responsible for the palpable errors and exaggerations that many of the rising generation recognize in the frontier theory as it is stated and applied today. At least they did not invent the safety-valve theory that now looks so dubious; they didn't misquote when they attributed political invention, and most of the reforms and the reformers, to the frontier; they weren't the first local and national patriots. In his work with his students, Turner seems to have been modest and tentative and open-minded to a degree; but in his essays he could be and was as inclusive and sweeping as any have been since.

What were the statements and attitudes which we regard as extreme or with which we would disagree? A number have just been alluded to, or were earlier marked and commented upon. But the treatment has been parenthetical and fragmentary. Let me conclude, therefore, with a brief organization of the most cogent reasons for regarding Turner's original doctrine on the frontier and American institutions as defective and in need of repair.

To begin with the details and proceed to the general, it seems first of all necessary to suggest that—whatever may later be decided about Turner's theory—his evidence and proofs leave much to be desired. I am not here referring to our difficulty in accepting Turner's reasons for believing that the frontier stimulated invention, liberal ideas, educational improvements, or humanitarian reforms—a difficulty that remains substantial enough in itself. Rather, it is the quantity of his evidence to which I would now call attention. How few were his concrete examples, and how often he would repeat them is really astonishing. For twenty-seven years he kept the same happy illustrations, in the same language often, and even perhaps without testing them by fresh investigation. In his first essay Turner invited such testing, and suggested the specific investigation of a number of different frontiers: "It would be a work worth the historian's labors to mark these various frontiers and in detail compare one with another." Yet if one goes to the later frontier essays for demonstration, one finds it only in the most general and vague terms. Undoubtedly, Turner was more interested in discovering than in proving. Undoubtedly, also, he must on occasion have carried his analysis of special areas and his search for positive proof somewhat deeper, particularly in his work with his graduate students and in his study of the different sections. Unfortunately, there is astonishingly little to show for that research in the later essays.

Did Turner, perhaps, on the other hand, put his effort into theory and philosophy, into developing and revising his first grand vision and interpretation? Once again, curiously, our examination indicates that he did not. For not only did he republish his first essay without substantial alteration, but his later essays show little if any advance beyond the position taken in his first. Not only is there small proof of fresh research; there is as little proof of fresh thinking.

Elaboration, progress in application, repetition, certainly, but distressingly little in the way of genuine reconsideration or modification. If anything, the later essays are more general, sweeping, and blurred—as if the hypothesis had somewhere already been proved. Yet when one turns back to the first statement one is startled to find in it reservations, moderation, and doubt.

A critic is reduced, therefore, to finding the same theory throughout, and is moved to protest at certain aspects of that theory. It is dangerous and ungenerous, I acknowledge, for a man living in a later climate of opinion to disparage the attitude of an earlier day. But since our problem concerns the *present applicability and future usefulness* of these frontier essays, certain assumptions and definitions cannot be allowed to pass without challenge.

As has been pointed out, first of all, the essays are in a high degree unsatisfactory in clarity, or definition. Turner's Master Force is defined and used as area, as population, as process. As if such inharmonious and confusing interpretations were not sufficiently inclusive, this force is then made to cover soil and mineral resources as well,—and at times everything Western, or pre-industrial, or non-European! I think it fair to say that the word "frontier" has been, and will be found again, a Pandora's box of trouble to historians, when opened to such wide interpretation.

Again, there seems to be haziness in the statement of *means*, and real doubt as to many of the *results* claimed for the frontier. At moments the wilderness, and even the flow of our population westward, seem to have been destructive rather than constructive experiences. And when the rebuilding is scrutinized, the proportion of invention looks surprisingly small. In particular, the contribution of the frontier to our educational, economic, and political institutions needs cautious reappraisal.

Once again, the emotional attitudes or assumptions of the author—and of his generation?—color his essays unmistakably. It would have been strange had they not done so. No personal censure is therefore intended. On the other hand, for the interpretation of American history in 1942, the emphasis of 1893 may become a serious handicap; it may even obscure or distort the elements in the theory that are still most meaningful. To be specific, the frontier hypothesis seems—as has been indicated several times already—too optimistic, too romantic, too provincial, and too nationalistic to be reliable in any survey of world history or study in comparative civilization. And it is too narrowly sectional and materialistic—in the sense of assigning deterministic forces to physical environment—to seem any longer a satisfactory gauge for internal cause-measurements. A thoughtful reading of the thirteen essays, or even of such materials as it has been possible to quote in this paper, ought to be conclusive on these defects. Yet perhaps a word more about one or two of them will not be out of place.

At an earlier point in the argument, the migration factor was isolated—as a sort of foreign substance—out of the frontier concept; and it was suggested that, at the least, a comparison with city-ward movements and with migrations the world around is in order. It now seems pertinent to suggest the extension of such comparisons from migration to the *whole story of settlement* or environmental adjustment in South America, Australia, and Africa. Did comparable situations always produce comparable results? Moreover, if we repeat such comparisons *within* the American experience, do we really find much similarity between the frontiers of Colonial Massachusetts, the Mississippi Delta, the Plains, and the mining country? If not, it would appear that the applicability of Turner's frontier hypothesis is far more limited than has been supposed.

Along another line of thought, I have suggested that Turner's views were deterministic. They were almost fatalistic. Again and again one gets the impression that western man was in the grip of overpowering forces. "The people of the United States have taken their tone from the incessant expansion which has not only been open but has even been forced upon them."

Now what makes this determinism particularly questionable is the fact that it is materialistic, yet in a high degree confused and cloudy in its statement of causes. Turner has been attacked by the economic determinists for not regarding commercialism, industrialism, and capitalism as more important than the continent—and the frontier essays certainly pay far too little attention to the commercial character of nineteenth-century American society, East or West. This school of critics is also quite correct in labelling Turner a geographer and a sociologist rather than a champion of the Marxian dialectic or interpretation. Nevertheless Turner remains, in his own way, almost as convinced a materialist as the author of *Das Kapital* himself. Only Turner's mastering force is a multiple thing, a cluster of causes singularly disparate and inharmonious. Part of the time the essays cite the natural environment, the physical continent, the wilderness; at other moments the source of change is located in the state of society: the sparseness, mobility, or indiscipline of settlement. Admittedly, America represented both physical hardship and social opportunity. The West was rough (a geographic factor) and it was empty (a sociological force). Perhaps, then, Turner's greatest achievement was his successful marriage of these two dissimilar forces in the single phrase: *free land*. He did not invent the term or the ideas it contains. But he most certainly popularized them.

If this sounds like a defense of Turner, it is intended rather as a clearer definition of his special materialism, which remains objectionable. And it remains so—even disregarding the untenable variations in his definition of "frontier"—because too much is attributed both to the land and to the fact that it was easy to acquire. A number of Turner's ablest friends and admirers regard his "free land" doctrine as a contribution of extraordinary insight and importance, and unquestionably it does seem impressive. Yet the modern observer cannot but be disturbed by the failure of some non-English groups, and even of a tremendous number of native Americans, to heed this call. The open spaces do not seem to have acted as a solvent on the Pennsylvanian Germans or the *habitants* of Lower Canada, and the migratory New England groups were only partially disintegrated, while an increasing number of farm boys gravitated to town and city (an even stronger solvent?) instead. It will bear repeating that Turner perhaps exaggerated the importance of "free land."

On the other hand, I cannot but feel that too small a role is allowed to man's own character and ambitions, to his capacity for change, and to the traditions and momentum of the society which came to use this free land. Thus the continent masters, destroys, commands, and creates—while man is surprisingly passive. Where many of us are inclined to regard the physical environment as permissive, or limiting in its influence, Turner in his essays tends to make it mandatory. Vice versa, where sociologists are today coming to recognize the factor of tradition and habit as very powerful, and where a man's ability to master circumstance is at times conceded to be extraordinary, the frontier hypothesis tends to ignore human origins and peculiarities, at least in the composition of American traits and American institutions. Thus first causes are made to lie in real estate, not state of mind. Hence, again, the first Colonial settlers are not examined with any care, but are treated as if they were *average* Europeans. And the later developments and changes in coastal society are handled as if they could have had only two sources: either a fresh migration or influence from Europe, or the powerful influence of an innovating frontier. Native invention in New England? Improvement in New York without the stimulus of the West? Apparently not.

THE CONTRADICTIONS AND OMISSIONS

It remains to add two final comments. They concern contradiction and omission.

However optimistic, nationalistic, one-sided, repetitious, fatalistic, undocumented, or erroneous a number of Turner's proposals may appear, the curious fact seems to be that one of the most striking weaknesses of the essays as a whole is internal inconsistency. As has been hinted throughout this paper, the frontier theory in its full development does not hang together. The nationalism of the frontier does violence to its sectional tendencies, innovations are derived from repetition, the improvement of civilization is achieved *via* the abandonment of civilization, and materialism gives birth to idealism. Such inconsistencies do not necessarily condemn the whole theory out of hand. But

they do unsettle conviction; they make it hard to remain complacent; they invite the most careful, open-minded restudy.

To this should be added the thought of what Turner did not write. Making all due allowances for the fact that the master's essays were composed in the period 1893–1920, it remains true that in the single field of economics he slighted the industrial revolution, he didn't seem to understand the commercial revolution, and he said nothing at all about the agricultural revolution. Yet it might be asserted that the last alone will be found to have produced more changes in American farming in the nineteenth century than all the frontiers put together! Again, it must be clear from our restatement that the frontier essays entirely failed to check the hypothesis by setting American experience against world experience. Because Turner was primarily a *Western* explorer, his pupils and followers have tended to neglect the all-important comparative approach. When, then, we review the questions with which this paper began, when we remember that the thirteen frontier essays treat the development of "American" and Middle-Western characteristics without reference to Romanticism, to Evangelism, to the eighteenth-century Enlightenment, to the scientific discoveries and the secularization of thought that in varying degrees have overtaken all Western peoples since the discovery of America, it may fairly be deduced that *for future purposes* these celebrated statements leave too much out.

Perhaps a conclusion may be stated in these terms:

In what it proposes, the frontier hypothesis needs painstaking revision. By what it fails to mention, the theory today disqualifies itself as an adequate guide to American development.

POSTSCRIPT

DID THE FRONTIER DETERMINE
THE COURSE OF AMERICAN HISTORY?

Turner's frontier thesis has proven to be more like honey than vinegar when it comes to attracting historians. His devotees greatly outnumber the critics. Also, Turner stands the test of time better than other historians who attempted to overhaul the way we look at the past. Beard on the Constitution and Jameson's causes and effects of the Revolution left themselves open to criticism more than Turner's study of the frontier. Nonetheless, Pierson raises many significant objections while, at the same time, carefully preserving the respect Turner enjoyed during his lifetime.

The question of the failure to provide supporting evidence remains at the heart of Pierson's revisionism. Obviously Turner did not think it was necessary to research specific aspects of his hypothesis. Only a mind so universal in its conceptualization could have attempted to synthesize all American history. At the same time, would a mind so fashioned regard the compiling of details as a necessary goal? Perhaps Pierson should have looked beyond Turner himself and asked if others, Turner's students and theirs as well, had not balanced the master's generalizations with the very evidence lacking in the original. Is it possible that Turner's apparent self-satisfaction with his thesis masked a constitutional inability to engage in specialized research which he left to others? Certainly the abstention had some positive effects: it generated research topics for hundres of graduate students, developed a new school of thought about American history second to none and stimulated historical subspecialties as well. Turner, of course, skated on thin ice when he omitted topics which might contradict his thesis as Pierson indicates. Studding his paragraphs with words like "free land," "democracy," "individualism," and "nationalism," but not defining them, also reduced the impact of his ideas. Pierson's criticism must undergo the same scrutiny as Turner's thesis. Has Pierson accurately summarized Turner? Has he criticized him fairly? Pierson's biases as well as Turner's must be analyzed. How have their basic assumptions delineated the subjects they address?

Turner's writings provided a lodestar for one historian in particular, Ray A. Billington, who wrote *The Far West Frontier, 1830–1860* (Harper, 1956), *America's Frontier Heritage* (Holt, 1966) and *Frederick Jackson Turner* (Oxford, 1973). Bernard de Voto's *The Year of Decision, 1846* (Little, Brown, 1943) and Francis Parkman's *The Oregon Trail* (Little, Brown, 1849) remain classics.

PART 4
CONFLICT AND
RESOLUTION

The changing nature of the American nation and the demands of its own principles finally erupted into violent conflict. Perhaps it was an inevitable step in the process of building a coherent nation from a number of distinct and diverse groups. The leaders, attitudes, and resources that were available to the North and the South were to determine the course of the war itself as well as how well the wounds were healed.

Was the South a Unique Section in American History?

Did the Democratic Process Fail During the Civil War?

Was Lincoln's Presidency Crucial to the North's Victory?

Was Reconstruction a Total Failure?

ISSUE 16

WAS THE SOUTH A UNIQUE SECTION IN AMERICAN HISTORY?

YES: C. Vann Woodward, from "The Search for Southern Identity," *The Burden of Southern History* (Random House, 1960)

NO: Thomas P. Govan, from "Americans Below the Potomac," Charles Grier Sellers, Jr., ed., *The Southerner as American* (University of North Carolina Press, 1960)

ISSUE SUMMARY

YES: Professor C. Vann Woodward argues that the South's different historical experiences of frustration and failure make a unique section in America.
NO: Professor Thomas P. Govan believes that historians have exaggerated sectional differences between the so-called industrial North and the agrarian South.

"The South is not quite a nation within a nation but it is the next thing to it," began the North Carolinian journalist Wilbur J. Cash in his classic statement on *The Mind of the South* (Knopf, 1941). Cash wrote his book on the eve of World War II, shortly before he committed suicide (some say because he dared to tell the truth about the South). Cash's death created a myth within a myth and helped solidify the popular image of the "tragic" South.

Since *The Mind of the South* first appeared novelists, journalists, and historians from all sections of the country and of various political persuasions have tried to explain the myths and realities of the American South. When the reader cuts through the multitude of adjectives used to describe the South, he concludes that there are actually only two— positive and negative.

An earlier generation of southern historians—Louis Wright, Clement Eaton, and Rollin G. Osterweis—have taken the myths of the plantation

South seriously enough to claim that with an addition of small doses of realism, such a place did in fact exist before the Civil War. Louis Wright claims the first gentlemen of Virginia had established an aristocracy of large land-owning farmers who developed great wealth from the profits on their tobacco estates. Although they were not descendents of British nobility, these planters lived in considerable splendor and developed a pattern of life modeled after the mother country's gentry. Dominating the colony's assemblies from its earliest years, the Virginia planter produced generations of leaders who, in the late eighteenth century, would be in the forefront of the American Revolution. Clement Eaton describes how the descendants of the coastal aristocrats carried the ideal of the country gentlemen with them as they migrated to other portions of the southwest in the early nineteenth century. Rollin G. Osterweis argues that the cult of chivalry permeated the South's romantic image of itself in the plantation system and that the institution of slavery shaped southern nationalism, eventually leading to secession and civil war.

A negative view of the South can still be gleaned from almost any person who lives north of the Mason-Dixon line. This Yankee who taught at a small liberal arts college in southern Alabama in the latter half of the 1960s has resisted the temptation to write a book about the South. Each year, during class discussions, however, I collect from my northern-bred students stereotyped impressions about white southerners. A partial list includes: hillbilly, redneck, agrarian, violent, militaristic, racist, Ku Klux Klan, gun freaks, lazy, slow moving, stupid, polite, courteous, friendly, and "speaks with a strange southern drawl." Aside from the fact that these epithets are often contradictory, the major implication is that southerners are not only different but also inferior to other Americans.

Howard Zinn, a white radical historian who spent many years teaching at a black southern college in Atlanta while actively participating in the civil rights movement in the 1960s, has turned these epithets on their heads. In his book *The Southern Mystique* (Knopf, 1964), he defines "southernism" as merely being an extension of the nation's worst qualities. There is no distinct South, he argues. Non-Southerners have merely projected onto the South those qualities which they least like about the American nation. Professor Zinn points out that more violence occurred in clashes between settlers and Indians on our western frontier than between masters and slaves in the antebellum South.

In the first selection, Professor C. Vann Woodward, the acknowledged dean of American historians, disagrees with Howard Zinn. He argues that the South has had a tragic history of failure, frustration, and defeat which distinguishes it from the history of success, omnipotence, and victory experienced by the whole American nation. In the second selection, Thomas P. Govan presents a tightly-knit description of the political and economic events confronting the South from 1790 to 1860. With the exception of the slavery issue, which becomes the paramount issue after 1850, Govan believes that historians have projected a false and oversimplified dicotomy of industrialism versus agrarianism and have exaggerated the differences between the North and the South.

YES   C. Vann Woodward

THE SEARCH FOR
SOUTHERN IDENTITY

The time is coming, if indeed it has not already arrived, when the Southerner will begin to ask himself whether there is really any longer very much point in calling himself a Southerner. Or if he does, he might well wonder occasionally whether it is worth while insisting upon the point. So long as he remains at home where everybody knows him the matter hardly becomes an issue. But when he ventures among strangers, particularly up North, how often does he yield to the impulse to suppress the identifying idiom, to avoid the awkward subject, and to blend inconspicuously into the national pattern, to act the role of the standard American? Has the Southern heritage become an old hunting jacket that one slips on comfortably while at home but discards when he ventures abroad in favor of some more conventional or modish garb? Or perhaps an attic full of ancestral wardrobes useful only in connection with costume balls and play acting—staged primarily in Washington, D. C. . . .

Asking himself some similar questions about the New England heritage, Professor George W. Pierson of Yale has come forth with some disturbing concessions about the integrity of his own region. Instead of an old hunting jacket, he suggests that we call New England "an old kitchen floor, now spatter-painted with many colors." He points out that roughly six out of every ten Connecticut "Yankees" are either foreign-born or born of foreign or mixed parentage, while only three have native forebears going as far back as two generations, and they are not necessarily New England forebears at that. "Like it or not," writes Pierson, "and no matter how you measure it—graphically, economically, racially, or religiously, there is no New England Region today." It has become instead, he says, "an optical illusion and a land of violent contrast and change." And yet in spite of the wholesale and damaging concessions of his essay, which he calls "A Study in Denudation," he concludes that, "as a region of the heart and mind, New England is still very much alive."

One wonders if the Southerner for his part can make as many damaging admissions of social change and cultural erosion as our New England friend has made and come out with as firm a conclusion about the vitality of his own regional heritage. More doubt than assurance probably come to mind at first. The South is still in the midst of an economic and social revolution that has by no means run its course, and it will not be possible to measure its results for a long time to come. This revolution has already leveled many of the old monuments of regional distinctiveness and may end eventually by erasing the very consciousness of a distinctive tradition along with the will to sustain it. The sustaining will and consciousness are also under the additional strain of a moral indictment against a discredited part of the tradition, an indictment more uncompromising than any since abolitionist times.

The Southerner may not have been very happy about many of those old monuments of regional distinctiveness that are now disappearing. He may, in fact, have deplored the existence of some—the one-horse farmer, one-crop agriculture, one-party politics, the sharecropper, the poll tax, the white primary, the Jim Crow car, the lynching bee. It would take a blind sentimentalist to mourn their passing. But until the day before yesterday there they stood, indisputable proof that the South was different. Now that they are vanished or on their way toward vanishing, we are suddenly aware of the vacant place they have left in the landscape and of our habit of depending upon them in final resort as landmarks of regional identification. To establish identity by reference to our faults was always simplest, for whatever their reservations about our virtues, our critics were never reluctant to concede us our vices and faults.

It is not that the present South has any conspicuous lack of faults, but that its faults are growing less conspicuous and therefore less useful for purposes of regional identification. They are increasingly the faults of other parts of the country, standard American faults, shall we say? Many of them have only recently been acquired, could, in fact, only recently be afforded. For the great changes that are altering the cultural landscape of the South almost beyond recognition are not simply negative changes, the disappearance of the familiar. There are also positive changes, the appearance of the strikingly new.

The symbol of innovation is inescapable. The roar and groan and dust of it greet one on the outskirts of every Southern city. That symbol is the bulldozer, and for lack of a better name this might be called the Bulldozer Revolution. The great machine with the lowered blade symbolizes the revolution in several respects: in its favorite area of operation for one, the area where city meets country; in its relentless speed for another; in its supreme disregard for obstacles, its heedless methods; in what it demolishes and in what it builds. It is the advance agent of the metropolis. It encroaches upon rural life to expand urban life. It demolishes the old to make way for the new. . . .

It is the conclusion of two Southern sociologists that the South's present drive toward uniformity "with national demographic, economic, and cultural norms might well hasten the day when the South, once perhaps the most distinctively 'different' American region, will have become in most such matters virtually indistinguishable from the other urban-industrial areas of the nation."

The threat of becoming "indistinguishable," of being submerged under a national steamroller, has haunted the mind of the

South for a long time. Some have seen it as a menace to regional identity and the survival of a Southern heritage. Premonitions of the present revolution appeared during the industrial boom that followed the First World War. Toward the end of the twenties two distinctive attempts were made by Southerners to dig in and define a perimeter of defense against further encroachment.

One of these entrenchments was that of the Twelve Southerners who wrote "I'll Take My Stand." They sought to define what they called "a Southern way of life against what may be called the American or prevailing way," and they agreed "that the best terms in which to represent the distinction are contained in the phrase, Agrarian *versus* Industrial." Agrarianism and its values were the essence of the Southern tradition and the test of Southern loyalty. Their credo held that "the whole way in which we live, act, think, and feel," the humanist culture, "was rooted in the agrarian way of life of the older South." They called for "anti-industrial measures" which "might promise to stop the advances of industrialism, or even undo some of them. ..."

Two years before the agrarian pronouncement appeared, another attempt was made to define the essence of the Southern tradition and prescribe the test of Southern loyalty. The author of this effort was the distinguished historian, Professor Ulrich B. Phillips. His definition had no reference to economic institutions but was confined to a preoccupation with race consciousness. The essential theme of continuity and unity in the Southern heritage, wrote Professor Phillips, was "a common resolve indomitably maintained" that the South "shall be and remain a white man's country." This indomitable conviction could be "expressed with the frenzy of a dema-gogue or maintained with a patrician's quietude," but it was and had been from the beginning "the cardinal test of a Southerner and the central theme of Southern history."

Professor Phillips' criterion of Southernism has proved somewhat more durable and widespread in appeal than that of the agrarians. It is not tied so firmly to an ephemeral economic order as was theirs. Nor does it demand—of the dominant whites, at least—any Spartan rejection of the flesh pots of the American Living Standard. Its adherents are able to enjoy the blessings of economic change and remain traditionalists at the same time. There are still other advantages in the Phillipsian doctrine. The traditionalist who has watched the Bulldozer Revolution plow under cherished old values of individualism, localism, family, clan, and rural folk culture has felt helpless and frustrated against the mighty and imponderable agents of change. Industrialism, urbanism, unionism, and big government conferred or promised too many coveted benefits. They divided the people and won support so that it was impossible to rally unified opposition to them.

The race issue was different. Advocates and agents of change could be denounced as outsiders, intruders, meddlers. Historic memories of resistance and cherished constitutional principles could be invoked. Racial prejudices, aggressions, and jealousies could be stirred to rally massive popular support. And with this dearly bought unity, which he could not rally on other issues, the frustrated traditionalist might at last take his stand for the defense of all the defiled, traduced, and neglected values of the traditional order. What then is the prospect of the Phillipsian "cardinal test" as a bulwark against change? Will it hold fast where other defenses have failed?

Recent history furnishes some of the answers. Since the last World War old racial attitudes that appeared more venerable and immovable than any other have exhibited a flexibility that no one would have predicted a dozen years ago. One by one, in astonishingly rapid succession, many landmarks of racial discrimination and segregation have disappeared and old barriers have been breached. Many remain, of course—perhaps more than have been breached—and distinctively Southern racial attitudes will linger for a long time. Increasingly the South is aware of its isolation in these attitudes, however, and in defense of the institutions that embody them. They have fallen into discredit and under condemnation from the rest of the country and the rest of the world.

Once more the South finds itself with a morally discredited Peculiar Institution on its hands. The last time this happened, about a century ago, the South's defensive reaction was to identify its whole cause with the one institution that was most vulnerable and to make loyalty to an ephemeral aspect which it had once led in condemning the cardinal test of loyalty to the whole tradition. Southerners who rejected the test were therefore forced to reject the whole heritage. In many cases, if they were vocal in their rejection, they were compelled to leave the South entirely and return only at their peril. Unity was thus temporarily achieved, but with the collapse of the Peculiar Institution the whole tradition was jeopardized and discredited for having been so completely identified with the part abandoned.

Historical experience with the first Peculiar Institution strongly discourages comparable experiments with the second. If Southernism is allowed to become identified with a last ditch defense of segregation, it will increasingly lose its appeal among the younger generation. Many will be tempted to reject their entire regional identification, even the name "Southern," in order to dissociate themselves from the one discredited aspect. If agrarianism has proved to be a second lost cause, segregation is a likely prospect for a third.

With the crumbling of so many defenses in the present, the South has tended to substitute myths about the past. Every self-conscious group of any size fabricates myths about its past: about its origins, its mission, its righteousness, its benevolence, its general superiority. But few groups in the New World have had their myths subjected to such destructive analysis as those of the South have undergone in recent years. Southern historians themselves have been the leading iconoclasts and their attacks have spared few of the South's cherished myths. . . .

While the myths of Southern distinctiveness have been waning, national myths have been waxing in power and appeal. National myths, American myths have proved far more sacrosanct and inviolate than Southern myths. Millions of European people of diverse cultural backgrounds have sought and found identity in them. The powerful urge among minority groups to abandon or disguise their distinguishing cultural traits and conform as quickly as possible to some national norm is one of the most familiar features in the sociology of American nationalism. European ethnic and national groups with traditions far more ancient and distinctive than those of the South have eagerly divested themselves of their cultural heritage in order to conform. . . .

Is there nothing about the South that is immune from the disintegrating effect of nationalism and the pressure for conformity? Is there not something that has not changed? There is only one thing that I can think of, and that is its history. By that I do not mean a Southern brand of Shintoism, the worship of ancestors. Nor do I mean written history and its interpretation, popular and mythical, or professional and scholarly, which has changed often and will change again. I mean rather the collective experience of the Southern people. It is in just this respect that the South remains the most distinctive region of the country. In their unique historic experience as Americans the Southerners should not only be able to find the basis for continuity of their heritage, but also make contributions that balance and complement the experience of the rest of the nation.

At this point the risks of our enterprise multiply. They are the risks of spawning new myths in place of the old. Awareness of them demands that we redouble precautions and look more cautiously than ever at generalizations.

To start with a safe one, it can be assumed that one of the most conspicuous traits of American life has been its economic abundance. From early colonial days the fabulous riches of America have been compared with the scarcity and want of less favored lands. Immense differentials in economic welfare and living standards between the United States and other countries still prevail. In an illuminating book called "People of Plenty," David Potter persuasively advances the thesis that the most distinguishing traits of national character have been fundamentally shaped by the abundance of the American living standard. He marshals evidence of the effect that plenty has had upon such decisive phases of life as the nursing and training of babies, opportunities for education and jobs, ages of marriage and childbearing. He shows how abundance has determined characteristic national attitudes between parents and children, husband and wife, superior and subordinate, between one class and another, and how it has moulded our mass culture and our consumer oriented society. American national character would indeed appear inconceivable without this unique experience of abundance.

The South has at times shared this national experience, and in very recent years has enjoyed more than a taste of it. But the history of the South includes a long and quite un-American experience with poverty. As recently as 1938, in fact, the South was characterized by the President as "The Nation's Economic Problem No. 1." And the problem was poverty, not plenty. It was a poverty emphasized by wide regional discrepancies in living standards, per capita wealth, per capita income, and the good things that money buys, such as education, health, protection, and the many luxuries that go to make up the celebrated American Standard of Living. This striking differential was no temporary misfortune of the great depression but a continuous and conspicuous feature of Southern experience since the early years of the Civil War. During the last half of the nineteenth and the first half of the twentieth centuries, when technology was multiplying American abundance with unprecedented rapidity, the South lagged far behind. In 1880 the per capita wealth of the South, based on estimated true valuation of property, was $376 as compared with $1,186 per capita in the states outside the South. In the same year the per capita wealth of the South was 27 per cent of that of the Northeastern states. That was just about the same ratio contemporaneously existing between the per capita wealth of Russia and that of Germany.

Generations of scarcity and want constitute one of the distinctive historical experiences of the Southern people, an experience too deeply embedded in their memory to be wiped out by a business boom and too deep not to admit of some uneasiness at being characterized historically as a "People of Plenty." That they should have been for so long a time a "People of Poverty" in a land of plenty is one mark of enduring cultural distinctiveness. In a nation known around the world for the hedonistic ethic of the American Standard of Living, the Southern heritage of scarcity is distinctive.

A closely related corollary of the uniquely American experience of abundance is the equally unique American experience of success. Some years ago Arthur M. Schlesinger made an interesting attempt to define the national character which he brought to a close with the conclusion that the American character "is bottomed upon the profound conviction that nothing in the world is beyond its powers to accomplish." In this he gave expression to one of the great American legends, the legend of success and invincibility. It is a legend with a firm foundation in fact, for much can be adduced from the American record to support it and explain why it has flourished. If the history of the United States is lacking in some of the elements of variety and contrast demanded of any good story, it is in part because of the very monotonous repetition of successes. Almost every major collective effort, even those thwarted temporarily, succeeded in the end. American history *is* a success story. Why should such a nation not have a "profound conviction that nothing in the world is beyond its power to accomplish"? Even the hazards of war— including the prospect of war against an unknown enemy with untried weapons— proves no exception to the rule. For these people have never known the chastening experience of being on the losing side of a war. They have solved every major problem

they have confronted—or had it solved for them by a smiling fortune. Success and victory are national habits of mind.

This is but one among several American legends in which the South can participate only vicariously or in part. Again the Southern heritage is distinctive. For Southern history, unlike American, includes large components of frustration, failure, and defeat. It includes not only an overwhelming military defeat but long decades of defeat in the provinces of economic, social, and political life. Such a heritage affords the Southern people no basis for the delusion that there is nothing whatever that is beyond their power to accomplish. They have had it forcibly and repeatedly borne in upon them that this is not the case. Since their experience in this respect is more common among the general run of mankind than that of their fellow Americans, it would seem to be a part of their heritage worth cherishing.

American opulence and American success have combined to foster and encourage another legend of early origin, the legend of American innocence. According to this legend Americans achieved a sort of regeneration of sinful man by coming out of the wicked Old World and removing to an untarnished new one. By doing so they shook off the wretched evils of feudalism and broke free from tyranny, monarchy, aristocracy, and privilege—all those institutions which, in the hopeful philosophy of the Enlightenment, accounted for all, or nearly all, the evil in the world. The absence of these Old World ills in America, as well as the freedom from much of the injustice and oppression associated with them, encouraged a singular moral complacency in the American mind. The self-image implanted in Americans was one of innocence as compared with less fortunate people of the Old World. They were a chosen people and their land a Utopia on the make. De Tocqueville's patience was tried by this complacency of the American. "If I applaud the freedom which its inhabitants enjoy, he answers, 'Freedom is a fine thing, but few nations are worthy to enjoy it.' If I remark on the purity of morals which distinguishes the United States," complained Tocqueville, " 'I can imagine,' says he, 'that a stranger, who has been struck by corruption of all other nations, is astonished at the difference.' "

How much room was there in the tortured conscience of the South for this national self-image of innocence and moral complacency? Southerners have repeated the American rhetoric of self admiration and sung the perfection of American institutions ever since the Declaration of Independence. But for half that time they lived intimately with a great social evil and the other half with its aftermath. It was an evil that was even condemned and abandoned by the Old World, to which America's moral superiority was an article of faith. Much of the South's intellectual energy went into a desperate effort to convince the world that its peculiar evil was actually a "positive good," but it failed even to convince itself. It writhed in the torments of its own conscience until it plunged into catastrophe to escape. The South's preoccupation was with guilt, not with innocence, with the reality of evil, not with the dream of perfection. Its experience in this respect was on the whole a thoroughly un-American one.

An age-long experience with human bondage and its evils and later with emancipation and its shortcomings did not dispose the South very favorably toward such popular American ideas as the doctrine of human perfectibility, the belief that every evil has a cure, and the notion that every human problem has a solution. For these reasons the utopian schemes and the gospel of progress that flourished above the Mason and Dixon Line never found very wide acceptance below the Potomac during the nineteenth century. In that most optimistic of centuries in the most optimistic part of the world, the South remained basically pessimistic in its social outlook and its moral philosophy. The experience of evil and the experience of tragedy are parts of the Southern heritage that are as difficult to reconcile with the American legend of innocence and social felicity as the experience of poverty and defeat with the legends of abundance and success.

One of the simplest but most consequential generalizations ever made about national character was Tocqueville's, that America was "born free." In many ways that is the basic distinction between the history of the United States and the history of other great nations. We skipped the feudal stage, just as Russia skipped the liberal stage. Louis Hartz has pointed up the infinitely complex consequences for the history of American political thought. To be a conservative and a traditionalist in America was a contradiction in terms, for the American Burke was forever conserving John Locke's liberalism, his only real native tradition. Even the South in its great period of reaction against Jefferson was never able fully to shake off the grip of Locke and its early self-image of liberalism. That is why its most original period of theoretical inspiration, the "Reactionary Enlightenment," came such a complete cropper and left almost no influence upon American thought.

There is still a contribution to be derived from the South's un-American adventure in feudal fantasy. The South was born Lockeian, but, as Hartz admits, it was long "an alien child in a liberal family, tortured and confused, driven to a fantasy life."

There *are* Americans, after all, who were not "born free." They are also Southerners. They have yet to achieve articulate expression of their uniquely un-American experience. This is not surprising, since white Southerners have only recently found expression of the tragic potentials of their past in literature. The Negro has yet to do that. His first step will be an acknowledgment that he is also a Southerner as well as an American. . . .

The most reassuring prospect for the survival of the South's distinctive heritage is the magnificent body of literature produced by its writers in the last three decades—the very years when the outward traits of regional distinctiveness were crumbling. The Southern literary renaissance has placed its writers in the vanguard of national letters and assured that their works will be read as long as American literature is remembered. The distinguishing feature of the Southern school, according to Allen Tate, is "the peculiar historical consciousness of the Southern writer." He defines the literary renaissance as "a literature conscious of the past in the present." The themes that have inspired the major writers have not been the flattering myths nor the romantic dreams of the South's past. Disdaining the polemics of defense and justification, they have turned instead to the somber realities of hardship and defeat and evil and "the problems of the human heart in conflict with itself." In so doing they have brought to realization for the first time the powerful literary potentials of the South's tragic experience and heritage. Such comfort as they offer lies, in the words of William Faulkner, in reminding us of "the courage and honor and hope and pride and compassion and pity and sacrifice" with which man has endured.

After Faulkner and Wolfe and Warren and Welty no literate Southerner could remain unaware of his heritage or doubt its enduring value. After this outpouring it would seem more difficult than ever to deny a Southern indentity, to be "merely American." To deny it would be to deny our history. And it would also be to deny to America participation in a heritage and a dimension of historical experience that America very much needs, a heritage that is far more closely in line with the common lot of mankind than the national legends of opulence and success and innocence. The South once thought of itself as a "peculiar people," set apart by its eccentricities, but in many ways modern America better deserves that description.

The South was American a long time before it was Southern in any self-conscious or distinctive way. It remains more American by far than anything else and has all along. After all, it fell to the lot of one Southerner to define America. The definition that he wrote voiced aspirations that were deeply rooted in his native region before the nation was born. The modern Southerner should be secure enough in his national identity to escape the compulsion of less secure minorities to embrace uncritically all the myths of nationalism. He should be secure enough also not to deny a regional heritage because it is at variance with national myth. It is a heritage that should prove of enduring worth to him as well as to his country.

NO

Thomas P. Govan

AMERICANS BELOW THE POTOMAC

The Old South, a part of the United States in which slavery continued for some sixty years after it had been given up in other areas, had a sense of unity within itself and of separation from the rest of the nation sufficiently strong to permit eleven of the states composing it to withdraw from the union and to fight for four years in an unsuccessful effort to maintain a separate existence as the Confederate States of America. To this extent, it was different, because no other area or group at any time in the national history challenged in such a way the continued unity of the American nation. Many historians, however, have not been satisfied with stating this substantial difference which did distinguish the Old South from the other areas of the country. They have insisted that by the time of the Civil War there were two divergent and irreconcilable social and economic systems, "two civilizations, in fact," in the United States.

The North, according to this point of view, was commercial-financial-industrial, the South agrarian, and these differences led to war between the two. One of the clearest statements of this conception is to be found in Morison and Commager's *Growth of the American Republic* where they write that the break between Jefferson and Hamilton was not personal but the "political expression of a deep lying antagonism between two great American interests—the planting-slaveholding interest, typified by Virginia; and the mercantile-shipping-financial interest, typified by Massachusetts. . . . American political history until 1865 is largely the story of these rival interests, capitalist and agrarian, Northern and Southern, contending for the control of the government."

This statement seems to mean that the planter with an investment in slaves, tools, and land, who raised staple crops to be sold at a profit in the markets of the United States and Europe, was somehow not a capitalist but an agrarian; that the merchants in the southern ports and interior towns were not engaged in mercantile activity; and that the southern bankers and brokers were not affiliated with the financial interest. The farmers who engaged in profitable agricultural operations in New York, Pennsylvania, New Jersey, Connecticut, New Hampshire, Vermont, Maine, Ohio, Indiana, Illinois, Michigan, Wisconsin, Iowa, and the territories, by this description were left completely out of account, as were those who engaged in the manufacture of tobacco in Virginia, North Carolina, South Carolina, Georgia, and Alabama; those who mined gold in Virginia, North Carolina, and Georgia; those who established iron foundries and coal mines in Virginia, North and South Carolina, Georgia, Tennessee, and Alabama; and the sugar mills which made every plantation from Baton Rouge to New Orleans an industrial as well as an agricultural enterprise.

What is even stranger about this widely accepted conception is the assertion of a supposed conflict of interest between the merchants, bankers, and shippers engaged in international trade and the producers of the commodities which were the basis of that trade. None of these groups could have prospered, or even existed, without the others. If there were a division of the American people into two segments with separate and conflicting economic interests, it was not between those who engaged in agriculture on the one side and those engaged in banking, merchandizing, and transportation on the other. Rather, it was between those whose primary concern was the market outside the United States, and those whose principal market was within the country. The growers of wool, sugar, hemp, and foodstuffs for domestic consumption had a different interest from those who grew cotton, rice, and tobacco, while the producers of wheat, whose market was sometimes mainly within the United States and at other times in the West Indies or Europe, wavered between the two.

Merchants, bankers, and shippers were as divided as the farmers since their interest coincided with that of whatever group of producers they served. If their principal activity was providing facilities for internal trade, then their interest led them to support measures which would increase that trade; but, if their facilities were used by the producers of export crops, then their interest was fostered by an increase in international trade. American manufacturers, confronted by competition from older and stronger industries of Great Britain and the continent, needed and desired protection, and they, almost as a unit, threw their influence in favor of measures that would discourage international trade and increase the consumption of domestic goods. This economic group was exceptional in its unity of interests, but until late in the nineteenth century it could not rival the influence or power of the earlier established, larger and wealthier agricultural, mercantile, and financial groups.

Southerners were to be found in each of these groups and shared their point of view and interest. Within the South, as in all the major geographical regions of the United States, there were distinctions in occupation based upon geological formations, climatic conditions, facilities for transportation, and other factors. Manufacturing was but a minor activity in the southern states during most of the period before 1865. The principal deposits of iron ore and coal were deep in the interior mountains, far from any market. Their exploitation had to wait until the railroads penetrated this area. The iron and coal of the northeast, on the other hand, were located in the vicinity of New York and Philadelphia, and were exploited earlier, as were those in the northwest at Pittsburgh, at the head of navigation of the Ohio River, which provided transportation to the great market of the Mississippi Valley. Southerners were not unaware of the importance of this activity, nor hostile to it, and whatever deposits of iron and coal were found in the areas that had transportation facilities— South Carolina, Virginia, or the Cumberland River valley of Tennessee— were developed and used.

In addition, the water power of the southern rivers was more difficult to utilize than that of the smaller rivers of New England, New Jersey, and Pennsylvania; and the fall line was more distant from the principal markets. These handicaps postponed the development of the textile and other industries. But the activities of William Gregg in South Carolina, the building of the power canal of Augusta, Georgia, as well as the mills at Athens, Columbus, and other towns on the fall line, followed very rapidly after the initial development of the textile industry in other regions.

The Old South, consequently, like the Northwest and part of New England, New York, Pennsylvania, and New Jersey, was primarily agricultural, but it was not united by this fact. Each of the major crops required different climatic conditions and different methods of cultivation. Rice, which needed ample water, was confined to the coastal regions. Sugar, essentially a semitropical growth, could be profitably raised only in the lower Southwest; and cotton, a hardier plant, became the basic product of the interior in the lower South. The great limestone areas of the mountain valleys and of the Lexington and Nashville basins, on the other hand, provided a soil that enabled its cultivators to engage in a mixed agriculture that had more in common with the agriculture of the northeastern United States than it did with the industrialized, single-crop agriculture of the cotton, rice, and sugar plantations in other areas of the South. Tobacco, a plant requiring relatively intense cultivation on small acreage, also had little in common with the other staple

crops, and if its cultivation was a bond of unity then it should have united those who grew it in the Connecticut valley with those who grew it in the South.

The people of the United States were not brought together or separated by these similarities and differences in sectional occupation and interest. The doctrine of sectional economic antagonism, though it had its origin in the early years of the American republic, was not an accurate reflection of economic reality in the United States; and it has been persuasive to twentieth-century historians largely because of their uncritical enthusiasm for that explanation of past events which views them as the determined result of economic forces and conflicts. This interpretation of the nature of the American economic society was never fully accepted by most Americans, and when Pierce Butler, a delegate from South Carolina to the Constitutional Convention, said that "he considered the interests of the [southern] and Eastern States to be as different as the interests of Russia and Turkey," Gouverneur Morris, a nationalist delegate from Pennsylvania, replied, "Either this distinction is fictitious or real; if fictitious, let it be dismissed and let us proceed with due confidence. If it be real, instead of blending incompatible things, let us at once take a friendly leave of each other."

The delegates chose to proceed with confidence, and the economic society they created was as united as their national government. A few political leaders, within the convention and afterwards, continued to use divisive sectional rhetoric when debating economic questions, but a majority of Americans, North and South, were unimpressed. Merchants, farmers, and bankers, most of the time, believed that their individual, local, and sectional prosperity was dependent upon economic conditions in the rest of the nation, and it was only in moments of financial or political crisis that the doctrine of sectional economic antagonism had any substantial number of adherents.

This doctrine was more influential in the South than in any other area, and the reason for its greater success in this section was closely connected with the career and ambitions of one of the nation's most effective and magnetic leaders, John C. Calhoun. This powerful South Carolinian began as a nationalist, and it would be difficult to find a more explicit rejection of sectionalism than his statement in the Congress following the War of 1812: "Blessed with a form of government at once combining liberality and strength, we may reasonably raise our eyes to a most splendid future, if we only act in a manner worthy of our advantages. If, however, neglecting them, we permit a low, sordid, selfish, and sectional spirit to take possession... this happy scene will vanish. We will divide and in its consequences will follow misery and degradation."

He was arguing in this speech for a federally financed system of roads and canals, which was vetoed by the President, but the same spirit was present in his more successful effort to charter the second Bank of the United States and to enact a protective tariff. Calhoun's nationalist measures did not have the effect that he and other sponsors anticipated, and the American economy, instead of being prosperous, was generally depressed between 1818 and 1828. The nation's import and export trade, and all those dependent upon it— farmers, merchants, bankers, and brokers, North, South, and West—suffered particularly; and Calhoun himself admitted in 1828 that "there is almost universal embarrassment among the people of the staple states, which they almost unanimously

attribute to the high duties."

The American tariff, despite this almost unanimous belief, had little to do with the low prices and reduced sales of the export crops of the South, the relatively small volume of the import and export trade in the ports, and the financial difficulties of this segment of the national economy. The principal cause of the depressed conditions between 1818 and 1822 was the improper management of the national bank, which forced the United States to liquidate the large private debt accumulated under the inflationary conditions of the War of 1812, through the painful processes of default, bankruptcy, and foreclosure. Virtually no one prospered during these four years, but, in 1822, the economy, aided by a change in management and policy at the Bank of the United States and by easy money and credit in Great Britain, began to recover.

Prices and business activity increased, and, by 1825, all trace of the earlier difficulties was gone. Just at this moment, however, the Bank of England, weakened and frightened by the speculative export of British capital to all areas of the world, contracted credit and precipitated one of the most severe crises in the history of Great Britain. The domestic segment of the American economy, protected and aided by the national bank, did not suffer as severely as it had in the earlier depression, but those engaged in international trade once more encountered major financial difficulties. The British markets for three years could absorb but a small volume of American exports at much reduced prices, and British merchants and manufacturers had little money or credit with which to finance American purchases of their manufactured goods.

These economic depressions were international and national in character, rather than sectional, and the connection between them and the American tariff was slight, if it existed at all. The relation between these depressions and the import and export trade, on the other hand, was direct, immediate, and decisive, and the volume and profits of this trade immediately revived in 1828 when the British pressure was removed. Producers of cotton, tobacco, rice, and other export staples began to make profits, as did the international merchants, bankers, and brokers, but this return of prosperity, instead of reducing the anti-tariff agitation, strengthened it and increased its virulence.

The center of the radical anti-tariff movement between 1828 and 1833 was South Carolina, and Calhoun, who had been the legislative sponsor of the protective system, was eventually compelled to become the most notable advocate of its repeal. He justified his reversal by returning to Butler's argument that the economic interests of the South and North were mutually antagonistic and conflicting, an argument which had been used effectively against him by his political enemies in South Carolina and other southern states, and he thus outwitted his local opponents by adopting their views. The tariff, according to Calhoun, was an instrument for the economic aggrandizement of the North, but his anti-tariff position received effective support from many powerful individuals and groups outside of the South. The builders of railroads and canals (private, public, and mixed) sought lowered tariff rates on iron and other building materials, and the northwestern wheat farmers, whose external market was greatly expanded after 1828, joined the growers of cotton, rice, and tobacco in opposing the protective system.

The northeastern seaports, with a permanent interest in international trade, continued their support of the anti-tariff move-

ment, and the manufacturers, miners, and the growers of a few agricultural products such as wool, sugar, and hemp, were thus left isolated in their need or desire for protection. The repeal of the protective tariff in 1833 was a victory, not for the South or any other section, but for those in all areas of the country whose interests lay in international rather than domestic trade, and, from this period on, the tariff was to be less important as a political issue between the sections than it had previously been made to appear.

The defeat of the protective system had little effect upon economic activity within the country. The years from 1828 to 1837, in contrast to the previous decade, were, on the whole, prosperous, but the fundamental cause of this prosperity was the general financial ease throughout the world, not American economic policy. The one interruption was during 1833–34, when the Bank of the United States, under political and financial attack by President Andrew Jackson and his administration, was forced to contract its loans for self-protection and to precipitate a severe but short domestic panic. The President, who had vetoed the bill rechartering the national institution in 1832, was determined to discredit it by proving it insolvent, but the Bank of the United States, soundly and intelligently managed, survived the attack. Economic activity, all over the country, was slowed down by this conflict, but when it ended, without a victory for either side, prosperity returned and continued for three years. . . .

The white inhabitants of the South, even in the 1850's, thought of themselves as Americans economically and in most other respects, and identified themselves politically and culturally with all people, except Indians and Negroes, who lived in the United States. State and sectional loyalty was a more important influence in their thought and conduct than it was with others, but this exaggeration of a point of view common to all Americans did not constitute a break in the essential cultural unity of the United States. The nation, from its beginning, was a single national society, an organic part of the unified western culture which had its origin in medieval Europe and which had been transformed by the Renaissance, the Reformation, the commercial, scientific, and industrial revolutions, and political democracy. The spiritual and intellectual fathers of this culture were the Hebraic, Greek, Hellenic, and European thinkers whose. teaching and writing shaped and formed the minds of all men in the West including those who lived in the southern United States.

Viewed against this background, the cultural distinctions which separated one group of Americans from another during the antebellum period seem minor and inconsequential, and no more important than the cultural distinctions between the inhabitants of the different counties of the small and unified kingdom of England. Deeply rooted and persistent provincial differences in language, customs, religion, and other major aspects of life, such as appear in Germany, Spain, Italy, or France (not to mention India or China), were foreign to the American experience and had no parallels in the slight differences to be found among the people of the antebellum period who lived in the various parts of this vast territory.

These distinctions and differences among Americans, as a general rule, coincided more nearly with the natural geographical regions than with state or sectional lines. Those who lived in the coastal plain, the regions behind the first fall line, and the valleys and coves of the mountains could be distinguished from the others by appearance, manner, and language; while those who lived in the Mississippi Valley, west of the Appalachians were different from those living in the East. Occasional enclaves, such as the Germans in Pennsylvania and the Valley of Virginia or the Creoles and Cajuns of southern Louisiana, further complicated the cultural patterns; but the greatest internal distinction to be found among the people of the United States was that between those who lived in the city and those who lived in the country, which existed in all parts of the nation, including the Old South, until its relatively recent modification by the paved road, electricity, and the consolidated school. In addition there were the distinctions between the sensible and the stupid, the educated and the uneducated, the genteel and the crude, the rich and the poor, the powerful and the weak, which are to be found in all societies at all times and in all places.

These cultural distinctions, as has been said before, were minor, and, like the differences in occupation and economic interest, give little support to those historians who insist that in the United States there were "two civilizations." The South did not secede because of differences in culture, nor even because of the tariff or the Bank of the United States, but rather because of its "peculiar" sectional interest. The one important sectional conflict in the nation's history arose from the fact that Negroes were held as slaves in the southern states until 1865. The defense of slavery against attacks from other areas of the country gradually affected the thinking of most white Southerners and led them to seek independence outside the American Union. . . .

The emancipation of the slaves eliminated the "peculiar institution" which distinguished the South from other areas of the country and eliminated the sole cause for its desire to be separate and independent. Its subsequent concern with the maintenance of white supremacy was not an evidence of its difference from other areas of the country, but of its unhappy identity with most men of European origin when they come into contact with large numbers of people of different origin, whether this be the Spanish with the Indians of Middle and South America, the Dutch in South Africa and the East Indies, the English in all parts of the colonial world, the French in North Africa and Indochina, or white Americans in California, Detroit, or Chicago.*

The South re-accepted membership in the national society with little or no change in basic attitudes and beliefs, because none was required. Its return to the nation was not an abandonment of its ancient tradition, but a return to it, and the subsequent changes, including industrialization, were a continuation of movements already well developed in the southern states before the outbreak of the war. The new South differed from the old only as the latter part of the nineteenth century differed from the earlier part, and most of the changes were the products of the scientific, industrial, and intellectual revolutions which were shared in common by all men of the western world.

*The moral and political criticism of white supremacy, which has steadily increased throughout the twentieth century, and the renewal of southern intransigence following the decision of the Supreme Court on segregation in schools, does not invalidate this statement. White and Negro Southerners have been among the leaders in voicing this criticism and defending the decision of the court, and they are effectively participating in the effort to eliminate this "glaring contradiction" to the expressed principles of the American nation.

POSTSCRIPT

WAS THE SOUTH A UNIQUE SECTION IN AMERICAN HISTORY?

Both Professors Woodward and Govan examine the southern experience with sophisticated approaches that avoid oversimplication of a complex historical process. Both are concerned with the question of race but neither views white supremacy as the central theme of southern history. Yet, both writers may have overstated their cases. Govan utilizes a more traditional approach to history. He tears down the vastly oversimplified industrial versus agrarian sectional dicotomy fashioned by earlier progressive historians. He denies the uniqueness of southern history by pointing out that its farmers, merchants, bankers, and politicians had much in common with the same groups in other parts of the country. He convincingly demonstrates that the Founding Fathers had created an economically unified nation. The policy splits that developed over the banking and tariff issues had more to do with the particular interests of an economic group (or the political ambitions of a major statesman) than with any major division between North and South. Govan admits, however, that the slavery question became the dominant issue which divided the country in the 1850s.

Professor Woodward, on the other hand, employs a cultural approach to history. He brilliantly contrasts the negative myths which characterize the unique southern historical consciousness with the more positive myths that prevail among the American public. He contrasts the southern experiences of slavery, poverty, military defeat, and reconstruction with the national experiences of freedom, abundance, and military invincibility. One might critique Woodward on several grounds. Don't the experiences Woodward is talking about apply more to the post-Civil War than the pre-Civil War South? Nor does the essay make clear whether the national experiences of abundance, innocence, and success are figments of the American public's imagination or whether these experiences can be demonstrated to be historically valid.

One final question remains. In 1958 Professor Woodward was worried about the South becoming indistinguishable from the rest of the nation. By 1972, he appeared to become even more apprehensive of a "Yankeefied" South. "Every new throughway, every new supermarket, every central city is an extension of it. . . . I wonder if what the South really wants is uncritical emulation of the North." Those who wish to ponder this question further should read Richard N. Current's delightfully short but highly-incisive lectures about *Northernizing the South* (Georgia, 1983).

ISSUE 17

DID THE DEMOCRATIC PROCESS FAIL DURING THE CIVIL WAR?

YES: Avery Craven, from "The 1840's and the Democratic Process," *The Journal of Southern History* (May 1950)

NO: Arthur M. Schlesinger, Jr., from "The Causes of the Civil War: A Note on Historical Sentimentalism," *Partisan Review* (October 1949)

ISSUE SUMMARY

YES: Professor Avery Craven emphasizes *how* the war came about, through a breakdown of the democratic process, is more important than the causes of the war.
NO: Professor Arthur M. Schlesinger, Jr., criticizes Craven and other revisionists because they ignore the moral issues which justified civil war as a means of ending slavery.

Professor Arthur Schlesinger's label for the Civil War, "our greatest national trauma," bears more than one interpretation. It describes, first of all, the actual event, the war years (1861–1865). On another level, however, the emotionalism of the event transfers itself to our understanding of the Civil War, particularly the causes of the conflict. The various causes of the war are, at once, complicated, interconnected and controversial. Consequently, historians must consider as many of them as possible in their evaluations, even if they choose to spotlight one or another as a major explanation.

Some of the factors prominently displayed in historical interpretations of the Civil War are: slavery and sectionalism, industrial development and agrarian conservatism, Manifest Destiny and the cotton kingdom, compromise and fanaticism. For example, some historians have featured the conflict between the industrial growth of the North and the agricultural interests of the South. This discussion focuses on issues such as tariffs, world trade and overall attitudes about economic development. The discussion, however, turns to debate when issues (states' rights, slavery, the railroads, the relationship between the western territories and the older sections of the country) intrude, as they must. While historians have tended to emphasize one cause, they cannot isolate themselves from the others. Many, however, have minimized the importance of slavery by pushing it as far into the background as possible. They have argued that, excepting perhaps the abolitionists, the slave issue was not a primary concern in the antagonism between the North and South. Some, like Professor Craven, suggest that the slavery issue masked the reality of the situation in the 1840s and 1850s. They argue for an interpretation based on realpolitik: how polticians act and react based on the hard truths of economics, demographics, territorial expansion, the feasibility of war and the use of their resources.

From a quite different point of view, there is the conflict between those historians who concentrate on the immediate causes occurring in the 1840s and 1850s compared to those who study the long-term origins. Again, however, complexity enters the picture. Whether historians choose to analyze the two decades before the attack on Fort Sumter or reach as far back as the Constitution, they must consider the topic of compromise (1787, 1820, 1850), westward expansion, the distribution of power between the federal government and the states as well as sectionalism. The situation of American blacks, whether slave or free, imposes itself on all these topics. The aftermath of the Revolution created sectional slavery. Massachusetts, the first colony to recognize slavery in the 1630s, became the first state to eradicate it, in 1790. The three-fifths compromise in 1787 reinforced slavery south of the Mason-Dixon line. The Northwest Ordinance, however, forbade involuntary servitude that same year in what became part of the Midwest. Article One, Section Nine of the Constitution, which forbade the importation of slaves after 1808, added to the muddled situation. The decision to count a slave as three-fifths of a white not only compromised them, it jeopardized the Constitution as well. It signaled the South that the North in 1787 placed a higher value on the union of the thirteen states than the slavocracy did and that acceptance of sectional slavery was the price of political unity.

Professor Craven argues, "If the breakdown of the democratic process is the significant thing about the coming of the Civil War, then the important question is not *what* the North and South were quarreling about half as much as it is *how* their differences got into such shape that they could not be handled by the process of rational discussion, compromise, or the tolerant acceptance of majority decision." Professor Schlesinger dissents emphatically. "Where have the revisionists gone astray?" he demands. A few paragraphs later he provides part of the answer: "By denying themselves insight into the moral dimension of the slavery crisis, in other words, the revisionists denied themselves a historical understanding of the intensities that caused the crisis." Schlesinger condemns the revisionists. "A society closed in the defense of evil institutions thus creates moral differences far too profound to be solved by compromise. Such a society forces upon every one, both those living at the time and those writing about it later, the necessity of a moral judgment; and the moral judgment in such cases becomes an indispensible factor in the historical understanding."

YES   Avery Craven

THE 1840's AND THE
DEMOCRATIC PROCESS

The most significant thing about the American Civil War is that it represents
a complete breakdown of the democratic process. After years of strain, men
ceased to discuss their problems, dropped the effort to compromise their differences, refused to abide by the results of a national election, and resorted to
the use of force. After four years of bloody civil strife, one side was beaten
into submission and the other had its way in national affairs. The emergence
of modern America was largely the product of that outcome.

If the breakdown of the democratic process is the significant thing about
the coming of the Civil War, then the important question is not *what* the North
and South were quarreling about half so much as it is *how* their differences
got into such shape that they could not be handled by the process of rational
discussion, compromise, or the tolerant acceptance of majority decision. The
question is not "What caused the Civil War?" but rather "How did it come
about?" The two questions are quite different, yet hopelessly tangled. The
effort to distinguish between them, however, is important and needs to be
stressed.

If one were to discuss the *causes* of the Civil War, he might begin with geography, move onto historical developments in time and place, trace the growth
of economic and social rivalries, outline differences in moral values, and then
show the way in which personalities and psychological factors operated. The
part which slavery played would loom large. It might even become the symbol of all differences and of all conflicts. State rights, territorial expansion, tariffs,
lands, internal improvements, and a host of other things, real and imagined,
would enter the picture. There would be economic causes, constitutional causes,
social causes, moral causes, political causes involving the breaking of old parties
and the rise of sectional ones, and psychological causes which ultimately permitted emotion to take the place of reason. There would be remote or background causes, and immediate causes, and causes resting on other causes,
until the most eager pedagogue would be thoroughly satisified.

From, "The 1840's and the Democratic Process," by Avery Craven, *Journal of Southern History,* May
1950. Copyright © 1950 by The Southern Historical Association. Reprinted by permission.

The matter of how issues got beyond the abilities of the democratic process is, on the other hand, a bit less complex and extended. It has to do with the way in which concrete issues were reduced to abstract principles and the conflicts between interests simplified to basic levels where men feel more than they reason, and where compromise or yielding is impossible because issues appear in the form of right and wrong and involve the fundamental structure of society. This is not saying, as some have charged, that great moral issues were not involved. They certainly were, and it is a matter of choice with historians as to whether or not they take sides, praise or condemn, become partisans in this departed quarrel, or use past events for present-day purposes.

As an approach to this second more modest problem, a correspondence which took place between Abraham Lincoln and Alexander H. Stephens between November 30 and December 22, 1860, is highly revealing.[1] On November 14, Stephens had delivered one of the great speeches of his life before the legislature of Georgia. It was a Union speech. He had begged his fellow Southerners not to give up the ship, to wait for some violation of the Constitution before they attempted secession. Equality might yet be possible inside the Union. At least, the will of the whole people should be obtained before any action was taken.[2]

Abraham Lincoln, still unconvinced that there was a real danger, wrote Stephens, as an old friend, for a revised copy of his speech. Stephens complied, and he ended his letter with a warning about the great peril which threatened the country and a reminder of the heavy responsibility now resting on the president-elect's shoulders. Lincoln answered with assurance that he would not "*directly, or indirectly,* interfere

with the slaves" or with the southern people about their slaves, and then closed with this significant statement: "I suppose, however, this does not meet the case. You think slavery is right and ought to be extended,, while we think it is *wrong* and ought to be restricted. That I suppose is the rub. It certainly is the only substantial difference between us."[3]

The reduction of "the only substantial difference" between North and South to a simple question of *right and wrong* is the important thing about Lincoln's statement. It revealed the extent to which the sectional controversy had, by 1860, been simplified and reduced to a conflict of principles in the minds of the northern people.

Stephens' answer to Lincoln's letter is equally revealing. He expressed "an earnest desire to preserve and maintain the Union of the States, if it can be done upon the principles and in furtherance of the objects for which it was formed." He insisted, however, that private opinion on the question of "African Slavery" was not a matter over which "the Government under the Constitution" had any control. "But now," he said, "this subject, which is confessedly on all sides outside of the Constitutional action of the Government so far as the States are concerned, is made the 'central idea' in the Platform of principles announced by the triumphant Party." It was this total disregard of the Constitution and the rights guaranteed under it that lay back of southern fears. It was the introduction into party politics of issues which projected action by Congress outside its constitutional powers that had made all the trouble. Stephens used the word "Constitution" seven times in his letter.[4]

The significant thing here is Stephens' reduction of sectional differences to the simple matter of southern rights under the

Constitution. He too showed how completely the sectional controversy had been simplified into a conflict of principles. And he with Lincoln, speaking for North and South, emphasized the fact that after years of strife the complex issues between the sections had assumed the form of a conflict between *right* and *rights*.

To the scholar it might be perfectly clear that this drastic simplification of sectional differences did not mean that either Lincoln or Stephens thought that all the bitter economic, social, and political questions could be ignored. It simply meant that *right* and *rights* had become the symbols or carriers of all those interests and values. Yet it is equally clear that as symbols they carried an emotional force and moral power in themselves that was far greater than the sum total of all the material issues involved. They suggested things which cannot be compromised—things for which men willingly fight and die. Their use, in 1860, showed that an irrepressible conflict existed.

The question as to whether the Civil War was "a needless war" has therefore, little to do with the bungling statesmanship of 1860-1861. It has much to do with the matter of how problems got beyond the ability of the democratic process. And as to that, we do know that the author of the Declaration of Independence, on which the Lincoln position rested, was a slaveholder. So was Madison and many other important leaders of the first great democratic drive in national life. The three men whom Arthur M. Schlesinger, Jr., names as the ones who carried the democratic torch on down to the age of Jackson[5]—John Randolph, Nathaniel Macon, and John Taylor of Carolina—were also slaveholders, as were Jackson himself and Thomas Hart Benton and Francis Preston Blair, his chief lieutenants. Even the father of Martin Van Buren held slaves.[6] Evidently, in these years only a generation away from Civil War, the belief that slavery was morally wrong did not constitute "the only substantial difference" between those who sought to forward government "of the people, by the people, for the people" and their reactionary opponents.

Nor, by the same token, was everyone in the early South agreed on the value of slavery or its constitutional right to immunity from public criticism and political action. In the Virginia constitutional convention of 1829-1830 and in the legislature of 1832, men questioned the economic benefits of slavery, pointed out its social dangers, and shamed its violation both of Christian and democratic values. Bills were introduced and voted upon. True, it was a case of a state discussing and acting upon its own domestic affairs, but these men were talking about slavery as an institution, not as just a Virginia practice, and they were thoroughly conscious of the larger national implications of what was going on. Robert Stanard spoke of the impulse begun in Virginia passing "with the rapidity of lightning across the whole extent of this Union." James Monroe frankly admitted that he looked "to the Union to aid in effecting" emancipation; and James M'Dowell, Jr., bitterly denounced slavery because it created "a political interest in this Union" and produced conflicts in Congress and dissension in the nation. He saw the day when a national crusade against slavery would unite all rival interests against the South.[7]

Slavery took its blows in other states as well, and there was anything but general agreement on how to protect constitutional rights when South Carolina took a try at nullification. However much they might dislike the tariff, the other southern states had not as yet returned to the old anticonsolidation state-rights position of their elder statesmen. The issue outside of South Carolina was generally one of the merits of the tariff rather than the constitutional rights of a state. The younger Southwest, moreover, had its own attitudes towards lands and internal improvements which kept these issues on the level of interest rather than on that of constitutionality.[8]

The next few years, however, brought important changes. The growing realization of failure to share equally in national expansion, the new demand for slaves with the spread of cotton, and the increasing agitation against slavery all contributed to a feeling of resentment and insecurity on the part of the South. Where the coming of the Industrial Revolution to the Northeast upset life to its very roots and forced a reconsideration of every old value and every relationship, Southerners, who had experienced only the extension of old agricultural patterns into new agricultural areas, knew no sharp break with their pasts and found no reason to question the soundness of old social and political institutions and relationships. Conditions under the Constitution, as the fathers had made it, were quite satisfactory.

Yet, the matchless material growth that had come to the nation in these years, the deep ferment of ideas, and the rapid increase in the means of communication denied the South the chance to live alone. The nation was, in fact, in a state of transition, politically, economically, and socially. The attempt to apply old forms to constantly changing conditions put heavy strain on institutions and agencies created in more simple times and tended to thrust forward for decision the questions of just what kind of a government we had set up in the United States, what provisions it made for the protection of minorities, and just what the relations were between government and business. Nor could southern institutions escape the scrutiny that was being given to all institutions and relationships in this age of transition. The whole Northeast, under the pressure of forces that would ultimately produce modern America, was rapidly becoming the center of social unrest and of efforts at reform. The new age was revealing too many contradictions between profession and practice. Where before in a simple rural order the true and the good were not beyond the comprehension of every man through a direct moral approach, and a good society was simply one composed of good men, they now found environment a force of major importance. The living of the many was passing into the hands of the few. Everywhere men were losing their independence, and forces quite beyond individual control were shaping the lives of the masses. Neither Christianity nor democracy seemed to be working. Something was wrong and it should be righted. The Declaration of Independence with its emphasis on freedom and equality ought again to become a force in American life.

Out of the welter of reform movements that resulted from such convictions came the antislavery impulse and the resulting struggle over antislavery petitions in Congress. Joining hands with the great religious revivals that were burning their way through the lives of men and women in a region spreading east and west from upper New York, a group of earnest souls had lighted the fires of moral indignation against the sin of slavery and were pouring a flood of petitions into Congress demanding various steps against the evil. The South thus found itself faced by danger on a new front. It was thrown on the defensive. The Constitution and its clear statements of rights also needed to be brought back into American consciousness.

Already, in the tariff controversy, Robert J. Turnbull had argued that under changing conditions it was the interest of the North and West to make the government "more national," while the interest of the South was to continue it "Federal."[9] In opposing Jackson's Force Bill, John C. Calhoun had insisted that the real issue was whether this was a federal union of states or a union of the American people in the aggregate. He made it perfectly clear that he thought it was the former, and that "To maintain the ascendency of the constitution over the law-making majority" was the great and essential thing for the preservation of the Union.[10] When the petition struggle developed, he quickly picked up the charge that slavery was "sinful and odious, in the sight of God and man," and pronounced it "a general crusade against us and our institutions." "The most unquestionable right may be rendered doubtful," he insisted, if slavery were "once admitted to be a subject of controversy." The subject was beyond the jurisdiction of Congress—"they have no right to touch it in any shape or form," he said, "or to make it the subject of deliberation or discussion." And then, ignoring his own words, he bluntly pronounced "the relation now existing in the slave-holding States" between the two races to be "a positive good." Even though opposition to the very popular right of petition might weaken friends in Congress and strengthen the abolitionists, the enemy must be met "on the frontier"; this was the southern "Thermopylae."[11]

Later, on December 27, 1837, he introduced a series of resolutions which carefully defined the character, purposes, and powers of the government under the Constitution. It had been adopted by the "free, independent and sovereign States" as security against all dangers, "*domestic* as well as foreign." The states retained the sole right over their domestic institutions, and any intermeddling with those institutions by other states or combinations of their citizens was unwarranted and "subversive of the objects for which the constitution was formed." And it was the duty of the government to resist all such meddling.

Negro slavery, he declared, was an important domestic institution in southern and western states and was such when the Constitution was formed. "No change of opinion or feeling, on the part of other States of the Union in relation to it, can justify them or their citizens in open and systematic attacks thereon." To do so was a "breach of faith, and a violation of the most solemn obligations, moral and religious." Furthermore, to attempt to abolish slavery in the District of Columbia, or in any of the territories, on grounds that it was immoral or sinful "would be a direct and dangerous attack on the institutions of all the slaveholding States"; and to refuse to increase the limits or population of these states by the annexation of new territory or states on the pretext that slavery was "immoral or sinful, or otherwise obnoxious" would destroy the equal "rights and advantages which the Constitution was intended to secure."[12] . . .

In this same period industry entered a new phase in the northeastern corner of the nation. Hard times and bitter competition wrecked weaker concerns and left the field to the large, well-financed corporations. Work was speeded up and wages remained low. Strikes became frequent. Gradually the native girls gave way before the Irish and French-Canadians, and the factory and the factory town reached maturity. Industry sent its spokesmen into legislative halls, and the ardent complaint against local ills gave way steadily to the attack on southern slavery. A general acceptance of the new age of interdependent nationalism, already a business reality, marked the section. The questioning and criticism represented in Fruitlands, Brook Farm, and the Fourier associations gradually lost force. A new feeling of being in step with progress took its place. The development of a complex industrial order was a part of the nation's manifest destiny. Men, therefore, fell into line on domestic issues, but they did not yield their tough Puritan estimates of the ways of other Americans. Meanwhile the growth of internal commerce, now far more important than foreign trade, fostered the growing cities along the Atlantic coast, and the canal and the railroad, as the great new agents of transportation, more and more linked the interests of the Northwest to those of the commercial-industrial Northeast.

By these quick and drastic developments, the problems of lands, internal improvements, tariffs, and expansion were thrust forward in aggravated forms. They took on the character of sectional struggles. They became part of the right and the effort to achieve a manifest destiny. Sooner or later every one of them became tangled with slavery and from it took new strength with which to wage their battles. Both Calhoun and the abolitionists connected slavery with the annexation of Texas. Benjamin Lundy declared the Texas revolution a scheme to wrest that territory from Mexico in order to establish a slave market, and John Quincy Adams and twelve associates denounced annexation as a proslavery scheme. Calhoun gave substance to their charge by insisting on annexation as necessary for the protection of southern slaveholders.[13] Others connected it with the tariff and internal improvements. Joshua Giddings of Ohio in May, 1844, called attention to the balance and rivalry between North and South which produced a deadlock in legislation. "So equally balanced has been the political power," he said, "that for five years past our lake commerce has been utterly abandoned; and such are the defects of the tariff, that for years our revenues are unequal to the support of government." The annexation of Texas, secured "obviously to enhance the price of human flesh in our slave-breeding states," would now place "the policy and the destiny" of this nation in southern hands.

"Are the liberty-loving democrats of Pennsylvania ready to give up our tariff?" he asked. "Are the farmers of the West, of Ohio, Indiana, and Illinois, prepared to give up the sale of their beef, pork, and flour, in order to increase the profits of those who raise children for sale, and deal in the bodies of women? Are the free states prepared to suspend their harbor and river improvements for the purpose of establishing their slave-trade with Texas, and to perpetuate slavery therein?" "Our tariff," he added at a later time, "is as much an anti-slavery measure as the rejection of Texas. So is the subject of internal improvements and the distribution of the proceeds of the public lands. The advocates of perpetual slavery oppose all of them, they regard them as opposed to slavery."[14]

Giddings represented an extreme position, but the proposed tax on tea and coffee brought from more moderate western men the charge that it was "a sectional tax." It was "wrong, unequal, and unjust," because while all free western laborers used these articles, the three million slave laborers scarcely touched them at all. President James K. Polk was asking for a war tax on tea and coffee "to make southern conquests, while northern territory [meaning Oregon] is given away by empires."[15]

Slavery was also blamed for Polk's veto of a river and harbor bill intended largely to benefit shipping on the Great Lakes. "Is it not strange that enlightened men of the South cannot be persuaded that our lakes are something more than goose ponds?" asked the Chicago *Democrat*. "If we were blessed with the glorious institution of slavery this comprehension would not be so difficult."[16] The Chicago *Daily Journal* was more blunt. It charged Southerners' opposition to western internal improvements to the fact that they were "slaveholders," but "not Americans." "If no measures for the protection and improvement of anything North or West are to be suffered by our Southern masters," it said, "if we are to be downtrodden, and all our cherished interests crushed by them, a signal revolution will eventually ensue."[17]

By the close of the Mexican War, which brought proslavery charges to a climax, some men were frankly saying that the whole business had become a struggle for power. The extension or nonextension of slavery in the territories acquired from Mexico was a matter of increasing or decreasing the strength of parties in Congress. Robert Barnwell Rhett of South Carolina was convinced that "Political power, the power of the different sections of the Union, seeking the mastery, is undoubtedly a strong element in the proposed exclusion of slavery from our territory."[18] George Oscar Rathbun of New York was more explicit. He had figured out that by its three-fifths representation of slaves the South gained some twenty-three members in Congress. With this vote the section had "turned the scale upon every important question that had divided this country for the last forty years." The South had by this advantage elected presidents,

filled the speakership, ruled the army and navy, and placed southern men in the office of Secretary of State during most of those years. Rathbun was, therefore, opposed to slavery in the territories because it gave "representation and political power." If the South would yield the three-fifths rule, he was willing for Southerners to go into any territory and freely to take their slaves with them.[19] Southerners made it just as clear that the exclusion of slavery from the territories meant the reduction of their section to the position of a permanent minority and the ultimate destruction of their institutions. They were contending for equality in the nation.

The Wilmot Proviso was unquestionably, in part, a move to check southern strength in Congress and to end the restraints placed on northern and western development. It was, however, considerably more than that. It was an assertion of the fact that North and West had now definitely caught step with the modern world and had reached the point where they knew both their minds and their strength. They knew that the future belonged to urban industrial and financial capitalism, to democracy, and to a more social Christianity. They understood that slavery, as an impediment to each of these things, had no place in a nation whose manifest destiny was to round out its boundaries on this continent and, perhaps, to right the social and political balances in the whole western world.

That understanding gave a positiveness to northern opposition to the extension of slavery that knew no yielding. It easily took on the flavor of a moral crusade. Politicians and "sober, deliberate, and substantial men," who had "the good of the country at heart," as Charles Hudson of Massachusetts described them, let it be known that slavery could not advance a foot farther.[20] Anyone who has read the debates in Congress on this issue knows that the question of whether slavery had reached its limits in the United States is a thoroughly academic one. And the answer has nothing to do with geography or profits. It could go no farther, for the simple reason that the North had made up its mind and had the strength to enforce its will.

And, regardless of how complex were the forces operating to produce this situation, the argument that carried the day was that slavery was a moral wrong and an impediment to progress. In the great debates on compromise which followed, Horace Mann and William H. Seward, not Daniel Webster, made the important northern statements. Mann insisted that to spread slavery was to "cast aside, with scorn, not only the teachings of Christianity, but the clearest principles of natural religion and of natural law." It was to sink back to the Dark Ages. To insist that men and women could rightly be called property was a trick for which any "juggler or mountebank" would be hissed off the stage in any respectable village. "I deliberately say, better disunion, better a civil or servile war—better anything that God in his providence shall send, than an extension of the boundaries of slavery."[21] Seward declared that we could be neither Christians nor real freemen if we imposed on another the chains we defied all human power to fasten on ourselves. He insisted that the Constitution had created a consolidated political state, in which the states had "submitted themselves to the sway of the numerical majority." The same Constitution had devoted the territories to freedom. And what was just as important, slavery itself in the long run would have to give way "to the salutary instructions of economy, and to the ripening influences of humanity." It was only a question of whether it be done peacefully or by force. And to those who offered the Constitution as an impediment to the forward sweep of material and moral progress, he offered the "higher law."[22]

Some day the historian will understand that there is no break between Henry David Thoreau's "Civil Disobedience," William Lloyd Garrison's burning of the Constitution, and Seward's higher law. He will also understand the obligation which northern men felt to bring profession and practice into harmony in a nation whose manifest destiny was to uphold Christianity and democracy throughout the western world.

The South, on its part, met the Wilmot Proviso with an uncompromising insistence on the right to an equal share in the territories won by the common blood of the nation. Calhoun, as usual, brouught forward a series of resolutions, declaring the territories to be the property of "the several States composing this Union" and denying the right of Congress to discriminate between the states or to deny to their citizens the full and equal opportunity to migrate to the territories with their property. Others took up the cry of "indefeasible right," and through their statements rang the word "Constitution" like the repeated call of the whippoorwill. "We invoke the spirit of the Constitution, and claim its guarantees," said the resolutions of the Nashville Convention. "I, for one, am for tearing asunder every bond that binds us together," said Alexander H. Stephens. "Any people capable of defending themselves, who would continue their allegiance to a Government which should deny to them a clear, unquestionable, constitutional right of the magnitude and importance of this to the people of the South, would deserve to be stigmatized as poltroons."[23] Jefferson Davis summed up the situation as one in which the North was determined to deny to slavery its constitutional rights for "the sole purpose of gaining political power."

Some day the historian will also understand that there is no break between southern abhorrence of the strife and ferment in northern and European society and its deep reliance on the Scriptures and the Constitution for defense of a stable order. He may even come to understand that few peoples on this earth have ever extended freedom of speech to the point of permitting agitation that would destroy a goodly percentage of their material wealth and completely upset the existing structure of society. Southerners too felt an obligation to manifest destiny.

The struggles of the 1840's had thus gone a long way toward becoming a matter of *right* and *rights*. Issues had been caught up in the great fundamental developments of the age. "Right" had become a part of what men were calling progress, a part of a nation's manifest destiny—its obligation to the democratic dogma and experiment. "Rights" too had become a part of something fundamental in terms of a superior way of life, a sound form of government, and a sane treatment of property.

It seemed for a time that the final crisis had been reached, that the Union would go to pieces. Some expressed the hope that it would. That it did not do so was due largely to the strength of political party ties. Whigs and Democrats, North and South, still felt the tug of party loyalty and still retained confidence in the integrity of their fellows. By a supreme effort they forced the conflict back to the concrete issues involved in the immediate difficulty and were able to secure a compromise. It was a slender thread, but it held. It promised, however, little for the future, for

third parties had already appeared and the rift in each of the dominant parties had perilously widened. They might not survive another crisis. And what was equally alarming was the growing tendency of issues, however material, to fall into the pattern of *right* and *rights* and to be linked to the matter of progress and national destiny. It might not be possible next time to throw aside this covering and to return to concrete issues.

The 1840's had certainly shown the weakness of the democratic process in dealing with issues cast as moral conflicts or having to do with the fundamental structure of society. It seemed to show, as Carl Becker has said, that "government by discussion works best when there is nothing of profound importance to discuss, and when there is plenty of time to discuss it. The party system works best when the rival programs involve the superficial aspects rather than the fundamental structure of the social system, and majority rule works best when the minority can meet defeat at the polls in good temper because they need not regard the decision as either a permanent or a fatal surrender of their vital interests."[24]

That, however, was only half of the difficulty. The 1840's had also shown that a democratic society cannot stand still. The conservative urge to hold fast to that which has been established may prove as fatal as the fanatic's prod to constant change. Those who profess a belief in democracy must ever remember that alongside the Constitution of the United States stands that other troublesome document, the Declaration of Independence, with its promise of greater freedom and equality. If politicians and parties do not sometimes give it heed, they may learn to their sorrow that the great document was written to justify revolt. That too may be a fatal weakness in the democratic process.

NOTES

1. Alexander H. Stephens, *A Constitutional View of the Late War Between the States; Its Causes, Character, Conduct and Results* (2 vols., Philadelphia, 1868–1870), II, 266-67 insert.

2. *Ibid.,* 279-300.

3. *Ibid.,* 266-67 insert.

4. *Ibid.,* 267-70.

5. Arthur M. Schlesinger, Jr., *The Age of Jackson* (Boston, 1945), 18-29.

6. William E. Smith, "Martin Van Buren," in Allen Johnson and Dumas Malone (eds.), *Dictionary of American Biography* (21 vols. and index, New York, 1928-1945), XIX, 152.

7. *Proceedings and Debates of the Virginia State Convention of 1829-30* (Richmond 1830), 306, 149; *Speech of James M'Dowell, Jr. in the House of Delegates of Virginia on the Slave Question: delivered Saturday, January 21, 1832* (2nd ed., Richmond, 1832).

8. Richmond *Enquirer,* April 24, December 13, 15, 1832; Charles S. Sydnor, *The Development of Southern Sectionalism, 1819-1848* (Baton Rouge, 1948), 208-09, 218-19.

9. Robert J. Turnbull (Brutus), *The Crisis: or, Essays on the Usurpations of the Federal Government* (Charleston, 1827), 11.

10. Richard K. Crallé (ed.), *The Works of John C. Calhoun* (6 vols., New York, 1853-1856), II, 197-262.

11. *Ibid.,* II, 481-90, 625-33.

12. *Ibid.,* III, 140-42.

13. Avery Craven, *The Coming of the Civil War* (New York, 1942), 189-96.

14. Joshua R. Giddings, *Speeches in Congress* (Boston, 1853), 98-105, 151-56; Giddings to Oran Follett, November 18, 1844, in Historical and Philosophical Society of Ohio, *Quarterly Publication* (Cincinnati, 1906-1923), X, 20.

15. Jacob Brinkerhoff of Ohio. *Cong. Globe,* 29 Cong., 1 Sess., Appendix, 784-85 (June 30, 1846).

16. Chicago *Democrat,* September 15, 1846.

17. Chicago *Daily Journal,* August 19, November 19, 1846.

18. *Cong. Globe,* 29 Cong., 2 Sess., Appendix, 246 (January 15, 1847).

19. *Ibid.,* 364-65 (February 9, 1847).

20. *Ibid.,* 51-52 (December 16, 1846).

21. *Ibid.,* 31 Cong., 1 Sess., Appendix, 219-24 (February 15, 1850).

22. *Ibid.,* Appendix, 260-69 (March 11, 1850).

23. *Ibid.,* 32 Cong., 1 Sess., 460 (April 27, 1852); M.W. Cluskey (ed.), *Political Text-Book, or Encyclopedia* (Washington, 1857), 597; Crallé (ed.), *Works of John C. Calhoun,* IV, 348.

24. Carl Becker, *New Liberties for Old* (New Haven, 1941), 106-107.

NO

Arthur Schlesinger, Jr.

THE CAUSES OF THE CIVIL WAR: A NOTE ON HISTORICAL SENTIMENTALISM

The Civil War was our great national trauma. A savage fraternal conflict, it released deep sentiments of guilt and remorse—sentiments which have reverberated through our history and our literature ever since. Literature in the end came to terms with these sentiments by yielding to the South in fantasy the victory it has been denied in fact; this tendency culminated on the popular level in *Gone with the Wind* and on the highbrow level in the Nashville cult of agrarianism. But history, a less malleable medium, was constricted by the intractable fact that the war had taken place, and by the related assumption that it was, in William H. Seward's phrase, an "irrepressible conflict," and hence a justified one.

As short a time ago as 1937, for example, even Professor James G. Randall could describe himself as "unprepared to go to the point of denying that the great American tragedy could have been avoided." Yet in a few years the writing of history would succumb to the psychological imperatives which had produced *I'll Take my Stand* and *Gone with the Wind;* and Professor Randall wouuld emerge as the leader of a triumphant new school of self-styled "revisionists." The publication of two vigorous books by Professor Avery Craven— *The Repressible Conflict* (1939) and *The Coming of the Civil War* (1942)— and the appearance of Professor Randall's own notable volumes on Lincoln— *Lincoln the President: Springfield to Gettysburg* (1945), *Lincoln and the South* (1946), and *Lincoln the Liberal Statesman* (1947—brought about a profound reversal of the professional historian's attitude toward the Civil War. Scholars now denied the traditional assumption of the inevitability of the war and boldly advanced the thesis that a "blundering generation" had transformed a "repressible conflict" into a "needless war."

The swift triumph of revisionism came about with very little resistance or even expressed reservations on the part of the profession. Indeed, the only adequate evaluation of the revisionist thesis that I know was made, not by an academic historian at all, but by that illustrious semi-pro, Mr. Bernard De

From, "The Causes of the Civil War: A Note on Historical Sentimentalism," by Arthur Schlesinger, Jr., *Partisan Review*, October 1949. Copyright © 1949. Reprinted by permission of *Partisan Review*.

Voto; and Mr. De Voto's two brilliant articles in *Harper's* in 1945 unfortunately had little influence within the guild. By 1947 Professor Allan Nevins, summing up the most recent scholarship in *Ordeal of the Union,* his able general history of the eighteen fifties, could define the basic problem of the period in terms which indicated a measured but entire acceptance of revisionism. "The primary task of statesmanship in this era," Nevins wrote, "was to furnish a workable adjustment between the two sections, while offering strong inducements to the southern people to regard their labor system not as static but evolutionary, and equal persuasions to the northern people to assume a helpful rather than scolding attitude."

This new interpretation surely deserves at least as meticulous an examination as Professor Randall is prepared to give, for example, to such a question as whether or not Lincoln was playing fives when he received the news of his nomination in 1860. The following notes are presented in the interests of stimulating such an examination.

The revisionist case, as expounded by Professors Randall and Craven, has three main premises. First:

1) that the Civil War was caused by the irresponsible emotionalization of politics far out of proportion to the real problems involved. The war, as Randall put it, was certainly not caused by cultural variations nor by economic rivalries nor by sectional differences; these all existed, but it was "stupid," as he declared, to think that they required war as a solution. "One of the most colossal of misconceptions" was the "theory" that "fundamental motives produce war. The glaring and obvious fact is the artificiality of war-marking agitation." After all, Randall pointed out, agrarian and industrial interests had been in conflict un-

der Coolidge and Hoover; yet no war resulted. "In Illinois," he added, "major controversies (not mere transient differences) between downstate and metropolis have stopped short of war."

Nor was the slavery the cause. The issues arising over slavery were in Randall's judgment "highly artificial, almost fabricated. . . . They produced quarrels out of things that would have settled themselves were it not for political agitation." Slavery, Craven observed, was in any case a much overrated problem. It is "perfectly clear," he wrote, "that slavery played a rather minor part in the life of the South and of the Negro."

What then was the cause of war? "If one word or phrase were selected to account for the war," wrote Randall, ". . . it would have to be such a word as fanaticism (on both sides), misunderstanding, misrepresentation, or perhaps politics." Phrases like "whipped-up crisis" and "psychopathic case" adorned Randall's explanation. Craven similarly described the growing sense of sectional differences as "an artificial creation of inflamed minds." The "molders of public opinion steadily created the fiction of two distinct peoples." As a result, "distortion led a people into bloody war."

If uncontrolled emotionalism and fanaticism caused the war, how did they get out of hand? Who whipped up the "whipped-up crisis"? Thus the second revisionist thesis:

2) that sectional friction was permitted to develop into needless war by the inexcusable failure of political leadership in the fifties. "It is difficult to achieve a full realization of how Lincoln's generation stumbled into a ghastly war," wrote Randall. ". . . If one questions the term 'blundering generation,' let him inquire how many measures of the time he would wish

copied or repeated if the period were to be approached with a clean slate and to be lived again."

It was the politicians, charged Craven, who systematically sacrificed peace to their pursuit of power. Calhoun and Adams, "seeking political advantage," mixed up slavery and expansion; Wilmot introduced his "trouble-making Proviso as part of the political game"; the repeal clause in the Kansas-Nebraska Act was "the after-thought of a mere handful of politicians"; Chase's Appeal to the Independent Democrats was "false in its assertions and unfair in its purposes, but it was politically effective"; the "damaging" section in the Dred Scott decision was forced "by the political ambitions of dissenting judges." "These uncalled-for moves and this irresponsible leadership," concluded Craven, blew up a "crack-pot" crusade into a national conflict.

It is hard to tell which was under attack here—the performance of a particular generation or democratic politics in general. But, if the indictment "blundering generation" meant no more than a general complaint that democratic politics placed a premium on emotionalism, then the Civil War would have been no more nor less "needless" than any event in our blundering history. The phrase "blundering generation" must consequently imply that the generation in power in the fifties was *below* the human or historical or democratic average in its blundering. Hence the third revisionist thesis:

3) that the slavery problem could have been solved without war. For, even if slavery were as unimportant as the revisionists have insisted, they would presumably admit that it constituted the real sticking-point in the relations between the sections. They must show therefore that there were policies with which a non-blundering gener-

ation could have resolved the slavery crisis and averted war; and that these policies were so obvious that the failure to adopt them indicated blundering and stupidity of a peculiarly irresponsible nature. If no such policies could be produced even by hindsight, then it would seem excessive to condemn the politicians of the fifties for failing to discover them at the time.

The revisionists have shown only a most vague and sporadic awareness of this problem. "Any kind of sane policy in Washington in 1860 might have saved the day for nationalism," remarked Craven; but he did not vouchsafe the details of these sane policies; we would be satisfied to know about one.* Similarly Randall declared that there were few policies of the fifties he would wish repeated if the period were to be lived over again; but he was not communicative about the policies he would wish pursued. Nevins likewise blamed the war on the "collapse of American statesmanship," but restrained himself from suggesting how a non-collapsible statesmanship would have solved the hard problems of the fifties.

In view of this reticence on a point so crucial to the revisionist argument, it is necessary to reconstruct the possibilities that might lie in the back of revisionism. Clearly there could be only two "solutions" to the slavery problem: the preservation of slavery, or its abolition.

Presumably the revisionists would not regard the preservation of slavery as a possible solution. Craven, it is true, has argued that "most of the incentives to honest and sustained effort, to a contented, well-rounded life, might be found under slav-

---

*It is fair to say that Professor Craven seems in recent years to have modified his earlier extreme position; see his article "The Civil War and the Democratic Process," *Abraham Lincoln Quarterly,* June 1947.

ery. . . . What owning and being owned added to the normal relationship of employer and employee is very hard to say." In describing incidents in which slaves beat up masters, he has even noted that "happenings and reactions like these were the rule [sic], not the exception." But Craven would doubtless admit that, however jolly this system might have been, its perpetuation would have been, to say the least, impracticable.

If, then, revisionism has rested on the assumption that the nonviolent abolition of slavery was possible, such abolition could conceivably have come about through internal reform in the South; through economic exhaustion of the slavery system in the South; or through some government project for gradual and compensated emancipation. Let us examine these possibilities.

1) *The internal reform argument.* The South, the revisionists have suggested, might have ended the slavery system if left to its own devices; only the abolitionists spoiled everything by letting loose a hysteria which caused the southern ranks to close in self-defense.

This revisionist argument would have been more convincing if the decades of alleged anti-slavery feeling in the South had produced any concrete results. As one judicious southern historian, Professor Charles S. Sydnor, recently put it, "Although the abolition movement was followed by a decline of antislavery sentiment in the South, it must be remembered that in all the long years before that movement began no part of the South had made substantial progress toward ending slavery. . . . Southern liberalism had not ended slavery in any state."

In any case, it is difficult for historians seriously to suppose that northerners could have denied themselves feelings of disapproval over slavery. To say that there "should" have been no abolitionists in America before the Civil War is about as sensible as to say that there "should" have been no anti-Nazis in the nineteen-thirties or that there "should" be no anti-Communists today. People who indulge in criticism of remote evils may not be so pure of heart as they imagine; but that fact does not affect their inevitability as part of the historic situation.

Any theory, in short, which expects people to repress such spontaneous aversions is profoundly unhistorical. If revisionism has based itself on the conviction that things would have been different if only there had been no abolitionists, it has forgotten that abolitionism was as definite and irrevocable a factor in the historic situation as was slavery itself. And, just as abolitionism was inevitable, so too was the southern reaction against it—a reaction which, as Professor Clement Eaton has ably shown, steadily drove the free discussion of slavery out of the South. The extinction of free discussion meant, of course, the absolute extinction of any hope of abolition through internal reform.

2) *The economic exhaustion argument.* Slavery, it has been pointed out, was on the skids economically. It was overcapitalized and inefficient; it immobilized both capital and labor; its one-crop system was draining the soil of fertility; it stood in the way of industrialization. As the South came to realize these facts, a revisionist might argue, it would have moved to abolish slavery for its own economic good. As Craven put it, slavery "may have been almost ready to break down of its own weight."

This argument assumed, of course, that southerners would have recognized the causes of their economic predicament and taken the appropriate measures. Yet such an assumption would be plainly contrary to history and to experience. From the beginning the South has always blamed its economic shortcomings, not on its own economic ruling class and its own inefficient use of resources, but on northern exploitation. Hard times in the eighteen-fifties produced in the South, not a reconsideration of the slavery system, but blasts against the North for the high prices of manufactured goods. The overcapitalization of slavery led, not to criticisms of the system, but to increasingly insistent demands for the reopening of the slave trade. Advanced southern writers like George Fitzhugh and James D.B. DeBow were even arguing that slavery was adapted to industrialism. When Hinton R. Helper did advance before the Civil War an early version of Craven's argument, asserting that emancipation was necessary to save the southern economy, the South burned his book. Nothing in the historical record suggests that the southern ruling class was prepared to deviate from its traditional pattern of self-exculpation long enough to take such a drastic step as the abolition of slavery.

3) *Compensated emancipation.* Abraham Lincoln made repeated proposals of compensated emancipation. In his annual message to Congress of December 1, 1862, he set forth a detailed plan by which States, on an agreement to abolish slavery by 1900, would receive government bonds in proportion to the number of slaves emancipated. Yet, even though Lincoln's proposals represented a solution of the problem conceivably gratifying to the slaveholder's purse as well as to his pride, they got nowhere. Two-thirds of the border representatives rejected the scheme, even when personally presented to them by Lincoln himself. And, of course, only the

pressure of war brought compensated emancipation its limited hearing of 1862.

Still, granted these difficulties, does it not remain true that other countries abolished slavery without internal convulsion? If emotionalism had not aggravated the situation beyond hope, Craven has written, then slavery "might have been faced as a national question and dealt with as successfully as the South American countries dealt with the same problem." If Brazil could free its slaves and Russia its serfs in the middle of the nineteenth century without civil war, why could not the United States have done as well?

The analogies are appealing but not, I think, really persuasive. There are essential differences between the slavery question in the United States and the problems in Brazil or in Russia. In the first place, Brazil and Russia were able to face servitude "as a national question" because it was, in fact, a national question. Neither country had the American problem of the identification of compact sectional interests with the survival of the slavery system. In the second place, there was no race problem at all in Russia; and, though there was a race problem in Brazil, the more civilized folkways of that country relieved racial differences of the extreme tension which they breed in the South of the United States. In the third place, neither in Russia nor in Brazil did the abolition of servitude involve constitutional issues; and the existence of these issues played a great part in determining the form of the American struggle.

It is hard to draw much comfort, therefore, from the fact that other nations abolished servitude peaceably. The problem in America was peculiarly recalcitrant. The schemes for gradual emancipation got nowhere. Neither internal reform nor economic exhaustion contained much promise for a peaceful solution. The hard fact, indeed, is that the revisionists have not tried seriously to describe the policies by which the slavery problem could have been peacefully resolved. They have resorted instead to broad affirmations of faith: if only the conflict could have been staved off long enough, then somehow, somewhere, we could have worked something out. It is legitimate, I think, to ask how? where? what?—at least, if these affirmations of faith are to be used as the premise for castigating the unhappy men who had the practical responsibility for finding solutions and failed.

Where have the revisionists gone astray? In part, the popularity of revisionism obviously parallels that of *Gone with the Wind*—the victors paying for victory by pretending literary defeat. But the essential problem is why history should be so vulnerable to this literary fashion; and this problem, I believe, raises basic questions about the whole modern view of history. It is perhaps stating the issue in too portentous terms. Yet I cannot escape the feeling that the vogue of revisionism is connected with the modern tendency to seek in optimistic sentimentalism an escape from the severe demands of moral decision; that it is the offspring of our modern sentimentality which at once evades the essential moral problems in the name of a superficial objectivity and asserts their unimportance in the name of an invincible progress.

The revisionists first glided over the implications of the fact that the slavery system was producing a closed society in the South. Yet that society increasingly had justified itself by a political and philosophical repudiation of free society; southern thinkers swiftly developed the anti-libertarian potentialities in a social system whose cornerstone, in Alexander H.

Stephens's proud phrase, was human bondage. In theory and in practice, the South organized itself with mounting rigor against ideas of human dignity and freedom, because such ideas inevitably threatened the basis of their own system. Professor Frank L. Owsley, the southern agrarian, has described inadvertently but accurately the direction in which the slave South was moving. "The abolitionists and their political allies were threatening the existence of the South as seriously as the Nazis threaten the existence of England," wrote Owsley in 1940; ". . . Under such circumstances the surprising thing is that so little was done by the South to defend its existence."

There can be no question that many southerners in the fifties had similar sentiments; that they regarded their system of control as ridiculously inadequate; and that, with the book-burning, the censorship of the mails, the gradual illegalization of dissent, the South was in process of creating a real machinery of repression in order more effectively "to defend its existence." No society, I suppose, encourages criticism of its basic institutions. Yet, when a democratic society acts in self-defense, it does so at least in the name of human dignity and freedom. When a society based on bond slavery acts to eliminate criticism of its peculiar institution, it outlaws what a believer in democracy can only regard as the abiding values of man. When the basic institutions are evil, in other words, the effect of attempts to defend their existence can only be the moral and intellectual stultification of the society.

A society closed in the defense of evil institutions thus creates moral differences far too profound to be solved by compromise. Such a society forces upon every one, both those living at the time and those writing about it later, the necessity for a moral judgment; and the moral judgment in such cases becomes an indispensable factor in the historical understanding.

The revisionists were commendably anxious to avoid the vulgar errors of the post-Civil War historians who pronounced smug individual judgments on the persons involuntarily involved in the tragedy of the slave system. Consequently they tried hard to pronounce no moral judgments at all on slavery. Slavery became important, in Craven's phrase, "only as a very ancient labor system, probably at this time rather near the end of its existence"; the attempt to charge this labor system with moral meanings was "a creation of inflamed imaginations." Randall, talking of the Kansas-Nebraska Act, could describe it as "a law intended to subordinate the slavery question and hold it in *proper* proportion" (my italics). I have quoted Randall's even more astonishing argument that, because major controversies between downstate and metropolis in Illinois stopped short of war, there was reason to believe that the Civil War could have been avoided. Are we to take it that the revisionists seriously believe that the downstate-metropolis fight in Illinois—or the agrarian-industrial fight in the Coolidge and Hoover administrations—were in any useful sense comparable to the difference between the North and South in 1861?

Because the revisionists felt no moral urgency themselves, they deplored as fanatics those who did feel it, or brushed aside their feelings as the artificial product of emotion and propaganda. The revisionist hero was Stephen A. Douglas, who always thought that the great moral problems could be solved by sleight-of-hand. The phrase "northern man of southern sentiments," Randall remarked, was "said opprobriously . . . as if it were a base thing for a northern man to work with his southern fellows."

By denying themselves insight into the moral dimension of the slavery crisis, in other words, the revisionists denied themselves a historical understanding of the intensities that caused the crisis. It was the moral issue of slavery, for example, that gave the struggles over slavery in the territories or over the enforcement of the fugitive slave laws their significance. These issues, as the revisionists have shown with cogency, were not in themselves basic. But they were the available issues; they were almost the only points within the existing constitutional framework where the moral conflict could be faced; as a consequence, they became charged with the moral and political dynamism of the central issue. To say that the Civil War was fought over the "unreal" issue of slavery in the territories is like saying that the Second World War was fought over the "unreal" issue of the invasion of Poland. The democracies could not challenge fascism inside Germany any more than opponents of slavery could challenge slavery inside the South; but the extension of slavery, like the extension of fascism, was an act of aggression which made a moral choice inescapable.

Let us be clear what the relationship of moral judgment to history is. Every historian, as we all know in an argument that surely does not have to be repeated [here], imports his own set of moral judgments into the writing of history by the very process of interpretation; and the phrase "every historian" includes the category "revisionist." Mr. De Voto in his paraphrases of the revisionist position has put admirably the contradictions on this point: as for "moral questions, God forbid. History will not put itself in the position of saying that any thesis may have been wrong, any cause evil. . . . History will not deal with moral values, though of course the Republican radicals were, well, culpable." The whole revisionist attitude toward abolitionists and radicals, repeatedly characterized by Randall as "unctuous" and "intolerant," overflows with the moral feeling which is so virtuously excluded from discussions of slavery.

An acceptance of the fact of moral responsibility does not license the historian to roam through the past ladling out individual praise and blame: such an attitude would ignore the fact that all individuals, including historians, are trapped in a web of circumstance which curtails their moral possibilities. But it does mean that there are certain essential issues on which it is necessary for the historian to have a position if he is to understand the great conflicts of history. These great conflicts are relatively few because there are few enough historical phenomena which we can confidently identify as evil. The essential issues appear, moreover, not in pure and absolute form, but incomplete and imperfect, compromised by the deep complexity of history. Their proponents may often be neurotics and fanatics, like the abolitionists. They may attain a social importance only when a configuration of non-moral factors—economic, political, social, military—permit them to do so.

Yet neither the nature of the context nor the pretensions of the proponents alter the character of the issue. And human slavery is certainly one of the few issues of whose evil we can be sure. It is not just "a very ancient labor system"; it is also a betrayal of the basic values of our Christian and democratic tradition. No historian can understand the circumstances which led to its abolition until he writes about it in its fundamental moral context. "History is supposed to understand the difference between a decaying economy

and an expanding one," as Mr. De Voto well said, "between solvency and bankruptcy, between a dying social idea and one coming to world acceptance. . . . It is even supposed to understand implications of the difference between a man who is legally a slave and one who is legally free."

"Revisionism in general has no position," De Voto continues, "but only a vague sentiment." Professor Randall well suggested the uncritical optimism of that sentiment when he remarked, "To suppose that the Union could not have been continued or slavery outmoded without the war and without the corrupt concomitants of war is hardly an enlightened assumption." We have here a touching afterglow of the admirable nineteenth-century faith in the full rationality and perfectibility of man; the faith that the errors of the world would all in time be "outmoded" (Professor Randall's use of this word is suggestive) by progress. Yet the experience of the twentieth century has made it clear that we gravely overrated man's capacity to solve the problems of existence within the terms of history.

This conclusion about man may disturb our complacencies about human nature. Yet it is certainly more in accord with history than Professor Randall's "enlightened" assumption that man can solve peaceably all the problems which overwhelm him. The unhappy fact is that man occasionally works himself into a log-jam; and that the log-jam must be burst by violence. We know that well enough from the experience of [past events]. Are we to suppose that some future historian will echo Professor Nevins' version of the "failure" of the eighteen-fifties and write: "The primary task of statesmanship in the nineteen-thirties was to furnish a workable adjustment between the United States and Germany, while offering strong inducements to the German people to abandon the police state and equal persuasions to the Americans to help the Nazis rather than scold them"? Will some future historian adapt Professor Randall's formula and write that the word "appeaser" was used "opprobriously" as if it were a "base" thing for an American to work with his Nazi fellow? Obviously this revisionism of the future (already foreshadowed in the work of Charles A. Beard) would represent, as we now see it, a fantastic evasion of the hard and unpleasant problems of the thirties. I doubt whether our present revisionism would make much more sense to the men of the eighteen-fifties.

The problem of the inevitability of the Civil War, of course, is in its essence a problem devoid of meaning. The revisionist attempt to argue that the war could have been avoided by "any kind of sane policy" is of interest less in its own right than as an expression of a characteristically sentimental conception of man and of history. And the great vogue of revisionism in the historical profession suggests, in my judgment, ominous weaknesses in the contemporary attitude toward history.

We delude ourselves when we think that history teaches us that evil will be "outmoded" by progress and that politics consequently does not impose on us the necessity for decision and for struggle. If historians are to understand the fullness of the social dilemma they seek to reconstruct, they must understand that sometimes there is no escape from the implacabilities of moral decision. When so-

cial conflicts embody great moral issues, these conflicts cannot be assigned for solution to the invincible march of progress; nor can they be by-passed with "objective" neutrality. Not many problems perhaps force this decision upon the historian. But, if any problem does in our history, it is the Civil War.

To reject the moral actuality of the Civil War is to foreclose the possibility of an adequate account of its causes. More than that, it is to misconceive and grotesquely to sentimentalize the nature of history. For history is not a redeemer, promising to solve all human problems in time; nor is man capable of transcending the limitations of his being. Man generally is entangled in insoluble problems; history is consequently a tragedy in which we are all involved, whose keynote is anxiety and frustration, not progress and fulfillment. Nothing exists in history to assure us that the great moral dilemmas can be resolved without pain; we cannot therefore be relieved from the duty of moral judgment on issues so appalling and inescapable as those involved in human slavery; nor can we be consoled by sentimental theories about the needlessness of the Civil War into regarding our own struggles against evil as equally needless.

One must emphasize, however, that this duty of judgment applies to issues. Because we are all implicated in the same tragedy, we must judge the men of the past with the same forbearance and charity which we hope the future will apply toward us.

POSTSCRIPT

DID THE DEMOCRATIC PROCESS FAIL
DURING THE CIVIL WAR?

The style and tone of these articles present as much contrast as their contents. Craven presents his views in a recognizable historical forum, using a traditional format to transfer historical information. Schlesinger, on the other hand, published his article in a periodical known for the discussion of controversial topics in a provocative manner. Craven presents an additional chapter in his revisionist interpretation, replete with historical documentation to convince his audience. Craven, however, seems unaware of the false dichotomy of his lead paragraph. Does an understanding of how the war came about preclude or, for that matter, negate why it occurred? These topics are not mutually exclusive as Craven would have us believe. Schlesinger attempts to convince by revealing the errors he thinks the revisionists have committed in trying to advance a kind of history which ignores fundamental moral questions. In addition to the close analysis in which he unmasks the weaknesses of the revisionist triumverate (Craven, Randall, Nevins) his essay includes statements which are turgid, rhetorical and (by his own admission) irrelevant. Perhaps Schlesinger's strongest argument is his insistence that morality is a crucial factor in interpreting history. It would appear that his salvos had some effect. Craven does more than pay lip service to the slavery question in his article which is the latest installment (1950) of work stretching back more than a decade. It was the early versions of that scholarship that Schlesinger targeted in 1949.

Is it possible that both historians are indulging in semantic rather than substantive debate? Are both interpretations excessively rhetorical? Shouldn't we consider the premises both historians assumed before putting pens to paper? Are their interpretations more heavily biased than usual?

The issue of compromise is at the center of both articles. Craven and Schlesinger assume diametrically opposed positions on the possibility of political compromise. Craven accepts compromise as an American tradition, a viable alternative, something to be relied on. Compromise is not possible to Schlesinger when moral issues are concerned. Here is a good starting place to examine the assumptions, biases and prejudices which add to the vitality of this historical debate.

Kenneth Stampp has edited a sample of contemporary and historical opinions about the Civil War called *The Causes of the Civil War* (Prentice-Hall, 1965). David M. Potter's *The Impending Crisis, 1848–1861* (Harper and Row, 1976) is the most recent detailed narrative.

ISSUE 18

WAS LINCOLN'S PRESIDENCY CRUCIAL TO THE NORTH'S VICTORY?

YES: David Donald, from *Lincoln Reconsidered: Essays on the Civil War Era* (Random House, 1956)

NO: Kenneth M. Stampp, from *The Southern Road to Appomattox* (Texas Western Press, 1969)

ISSUE SUMMARY

YES: Professor Donald argues that Lincoln concentrated all his energies and presidential powers on winning the war.
NO: Professor Stampp explains why the South subconsciously desired to lose.

Generations of historians have ranked Abraham Lincoln as one of our greatest presidents, perhaps *the* most outstanding. They have argued that without him, there might not be a United States today. Because of the Emancipation Proclamation, his reputation as our noblest folk hero adds to this high esteem. Lincoln has come to personify national unity; yet the other side of the story indicates Lincoln also had divisive effects.

He barely squeezed by the three other candidates in the election of 1860. He obtained only 40 percent of the popular vote (although the electoral college formula increased it to 58). Lincoln's victory motivated South Carolina, followed by Mississippi, Florida, Alabama, Georgia, Louisiana and Texas, to secede from the union. One of the new president's first executive orders, a summons for a militia of 75,000 men to suppress this "insurrection" as Lincoln called it, pushed Virginia, Arkansas, Tennessee and North Carolina into the arms of the Confederacy. The election of 1864 did not seem to contribute to a notion of Lincoln's greatness either. Lincoln received only 55 percent of the popular vote in

November 1864, two years after the Emancipation Proclamation and while General Sherman's troops were devastating Georgia, rending apart the South, and forcing the war to a conclusion.

Lincoln's role in precipitating the secession crisis seems easier to assess than his impact as commander in chief during the hostilities. Did the sixteenth president's greatness escape his contemporaries? Are his outstanding qualities more apparent in retrospect? The complexities of this issue unfold in many ways. Certainly people are a fundamental part of historical events but in an episode of the Civil War's magnitude, one particular individual, even the president of the United States, must not be disproportionately overrated. Did Lincoln run the country in a vacuum? Were not some members of his cabinet (Seward, Stanton, Chase) vigorous leaders? Military officials, members of Congress and the jurists of the Supreme Court also influenced the decisions made, or judged the constitutionality of their effects.

Larger factors helped determine the results of the conflict as much as any one person. Economic, demographic and technological circumstances at the beginning of the war must be evaluated. The changes which occurred in these material forces over the four years of fighting need consideration also. The South's demographic weakness, nine million inhabitants (over one third in bondage) compared to twenty-two million in the North, did not inhibit the Confederacy's military efforts at least during the initial years of the war. The North and its industrial might faced tremendous readjustments with an important source of domestic raw materials in the hands of its adversary.

In the search for some conclusions among the circumstances of the North's victory and the importance of Lincoln's direction of United States policy, there seems to have been one constant, time. Was not the length of the war a decisive factor? Perhaps *the* decisive factor? Would not the victory belong to whichever side could use attrition to its advantage?

Donald emphasized Lincoln's decisive personality, casting him as a great man of history. "Lincoln took quite literally the constitutional provision that 'the President shall be Commander in Chief of the Army and Navy of the United States,'" he wrote. "He not merely appointed and removed generals; he attempted to plan their campaigns." Stampp prefers a macroscopic explanation. Historical circumstance and group psychology are more significant to him than the importance of one highly-placed individual. He asked, "What circumstantial evidence is there to suggest that Southerners lost the Civil War, in part, because a significant number of them unconsciously felt that they had less to gain by winning than by losing?" Stampp partially answers his own question with this conclusion: "The history of the Confederacy is not that of a people with a sense of deep commitment to their cause—a feeling that without victory there is no future—for too many of them declined to make the all-out effort that victory would have required."

YES   David Donald

ABRAHAM LINCOLN AND THE
AMERICAN PRAGMATIC TRADITION

Everybody admits that Abraham Lincoln was a great statesman, but no two writers seem to agree upon the basis of his greatness. Some think he merits immortality as the spokesman of Republican principles—whatever they may be—but others give him most credit for being a kind of crypto-Democrat. In recent years major historians have debated whether Lincoln was the embodiment of the American conservative tradition or the personification of American liberalism.

Such arguments on the whole reveal more about their authors than about Lincoln, and often they evidence more an inclination to annex a major folk hero to some current cause than a desire to accept the past upon its own terms. To most men of his own day Lincoln seemed neither liberal nor conservative statesman; he was simply a rather ineffectual President. It is hard to remember how unsuccessful Lincoln's administration appeared to most of his contemporaries. He was, as J.G. Randall has pointed out in a brilliant essay, "The Unpopular Mr. Lincoln," a man censured and distrusted by all parties. Friendly critics viewed him as honest, well intentioned, but rather lacking in force; hostile ones, as weak, vacillating, and opportunistic. They agreed in sensing an absence of direction in Lincoln's administration, a seeming and puzzling lack of policy.

As President, he appeared not to take hold. Before he was inaugurated, seven worried states of the Deep South seceded, but Lincoln did little to avert a crisis. He issued no public statements, announced no plans for peace, and apparently spent his time growing a set of whiskers. On his way to Washington in February 1861 his speeches bore the obviously erroneous refrain: ". . . There is nothing going wrong. . . . There is nothing that really hurts anybody." After he was inaugurated, war broke out and four more states deserted Lincoln's government for the Confederacy. The President called for 75,000 nine-month volunteers to fight a war that was ultimately to enroll more than 2,000,000 soldiers on both sides and to cost $20,000,000,000. Northern newspapermen and politicians demanded a prompt advance against the Confederate armies, and under their pressure the President yielded and ordered the army "On to Richmond"—and on to Bull Run. Other disasters followed with monotonous regularity—the Peninsula campaign; Second Bull Run; Fredericksburg; Chancellorsville—and the few Federal victories were as costly as the defeats.

The President seemed unable to cope with the crisis. As an administrator, he appeared hopelessly incompetent. He was a born enemy of rules. His secretaries fought a constant and losing battle to systematize his schedule. For a long while he refused to put any restrictions upon the throngs of visitors, petitioners, and office-seekers who besieged his White House office. "They do not want much," he explained, "and they get very little . . . I know how I would feel in their place." Finally, under the pressure of urgent war business, the President was persuaded to limit these tiring visitors' hours, but even then he was constantly making exceptions for needy cases.

His Cabinet was of little help in organizing the war effort. For a while he held no regular Cabinet meetings at all. Then, when they were held, they seldom dealt with serious matters of policy. As a usual thing, Lincoln permitted each Cabinet officer to run his own department without control, guidance, or interference. When Secretary Chase presented proposed financial measures for his consideration, the President agreed without a question, saying; "You understand these things. I do not." But along with this aloofness, Lincoln also had a fondness for what seemed to be random meddling with his administrators. Just when a Cabinet officer had worked out some systematic plan for handling his department's business, he would unexpectedly be greeted by petitioners bearing brief but authoritative notes signed by the President: "Let this woman have her son out of Old Capital Prison." "Attorney-General, please make out and send me a pardon in this case." "Injustice has probably been done in this case, Sec. of War please examine it."

As the war dragged on and defeat followed defeat, nearly every segment of Northern opinion showed distrust of the unsuccessful President. Copperheads, Radicals, War Democrats, Conservative Republicans—all attacked Lincoln. Day after day indignant Senators and irate Representatives stalked into the White House, blustering, threatening, cajoling, all demanding that the President take a firm stand and do something—indeed, do almost anything—positive. "Let him," wrote Lincoln's disillusioned law partner, Herndon, "hang some Child or woman, if he has not Courage to hang a *man*." "Does he suppose he can crush—squelch out this huge rebellion by pop guns filled with rose water."

To such critics Lincoln amiably gave the often repeated reply: "My policy is to have no policy." To men with plans, to men with axes to grind or hatchets to use, the President's remark was incomprehensible. Self-righteous Secretary Salmon P. Chase snorted that it was an "idiotic notion." But Lincoln was not being flippant or evasive; he was enunciating the basic premise of his political philosophy and at the same time expressing the fundamental pragmatic element in the American political tradition.

The President's statement sounded simple, and if it had come from another man, it might have revealed nothing more than simple-mindedness. But when Lincoln said: "My policy is to have no policy," he was enunciating, either directly or by implication, a series of fundamental political principles.

(1) He was rejecting the doctrinaire approach to problems, declining to become attached to inflexible solutions or to ideological labels. Consistency meant little to Lincoln, and he refused to measure his associates by rigid tests of doctrinal purity. He was concerned with results. Long before the war, in 1844, he had energetically supported Henry Clay for President, believing that the Kentuckian, though himself a slaveholder, would not permit the further expansion of slavery. Simon-pure abolitionists took the opposing view—how could a real antislavery man vote for a slaveholder?—and they wasted their votes on the doctrinally pure but politically hopeless third-party candidate. Their vote helped elect James K. Polk and to bring on the Mexican War. To Lincoln the abolitionists' way of thinking seemed "wonderful." To their contention that "We are not to do *evil* that *good* may come," he countered with another, more apt Biblical injunction: "By the *fruit* the tree is to be known."

A decade later, ironically enough, the situation was reversed, for conservative Whigs hesitated to oppose Stephen A. Douglas's Kansas-Nebraska scheme because they disliked to join the suspected abolitionists. "Good humoredly" Lincoln told his Whig friends that they were being "very silly," and he gave them some practical advice: "Stand with anybody that stands RIGHT." Stand with him while he is right and PART with him when he goes wrong. Stand WITH the abolitionist in restoring the Missouri Compromise; and stand AGAINST him when he attempts to repeal the fugitive slave law.

So pragmatic an attitude was, of course, shocking to those Americans who lived by dogmas, by the hoary certainties of the past. No one could have exceeded Lincoln in his admiration for the founders of the Republic. "I have never had a feeling politically that did not spring from the sentiments embodied in the Declaration of Independence," he declared, and he spoke reverently of the "great authority" of the Revolutionary Fathers. But he warned his own age not to be bound by history. "The dogmas of the quiet past," he wrote, in an annual message to Congress, "are inadequate to the stormy present. The occasion is piled high with difficulty, and we must rise with the occasion. As our case is new, so we must think anew, and act anew. We must disenthrall ourselves, and then we shall save our country."

(2) Rejecting ideological labels, Lincoln tried to face political reality as it was, not as he would have it become. No man more carefully distinguished between "is" and "ought to be." On slavery, for example, Lincoln's personal views had long been a matter of public record. "If slavery is not wrong," he said simply, "nothing is wrong." But the President of the United States could not act as Abraham Lincoln wished. He was President not of the antislavery forces but of a disunited and divided people, and he must serve the general welfare. "I am naturally antislavery," the President declared. "And yet I have never understood that the Presidency conferred upon me an unrestricted right to act officially upon this judgment and feeling."

As a man he wished to eliminate slavery everywhere, but as President it became his official and painful duty to rebuke his subordinates who took extralegal steps to uproot the peculiar institution. When Generals John Charles Frémont and

David Hunter issued edicts liberating the slaves in their military commands, Lincoln promptly overruled both commanders. Their hasty action would have cost the Union the support of the loyal slaveholders of Kentucky, and if Kentucky seceded, Missouri and Maryland might well follow. "These all against us," Lincoln explained, "and the job on our hands is too large for us. We would as well consent to separation at once, including the surrender of this capitol."

While Radical antislavery men grumbled about Lincoln's subservience to "negrophobic" counsels, the President was realistically warning his Southern friends that the war meant death for slavery. As Federal troops advanced into the South, flocks of Negroes left the plantations and fled to freedom. Whenever a raiding party returned from Virginia or Tennessee, it had behind it "an outlandish tatterdemalion parade of refugees, men and women and helpless children, people jubilant and bewildered and wholly defenseless, their eyes on the north star." It was not possible, the President advised their owners, to reduce these people again to slavery; there was no law that could remove the idea of freedom from the heart of a Negro. Earnestly Lincoln advised the border states to move toward gradual, compensated emancipation while there was still time.

Equally realistic was Lincoln's advice to the Negroes themselves. The President himself was color-blind; he shared neither the antislavery man's idealization of the Negro as God's image in ebony nor the slaveholder's view of the Negro as an inferior race. He had warm friends and countless admirers among the Negro people, and he thought of the black man first of all as a man. But again he separated his personal feelings from what he regarded as his official duty when he summoned a group of Northern free Negro leaders to the White House in August 1862. Plainly and painfully he told them the facts of life: "You and we are different races. We have between us a broader difference than exists between almost any other two races." Right or wrong, he continued, the difference meant that the Negro was unassimilable in American society. Freedom would not solve their problems. ". . . Even when you cease to be slaves, you are yet far removed from being placed on an equality with the white race. You are cut off from many of the advantages which the other race enjoy." If the Negroes wanted to avoid a future of menial subjection, they should think of colonizing, under United States protection, say in Haiti or in Central America. "It is better for us both," the President concluded, "to be separated." Such advice seemed inhuman to the idealists of the time, and it is unpalatable to the present-day liberal as well; yet clearly Lincoln had correctly analyzed the current state of American popular sentiment.

(3) Refusing to force reality to fit a formula, Lincoln insisted that every problem was unique, that issues could only be decided one at a time, that conflicts need be resolved only when they actually arose. Again and again he told anecdotes to illustrate his view. "The pilots on our Western rivers steer from *point to point* as they call it—setting the course of the boat no farther than they can see," he said "and that is all I propose to myself. . . ." He was not, he told a questioner, going "to cross 'Big Muddy' until he reached it."

War-torn and politics-ridden Missouri presented to President Lincoln a never-ending source of problems. Radicals and Conservative Republicans fought the secessionists, each other, and also the Federal military commanders in that state with about equal ferocity. All factions kept sending deputations to Washington, calling upon Lincoln to take a firm stand and commit himself to a clear-cut solution. The temptation must have been almost irresistible to take sides, to apply some simple formula to the Missouri problem in order to end the strife. Lincoln rejected the temptation. The governor of Missouri demanded that the President recognize his right to appoint the commanding officers of the state militia; his political opponents urged that, as the militia was now in the Federal service, the appointments must be made by Washington. Quietly Lincoln bypassed the issue. He permitted the Missouri governor to commission the officers first—and then he recommissioned them himself. "After a good deal of reflection," he explained to the governor, "I concluded that it was better to make a rule for the practical matter in hand . . . than to decide a general question, . . . which, while it might embrace the practical question mentioned, might also be the nest in which forty other troublesome questions would be hatched. I would rather meet them *as* they come, than *before* they come, trusting that some of them may not come at all."

(4) The ability to face reality means, of course, a willingness to change with events. Lincoln willingly admitted that his opinions and his actions were shaped by forces beyond his control. His shifting position on emancipation clearly illustrates his flexibility. At first Lincoln and his administration were committed to the Crittenden Resolution, declaring that the purpose of the war was simply to restore the Union without disturbing slavery at all. Then the pressures for emancipation began mounting. By 1862 American diplomats warned that only a firm antislavery stand would check the pro-Confederate sympathies of France and England. Northern governors bluntly told the President

that their antislavery young men were unwilling to enlist in an army still legally bound to preserve the hated institution. Military leaders like General Grant demanded more men and pointed to the large numbers of Negroes who would willingly serve for their freedom.

As events moved, so moved the President. He was not going to act blindly, he assured a group of antislavery churchmen; there was certainly no point in issuing proclamations that "must necessarily be inoperative, like the Pope's bull against the comet." But he did act when ends and means were fitted, and the Emancipation Proclamation was a masterpiece of practical political sagacity. Lincoln rightly regarded the Proclamation as his chief claim to historical fame, but he was always careful to insist that it was a product of circumstances. He had responded to the changing times. In 1864 he wrote to an admirer: "I claim not to have controlled events, but confess plainly that events have controlled me."

(5) As a pragmatic politician, Lincoln was careful not to make irredeemable pledges against the future. Characteristically, he approached the difficult problem of reconstruction with an open mind and an absence of commitment. When Federal troops overran Louisiana and Arkansas, some sort of civil government had to be re-established, and the President, as commander-in-chief, had to act. He offered a lenient program of amnesty and reconstruction, under which the states would be restored to the Union if only ten per cent of the 1860 voting population assented. He did not attempt to set up loyalty tests that would disqualify former Confederates from participating in the elections. "On principle I dislike an oath which requires a man to swear he *has* not done wrong," he told Secretary Stanton.

"It rejects the Christian principle of forgiveness on terms of repentance. I think it is enough if the man does no wrong here-after."

Lincoln's hopes for generous amnesty and quick restoration in the South have often been distorted by historians, who speak of "Lincoln's plan of reconstruction" as though the President had a blueprint for peace. It is true that later, in the unskillful hands of Andrew Johnson, Lincoln's suggestions were converted into dogmas, but it is important to remember that while Lincoln was alive his views on reconstruction were constantly changing. A shrewd observer like James G. Blaine felt "that Mr. Lincoln had no fixed plan for the reconstruction of the States." . . .

For the view that Lincoln dramatically extended the range of executive power there is certainly abundant evidence. In 1861 when the Confederates fired upon Fort Sumter, he acted with such vigorous promptness that his critics cried out against his "dictatorship." Without consulting Congress, he decided that a state of war existed, summoned the militia to defeat this combination "too powerful to be suppressed by the ordinary course of judicial proceedings," and enlarged the size of the regular United States army. Without congressional appropriation or approval he entrusted two million dollars of government funds to his private agents in New York in order to pay for "military and naval measures necessary for the defense and support of the government." Directing General Winfield Scott "to suspend the writ of Habeas Corpus for the public safety," he authorized the arbitrary arrest of suspected secessionists and other enemies of the government.

As the war progressed, Lincoln further extended his executive powers, even in the loyal states of the Union. "[B]y degrees," as he explained in 1863, he had come to feel that "strong measures" were "indispensable to the public Safety." Civil rights throughout the North were drastically curbed. Both Secretary of State William H. Seward, who was in charge of the arbitrary arrests made during 1861, and Secretary of War Edwin M. Stanton, who took control in the following year, exercised power "almost as free from restraint as a dictator or a sultan." Nobody knows how may Northern civilians were imprisoned without due process of law; estimates range from fifteen thousand to thirty-eight thousand. It required but a line from the President to close down a censorious newspaper, to banish a Democratic politician, or to arrest suspected members of a state legislature.

Over the Union armed forces, too, Lincoln exercised unprecedented authority. Presidential order, not congressional enactment, instituted in 1862 the first national program of conscription in United States history. Disregarding the explicit constitutional provision that Congress should "make Rules for the Government and Regulation of the land and naval Forces," Lincoln authorized Professor Francis Lieber to draw up and General Henry W. Halleck to proclaim General Orders No. 100, spelling out the legal rules for the conduct of the war.

Lincoln took quite literally the constitutional provision that "the President shall be Commander in Chief of the Army and Navy of the United States." He not merely appointed and removed generals; he attempted to plan their campaigns. At his insistence General Irvin McDowell advanced to First Bull Run and to defeat in July 1861. Lincoln's unsolicited strategic advice drove General George B. McClellan, McDowell's successor, into hiding at the house of a friend so as to escape "browsing presidents." During the winter of 1861 when McClellan, ill with typhoid, did not advance, Lincoln issued his unprecedented President's General War Order No. 1, taking personal direction of five Union armies and two naval flotillas and ordering them simultaneously to advance on February 22. The fact that General McClellan, upon recovering, persuaded Lincoln to abandon his plan did not mean the end of presidential war-making. In fact, even at the end of the war, after Lincoln had named U. S. Grant general-in-chief, the President continued to have a personal hand in shaping Union strategy. Lincoln himself bluntly declared that should he think any plan of campaign ill-advised, he "would scarcely allow the attempt to be made, if the general in command should desire to make it."

To an even greater extent Lincoln asserted his presidential powers over the rebellious South. His Emancipation Proclamation, which Charles A. Beard called "the most stupendous act of sequestration in the history of Anglo-Saxon jurisprudence," was a presidential act, performed without authorization from Congress— performed, indeed, when the President thought Congress had no power to authorize it. Lincoln's December 1863 proclamation of amnesty and pardon marked another major expansion of presidential powers. Without the approval of Congress he established provisional courts in conquered Southern states and gave them "the unlimited power of determining every question that could be the subject of judicial decision." In naming military governors for the states of Louisiana, Arkansas, and Tennessee, the President, again without congressional authorization, created offices unknown to the American Constitution. In establishing new and securely loyal ad-

ministrations in these ex-Confederate states, the military governors were not obliged to observe normal constitutional procedures. Lincoln himself directed them: "Follow forms of law as far as convenient. . . ."

Lincoln's record, then, abundantly justifies the conclusion of George Fort Milton that no other President in American history has "found so many new sources of executive power, nor so expanded and perfected those others already had used." . . .

The party to which Lincoln belonged for most of his life originated in objections to the "executive usurpation" of Andrew Jackson. Whig leaders concealed their economic motives and personal aspirations under denunciation of Jackson as "a detestable, ignorant, reckless, vain and malignant tyrant." Just as their ancestors of 1776 had stood against another executive usurper, so the Whigs of the 1830's fought against the "dictator" in the White House. Henry Clay and Daniel Webster bewailed the policy of the Democrats, which was tending rapidly toward "a total change of the pure republican character of our government, and to the concentration of all power in the hands of one man." William Henry Harrison, the first Whig President, made his inaugural address a classic exposition of his party's creed: ". . . it is preposterous to suppose that . . . the President, placed at the capital, in the center of the country could better understand the wants and wishes of the people than their own immediate representatives who spend a part of every year among them . . . and [are] bound to them by the triple tie of interest, duty, and affection." Zachary Taylor, the only other President elected by the Whig party, held the same views: "The Executive . . . has authority to recommend (not to dictate) measures to Congress. Having performed that duty, the Executive department of the

Government cannot rightfully control the decision of Congress on any subject of legislation . . . the . . . veto will never be exercised by me except . . . as an extreme measure, to be resorted to only in extraordinary cases. . . .". . .

Lincoln was, of course, too strong a personality to submit to such dictation. Indeed, even during the Taylor administration he had realized that the Whig theory of Cabinet responsibility gave "The President the . . . ruinous character of being a mere man of straw." Consequently, when Seward in April 1861 proposed to become virtual premier of the new administration in order to lead it on a daring new policy of foreign embroilments, Lincoln quietly squelched him, declaring: ". . . if this must be done, I must do it." Similarly, when preparing to issue the Emancipation Proclamation, Lincoln told his Cabinet advisers: "I have got you together to hear what I have written down. I do not wish your advice about the main matter—for that I have determined for myself. . . . If there is anything in the expressions I use, or in any other minor matter, which anyone of you thinks had best be changed, I shall be glad to receive the suggestions."

On key policies, therefore, especially those involving the use of the war power, Lincoln, like Harrison and Taylor before him, departed from the Whig theory of Cabinet responsibility, but he could not rid himself of the political ideas with which he had been raised. Given the alternatives of imposing his own will upon his Cabinet or of submitting to their majority opinion, Lincoln evaded the decision by treating the Cabinet as an unnecessary nuisance, allowing it to consider only insignificant matters. Since there was no real consultation to formulate common policy and since the President could not personally oversee the details of everyday administration, each secretary, however disagreeable, self-promoting, or even conspiratorial, had a free hand in conducting his own department's affairs.

These weaknesses of Lincoln's administration seem to stand in sharp contrast with the President's energetic assertion of his powers over civil liberties, over the military forces, and over the rebellious South, but there is no evidence that Lincoln himself was troubled by any inconsistency in his roles. Necessity, not political theory, caused him to make his first sweeping assertions of executive authority during the secession crisis. The onset of civil war posed the immediate, practical dilemma, he declared later, "whether, using only the existing means, agencies, and processes which Congress had provided, I should let the government fall at once into ruin, or whether, availing myself of the broader powers conferred by the Constitution in cases of insurrection, I would make an effort to save it with all its blessings for the present age and for posterity." When the question was so posed, the answer became simple. "Necessity knows no law," he thought; consequently it was obligatory for him in this crisis to take strong measures, "some of which," he admitted, "were without any authority of law," in order to save the government.

When it did become necessary for Lincoln to justify his actions, he found his defense in the war powers granted him under the Constitution. ". . . as Commander in Chief of the Army and Navy, in time of war," he asserted, "I suppose I have a right to take any measure which may best subdue the enemy." Though critics claimed that the President was asserting dictatorial authority, it is clear that Lincoln himself took a narrower view of his powers. For example, he rejected the application of a general to construct a railroad in Missouri, which, it was claimed, would have some military utility. Since real military necessity was not shown, Lincoln felt this was an unwarranted extension of executive power. "... I have been," he assured Congress, "unwilling to go beyond the pressure of necessity in the unusual exercise of power."

The complex problem of emancipation shows the degree to which Lincoln's conception of his war powers served both as a source for executive action and as a restriction upon such action. His personal preferences, the expediencies of politics, the thundering pressure from Northern governors, and the growing sentiment that emancipation would aid the Union cause abroad all urged him during 1861 and 1862 to move against slavery. He delayed, not because he doubted his constitutional power, but because he questioned the necessity. "The truth is," he told a Louisiana loyalist, "that what is done, and omitted, about slaves, is done and omitted on the same military necessity." By late 1862 when necessity clearly demanded the abolition of slavery, Lincoln issued his proclamation of freedom, "as Commander in Chief, of the Army and Navy of the United States in time of actual armed rebellion against authority and government of the United States, and as a fit and necessary war measure for suppressing said rebellion." The Emancipation Proclamation, he declared later, had "no constitutional or legal justification, except as a military measure." ...

NO

Kenneth M. Stampp

THE SOUTHERN ROAD
TO APPOMATTOX

Not long ago one of America's best political commentators made an observation about the problem of causation in history that every responsible historian
would surely endorse:

> I hold a kind of Tolstoyan view of history and believe that it is hardly ever possible
> to determine the real truth about how we got from here to there. Since I find it ex-
> tremely difficult to uncover my own motives, I hesitate to deal with those of other
> people, and I positively despair at the thought of ever being really sure about what
> has moved whole nations and whole generations of mankind. No explanation of
> the causes and origins of any war—of any large happening in history—can ever be
> for me much more than a plausible one, a reasonable hypothesis.

This is a position to which I fully subscribe, and I believe that it is as valid
for explanations of why a war was won or lost as for explanations of why a
war began.

With this cautionary statement in mind, I am going to suggest one of the
conditions, among several, that may help to explain why the South lost the
Civil War. I think there is reason to believe that many Southerners—how many
I cannot say, but enough to affect the outcome of the war—who outwardly
appeared to support the Confederate cause had inward doubts about its validity,
and that, in all probability, some unconsciously even hoped for its defeat. Like
all historical explanations, my hypothesis is not subject to definitive proof; but
I think it can be established as circumstantially plausible, because it is a reasonable explanation for a certain amount of empirical evidence.

All interpretations of the defeat of the Confederacy fall into two broad
categories: those that stress the South's physical handicaps, and those that
stress human failings. Explanations in the first category emphasize the overwhelming preponderance of northern manpower and economic resources.
To some historians it is enough to note that the North had four times as many
men of military age as the South, ten times as productive an industrial plant,
three times as many miles of railroads in operation, and far greater supplies

of raw materials. Moreover, the North had a large merchant marine and sufficient naval power to establish an effective blockade of southern ports, whereas the South had virtually no merchant marine and no navy at all. "The prime cause [of Confederate defeat] must have been economic," argues Richard N. Current. "Given the vast superiority of the North in men and materials, in instruments of production, in communication facilities, in business organization and skill—and assuming for the sake of the argument no more than rough equality in statecraft and generalship—the final outcome seems all but inevitable." . . .

The theme of political failure has several variations. According to one of them, the widespread assertion of the constitutional doctrine of state rights during the war crisis made southern defeat certain. Frank L. Owsley maintains that "if the political system of the South had not broken down under the weight of an impracticable doctrine put into practice in the midst of a revolution, the South might have established its independence." He suggests that on the gravestone of the Confederacy should be carved these words: "Died of State Rights." Owsley provides ample illustrations of the extremes to which some Confederate politicians went in defense of the sovereignty of the states.

Unquestionably the state-rights doctrinaires helped to paralyze the hands of the Confederate government and thus grievously injured their own cause. But this explanation of Confederate defeat also raises questions, because before the war most southern politicians had not been consistent state-rights doctrinaires. Instead, like Northerners, they had shown a good deal of flexibility in their constitutional theories, and they had been willing to tolerate a relatively vigorous federal government as long as it heeded southern needs. They had not objected to a federally subsidized transcontinental railroad—along a southern route; they had not objected to federal appropriations for internal improvements—if the appropriations were for the improvement of transportation along southern rivers; and they showed no fear of creeping federal tyranny when they demanded effective federal action to recover fugitive slaves or to protect slavery in the territories. Indeed, some southern politicians seemed to show less constitutional flexibility in dealing with a government of their own creation than they had in dealing with the federal government before 1861.

David Donald offers another variation on the theme of Confederate political failure. He argues that the basic weakness of the Confederacy was that "the Southern people insisted upon retaining their democratic, individualistic rights." In the North civil rights were more severely compromised, the soldier was better disciplined, and regimentation was more readily accepted. Therefore, Professor Donald concludes, "we should write on the tombstone of the Confederacy: 'Died of Democracy.'"

Before the Civil War, needless to say, the South had not been notably more democratic than the North; and at some points Donald seems to equate democracy with poor organization, political ineptitude, and chaos. But there is truth in his generalization, which raises still another question: Why was it that Northerners, who were every bit as democratic and almost as individualistic as Southerners, by and large were willing to tolerate more regimentation for the sake of their cause than Southerners appeared ready to tolerate for the sake of theirs? The question, of course, is one of degree, for many

Northerners also resisted war measures such as conscription and encroachments on civil liberties.

Bell I. Wiley adds a final touch to the behavioral approach to Confederate defeat. "Perhaps the most costly of the Confederacy's shortcomings," he suggests, "was the disharmony among its people. A cursory glance at the Confederacy reveals numerous instances of bitter strife. . . . Behind the battle of bullets waged with the invaders was an enormous war of words and emotions among Confederates themselves which began before secession and which eventually became so intense that it sapped the South's vitality and hastened Northern victory." In a recent study of Confederate politics, Eric L. McKitrick was also struck by the bickering "that seeped in from everywhere to soften the very will of the Confederacy."

Collectively, all these behavioral problems—the failure of political leadership, the absurd lengths to which state rights were carried, the reluctance of Southerners to accept the discipline that war demanded, and the internal conflicts among the southern people—point to a Confederate weakness that matched in importance its physical handicaps. This was a weakness of morale. Assuming rough equality in military training and similar military traditions, a country with inferior resources and manpower can hope to defeat a more powerful adversary only if it enjoys decidedly superior morale in its civilian population. High morale is the product of passionate dedication to a cause, which creates a willingness to subordinate personal interests to its success. This is what has sometimes enabled small states to resist successfully the aggression of stronger neighbors, and nationalist movements to succeed against colonial powers. In such cases the fires of patriotism, fed by a genuine national identity, burned fiercely, and the longing for political freedom produced a spirit of self-sacrifice. When the partisans of a cause have no doubts about its validity, when they view the consequences of defeat as unbearable, morale is likely to be extremely high. . . .

That southern morale was not high enough and dedication to the cause fierce enough to offset the Confederacy's physical handicaps has sometimes been attributed to the failure of its leaders to perform their duties as propagandists and morale builders. Charles W. Ramsdell holds the politicians responsible for failing to build an efficient propaganda organization or to portray some compelling issue for which the southern people would have made great sacrifices. Similarly, Bell I. Wiley blames both Jefferson Davis and the Confederate Congress for not realizing "the necessity of winning the hearts and minds of the people." To David M. Potter the prime responsibility for the failure to dramatize the southern cause belonged to President Davis. One of his major shortcomings was his inability to "communicate with the people of the Confederacy. He seemed to think in abstractions and to speak in platitudes."

If Davis had a penchant for abstract and platitudinous discourse, most other Confederate politicians and publicists, when upholding the Confederate cause, seemed to suffer from the same defect. Yet the South had more than its share of able speakers and editors, who exploited as best they could the available issues: the menace of a ruthless northern invader, the need to defend the constitutional principles of the Founding Fathers, and the threat to southern civilization posed by northern abolitionists and their doctrine of racial equality. Significantly, however, only occasionally did they identify the Confederacy with slavery. "Our new Government," Vice President Alexander H. Stephens once boldly proclaimed, "is founded upon . . . the great truth that the negro is not equal to the white man; that slavery, subordination to the superior race, is his natural and moral condition. This, our new Government, is the first, in the history of the world, based upon this great physical, philosophical and moral truth." In his message to Congress, April 29, 1861, President Davis declared that "the labor of African slaves was and is indispensable" to the South's economic development. "With interests of such overwhelming magnitude imperiled, the people of the Southern States were driven by the conduct of the North to the adoption of some course of action to avert the danger with which they were openly menaced." This rhetoric was hardly inspiring, but, more important, neither was the cause it supported. Confederate propagandists apparently found the defense of slavery a poor tool with which to build southern morale, and they usually laid stress on other issues.

This reluctance of southern propagandists candidly to identify the Confederacy with slavery helps to explain their sterile rhetoric and their dismal failure; for, in my opinion, slavery was the key factor that gave the antebellum South its distinct identity, and the supposed northern threat to slavery was the basic cause of secession. To understand why southern propagandists failed, one must, in addition to evaluating their skill and techniques, compare the issues at their disposal with those at the disposal of their antagonists. Northern propagandists exploited all the historic traditions associated with the federal Union; reaffirmed America's mission and manifest destiny; proclaimed that democracy and self-government were on trial; above all,

identified their cause with the principles of the Declaration of Independence. These were the themes that Lincoln developed in the letters, speeches, and state papers which we remember a century later. It is of the utmost significance that no southern leader, even if he had had Lincoln's skill with words, could have claimed for the Confederacy a set of war aims that fired the nineteenth-century imagination as did those described in the Gettysburg Address. One wonders what Lincoln could have done with the issues available to him in the South, what even Jefferson Davis might have done with those that every northern politician had available to him.

When southern propagandists found it expedient, for reasons of domestic policy as well as foreign, to soft-pedal the very *cause* of the war, the Confederacy was at a considerable disadvantage as far as its moral position was concerned. This may help to explain why the Confederate Congress contained no group as fiercely dedicated to the southern cause as the Radical Republicans were to the northern cause. It illuminates Roy F. Nichols' impression that southern leaders were "beset by psychological handicaps." In short, it locates one of the fundamental reasons for the weakness of southern morale. It was due not only to the failure of those who tried to uphold the cause, important as that may have been; but, viewed as an appeal to the minds and emotions of nineteenth-century Americans, it was also due to the inherent frailty of the cause itself.

At this point, keeping the southern morale problem in mind, I would like to introduce my hypothesis that many seemingly loyal Confederates lacked a deep commitment to the southern cause and that some unconsciously even desired to lose the war. In the study of human behavior we frequently encounter cases of persons involved in conflicts which outwardly they seem to be striving to win, when, for reasons of which they are hardly conscious, they are in fact inviting defeat. I believe that there is considerable circumstantial evidence indicating that an indeterminate but significant number of Southerners were behaving in this manner, and I would like to suggest two reasons why unconsciously they might have welcomed defeat, or at least declined to give that "last full measure" which might have avoided it.

The first reason is related to the circumstances of southern secession. Fundamentally this movement was not the product of genuine southern nationalism; indeed, except for the institution of slavery, the South had little to give it a clear national identity. It had no natural frontiers; its white population came from the same stocks as the northern population; its political traditions and religious beliefs were not significantly different from those of the North; and the notion of a distinct southern culture was largely a figment of the imaginations of proslavery propagandists. Few of the conditions that underlay nineteenth- and twentieth-century nationalist movements in other parts of the world were present in the antebellum South. . . .

Defeat gave Southerners another reward: a way to rid themselves of the moral burden of slavery. This is the second reason why I think that some of them, once they found themselves locked in combat with the North, unconsciously wanted to lose. To suggest as I do that slavery gave the South such identity as it had, caused secession and war, and at the same time gave some Southerners a reason for wanting to lose the war will, I admit, take some explaining.

Let me begin with what I believe to be a fact, namely, that a large number of white Southerners, however much they tried, could not persuade themselves that slavery was a positive good, defensible on Christian and ethical principles. In spite of their defense of slavery and denial of its abuses, many of them, as their unpublished records eloquently testify, knew that their critics were essentially right. In saying this, I do not think I am judging nineteenth-century men by twentieth-century standards, for among the romanticists of the nineteenth century there was no greater moral good than individual liberty. Hence, the dimensions of the South's moral problem cannot be appreciated unless one understands that slavery was, by the South's own values, an abomination. The problem would not have been nearly as serious for Southerners if abolitionist criticism, strident and abrasive though it often was, had not been a mere echo of their own consciences.

No analysis of the Old South, writes Professor Sellers, "that misses the inner turmoil of the antebellum Southerner can do justice to the central tragedy of the southern experience. . . . Southerners were at least subconsciously aware of the 'detestable paradox' of 'our every-day sentiments of liberty' while holding beings in slavery." Their general misgivings about slavery "burrowed beneath the surface of the southern mind, where they kept gnawing away the shaky foundations on which Southerners sought to rebuild their morale and self-confidence as a slave-holding people." Wilbur J. Cash insists that the Old South "in its secret heart always carried a powerful and uneasy sense of the essential rightness of the nineteenth century's position on slavery. . . . This Old South, in short, was a society beset by the specters of defeat, of shame, of guilt—a society driven by the need to bolster its morale, to nerve its arm against waxing odds, to justify itself in its own eyes and in those of the world."

To be sure, a basic purpose of the pro-slavery argument, with its historical, biblical, philosophical, and scientific defenses, was to soothe the troubled consciences of slaveholders. This is evident in the frequency with which they recited the argument to themselves and to each other in their diaries and letters. But it did not seem to be enough. No people secure in their conviction that slavery was indeed a positive good and unaware of any contradictions between theory and practice would have quarreled with the outside world so aggressively and reassured themselves so often as the slaveholders did. "The problem for the South," William R. Taylor believes, "was not that it lived by an entirely different set of values and civic ideals but rather that it was forced either to live with the values of the nation at large or—as a desperate solution—to invent others, others which had even less relevance to the Southern situation. . . . More and more it became difficult for Southerners to live in peace with themselves: to accept the aspirations and the ideals of the nation and, at the same time, accept the claims and rationalizations produced by the South's special pleaders. Almost invariably they found themselves confronted with contradictions of the most troubling and disquieting kind."

I do not mean to suggest that every slaveholder was guilt-ridden because of slavery. The private papers of many of them give no sign of such a moral crisis—only a nagging fear of slave insurrections and bitter resentment at outside meddling in the South's affairs. Countless slaveholders looked upon Negroes as subhuman, or at least so far inferior to whites as to be suited only for bondage, and some showed little sensitivity about the ugly aspects of slavery. On the other hand, many slaveholders, perhaps most, were more or less tormented by the dilemma they were in. They could not, of their own volition, give up the advantages of slavery—a profitable labor system in which they had a $2 billion capital investment. They dreaded the adjustments they would have to make if they were to live in the same region with four million free Negroes, for their racial attitudes were much like those of most other white Americans, North and South. Yet they knew that slavery betrayed the American tradition of individual liberty and natural rights and that the attack on it was in the main valid. . . .

Indeed, I believe that under these circumstances not only the Civil War but the outcome as we know it was unavoidable. Southerners, many of whom were unsure of their goals and tormented by guilt about slavery, having founded a nation on nothing more substantial than anger and fear, were in no position to overcome the North's physical advantages. Moreover, at least some of them must have been troubled, at some conscious or unconscious level, by the question of what precisely was to be gained from winning the war— whether more in fact might be gained from losing it. For it soon became evident that, in addition to restoring the South to the Union, defeat would be the doom of slavery. Thus President Lincoln and the Union Congress would do for the slaveholders what even the more sensitive among them seemed unable to do for themselves— resolve once and for all the conflict between their deeply held values and their peculiar and archaic institution.

What circumstantial evidence is there to suggest that Southerners lost the Civil War in part because a significant number of them unconsciously felt that they had less to gain by winning than by losing? There is, first of all, the poor performance of some of the South's talented and experienced political leaders; the uninspiring record of the Confederate Congress; the aggressive assertion of state rights even though it was a sure road to defeat; and the internal bickering and lack of individual commitment that would have made possible the discipline essential to victory. The history of the Confederacy is not that of a people with a sense of deep commitment to their cause—a feeling that without victory there is no future—for too many of them declined to make the all-out effort that victory would have required.

Equally significant was the behavior of Confederate civilians in areas occupied by Union military forces. One must be cautious in the use of historical analogies, but it is worth recalling the problems that plagued the German Nazis in the countries they occupied during the second World War. Everywhere they met resistance from an organized underground that supplied information to Germany's enemies, committed acts of sabotage, and made life precarious for collaborators and German military personnel. At the same time, bands of partisans gathered in remote places to continue the war against the Nazis. The French had a similar experience in Algeria after the second World War. The Algerian nationalists struggled with fanatical devotion to their cause; every village was a center of resistance, and no Frenchman was safe away from the protection of the French army. The country simply could not be pacified, and France, in spite of its great physical superiority, had to withdraw.

In the Confederate South, apart from border-state bushwhacking, there was only one example of underground resistance even remotely comparable to that demonstrated in Nazi-occupied Europe or French-occupied Algeria. This example was provided not by southern nationalists but by East Tennessee Unionists against the Confederacy itself. The counties of East Tennessee had been strongly opposed to secession, and so great was the disaffection that by the fall of 1861 some 11,000 Confederate infantry, cavalry, and artillery occupied them. In response some two thousand Union partisans fled to Kentucky to begin training as an army of liberation, while others drilled in mountain fastnesses in preparation for the arrival of federal forces. Still other East Tennesseans organized an underground and engaged in such activities as cutting telegraph wires and burning bridges. The most strenuous Confederate efforts at pacification failed to suppress these dedicated Unionists, and East Tennessee remained a cancer in the vitals of the Confederacy.

Nowhere in the South was there impressive resistance to the federal occupation, even making allowance for the fact that most able-bodied men of military age were serving in the Confederate armies. In 1862 Middle Tennessee, West Tennessee, part of northern Mississippi, and New Orleans fell under federal military occupation, but no significant underground developed. In 1864, General Sherman marched through Georgia and maintained long lines of communication without the semblance of a partisan resistance to trouble him. In commenting on this remarkable phenomenon, Governor Zebulon Vance of North Carolina wrote: "With a base line of communication of 500 miles in Sherman's rear, through our own country, not a bridge has been burnt, a car thrown from its track, nor a man shot by our people whose country has been desolated! They seem everywhere to submit. . . . It shows what I have always believed, that the great *popular heart* is not now and never has been in this war!" The absence of civilian resistance was quite as remarkable when, early in 1865, Sherman's army turned northward from Savannah into South Carolina. In the spring, when the Confederate armies surrendered, there were no partisans to take refuge in the mountains for a last desperate defense of southern nationalism. The Confederate States of America expired quietly, and throughout the South most people were reconciled to its death with relative ease. We hear much of unreconstructed southern rebels, but the number of them was not very large; the great majority of Southerners made haste to swear allegiance to the Union.

Finally, and to me most significant of all, was the readiness, if not always good grace, with which most Southerners accepted the abolition of slavery—a readiness that I do not think is explained entirely by the circumstances of defeat. Probably historians have given too much emphasis to the cases of recalcitrance on this matter in the months after Appomattox, when, actually, slavery collapsed with remarkably little resistance. Just a few years earlier it had been impossible publicly to oppose slavery in all but the border slave states, and southern politicians and publicists had aggressively asserted that slavery was a positive good; yet soon after the Confederate surrender no Southerner except an occasional eccentric would publicly affirm the validity of the proslavery argument. In-

deed, I believe that even in the spring of 1866, if Southerners had been permitted to vote for or against the reestablishment of slavery, not one southern state would have mustered a favorable majority. Only two weeks after Appomattox, when a group of South Carolina aristocrats looked to the years ahead, though one of them could see only "poverty, no future, no hope," another found solace in the fact that at least there would be "no slaves, thank God!" In July another South Carolinian said more crudely: "It's a great relief to get rid of the horrid negroes."

Very soon, as a matter of fact, white Southerners were publicly expressing their satisfaction that the institution had been abolished and asserting that the whites, though perhaps not the blacks, were better off without it. Many were ready now to give voice to the private doubts that they had felt before the war. They denied that slavery had anything to do with the Confederate cause, thus decontaminating it and turning it into something they could cherish. After Appomattox Jefferson Davis claimed that slavery "was in no wise the cause of the conflict," and Alexander H. Stephens argued that the war "was not a contest between the advocates or opponents of that Peculiar Institution." The speed with which white Southerners dissociated themselves from the cause of slavery is an indication of how great a burden it had been to them before Appomattox . . . .

POSTSCRIPT

WAS LINCOLN'S PRESIDENCY
CRUCIAL TO THE NORTH'S VICTORY?

Is it possible to evaluate Lincoln's role in the Civil War? An important advantage the North possessed was its vast transportation network which moved troops and war materiel quickly and cheaply. This system of roads, canals and railroads had been constructed over decades, starting in the early part of the century as had the factories which sustained the North's military forces. Doesn't spotlighting the intentions of one man distort these important economic considerations?

Lincoln's intangible assets (his eloquence, the moral cause in which he mantled himself) cannot be calculated with the precision of the North's railroads or counted like the large number of West Point graduates in the southern army in 1861. But they cannot be ignored either. The moral cause was as potent a force here as it has been in other countless battles. Lincoln's greatest moral asset, his belief in the Union and his determination to insure its survival, must not be minimized. Less apparent but also crucial was Lincoln's possible realization that time was on his side. Certainly it was possible that he learned a lesson from his checkered career in national politics: a one-term Congressman in 1848-49 and a defeated candidate for the United States Senate in 1854 who became a minority president in 1860. To preserve the Union meant to persevere.

Abraham Lincoln by Benjamin Thomas (Alfred A. Knopf, 1952), is readable and sufficiently detailed to give a sound picture. Allan Nevins's eight-volume *Ordeal of the Union* (Charles Scribner's Sons, 1947-1971), begins in 1847 and has an interesting summary, a balance sheet of the war in 1863, at the beginning of volume seven, *The War for the Union*. Gore Vidal's latest volume of historical fiction, *Lincoln* (Random House, 1984), offers the reader a panorama of local color while keeping the "dramatis personae" in very clear focus. Vidal gives the variety of people around the president considerable attention.

ISSUE 19

WAS RECONSTRUCTION A TOTAL FAILURE?

YES: J.G. Randall, from "Reconstruction Debacle," *The Civil War and Reconstruction** (D.C. Heath and Company, 1937)

NO: Eric Foner, "The New View of Reconstruction," *American Heritage,* October/November 1983

ISSUE SUMMARY

YES: Author Randall argues that reconstruction failed because carpet-baggers and their Negro allies misgoverned the South and looted its treasuries.
NO: Professor Eric Foner believes that, although reconstruction was nonrevolutionary and conservative, it was a splendid failure because it offered blacks a temporary vision of a free society.

The Reconstruction Era (1865-1877) contains a mythological history which has been impossible for professional historians to dislodge. While the Civil War has been portrayed as an heroic era for both sides, reconstruction has been categorized as a tragedy for all Americans— northerners, southerners, whites, and blacks. According to the mythology a vengeful Congress, dominated by radical Republicans, imposed military rule upon the southern states. Carpetbaggers from the North, along with traitorous white scalawags and their ignorant Negro ac- complices, rewrote the state constitutions, disenfranchised former Con- federate whites, controlled the legislature, passed laws which enabled them to raise taxes, looted the coffers of the government, and stole the possessions of the good white northerners. This farce came to an end in 1877 when a deal was made to allow Rutherford B. Hayes to assume the office of the Presidency. Hayes was given fifteen disputed electoral col- lege votes (which enabled him to defeat his opponent Samuel J. Tilden by one vote). In return, the President agreed to end reconstruction by withdrawing federal troops from the southern states.

Between the years 1890 and 1930, this mythological portrait of reconstruction dominated the historical profession. The reasons for this are obvious; White southerners who wrote about this period made two basic assumptions: (1) that the South was capable of solving its own pro- blems without federal government interference and (2) that blacks were intellectually inferior to whites and incapable of running a government (much less one in which whites would be their subordinates). Furthermore, the events of the times made this interpretation seem plausible. By the 1890s, most social scientists believed that the White Anglo-Saxon Protestants (WASPs) were biologically superior to Negroes, Orientals, Catholics, and Jewish immigrants. Segregation was legalized by statute in the southern states and the Supreme Court, and the rest of the nation wanted to heal the wounds of the Civil War and allowed the South to handle its own "problem." As a result of the Spanish American War in 1898, the United States acquired an empire in South America and the Pacific and forcibly ruled over non-white inhabitants.

Professional historians now reject this interpretation of the Reconstruction Era. The general public, however, still learns most of its history from fiction, movies, and the televised docudramas. Two of the greatest movies ever made dealt with the Civil War and the reconstruction period. In 1915 the silent film epic "The Birth of a Nation" mythologized the pre- and post-Civil War South and made heros of the Ku Klux Klan. (It was, said President Woodrow Wilson, "cultural history written with lightening.") In 1939 another great epic movie "Gone With the Wind" romanticized the South for the current generation of Americans and is still shown to large television audiences.

The traditional interpretation of reconstruction has been under attack by historians for the past fifty years. Corruption, for example, existed in some reconstruction states but it also existed in northern states. (The Grant administration in Washington has been called the "era of good stealings.") Even after reconstruction ended, many other southern states became more corrupt than they had been during reconstruction.

Progressive historians printed a more positive picture of reconstruction. New state constitutions were written during this era that outlasted the politicians who wrote them; improvements were made in local administrations; the court systems were revised; and state-supported public schools were established for both whites and blacks.

Revisionist historians sharply attacked the notion that blacks had dominated the politics of the reconstruction South. They pointed out that there were no black governors, only two black senators, and fifteen black congressmen during this period. In no southern state did blacks control both houses of the legislature. Black politicians were usually better educated than their constituents and, contrary to legend, generally followed moderate policies favoring black equality; through the adoption of the Fourteenth and Fifteenth Amendments blacks were granted citizenship and adult males were given the right to vote.

In a selection that represents the traditional view of reconstruction, the Lincoln scholar, J.G. Randall, argues that reconstruction failed because the carpetbagger-Negro coalition of radical Republicans mismanaged the state governments and robbed its citizens. Searching for a new synthesis which moves beyond the negative post-revisionist studies, Professor Eric Foner concedes that reconstruction was not very radical, much less revolutionary. Nevertheless, it was a splendid failure because it offered blacks a vision of what a free society should look like.

YES

J. G. Randall

RECONSTRUCTION DÉBÂCLE

I

For the seceded states the Grant period constituted the darkest days of "reconstruction." Coming south after the war to make money and seize political power, the Northern "carpetbagger" became the dominant figure in Southern politics for a decade. In collusion with the carpetbaggers were the "scalawags," native whites in the South who took advantage of the chance for aggrandizement which the postwar régime offered. Southern as they were, familiar with Negro characteristics and unembarrassed by the extravagance and gaucherie of the carpetbaggers, they obtained control of numerous offices and became a power in local politics. Aided by a system which gave the vote to the Negro while it disfranchised the more substantial element among the whites, these political adventurers improved upon the system and added extra-legal touches of their own.

Elections in the South became a byword and a travesty. Ignorant blacks by the thousands cast ballots without knowing even the names of men for whom they were voting.[1] Southern communities in their political, social, and economic interests were subjected to the misguided action of these irresponsible creatures directed by white bosses. Election laws were deliberately framed to open the way for manipulation and fraud. Ballots were inspected before going into the box, and Negroes seeking to cast Democratic ballots were held up by objections and by an effort to change their votes.[2] Registration lists showed Negroes in proportion to population at a much higher ratio than the actual fact. Vote-buying became so common that Negroes came to expect it; much of the bacon and ham mentioned as "relief" was distributed with an eye to election-day results.[3] To colored voters in Florida, acting under instructions from Radical leaders, the motto seemed to be "Vote early and often." Starting in early morning they moved along in groups, voting "at every precinct" on a long "line of march," each time under assumed names.[4] In advance of the voting hour ballots would be fraudulently deposited in the box. Party conventions were manipulated by Radical leaders, and nominations were forced by the bosses (sometimes military officers) in control. Reporting on the election of 1872 in Louisiana a committee of Congress stated that in their determination to have a legislature of their own party, the Republican returning board juggled election returns, accepted false affidavits, and in some cases merely estimated "what the vote ought to have been." The whole proceeding was characterized as a "comedy of blunders and frauds."[5]

By 1867 the Union League had become strongly intrenched in the South; and it proved an effective instrument in the organization of the Radical Republican party among the blacks. It was stated in October, 1867, that the League had eighty-eight chapters in South Carolina, and that almost every Negro in the state was enrolled in the order.[6] According to a statement of a Leaguer, every member was oath-bound to vote for those nominated by the order. The league, he said, existed "for no other purpose than to carry the elections. . . ."[7] Ritual, ceremony, high-flown phrases about freedom and equal rights, sententious references to the Constitution and the Declaration of Independence, accompanied by song, prayer, and oratory, had a compelling effect upon Negro emotions, while the black man's instinctive dependence upon whites made conquest easy, so that the sanctimonious League functioned with remarkable success in capturing and delivering the Negro vote. The Leagues "voted the Negroes like 'herds of senseless cattle'" is the statement of competent observers, borne out by numerous instances similar to that of a South Carolina black who explained his vote by saying that the League

was the "place where we learn the law." Another typical case was that of a Negro who was asked why he voted Republican and replied, "I can't read, and I can't write... We go by instructions. We don't know nothing much."[8]

As the processes of carpetbag rule unfolded, honest men in the South felt increasing disgust. Conservative editors referred to the fancy state conventions as "black and tan" gatherings, "ring-streaked and speckled" conventions, or as assemblies of "baboons," "ragamuffins," or "jailbirds."[9] "The maddest, most... infamous revolution in history," was the comment of the Fairfield (South Carolina) Herald.[10] In the carpetbag constitutional convention of South Carolina (1868) 76 of the 124 delegates were colored, two-thirds of the Negroes being illiterates just emerging from slavery. These black members comported themselves in "bashful silence" while the whites attended to matters.[11] Of the whites one was put in jail for stealing his fellow members' belongings; others were accused of graver crimes; and in general it was remarked by the New York Times that hardly a white among the lot had a character that "would keep him out of the penitentiary."[12]

II

Supported by the Grant administration and fortified by military power, the Radical Republican state machines plunged the Southern commonwealths into an abyss of misgovernment. A congressional committee reported that one of the leading carpetbag governors made over $100,000 during his first year though his salary was $8000, while one of his appointees received fees exceeding $60,000 a year.[13] Another carpetbag governor was charged with stealing and selling the food of the freedmen's bureau intended for the relief of helpless and ragged ex-slaves. One of his associates was accused of falsely arresting Democratic members of the Florida state legislature in order to produce a carpetbag majority. F. J. Moses, scalawag, stated that he received $15,000 while governor of South Carolina for approving a large printing bill, $25,000 when speaker, and various other sums.[14]

Southern legislatures were composed largely, sometimes predominantly, of Negroes. J. S. Pike, in a passage that has become classic, described the dense Negro crowd which, amid clamor and disorder, did the debating, squabbling, and lawmaking in South Carolina. Speaker, clerk, doorkeepers, pages, and chaplain were black. No one talked more than five minutes, said Pike, without interruption. Their "bellowings and physical contortions" baffled description. It seemed to him barbarism overwhelming civilization with physical force; yet there was a curious earnestness about it all. In the confusion and uproar, with guffaws greeting the speaker as he rapped for order, the uncouth lawmakers were taking themselves seriously. "Seven years ago these men were raising corn and cotton under the whip of the overseer. Today they are raising points of order and questions of privilege. ... It is easier and better paid. ... It is their day of jubilee.[15]

Some of the justices put into office by the Radicals could not write. According to a report of conditions in Mississippi, where the Ames Republicans[16] controlled the Negro vote and used it "as a solid mass," the legislature contained Negroes who could neither read nor write, members of grand juries were "totally illiterate," and the Republicans nominated as mayor of Vicksburg a man who was under indictment for twenty-three offenses.[17] Taking a leaf out of the carpetbaggers' book, Negro members of the Florida legislature were said to have formed a caucus with a

"smelling committee" to "ferret out all . . . money schemes." The arrangement broke down when it was found that the colored caucus chairman appropriated to himself the moneys intended to be distributed among members for the fixing of legislative votes.[18] A Negro leader in South Carolina, admitting the receipt of $5000 "in connection with" legislative matters, stated that he voted for the legislative measures because he thought they were right, and that by taking the money he was keeping it in the state! Refreshments supplied at public expense to South Carolina legislators included the finest wines, ales, whiskeys, and cigars; indeed the porter thought it impossible for men to drink so much whiskey and attend to any business.[19] State house "supplies" paid for out of public funds included many varieties of liquors, costly table delicacies, luxurious furniture in lavish amounts, horses, and carriages. For the one item of printing in South Carolina the cost per month under Republican rule was more than a hundred times that of the subsequent Hampton administration. In fifteen months under the Republican administration $835,000 was spent for printing as compared to $609,000 for seventy-eight years under the old régime.[20] In the matter of "state aid" to railroad building in Alabama the notorious Stantons (John C. and Daniel N. of Boston) found their opportunity. Bringing no money into the state, they organized and promoted the Alabama and Chattanooga Railroad Company, obtained millions of state money from a bribed Radical legislature, built a hotel and opera house with some of the money, obtained fraudulent bond endorsements from the scalawag governor (William H. Smith), and left the state a wretched heritage of defaulted obligations.[21]

Huge debts were saddled upon the Southern states with the meagerest improvements to show for them. Millions in bonds in South Carolina were issued contrary to law, taxation being greatly increased, while the total assessed value of property in the state declined from $489,000,000 in 1860 to $90,000,000 in 1866.[22] Delicate women were reported selling provisions needed for their hungry children, in order to pay taxes; while for failure to pay taxes Southern whites were losing lands which were brought up by Negroes or Northern speculators.[23] South Carolina newspapers were "full of reports of sheriff's sales," 74,000 acres being put under tax sales in a brief period in Darlington County, 86,000 acres in Williamsburg County, and more than two thousand pieces of real estate in Charleston.[24] Tax rates in Mississippi were fourteen times as great in 1874 as in 1869, the public debt being piled up annually at the rate of $664,000.[25] Grants under the scalawag Holden régime to railroad companies in North Carolina exceeded $27,000,000.[26]

One of the flagrant evils of misgovernment was seen in the militia of carpetbag times. White desperadoes from Missouri, enlisted as Arkansas miltiamen, tore up and down the state smashing property, destroying crops, and committing murder.[27] Groups of Negro militia in the same state became murderous mobs, with defiance born of the belief "that crimes committed... as a mob... [would] not subject them to... punishment."[28] A Negro militia detachment of more than a hundred men dashed into an Arkansas town and galloped about, cursing, threatening, raiding a grocery store, and breaking into the jail.[29] Because of the terrorism practiced by the militia in North Carolina, Governor Holden was impeached and removed from office.[30] In South Carolina militia troubles developed into a war of races as outraged whites organized to protect their property and

lives against armed Negro militiamen.[31] In this commonwealth the militia was almost entirely colored, and it was reported that at least two-thirds of the militia expenditures were a "huge fraud," the amount being in reality used for "political services."[32]

To use a modern phrase, government under Radical Republican rule in the South had become a kind of "racket." A parasitic organization had been grafted on to the government itself, so that the agencies of rule and authority were manipulated for private and partisan ends. Often in the reconstructed states government bore a bogus quality: that which called itself government was an artificial fabrication. Where the chance of plunder was so alluring it was no wonder that rival factions would clash for control of the spoils, nor that outraged citizens, seeking to recover the government for the people, should resort to irregular and abnormal methods. At times this clash of factions created the demoralizing spectacle of dual or rival governments. In Louisiana the Warmoth-McEnery faction battled furiously with the Kellogg-Casey faction.[33] In South Carolina "was seen the... spectacle of two speakers and two Houses conducting deliberations in the same hall. Motions, ... [etc.] were heard by the respective speakers; neither speaker, however, recognized members of the other House."[34] In Arkansas similar conditions produced the cheap melodrama of the "Brooks-Baxter war," with rival "armies" facing each other in support of their "governments," resulting in some actual bloodshed, various arrests for treason, sundry impeachments, not a little *opéra bouffe* comedy, and general confusion.[35]

Such, in brief, was the nature of carpetbag rule in the South. The concept which the Radicals sought to disseminate was that the problems of restoration had all been neatly solved, the country saved, and the South "reconstructed" by 1868. That dignified publication known as the *American Annual Cyclopedia* began its preface for the year 1868 with the following amazing statement: "This volume of the *Annual Cyclopedia,* for the year 1868, presents the complete restoration, as members of the Union, of all the Southern states except three [Virginia, Mississippi, Texas], and the final disappearance of all difficulties between the citizens of those States and the Federal Government." The fact of the matter was that this "complete restoration" was merely the beginning of the corrupt and abusive era of carpetbag rule by the forcible imposition of Radical governments upon an unwilling and protesting people. Before this imposition took place the Southern states already had satisfactory governments. It is a serious misconception to suppose that Johnson's efforts in the South had been altogether a "failure." On the contrary, in the years from 1865 to 1868, when Congress had not "reconstructed" a state except Tennessee, and when state governments in the South were imperatively needed for domestic purposes, such governments were set up by Johnson. It must not be forgotten that these were native white governments genuinely supported and put into power by the Southern people, and that they functioned in the preservation of order and internal government in those important years that intervened between the surrenders and the establishment of carpetbag misrule by Congress. If one would seek to measure the importance of this, let him contemplate what would have been the result if these commonwealths had made no such adjustment and had waited several years for Congress to supply the pattern for state governments. Instead of saying that reconstruction had been solved by Congress in 1868, the truer generalization would be

that the transition to normal polity in the South had been pretty well worked out by Johnson, that it was violently interrupted by the Radicals, and that only after the overthrow of the Radical régime (about 1877) did genuine political reconstruction get under way with any fair prospect for the future.

Another unfair conclusion is to attribute the excesses of the carpetbag period to the Negro. Though the Radicals used Negro voting and officeholding for their own ends, Republican governments in the South were not Negro governments. Even where Negroes served, the governments were under white control. It is the contention of Carter G. Woodson that "most of the local offices... were held by the white men, and [that] those Negroes who did attain some of the higher offices were... about as competent as the average whites thereto elected." He also argues that illiteracy among Negro officeholders has been exaggerated.[36] That the first phase of the Negro's experience of freedom after centuries of slavery should occur under the degrading conditions of these carpetbag years was not the fault of the Negro himself, but of the whites who exploited him....

NOTES

1. W. L. Fleming, ed., *Documentary History of Reconstruction,* II, 44.
2. *Ibid.,* II, 81–82.
3. *Ibid.,* II, 83.
4. *Ibid.,* II, 85–86.
5. H. C. Warmoth, *War, Politics and Reconstruction: Stormy Days in Louisiana,* 225.
6. Simkins and Woody, *South Carolina during Reconstruction,* 75 n.
7. *Ibid.,* 79.
8. *Ibid.,* 80.
9. E. P. Oberholtzer, *Hist. of the U. S. since the Civil War,* II, 45.
10. Quoted in Simkins and Woody, 110.
11. *Ibid.,* 91.
12. *Ibid.,* 92–93.
13. Fleming, *Doc. Hist.,* II, 39.
14. *Ibid.,* II, 41.

15. J. S. Pike, *The Prostrate State*, 12 ff., quoted in Fleming, *Doc. Hist.*, II, 51 ff.

16. So named after General Adelbert Ames of Maine, who was provisional governor, United States senator, and then governor of Mississippi in the carpetbag period, and under whose Radical rule there was violent opposition among the whites, leading to terrorism over the state and a serious race riot at Vicksburg on December 7, 1874.

17. Fleming, *Doc. Hist*, II, 42–43.

18. *Ibid.*, II, 50–51.

19. *Ibid.*, II, 59.

20. *Ibid.*, II, 69.

21. A. B. Moore, "Railroad Building in Alabama During the Reconstruction Period," *Jour. of Southern Hist.*, I, 421–441 (Nov., 1935), especially 427–430.

22. Simkins and Woody, 175.

23. *Ibid.*, 178–179.

24. *Ibid.*, 180–181.

25. Fleming, *Doc. Hist.*, II, 71.

26. J. G. de R. Hamilton, *Reconstruction in North Carolina*, 448.

27. Fleming, *Doc. Hist.*, II, 73 ff.

28. *Ibid.*, II, 77.

29. *Ibid.*, II, 76.

30. *Ibid.*, II, 78.

31. Simkins and Woody, 485.

32. Fleming, *Doc. Hist.*, II, 79.

33. See below (sec. vi of the present chapter); see also H. C. Warmoth, *War, Politics and Reconstruction... in Louisiana*, 233, and *passim*.

34. Simkins and Woody, 524.

35. J. M. Harrell, *The Brooks and Baxter War: A History of the Reconstruction Period in Arkansas.*

36. Carter G. Woodson, *The Negro in Our History*, 403 ff.

NO   Eric Foner

THE NEW VIEW OF
RECONSTRUCTION

In the past twenty years, no period of American history has been the subject
of a more thoroughgoing reevaluation than Reconstruction—the violent,
dramatic, and still controversial era following the Civil War. Race relations,
politics, social life, and economic change during Reconstruction have all been
reinterpreted in the light of changed attitudes toward the place of blacks within
American society. If historians have not yet forged a fully satisfying portrait of
Reconstruction as a whole, the traditional interpretation that dominated
historical writing for much of this century has irrevocably been laid to rest.

Anyone who attended high school before 1960 learned that Reconstruction
was an era of unrelieved sordidness in American political and social life. The
martyred Lincoln, according to this view, had planned a quick and painless
readmission of the Southern states as equal members of the national family.
President Andrew Johnson, his successor, attempted to carry out Lincoln's
policies but was foiled by the Radical Republicans (also known as Vindictives or
Jacobins). Motivated by an irrational hatred of Rebels or by ties with Northern
capitalists out to plunder the South, the Radicals swept aside Johnson's lenient
program and fastened black supremacy upon the defeated Confederacy. An
orgy of corruption followed, presided over by unscrupulous carpetbaggers
(Northerners who ventured south to reap the spoils of office), traitorous
scalawags (Southern whites who cooperated with the new governments for
personal gain), and the ignorant and childlike freedmen, who were incapable of
properly exercising the political power that had been thrust upon them. After
much needless suffering, the white community of the South banded together to
overthrow these "black" governments and restore home rule (their euphemism
for white supremacy). All told, Reconstruction was just about the darkest page in
the American saga.

Originating in Anti-Reconstruction propaganda of Southern Democrats
during the 1870s, this traditional interpretation achieved scholarly legitimacy

around the turn of the century through the work of William Dunning and his students at Columbia University. It reached the larger public through films like *Birth of a Nation* and *Gone With the Wind* and that best-selling work of myth-making masquerading as history, *The Tragic Era* by Claude G. Bowers. In language as exaggerated as it was colorful, Bowers told how Andrew Johnson "fought the bravest battle for constitutional liberty and for the preservation of our institutions ever waged by an Executive" but was overwhelmed by the "poisonous propaganda" of the Radicals. Southern whites, as a result, "literally were put to the torture" by "emissaries of hate" who manipulated the "simple-minded" freedmen, "inflaming the negroes' egotism" and even inspiring "lustful assaults" by blacks upon white womanhood.

In a discipline that sometimes seems to pride itself on the rapid rise and fall of historical interpretations, this traditional portrait of Reconstruction enjoyed remarkable staying power. The long reign of the old interpretation is not difficult to explain. It presented a set of easily identifiable heroes and villains. It enjoyed the imprimatur of the nation's leading scholars. And it accorded with the political and social realities of the first half of this century. This image of Reconstruction helped freeze the mind of the white South in unalterable opposition to any movement for breaching the ascendancy of the Democratic party, eliminating segregation, or readmitting disfranchised blacks to the vote.

Nevertheless, the demise of the traditional interpretation was inevitable, for it ignored the testimony of the central participant in the drama of Reconstruction—the black freedman. Furthermore, it was grounded in the conviction that blacks were unfit to share in political power. As Dunning's Columbia colleague John W.

Burgess put it, "A black skin means membership in a race of men which has never of itself succeeded in subjecting passion to reason, has never, therefore, created any civilization of any kind." Once objective scholarship and modern experience rendered that assumption untenable, the entire edifice was bound to fall.

The work of "revising" the history of Reconstruction began with the writings of a handful of survivors of the era, such as John R. Lynch, who had served as a black congressman from Mississippi after the Civil War. In the 1930s white scholars like Francis Simkins and Robert Woody carried the task forward. Then, in 1935, the black historian and activist W. E. B. Du Bois produced *Black Reconstruction in America,* a monumental reevaluation that closed with an irrefutable indictment of a historical profession that had sacrificed scholarly objectivity on the altar of racial bias. "One fact and one alone," he wrote, "explains the attitude of most recent writers toward Reconstruction; they cannot conceive of Negroes as men." Du Bois's work, however, was ignored by most historians.

It was not until the 1960s that the full force of the revisionist wave broke over the field. Then, in rapid succession, virtually *every* assumption of the traditional viewpoint was systematically dismantled. A drastically different portrait emerged to take its place. President Lincoln did not have a coherent "plan" for Reconstruction, but at the time of his assassination he had been cautiously contemplating black suffrage. Andrew Johnson was a stubborn, racist politician who lacked the ability to compromise. By isolating himself from the broad currents of public opinion that had nourished Lincoln's career, Johnson created an impasse with Congress that Lincoln would certainly have avoided, thus throwing away his political power and destroying his own plans for reconstructing the South.

The Radicals in Congress were acquitted of both vindictive motives and the charge of serving as the stalking-horses of Northern capitalism. They emerged instead as idealists in the best nineteenth-century reform tradition. Radical leaders like Charles Sumner and Thaddeus Stevens had worked for the rights of blacks long before any conceivable political advantage flowed from such a commitment. Stevens refused to sign the Pennsylvania Constitution of 1838 because it disfranchised the state's black citizens; Sumner led a fight in the 1850s to integrate Boston's public schools. Their Reconstruction policies were based on principle, not petty political advantage, for the central issue dividing Johnson and these Radical Republicans was the civil rights of freedmen. Studies of congressional policy-making, such as Eric L. McKitrick's *Andrew Johnson and Reconstruction,* also revealed that Reconstruction legislation, ranging from the Civil Rights Act of 1866 to the Fourteenth and Fifteenth Amendments, enjoyed broad support from moderate and conservative Republicans. It was not simply the work of a narrow radical faction.

Even more startling was the revised portrait of Reconstruction in the South itself. Imbued with the spirit of the civil rights movement and rejecting entirely the racial assumptions that had underpinned the traditional interpretation, these historians evaluated Reconstruction from the black point of view. Works like Joel Williamson's *After Slavery* portrayed the period as a time of extraordinary political, social, and economic progress for blacks. The establishment of public school systems, the granting of equal citizenship to blacks, the effort to restore the devastated Southern economy, the attempt to construct an interracial political democracy from the ashes of slavery, all these were commend-

able achievements, not the elements of Bowers's "tragic era."

Unlike earlier writers, the revisionists stressed the active role of the freedmen in shaping Reconstruction. Black initiative established as many schools as did Northern religious societies and the Freedmen's Bureau. The right to vote was not simply thrust upon them by meddling outsiders, since blacks began agitating for the suffrage as soon as they were freed. In 1865 black conventions throughout the South issued eloquent, though unheeded, appeals for equal civil and political rights.

With the advent of Radical Reconstruction in 1867, the freedmen did enjoy a real measure of political power. But black supremacy never existed. In most states blacks held only a small fraction of political offices, and even in South Carolina, where they compromised a majority of the state legislature's lower house, effective power remained in white hands. As for corruption, moral standards in both government and private enterprise were at low ebb throughout the nation in the postwar years—the era of Boss Tweed, the Credit Mobilier scandal, and the Whiskey Ring. Southern corruption could hardly be blamed on former slaves.

Other actors in the Reconstruction drama also came in for reevaluation. Most carpetbaggers were former Union soldiers seeking economic opportunity in the postwar South, not unscrupulous adventurers. Their motives, a typically American amalgam of humanitarianism and the pursuit of profit, were no more insidious than those of Western pioneers. Scalawags, previously seen as traitors to the white race, now emerged as "Old Line" Whig Unionists who had opposed secession in the first place or as poor whites who had long resented planters' domination of Southern life and who saw in Reconstruction a chance to recast Southern society along more democratic lines. Stongholds of Southern white Republicanism like east Tennessee and western North Carolina had been the scene of resistance to Confederate rule throughout the Civil War; now, as one scalawag newspaper put it, the choice was "between salvation at the hand of the Negro or destruction at the hand of the rebels."

At the same time, the Ku Klux Klan and kindred groups, whose campaign of violence against black and white Republicans had been minimized or excused in older writings, were portrayed as they really were. Earlier scholars had conveyed the impression that the Klan intimidated blacks mainly by dressing as ghosts and playing on the freedmen's superstitions. In fact, black fears were all too real: the Klan was a terrorist organization that beat and killed its political opponents to deprive blacks of their newly won rights. The complicity of the Democratic party and the silence of prominent whites in the face of such outrages stood as an indictment of the moral code the South had inherited from the days of slavery.

By the end of the 1960s, then, the old interpretation had been completely reversed. Southern freedmen were the heroes, the "Redeemers" who overthrew Reconstruction were the villains, and if the era was "tragic," it was because change did not go far enough. Reconstruction had been a time of real progress and its failure a lost opportunity for the South and the nation. But the legacy of Reconstruction—the Fourteenth and Fifteenth Amendments—endured to inspire future efforts for civil rights. As Kenneth Stampp wrote in *The Era of Reconstruction*, a superb summary of revisionist findings published in 1965, "If it was worth four years of civil war to save the Union, it was worth a few years of radical reconstruction to give the American Negro the ultimate promise of equal civil and political rights."

As Stampp's statement suggests, the reevaluation of the first Reconstruction was inspired in large measure by the impact of the second—the modern civil rights movement. And with the waning of that movement in recent years, writing on Reconstruction has undergone still another transformation. Instead of seeing the Civil War and its aftermath as a second American Revolution (as Charles Beard had), a regression into barbarism (as Bowers argued), or a golden opportunity squandered (as the revisionists saw it), recent writers argue that Radical Reconstruction was not really very radical. Since land was not distributed to the former slaves, they remained economically dependent upon their former owners. The planter class survived both the war and Reconstruction with its property (apart from slaves) and prestige more or less intact.

Not only changing times but also the changing concerns of historians have contributed to this latest reassessment of Reconstruction. The hallmark of the past decade's historical writing has been an emphasis upon "social history"—the evocation of the past lives of ordinary Americans—and the downplaying of strictly political events. When applied to Reconstruction, this concern with the "social" suggested that black suffrage and officeholding, once seen as the most radical departures of the Reconstruction era, were relatively insignificant.

Recent historians have focused their investigations not upon the politics of Reconstruction but upon the social and economic aspects of the transition from slavery to freedom. Herbert Gutman's influential study of the black family during and after slavery found little change in family structure or relations between men and women resulting from emancipation. Under slavery most blacks had lived in nuclear family units, although they faced the constant threat of separation from loved ones by sale. Reconstruction provided the opportunity for blacks to solidify their preexisting family ties. Conflicts over whether black women should work in the cotton fields (planters said yes, many black families said no) and over white attempts to "apprentice" black children revealed that the autonomy of family life was a major preoccupation of the freedmen. Indeed, whether manifested in their withdrawal from churches controlled by whites, in the blossoming of black fraternal, benevolent, and self-improvement organizations, or in the demise of the slave quarters and their replacement by small tenant farms occupied by individual families, the quest for independence from white authority and control over their own day-to-day lives shaped the black response to emancipation.

In the post-Civil War South the surest guarantee of economic autonomy, blacks believed, was land. To the freedmen the justice of a claim to land based on their years of unrequited labor appeared self-evident. As an Alabama black convention put it, "The property which they [the planters] hold was nearly all earned by the sweat of *our* brows." As Leon Litwack showed in *Been in the Storm So Long,* a Pulitzer Prize-winning account of the black response to emancipation, many freedmen in 1865 and 1866 refused to sign labor contracts, expecting the federal government to give them land. In some localities, as one Alabama overseer reported, they "set up claims to the plantation and all on it."

In the end, of course, the vast majority of Southern blacks remained propertyless and poor. But exactly why the South, and especially its black population, suffered from dire poverty and economic retardation in the decades following the Civil War is a matter of much dispute. In *One Kind of Freedom,* economists Roger Ransom and Richard Sutch indicted country merchants for monopolizing credit and charging usurious interest rates, forcing black tenants into debt and locking the South into a dependence on cotton production that impoverished the entire region. But Jonathan Wiener, in his study of postwar Alabama, argued that planters used their political power to compel blacks to remain on the plantations. Planters succeeded in stabilizing the plantation system, but only by blocking the growth of alternative enterprises, like factories, that might draw off black laborers, thus locking the region into a pattern of economic backwardness.

If the thrust of recent writing has emphasized the social and economic aspects of Reconstruction, politics has not been entirely neglected. But political studies have also reflected the postrevisionist mood summarized by C. Vann Woodward when he observed "how essentially nonrevolutionary and conservative Reconstruction really was." Recent writers, unlike their revisionist predecessors, have found little to praise in federal policy toward the emancipated blacks.

A new sensitivity to the strength of prejudice and laissez-faire ideas in the nineteenth-century North has led many historians to doubt whether the Republican party ever made a genuine commitment to racial justice in the South. The granting of black suffrage was an alternative to a long-term federal responsibility for protecting the rights of the former slaves. Once enfranchised, blacks could be left to fend for themselves. With the exception of a few Radicals like Thaddeus Stevens, nearly all Northern policy-makers and educators are criticized today for assuming that, so long as the unfettered operations of the market-place afforded blacks the opportunity to advance through diligent labor, federal efforts to assist them in acquiring land were unnecessary.

Probably the most innovative recent writing on Reconstruction politics has centered on a broad reassessment of black Republicanism, largely undertaken by a new generation of black historians. Scholars like Thomas Holt and Nell Painter insist that Reconstruction was not simply a matter of black and white. Conflicts within the black community, no less than divisions among whites, shaped Reconstruction politics. Where revisionist scholars, both black and white, had celebrated the accomplishments of black political leaders, Holt, Painter, and others charge that they failed to address the economic plight of the black masses. Painter criticized "representative colored men," as national black leaders were called, for failing to provide ordinary freedmen with effective political leadership. Holt found that black office-holders in South Carolina mostly emerged from the old free mulatto class of Charleston, which shared many assumptions with prominent whites. "Basically bourgeois in their origins and orientation," he wrote, they "failed to act in the interest of black peasants."

In emphasizing the persistence from slavery of divisions between free blacks and slaves, these writers reflect the increasing concern with continuity and conservatism in Reconstruction. Their work reflects a startling extension of revisionist premises. If, as has been argued for the past twenty years, blacks were active agents rather than mere victims of manipulation, then they could not be absolved of blame for the ultimate failure of Reconstruction.

Despite the excellence of recent writing and the continual expansion of our knowl-edge of the period, historians of Reconstruction today face a unique dilemma. An old interpretation has been overthrown, but a coherent new synthesis has yet to take its place. The revisionists of the 1960s effectively established a series of negative points: the Reconstruction governments were not as bad as had been portrayed, black supremacy was a myth, the Radicals were not cynical manipulators of the freedmen. Yet no convincing overall portrait of the quality of political and social life emerged from their writings. More recent historians have rightly pointed to elements of continuity that spanned the nineteenth-century Southern experience, especially the survival, in modified form, of the plantation system. Nevertheless, by denying the real changes that did occur, they have failed to provide a convincing portrait of an era characterized above all by drama, turmoil, and social change.

Building upon the findings of the past twenty years of scholarship, a new portrait of Reconstruction ought to begin by viewing it not as a specific time period, bounded by the years 1865 and 1877, but as an episode in a prolonged historical process—American society's adjustment to the consequences of the Civil War and emancipation. The Civil War, of course, raised the decisive questions of America's national existence: the relations between local and national authority, the definition of citizenship, the balance between force and consent in generating obedience to authority. The war and Reconstruction, as Allan Nevins observed over fifty years ago, marked the "emergence of modern America." This was the era of the completion of the national railroad network, the creation of the modern steel industry, the conquest of the West and final subduing of the Indians, and the expansion of the mining frontier. Lincoln's America—the world of the small farm and artisan shop—gave way to a rapidly industrializing economy. The issues that galvanized postwar Northern politics—from the question of the greenback currency to the mode of paying holders of the national debt—arose from the economic changes unleashed by the Civil War.

Above all, the war irrevocably abolished slavery. Since 1619, when "twenty negars" disembarked from a Dutch ship in Virginia, racial injustice had haunted American life, mocking its professed ideals even as tobacco and cotton, the products of slave labor, helped finance the nation's economic development. Now the implications of the black presence could no longer be ignored. The Civil War resolved the problem of slavery but, as the Philadelphia diarist Sydney George Fisher observed in June 1865, it opened an even more intractable problem: "What shall we do with the Negro?" Indeed, he went on, this was a problem "*incapable* of any solution that will satisfy both North and South."

As Fisher realized, the focal point of Reconstruction was the social revolution known as emancipation. Plantation slavery was simultaneously a system of labor, a form of racial domination, and the foundation upon which arose a distinctive ruling class within the South. Its demise threw open the most fundamental questions of economy, society, and politics. A new system of labor, social, racial, and political relations had to be created to replace slavery.

The United States was not the only nation to experience emancipation in the nineteenth century. Neither plantation slavery nor abolition were unique to the United States. But Reconstruction was. In a comparative perspective Radical Reconstruction stands as a remarkable experiment, the only effort of a society experiencing abolition to bring the former slaves within the um-

brella of equal citizenship. Because the Radicals did not achieve everything they wanted, historians have lately tended to play down the stunning departure represented by black suffrage and officeholding. Former slaves, most fewer than two years removed from bondage, debated the fundamental questions of the polity: What is a republican form of government? Should the state provide equal education for all? How could political equality be reconciled with a society in which property was so unequally distributed? There was something inspiring in the way such men met the challenge of Reconstruction. "I knew nothing more than to obey my master," James K. Greene, an Alabama black politician later recalled. "But the tocsin of freedom sounded and knocked at the door and we walked out like free men and we met the exigencies as they grew up, and shouldered the responsibilities."

"You never saw a people more excited on the subject of politics than are the negroes of the south," one planter observed in 1867. And there were more than a few Southern whites as well who in these years shook off the prejudices of the past to embrace the vision of a new South dedicated to the principles of equal citizenship and social justice. One ordinary South Carolinian expressed the new sense of possibility in 1868 to the Republican governor of the state: "I am sorry that I cannot write an elegant stiled letter to your excellency. But I rejoice to think that God almighty has given to the poor of S. C. a Gov. to hear to feel to protect the humble poor without distinction to race or color. . . . I am a native borned S. C. a poor man never owned a Negro in my life nor my father before me. . . . Remember the true and loyal are the poor of the whites and blacks, outside of these you can find none loyal."

Few modern scholars believe the Reconstruction governments established in the South in 1867 and 1868 fulfilled the aspirations of their humble constituents. While their achievements in such realms as education, civil rights, and the economic rebuilding of the South are now widely appreciated, historians today believe they failed to affect either the economic plight of the emancipated slave or the ongoing transformation of independent white farmers into cotton tenants. Yet their opponents did perceive the Reconstruction governments in precisely this way—as representatives of a revolution that had put the bottom rail, both racial and economic, on top. This perception helps explain the ferocity of the attacks leveled against them and the pervasiveness of violence in the postemancipation South.

The spectacle of black men voting and holding office was anathema to large numbers of Southern whites. Even more disturbing, at least in the view of those who still controlled the plantation regions of the South, was the emergence of local officials, black and white, who sympathized with the plight of the black laborer. Alabama's vagrancy law was a "dead letter" in 1870, "because those who are charged with its enforcement are indebted to the vagrant vote for their offices and emoluments." Political debates over the level and incidence of taxation, the control of crops, and the resolution of contract disputes revealed that a primary issue of Reconstruction was the role of government in a plantation society. During presidential Reconstruction, and after "Redemption," with planters and their allies in control of politics, the law emerged as a means of stabilizing and promoting the plantation system. If Radical Reconstruction failed to redistribute the land of the South, the ouster of the planter class from control of politics at least ensured that the sanctions of the criminal law would

not be employed to discipline the black labor force.

An understanding of this fundamental conflict over the relation between government and society helps explain the pervasive complaints concerning corruption and "extravagance" during Radical Reconstruction Corruption there was aplenty; tax rates did rise sharply. More significant than the rate of taxation, however, was the change in its incidence. For the first time, planters and white farmers had to pay a significant portion of their income to the government, while propertyless blacks often escaped scot-free. Several states, moreover, enacted heavy taxes on uncultivated land to discourage land speculation and force land onto the market, benefiting, it was hoped, the freedmen.

As time passed, complaints about the "extravagance" and corruption of Southern governments found a sympathetic audience among influential Northerners. The Democratic charge that universal suffrage in the South was responsible for high taxes and governmental extravagance coincided with a rising conviction among the urban middle classes of the North that city government had to be taken out of the hands of the immigrant poor and returned to the "best men"—the educated, professional, financially independent citizens unable to exert much political influence at a time of mass parties and machine politics. Increasingly the "respectable" middle classes began to retreat from the very notion of universal suffrage. The poor were no longer perceived as honest producers, the backbone of the social order; now they became the "dangerous classes," the "mob." As the historian Francis Parkman put it, too much power rested with "masses of imported ignorance and hereditary ineptitude." To Parkman the Irish of the Northern cities and the blacks of the South were equally incapable of utilizing the ballot: "Witness the municipal corruptions of New York, and the monstrosities of negro rule in South Carolina." Such attitudes helped to justify Northern inaction as, one by one, the Reconstruction regimes of the South were overthrown by political violence.

In the end, then, neither the abolition of slavery nor Reconstruction succeeded in resolving the debate over the meaning of freedom in American life. Twenty years before the American Civil War, writing about the prospect of abolition in France's colonies, Alexis de Tocqueville had written, "If the Negroes have the right to become free, the [planters] have the incontestable right not to be ruined by the Negroes' freedom." And in the United States, as in nearly every plantation society that experienced the end of slavery, a rigid social and political dichotomy between former master and former slave, an ideology of racism, and a dependent labor force with limited economic opportunities all survived abolition. Unless one means by freedom the simple fact of not being a slave, emancipation thrust blacks into a kind of no-man's land, a partial freedom that made a mockery of the American ideal of equal citizenship.

Yet by the same token the ultimate outcome underscores the uniqueness of Reconstruction itself. Alone among the societies that abolished slavery in the nineteenth century, the United States, for a moment, offered the freedmen a measure of political control over their own destinies. However brief its sway, Reconstruction allowed scope for a remarkable political and social mobilization of the black community. It opened doors of opportunity that could never be completely closed. Reconstruction transformed the lives of Southern blacks in ways unmeasurable by statistics and unreachable by law. It raised their expectations and aspirations, redefined their status in relation to the larger society, and allowed space for the creation of institutions that enabled them to survive the repression that followed. And it established constitutional principles of civil and political equality that, while flagrantly violated after Redemption, planted the seeds of future struggle.

Certainly, in terms of the sense of possibility with which it opened, Reconstruction failed. But as Du Bois observed, it was a "splendid failure." For its animating vision— a society in which social advancement would be open to all on the basis of individual merit, not inherited caste distinctions—is as old as America itself and remains relevant to a nation still grappling with the unresolved legacy of emancipation.

POSTSCRIPT

WAS RECONSTRUCTION A TOTAL FAILURE?

Both the traditional and revisionist writers of reconstruction history have treated blacks in a passive manner. Traditionalists like Randall, who assumed the intellectual inferiority of Negroes to whites, argued that black politicians were the junior partners of the white carpetbaggers and scalawags in looting the reconstruction governments. Revisionists like Kenneth Stampp, who believed in the biological equality of all human races, maintained that the black politicians did not constitute a majority in the reconstruction government, were not totally corrupt, and did not want to disenfranchise whites but only desired their political and social constitutional rights. Writing at the peak of the civil rights movement in 1965, it appears that Stampp was trying to assure his readers that blacks only wanted to become good Americans and obtain (in this second Reconstruction Era) what had been denied them a century ago.

Professor Foner's essay makes it clear that the Reconstruction Era is in search of a new synthesis. One area that deserves further investigation is the role of the era's ex-slaves. In recent years, slavery has been reinterpreted from the point of view of the slaves rather than the slave owners. Post-revisionist writers must look at the newly freed blacks as actively struggling to achieve their rights and to assume their new responsibilities in the post-Civil War society.

Recent writers of this period have taken two different approaches—local history and comparative history. Thomas Holt's *Black Over White* (Illinois, 1977) is a sophisticated study of Negro political leadership in South Carolina during reconstruction. Combining traditional sources like old letters, military service records, and newspapers with sophisticated quantitative analyses of voting records, Holt gives a complex picture of the reconstructed state with the largest number of "black peasants" (p. 3). Reconstruction failed in South Carolina, says Holt, not because of corruption but because Negro leaders failed to develop a clear and unifying ideology to challenge whites who wanted to restore white supremacy.

Clearly, Holt is arguing from a "pessimistic" viewpoint which believes that reconstruction accomplished very little because the federal government did not break up "the planter class" and give every former slave "forty acres and a mule." More hopeful about the achievements of the Reconstruction Era is Professor Eric Foner. In a series of essays published in 1984 by the Louisiana State University Press, Foner's *Nothing But Freedom: Emancipation and Its Legacy* compares American ex-slaves with those newly emancipated in Haiti and the British West Indies. Only in America were the freed men given voting and economic rights. Though these rights had been taken away from the majority of blacks by 1900 reconstruction had, nevertheless, created a legacy of freedom which inspired succeeding generations of blacks.

CONTRIBUTORS
TO THIS VOLUME

EDITORS

EUGENE KUZIRIAN, a native Californian, has been attracted to historical inquiry since the eighth grade when he discovered that asking questions is as important as trying to uncover the answers. Professors John Bohnstedt at the California State University (Fresno) and Professor Emeritus Margaret Judson at Rutgers, encouraged this interest by teaching through inquiry. In the courses he teaches at the University of Texas at El Paso, historical inquiry has developed into student-centered questioning. He has written articles on this subject, and read papers on historical inquiry at meetings in this country, Japan, and the Federal Republic of Germany. His short biographies of women in history, "Clio's Daughters," appeared on KTEP, a PBS affiliate.

LARRY MADARAS was born in Bayonne, New Jersey, in 1937. He attended Xavier High School in New York City and received his Bachelor's degree from Holy Cross College in 1959, an M.A. from New York University in 1961, and a Ph.D. from New York University in 1964. He has taught at Spring Hill College, the University of South Alabama, the University of Maryland at College Park and is currently teaching history and political science full-time at Howard Community College in Columbia, Maryland. He has been a Fulbright fellow and has held two fellowships from the National Endowment for the Humanities. He is the author of dozens of journal articles and book reviews and contributed to *Using Taking Sides in the Classroom: Methods, Systems and Techniques for the Teaching of Controversial Issues.*

AUTHORS

T.D. ALLMAN is a political journalist who writes frequently for weekly political magazines and is the author of *Unmanifest Destiny*.

The late CHARLES A. BEARD taught politics at Columbia University from 1910 to 1917, authored numerous books on American government and history and was elected president of the American Government Association in 1933.

MORTON BORDEN is professor of history at the University of California at Santa Barbara and has written several books on the Federalist era.

PAUL BOYER is professor of history at the University of Wisconsin, Madison.

The late AVERY CRAVEN was emeritus professor of American history at the University of Chicago.

DAVID DONALD is Charles Warren Professor of History at Harvard University.

STANLEY ELKINS is professor of history at the University of Chicago.

ROBERT H. FERRELL is professor of diplomatic history at the University of Indiana and the author of numerous books including *Woodrow Wilson and World War I: 1917-1921* in the New American Nation series.

ERIC FONER is professor of history at Columbia University and is currently writing the synthesis of the Reconstruction era for the New American Nation series.

EUGENE GENOVESE is professor of history at the University of Rochester and author of the major synthesis on slavery entitled *Roll Jordan Roll*.

The late LAWRENCE HENRY GIPSON was professor emeritus of history at Lehigh University at the time of his death.

THOMAS P. GOVAN taught history for many years at New York University and the University of Oregon and is the author of *Nicholas Biddle*.

CHADWICK HANSEN is professor of English literature at the University of Illinois, Chicago Circle.

The late CARLTON J.H. HAYES taught European history at Columbia University from 1910 to 1950, served as United States ambassador to Spain from 1942 to 1945, and was elected president of the American Historical Association in 1946.

The late J. FRANKLIN JAMESON taught history for many years at Johns Hopkins University, Brown Unioversity and the University of Chicago.

RICHARD R. JOHNSON is associate professor of history at the University of Washington.

GERDA LERNER is Robinson-Edwards Professor of History at the University of Wisconsin, Madison.

LEONARD W. LEVY, professor of history at Claremont Graduate School, is a member of the editorial board of *Reviews in American History* and author of the substantially revised *Emergence of a Free Press*.

RICHARD P. McCORMICK is professor emeritus of history at Rutgers University and author of numerous works on nineteenth-century politics including *The Presidential Game: The Origins of American Presidential Politics.*

FORREST McDONALD is professor of history at the University of Alabama and distinguished senior fellow at the Center for Study of Southern History.

STEPHEN NISSENBAUM is professor of history at the University of Massachusetts, Amherst.

The late ULRICH B. PHILLIPS taught at Yale University at the time of his death.

GEORGE W. PIERSON is emeritus professor of history at Yale University.

J.G. RANDALL was the author of the standard textbook on *The Civil War and Reconstruction* as well as a four-volume biography of Abraham Lincoln.

ROBERT V. REMINI is professor of history at the University of Illinois at Chicago Circle and is the author of six books about Andrew Jackson.

The late CLINTON ROSSITER was John L. Senior Professor of American Institutions at Cornell University.

ARTHUR M. SCHLESINGER, Jr., won the Pulitzer prize for history in 1945, served as special assistant to President Kennedy from 1961 to 1964, and is Albert Schweitzer Professor of Humanities at the City University of New York.

The late ARTHUR M. SCHLESINGER, Sr., taught American history at Harvard from 1924 to 1954 and served as president of the American Historical Association in 1943.

ALAN SIMPSON is emeritus president and emeritus professor of history at Vassar College.

KENNETH M. STAMPP is Morrison Professor of History emeritus at the University of California, Berkeley.

FREDERICK B. TOLLES is emeritus professor of history at Swarthmore College.

The late FREDERICK J. TURNER was professor of history at Harvard University at the time of his death, and served as president of the American Historical Association in 1910.

ALDEN T. VAUGHAN is professor of history at Columbia University.

RONALD G. WALTERS is professor of history at Johns Hopkins University and a National Endowment for the Humanities younger humanist fellow.

The late THOMAS J. WERTENBAKER taught at Princeton University for many years, was an Edwards Professor of American History from 1925 to 1947 and was elected president of the American Historical Association in 1947.

NANCY WOLOCH has taught at several universities and has been a fellow of the National Endowment for the Humanities.

C. VANN WOODWARD is professor emeritus at Yale University and a past president of the American Historical Association. His book on *The Origins of the New South* is considered one of the five most important history books written since the end of World War two. His lectures on *The Strange Career of Jim Crow* have been read by two generations of students.

INDEX

Griggs, William, 43
Grimké, Angelina, 193
Grimké, Sarah, 193
Growth of the American Republic, 300
Guadalupe Hidalgo, Treaty of (1848), 226-227
Gutman, Herbert, 361

Hale, John, 35, 42
Hale, Sarah, 176, 179, 182
Haley, Alex, 265
Halfway Covenant, 108
Halleck, Henry W., 337
Hamilton, Alexander, 139, 140, 162, 165, 166, 167, 188, 239; and Jefferson, 300; and split with Adams, 163
Hammond, James H., 87, 93, 94
Hand, Learned, 155, 156
Hansen, Chadwick, 32, 33, 41-46, 47
Hargreave, James, 77
Harrison, Benjamin, 206
Harrison, William Henry, 273, 338, 339
Hartz, Louis, 298
Harvard University, 108
Hayes, Carlton J.H., 12, 13, 23-30, 31
Hayes, Rutherford B., 350
Helms, Jesse, 213
Helper, Hinton R., 324
Henry, Patrick, 79
Henson, Josiah, 258
Hermitage, the, 206
History of American Life (Schlesinger), 28
History of England, 117
History of the Monroe Doctrine, A, 215, 229
Hoffman, Ross, 26
Hogarth, William, 77
Holmes, Oliver Wendell, 155-156
Holt, Thomas, 363, 367
Holy Experiment, 108
Home Treatment for Sexual Abuses, 241
Horsman, Reginald, 63
Houston, Sam, 224
Hubbard, Elizabeth, 45
Hudson, Charles, 316
Hughes, Hugh Price, 104
Huguenots, in early North America, 71
Hume, David, 76, 117
Hunt, Harriot, 181, 186
Hunter, David, 335
Hutchinson, Anne, 108, 235

Idaho, 271
Ideological Origins of the American Revolution, The, 135
Illinois, 199, 206, 207
I'll Take My Stand, 320
Impending Crisis, The, 329
imperialism, U.S., in 19th century, 210-229
indentured service, effect of Revolution on, 119-120, 130; in the South, 86

Indiana, 200
Indian Removal, 63
Indians, *see* Native Americans
individualism, role of, in American character, 21
industrialization, and the Civil War, 308; impact of, on slavery issue, 314-315, 323-324; role of women in, 188, 189
Irish settlers, 64-65, 69, 72
iron industry, in the North, 301; in the South, 301
Iroquois, 57, 58, 60
isolationism, and Monroe Doctrine, 211; role of, in American character, 30
Iturbide, Agustin de, 222

Jackson, Andrew, 19, 62, 239-240, 304; and American West, 223, 224-225, 273, 280; and 1828 election, 196-209, 239
Jacksonian democracy, 196-197, 203; effect of, on voting behavior, 198-202; *see also,* Democratic party
Jacobins, *see* Radical Republican party, 358
Jacobs, Jr., George, 39
James, William, 156
Jameson, J. Franklin, 114, 115, 116-126, 128, 129, 130, 132, 133, 134, 135, 287
Jay, John, 24, 139
Jefferson, Thomas, 24, 77, 109, 114, 130, 162, 300; and civil liberties, 152-169; inaugural address of, 163-164; and Louisiana Territory, 210, 275; and slavery, 236, 312; *see also,* Declaration of Independence; Lousiana Purchase
Jefferson and Civil Liberties, 152
Jeffersonianism, 164
Jensen, Merrill, 151
Jews, in colonial North America, 65, 71, 79
Johnson, Adeline, 261
Johnson, Andrew, 337, 356, 358, 359
Johnson, Lyndon, 218
Johnson, Matthew, 67
Johnson, Richard, M., 240
Johnson, Richard R., 48, 49, 57-62, 63
Johnson, Samuel, 76
Johnson, William, 256
Jordan, Winthrop, 54, 97

Kansas, 270, 280
Kansas-Nebraska Act, 322, 326, 334
Kentucky, 162, 200, 206, 335
Kentucky Resolutions of 1798-1799, 154
King, Rufus, 143
King Philip's War (1675-1676), 49, 52, 53, 58, 61, 62, 185
King William's War, 52
Kittridge, G.L., 47
Knights of Labor, 237
Know-Nothing party, 239